...TORY

RICHLAND PLACE LIBRARY

Cumberland River

Rockcastle R.

South Fork

Obas R.

Clinch R.

Ress's Iron Works

KNOXVILLE

Holston

French Broad

Nolachucky

Coyeta

Tennessee

Chota

To Pen's

A Cold the way nearly level

Talasse

Chilhowee

N. CAROLINA

S. CAROLINA

Savannah R.

ckajack T.

Cherokee T.

Eftenauhly

G I A

D1800461

RICHLAND PLACE

The Southwest Territory
1790-1796

*To Betty Jacobs, "my partner,"
with sincere best wishes!
Walter Durham
December 12, 1990*

Before Tennessee:

The Southwest Territory

1790-1796

A Narrative History of the
Territory of the United States
South of the River Ohio

By Walter T. Durham

Rocky Mount Historical Association
Rocky Mount Parkway — Rt. 11E
Piney Flats, Tennessee 37686

Copyright © 1990 by Walter T. Durham
Published by the Rocky Mount Historical Association
Piney Flats, Tennessee

Library of Congress Catalogue Number: 90-62183
ISBN 0-9627696-0-6

Manufactured By
The Overmountain Press
Johnson City, Tennessee, United States of America

To My Grandchildren
Samantha Durham Lindsey, Stanley Doak Lindsey,
and Robert Leland Windrow

Also By The Author:

The Great Leap Westward, A History of Sumner County, Tennessee, From Its Beginnings to 1805.

Old Sumner, A History of Sumner County, Tennessee, From 1805 to 1861.

A College for this Community.

Daniel Smith, Frontier Statesman.

The Building Supply Dealer in Tennessee, A History of the Tennessee Building Material Association, 1925-1976.

James Winchester, Tennessee Pioneer.

Rebellion Revisited, A History of Sumner County, Tennessee, From 1861 to 1870.

Nashville The Occupied City, The First Seventeen Months— February 16, 1862, to June 30, 1863.

(With James W. Thomas) *A Pictorial History of Sumner County, Tennessee, 1786-1986.*

Reluctant Partners, Nashville and the Union, July 1, 1863, to June 30, 1865.

Contents

Preface ....

Chapter
- I. Independent Spirit—and Space for It 1
- II. Westerners Unite for Cession 17
- III. The Territory of the United States South of the River Ohio .. 31
- IV. Indian Neighbors and the Treaty of Holston 47
- V. Beyond Treaties 69
- VI. Conquering the Frontier 93
- VII. Is Peace Possible? 111
- VIII. A Trying Scene 131
- IX. Representative Government 150
- X. Terror and Violence Exchanged 165
- XI. Indian Relations and the General Assembly 188
- XII. Peace at Hand 202
- XIII. The People and the Land 212
- XIV. Commerce, Trade, and Travel 224
- XV. In Community 240
- XVI. The State of Tennessee 252

Bibliography 273

Index 283

List of Photographs

1. Rocky Mount
2. Rocky Mount Kitchen
3. Shingle Making
4. Act Creating Territory South of the River Ohio
5. William Blount
6. James Winchester
7. John Sevier
8. Andrew Jackson
9. William Cocke
10. James Robertson
11. Archibald Roane
12. John Overton
13. Samuel Doak
14. The Blount Mansion
15. Blount's Office
16. Office Interior
17. Chisholm's Tavern
18. William Bowen House
19. Rock Castle
20. Knoxville Barracks
21. Mansker's Fort (reconstructed)
22. Map of the Tennessee Government
23. Bledsoe's Fort Artifacts
24. Bledsoe's Fort Artifacts
25. The Nashville Inn
26. Territorial Warrant to Pay Militia
27. Map of the State of Kentucky and the Tennassee Government
28. Constitution of the State of Tennessee

Photo Credits: 1, 2, 3—Rocky Mount Historical Association, Piney Flats, Tennessee; 4—Library of Congress; 5, 19, 26, 28— Tennessee State Library and Archives, Nashville; 6—Sumner County Chapter, APTA, Gallatin; 7, 12, 13—Tennessee State Museum, Tennessee Historical Society Collection, Nashville; 8—Special Collections, Hoskins Library, University of Tennessee, Knoxville; 9, 10—Tennessee State Library and Archives, Tennessee Historical Society Collection; 11—Tennessee State Museum; 14, 15, 16—The Blount Mansion Association, Knoxville; 17, 20—McClung Historical Collection, Knox County Public Library System, Knoxville; 18, 21, 23, 24—James Thomas; 22, 27, and end papers—The Robert A. McGaw Tennessee Map Collection, Special Collections, Vanderbilt University, Nashville; 25—Nashville Room, Ben West Public Library, Nashville.

End Papers. Front, Map of the *S.W. Territory;* back, Map of *Tennassee lately the S.Wn. Territory.*

Sketch maps by Robert C. Durham.

PREFACE

The Northwest Territory and the landmark Ordinance of 1787 that created it have been the subjects of inquiry and evaluation by American historians for the better part of the last two centuries. The location of the territory "north-west of the river Ohio" in the American heartland, the vast sweep of its lands and waters, and its potential for contributing several states to the Union have combined to attract students investigating the many aspects of the westward movement. The Ordinance of 1787 has emerged as one of the great documents of American political history rivaling the Constitution itself and provoking the curiosity of political scientists, historians, and other students of representative government.

The Territory of the United States South of the River Ohio, known subsequently as the Southwest Territory, was created in 1790, the second great federal territory. Comparatively small in size, it has been regarded by most as only an interlude in the developing history of the state of Tennessee that began with the first settlements in the western lands of North Carolina.

Yet the Southwest Territory, governed principally under the terms of the Ordinance of 1787, first followed the three-step progression to statehood set forth in that instrument. The Southwest Territory first produced a state—Tennessee—and demonstrated that the provisions of the ordinance were indeed workable. Although only one state was created from the entire territory, its creation was a signal to those looking to the West that there was a proven path to statehood for newly settled areas. The prospect of a system of western colonies bereft of a vote and voice in government had been firmly put aside.

It is this special role in the developing West played by the Southwest Territory that attracted the author. The resulting book is a narrative history that includes something of the settlement of the territory, the Indian wars, the greed of the land speculators, the growth of commerce, the rise of new leaders, and the development of government at all levels. Because of the power of his office, the records he left, and his innumerable activities as a land speculator and businessman, Governor William Blount is the central figure in the story. The various Indian nations in the region share the spotlight with him, but on his terms, not theirs, because they passed on little written material to enlighten the researcher. Their brutal excesses are well documented by the whites, but Indian claims against white excesses are known only from records kept—or not kept—by whites.

The many accounts of Indian raids on the settlers are included not to indict the raiders but to show that the whites lived under a barrage of reports and acts that were frightening in the extreme. On the other hand, the Indians believed their action was justified because they took it in defense of their homelands against the intrusion of the whites.

Simply put, the development of the Southwest Territory was an exercise in acquiring land from the Indians and bringing settlers in to occupy it. Whether the land was obtained by purchase, conquest, intrusion, or fraud, the Indians gave it up because of the superior power of the whites. They were forced off the land, piece by piece. In the process both settlers and Indians suffered; both were guilty of heinous acts.

In the research for this project, help has come from many sources. The author is grateful to Fran Schell, Marylin Hughes, and their helpful colleagues at the Tennessee State Library and Archives, Nashville; to Mary Glenn Hearne and her associates in the Nashville Room of the Public Library of Nashville and Davidson County; and to the Special Collections staff of the Jean and Alexander Heard Library of Vanderbilt University.

Willing cooperation was offered by the Special Collections staff of the Hoskins Library, University of Tennessee, Knoxville; the staff of the McClung Collection, East Tennessee Historical Society, Knoxville; Kent Whitworth of the Blount Mansion Association, Knoxville; and by Samuel D. Smith of the Tennessee State Department of Archeology and Herbert Harper and Stephen T. Rogers of the Tennessee Historical Commission, Nashville.

Important assistance came from the Tennessee State Museum; the William R. Perkins Library of Duke University, Durham, North Carolina; the Southern Historical Collection, University of North Carolina, Chapel Hill; the Jessie Ball duPont Library, University of the South, Sewanee, Tennessee; the Library of the State Historical Society of Wisconsin, Madison; and the Library of Congress and the National Archives, Washington, D.C.

The encouragement and support of Lucy Kennerly Gump, president, and E. Alvin Gerhardt, Jr., executive director of the Rocky Mount

PREFACE

Historical Association at Rocky Mount, site of the first seat of government for the Southwest Territory, have been crucial to the undertaking. The commitment of the association to publish this volume is gratefully acknowledged.

Any book represents the work of many. This one is no exception. I am indebted again to Bernarr Cresap for a thorough reading of the manuscript and for the suggestions resulting from it. The patient editing of Dimples Kellogg has contributed immeasureably to the final product. Glenda Brown Vanatta, my secretary and research associate, has cheerfully endured this eleventh book of our doing.

The ration of my time invested in this undertaking was made available by my wife, Anna Coile Durham, and my business partner, John R. Phillips, Sr. For their understanding and generosity, I will be eternally grateful.

Walter T. Durham
Gallatin, Tennessee
September 14, 1990

CHAPTER I

INDEPENDENT SPIRIT—AND SPACE FOR IT

On May 26, 1790, President George Washington signed into law an act of Congress passed earlier in the month that established the Territory of the United States South of the River Ohio. Embracing the western lands ceded by the state of North Carolina on December 22, 1789, the new territory was to be governed under the terms of the Ordinance of 1787, which created its predecessor, the Northwest Territory.

Either appellation, the Territory of the United States South of the River Ohio or the Southwest Territory, the name by which it soon became popularly known, suggested a possible sweep of territory more extensive than that encompassed by the North Carolina cession. Perhaps the descriptive name was made broad enough to include Virginia's western lands if that state's negotiations with its western citizens should fail to result in a new state. It might have been intended to have a territory ready-made to receive a possible cession from Georgia as the United States owned all of the area east of the Mississippi and north of the thirty-first parallel. It is more likely that the name was suggested by the 1786 federal division of the Indian country into two districts, one north and the other south of the Ohio River.[1]

The extent of the new territory, however, was well defined. Containing about forty-three thousand square miles of land, it was restricted to North Carolina's western district bounded on the north by the boundary of North Carolina and Virginia in the parallel of latitude 36 1/2 degrees north from the equator, on the west by a line in the middle of the Mississippi River, on the south by the parallel 35 degrees north, and on the east by a jagged, less clearly identified line running from

---

1. Clarence Edwin Carter, comp. and ed., *The Territorial Papers of the United States, Territory of the United States South of the River Ohio, 1790-1796*, Vol. IV (Washington, D.C.: Government Printing Office, 1936), pp. 18-19 (hereinafter cited as Carter, ed., *Territorial Papers, SWT*, IV); Donald L. McMurry, "The Indian Policy of the Federal Government and the Economic Development of the Southwest, 1789-1801," *Tennessee Historical Magazine*, Vol. I (March 1915), p. 30; Jack D.L. Holmes, "Spanish-American Rivalry Over the Chickasaw Bluffs, 1780-1795," East Tennessee Historical Society *Publications*, No. 34 (1962), p. 28; Clarence Edwin Carter, comp. and ed., *Territorial Papers of the United States, Northwest Territory, 1787-1803*, Vol. II (Washington, D.C.: Government Printing Office, 1934), p. 20 (hereinafter cited as Carter, ed., *Territorial Papers, NWT*, II).

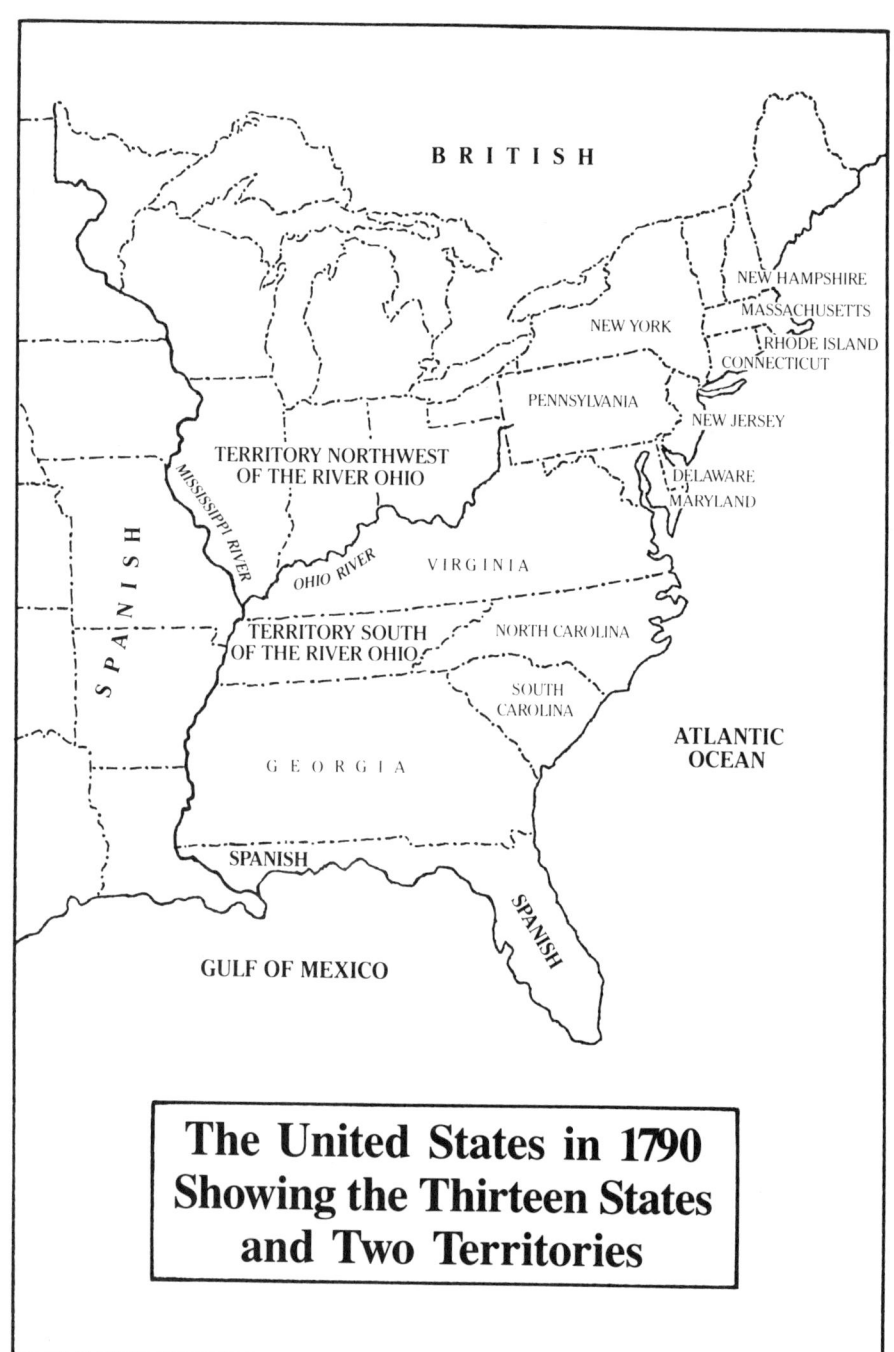

The United States in 1790 Showing the Thirteen States and Two Territories

northeast to southwest connecting some dominant mountain peaks. It was the territory that in 1796 would become the state of Tennessee.[2]

The new territory and its government were created in response to four major concerns. The first was the determination of the settlers to enjoy the protection of the national government in their ongoing encounters with the southern Indians. North Carolina had been able to afford little assistance to them, and they believed that their survival was at stake.

The second concern was that of the federal government itself, which faced the burdensome national debt amassed during the American Revolution. Many individuals in positions of responsibility believed that the debt might be retired successfully by the sale of lands beyond the Appalachians, if the states would cede them promptly.

North Carolina's concern was that if it did not cede the western territory, all of the land entered there would be included in the total acreage used to compute its part of the national debt. Because the state was already financially destitute, its leaders were looking for ways to minimize its tax liability to the confederation government. Cession forestalled what was generally regarded as a ruinous tax burden and also brought welcome relief from the urgent petitions of the westerners for military and financial assistance.

The fourth concern had grown out of the federal government's need to control all of the lands won by conquest from Great Britain and recognized in the Treaty of 1783. Separatist movements had been formed in the western districts of both Virginia and North Carolina in the prior decade, and it behooved the central government to protect the integrity of its holdings, lest the overmountain areas east of the Mississippi River be picked off in fragments by Spain, France, or Great Britain or by coalitions of settlers themselves. But of these concerns none was more urgent nor more heavily lobbied than the passion of the settlers for survival.[3]

---

2. [Daniel Smith], *A Short Description of the Tennassee Government, or the Territory of the United States South of the River Ohio, To Accompany and Explain a Map of that Country* (Philadelphia: Mathew Carey, Bookseller, 1793), p. 3; "A Map of the Tennassee Government formerly Part of North Carolina taken chiefly from surveys by Gen'l D. Smith and Others, J.T. Scott, sculp.," *Guthrie's Geography* (Philadelphia: Mathew Carey, 1794), plate 31; Robert E. Corlew, *Tennessee, A Short History*, 2d ed. (Knoxville: University of Tennessee Press, 1981), p. 90.

3. Walter Clark, ed., *The State Records of North Carolina*, Vol. 25, Part 1 (Goldsboro, North Carolina: Nash Brothers, 1906), pp. 4-6.

Although the British King George III had sought to prevent settlement west of the mountains in his proclamation of 1763, white settlers from the East, often accompanied by black slaves, had come into the near valleys of the forbidden land as early as 1769. The first family was probably that of William Bean. One of the largest contingents to occupy the Watauga Valley included sixteen families; it was conducted across the mountains in 1771 by young James Robertson, already a frontier leader. Thousands would follow.[4]

Before and during settlement, explorers discovered the dominant characteristics of the western terrain. The ridges forming the mountain fastness in the eastern extremity of the territory were its most prominent physical features. A great river, called the Holston along its upper reaches and the Tennessee along its lower and longer passage, drained the eastern one-third of the territory and part of its south central area. Rising in Virginia, the river crossed the territory in a southwesterly direction through a wide valley before leaving it to flow westwardly across part of the later states of Alabama and Mississippi. It turned abruptly northward at a point about 150 miles east of the Mississippi River, crossed the territory again, and continued across the north-south width of Virginia to empty into the Ohio River about 40 miles above its mouth. Along its course it was fed by the waters of the Watauga, French Broad, Clinch, Little Tennessee, Hiwassee, Sequatchie, Elk, and Duck river systems.

The central or middle section of the territory was drained principally by the Cumberland River that entered from the north, cut a semicircular ravel through the forested hills and rolling countryside before reentering Virginia to cross it and empty into the Ohio River about eight miles above the mouth of the Tennessee. The waters of the Cumberland were supplemented by the runoff from the drainage sheds of Obed's, Caney Fork, Stone's, Harpeth, and Red rivers. The eastern and southeastern rim of this section was formed by the Cumberland Plateau that rose to an elevation of approximately two thousand feet above sea level. Chains of lower hills defined the southwestern, western, and northern limits of the area, later known as the middle grand division or Middle Tennessee.

West of the north-flowing Tennessee River explorers found the

---

4. Allen Nevins, *The American States During and After the Revolution, 1775-1789* (New York: The Macmillan Company, 1927), p. 667.

territory was cut from part of the extensive flatlands of the Mississippi River valley. Five slow-flowing rivers of short length drained the area directly into the Mississippi: the Wolf, Hatchee, Forked Deer, Obion, and Reelfoot.[5]

Abundant water and a long growing season combined with a plentiful supply of game to make settlement attractive. Other practical needs were met by the scattered presence of salt licks and the omnipresence of heavily timbered lands. That combination had already attracted native American Indians. In the east were the towns and villages of the Cherokee; in the west was the land of the Chickasaw. Immediately south of the territory were the Creek and Choctaw tribes. The middle district had no permanent Indian settlements; it was a hunting ground jointly held by the Cherokee, Chickasaw, and Shawnee. The latter tribe had once occupied part of that area but had been driven out, probably during the prior century. In 1790 their tribal home ground was immediately northeast of the junction of the Ohio and Mississippi rivers.

In 1789 there were no more than 2,650 Cherokee warriors, 1,200 Chickasaw, 6,000 Choctaw, and 6,000 Creek. That count indicated a combined population of 70,000 to 80,000 persons. The size of the Indian populations was known only by estimate, and sometimes the estimates varied considerably.[6]

The Cherokee lived in villages and, by European standards, appeared the most advanced. Their males not only hunted game, but engaged in rudimentary agriculture by cultivating the ground, herding sheep, and breeding cattle. The women, interested in imitating European dress, were eagerly learning how to raise cotton and flax, how to shear wool, and how to spin and weave all three. The Creek had responded more slowly to their contacts with European culture but had begun to cultivate corn and potatoes and had cattle, horses, and a few slaves. Hunting deer and small game was the principal occupation of Creek men.

The Chickasaw and Choctaw, who had the least contact with Europeans, were least affected by them. Both tribes often suffered from

---

5. [Smith], *A Short Description of the Tennassee Government*, pp. 3-8.
6. Albert C. Holt, "The Economic and Social Beginnings of Tennessee," *Tennessee Historical Magazine*, Vol. VII (October 1921), p. 229; McMurry, "The Indian Policy of the Federal Government and the Economic Development of the Southwest, 1789-1801," pp. 22-23; Walter Lowrie and Matthew St. Clair Clarke, eds., *American State Papers, Class II, Indian Affairs*, Vol. I (Washington, D.C.: Gales and Seaton, 1832), pp. 78-79 (hereinafter cited as *ASP, II, Indian Affairs*).

hunger; sometimes they were without clothing, were poorly armed, and had little ammunition for their few guns.[7]

By 1790, Indian tribes living in or near the new territory had many reasons to be apprehensive of the white man's intentions. Not only had succeeding treaties resulted in Indian lands being ceded or sold to whites,[8] but white settlers had plunged past the Avery line of 1777,[9] reconfirmed by the Treaty of Hopewell with the Cherokee in 1785, and had made the great leap westward in 1779-1780 to settle in the prized hunting grounds along the Cumberland River.[10] As early as 1784, speculators had entered land claims for large tracts along the Mississippi River under the North Carolina "land grab" act of the prior year. In 1785 a Spanish agent reported from Cumberland that there was great excitement at Nashville about the possible settlement of the Chickasaw Bluffs on the eastern bank of the river, although it was reckoned the Chickasaw would resist. When a handful of American traders set up a post on one of the Chickasaw Bluffs in 1787, the Creek, aroused by mistaken reports that the Chickasaw had ceded the land for that purpose, killed eight and dispersed the remainder. And in 1788, a speculator who occupied a high place in government had proposed to rent vacant Chickasaw lands for the use of settlers.[11] Even though the westernmost section would remain in Chickasaw hands until the Jackson Purchase of 1819, the prospect that the whites would occupy the territory from the mountains to the Mississippi could not have been reassuring to the natives.

The Indian leaders surely remembered their experiences with the whites during the various wars of the last half of the eighteenth century. The French War of 1755 had found the Cherokee on the side of

---

7. McMurry, "The Indian Policy of the Federal Government and the Economic Development of the Southwest, 1789-1801," pp. 22-23.

8. The Proclamation Line, 1763; Treaty of Fort Stanwix, 1766; the Henderson "purchase" at Watauga, 1775; Treaty of Fort Henry, 1777; and Treaty of Hopewell, 1785. John Haywood, *The Civil and Political History of the State of Tennessee* (reprint, Knoxville: The Tenase Company, 1969), pp. 29-33, 220, 225, 501.

9. Waightstill Avery, a North Carolina Commissioner for treating with the Cherokee, established this line in conference with the Indians at Long Island of the Holston in 1777. Later he negotiated successfully with them for the right to a trace across the wilderness to the Cumberland country. Haywood, *The Civil and Political History of the State of Tennessee*, pp. 68, 501-4.

10. Walter T. Durham, *The Great Leap Westward* (Gallatin, Tennessee: Sumner County Library Board, 1969), pp. vii, 39-54.

11. Holmes, "Spanish-American Rivalry Over the Chickasaw Bluffs, 1780-1795," pp. 31, 32-33; Shelby County, Tennessee, Records, Grant Book 1, Microfilm, Tennessee State Library and Archives, Nashville, pp. 51, 110, 158. (The Tennessee State Library and Archives are hereinafter cited as TSLA.) John Sevier to Piomingo, December 15, 1788, in Clark, ed., *The State Records of North Carolina*, Vol. 22, Part 2 (Goldsboro, North Carolina: Nash Brothers, 1907), pp. 704-5.

the French against the British; a year later they were allied with the British against the French. A few years later in the French and Indian War, they joined forces with the French against the British colonists. During the American Revolution 1776-83, most tribes fought for the British against the Americans; and in the period 1783-89, the southern tribes were clients of Spain, seeking to block the extension of American colonial power westward. In those wars they lost hundreds of thousands of acres of land, thousands of warriors fell, and many of their villages were destroyed by frontier militiamen. The Indians gained little more than an uncertain supply of arms and ammunition and a few worthless trinkets. They were made hapless pawns in a shifting power struggle between the colonial powers of Europe, their colonies in North America, and the emerging new United States.[12]

When created by Congress, the Territory of the United States South of the River Ohio had two centers of population approximately 150 miles apart, separated by the Cumberland Mountains, then commonly referred to as "the wilderness." The larger population, some twenty-eight thousand, was in the eastern part of the territory in a corridor from 25 to 60 miles wide that extended from the Virginia line down the Holston River Valley about 110 miles to the southwest. Settlements were clustered along the Holston, Watauga, Nolichucky, French Broad, and Little rivers and their tributaries. The smaller Cumberland settlements of perhaps seven thousand were located along an 80-mile stretch of the Cumberland River from Bledsoe's Lick in the east to Clarksville in the west.[13] Just two years earlier, in 1788, Avery's Trace was opened to provide a crude road between the two pockets of western settlement.[14] The Indians regarded settlements in the Cumberland area and in certain parts of the Holston Valley as encroachments on their territory.

Although most of the eastern settlers had established themselves on treaty lands north of the French Broad River, many had crossed the river into territory guaranteed to the Cherokee by the Treaty of Hopewell. By 1790, at least 500 families had taken possession of approximately three hundred thousand acres clearly belonging to the Indians. The

---

12. Haywood, *The Civil and Political History of the State of Tennessee*, pp. 41, 47, 49, 253.
13. William Henry Masterson, *William Blount* (New York: Greenwood Press, 1969), pp. 185-86.
14. Authorized by the North Carolina General Assembly, the road was cleared by three militia companies commanded by Captains William Martin, Joshua Hadley, and John Hunter and opened September 25, 1788. John Dawson Boniol, Jr., "The Walton Road," *Tennessee Historical Quarterly,* Vol. XXX (Winter 1971), pp. 402-3.

enumeration of inhabitants made in 1791 totaled 3,619 persons, free and slave, living south of the French Broad.[15]

From the beginning the self-reliant settlers were committed to providing their own needs. When the Watauga settlements were flowering in 1772, the inhabitants organized the Watauga Association, an independent self-government that was not sanctioned by the Crown. Lord Dunmore, governor of the colony of Virginia, reported to London that the Wataugans had "erected themselves into . . . a separate state." Although the state was "inconsiderable," he said it constituted "a dangerous example to the people of America by forming governments distinct from and independent of his majesty's authority."

The association, administered by five commissioners, provided local government services that were not otherwise available. It continued to govern until 1777 when other newer, nearby settlements joined the Wataugans to send representatives to the North Carolina convention at Halifax. There the county and district of Washington were established to include them all, and the Watauga Association was disbanded.[16]

In 1784 Congress passed an act drafted by Thomas Jefferson of Virginia that called for "incipient states in the Northwest and old Southwest" to be created from lands to be ceded to the national government by the original member states of the confederation. Other provisions of the bill seem to have rendered it inoperable, but it may have paved the way for the creation of territories as an interim step to statehood.[17] Passage of the act provided clear evidence that the national government coveted the states' western lands; it did not go unnoticed in the transmontane West.

The settlers in Washington District, representing the counties of Washington, Sullivan, and Greene, watched anxiously in 1784 as North Carolina voted to yield its western territory to the central government.

---

15. Carl Driver, *John Sevier, Pioneer of the Old Southwest*, 2d ed. (Nashville: Charles and Randy Elder, Booksellers, 1973), pp. 66-67; *ASP, II, Indian Affairs*, Vol. I, Series No. 7, p. 83; *Return of the Whole Number of Persons Within the Several Districts of the United States, According to "An Act providing for the enumeration of the inhabitants of the United States," passed March the first, seventeen hundred and ninety-one* (Washington City: Printed by William Duane, 1802), p. 52 (hereinafter cited as *Enumeration of 1791*). Some estimates placed the number of families as high as 1,500. Clark, ed., *The State Records of North Carolina*, Vol. 21, Part 1 (Goldsboro, North Carolina: Nash Brothers, 1903), p. 501.

16. Ben Allen and Dennis T. Lawson, "The Wataugans and the 'Dangerous Example,'" *Tennessee Historical Quarterly*, Vol. XXVI (Summer 1967), pp. 139, 145, 146; Haywood, *The Civil and Political History of The State of Tennessee*, pp. 69, 70.

17. Samuel C. Williams, *The Lost State of Franklin*, rev. ed. (New York: The Press of the Pioneers, 1933), pp. 28-29.

The cession was made with the provision that if Congress should not accept it within twelve months, the act would become null and void. Until accepted by Congress, the ceded western lands would continue to be part of the state of North Carolina, governed by its laws.[18]

Federal ownership appealed to many frontier people who believed that concurrently federal power would be extended to protect them from their Indian neighbors. Yet the possibility of having to wait two years for a final determination of their future as a territory or as a part of North Carolina caused grave concern, especially in the Holston settlements. If neither North Carolina nor the United States safeguarded them in the interim, how would they be able to carry on the functions of local government or fund the payrolls of their own militia for defense against the Indians?[19]

To consider what they could do to provide those urgent needs, the three counties of Washington District sent deputies to meet at Jonesborough on August 23, 1784. There the seeds of a separate government were planted as the delegates freely discussed their options to form a new state, being "invited" into such a discussion by North Carolina's cession and by various "resolves" of the Confederation Congress relative to the development of new states from the western lands generally. No action was taken on "a separate government" *per se,* but those assembled agreed that they enjoyed the right of convention and that they would gather again in the autumn for further consideration of issues affecting them.[20]

The first autumn session, convened in September, accomplished little. Another attempt to hold a meeting in November ended in confusion, but not before the delegates agreed to convene again December 14 at Jonesborough.[21]

Rallying their forces, promoters of governmental independence west of the mountains generated public enthusiasm for the December meeting. On the appointed day, five representatives from each of the three counties met at Jonesborough. They elected the popular frontier leader John Sevier, Sr., to preside.

Declaring for a "separate and distinct state at this time," the delegates

---

18. Haywood, *The Civil and Political History of the State of Tennessee,* pp. 147, 148.
19. Ibid., p. 149.
20. Ibid., pp. 151-53.
21. Ibid., pp. 153-54.

considered two drafts of a constitution for the new state, named it Franklin, and called a convention for a year hence when they would hammer out a final version of the constitution. The delegates ordained, also, that in the meantime a general assembly should be elected and assembled to organize the new government under a provisional constitution.[22]

The December convention adjourned before news reached Jonesborough that the North Carolina General Assembly had repealed the cession act at its October term. In addition, the state had taken steps to demonstrate its sense of responsibility to the western country. An act created a new Washington District that included the counties of Washington, Sullivan, Greene, and Davidson and provided an assistant judge and attorney general for the superior court to sit at the Washington County Courthouse. Provision was made for additional compensation for a judge or judges from east of the mountains who would preside in that court.

Another act organized the militia of the district into a brigade and placed John Sevier, who had advocated separation, in command as brigadier general, a move that briefly returned his wavering loyalty to North Carolina and won the support of many militiamen. Sevier made a written declaration of his position on January 1, 1785, in a letter to the people of Greene County begging them to abandon all support of the new, separate government.[23]

Notwithstanding Sevier's change of heart in January, the separatist movement gained momentum. Its delegates meeting in general assembly for the first time in March, 1785, elected the officers of the new government. They chose John Sevier, who had returned to the fold of the separatists, as governor; David Campbell, judge of the superior court; Joshua Gist and John Anderson, assistant judges; Landon Carter, speaker of the senate; and William Cage, speaker of the house of representatives. Before the end of the session, Cage would be elected treasurer of Franklin and Joseph Hardin of Greene County would succeed him as speaker. Most lesser offices were filled by those holding them under the laws of North Carolina.[24]

---

22. Ibid., pp. 154-55; Williams, *The Lost State of Franklin*, pp. 39-41; Hugh T. Lefler and Albert R. Newsom, *North Carolina, The History of a Southern State* (Chapel Hill: University of North Carolina Press, 1954), p. 260.
23. Williams, *The Lost State of Franklin*, p. 43.
24. Ibid., pp. 57-58, 61-62.

Speakers Carter and Cage notified Governor Alexander Martin of North Carolina that the new state had been established to enable its citizens to have the governmental services needed on the frontier. They reminded him that they and their fellow westerners had paid taxes to North Carolina, but had not shared all the blessings of government.

Passage of the North Carolina cession act had been construed in the West as legislative countenance for the creation of a new state under provisions of the constitution of North Carolina, the Franklin spokesmen explained. The "resolutions of Congress held out from time to time encouraging the erection of new states" were seen as sufficient federal encouragement for the undertaking. Noting the mountain barrier separating the mother state from her western lands and the vast distances from the Holston Valley to the North Carolina capital, the speakers contended that "our interest is also in many respects distinct from the inhabitants on the other side and much injured by a union with them." They concluded, "We unanimously agree that our lives, liberties, and property can be more secure and our happiness much better propagated by our separation . . . into a new independent state."[25]

A concurrent letter from Governor Sevier to Governor Martin explained the state of Franklin in terms of western anger. "The people . . . consider themselves illy treated," he wrote. "First being ceded without their consent. Secondly, by repealing the act in the same manner." Too, North Carolina had stopped shipments of goods due the Indians as payment for earlier land cessions, raising their ire and, in Sevier's opinion, causing them to attack travelers and to menace the settlements. He said the settlers perceived "a neglect and coolness, and the language of many of your most leading members convinced them they were altogether disregarded." Carter and Cage reported comments at the general assembly in 1784 that characterized the inhabitants of the western country as "the offscourings of the earth [and] fugitives from justice."[26]

The leaders of the two governments exchanged strong statements. At first both were unyielding. Turning to the central government, Franklin officials sent the Virginia-born attorney William Cocke to deliver their appeal for statehood to the Confederation Congress then

---

25. Clark, ed., *The State Records of North Carolina*, Vol. 22, Part 2, pp. 637-40.
26. Ibid., pp. 637, 640-41; Jared Sparks, *The Works of Benjamin Franklin*, Vol X (Boston: Tappan and Whittemore, 1840), pp. 260, 266, 290.

in session at New York. There sympathetic congressmen were unable to muster the votes required to win favorable action for them.[27]

In the meantime, Franklin and North Carolina continued to exchange views. In a conciliatory gesture, the North Carolina General Assembly passed an act on November 19, 1785, by which it declared its intent to provide the "benefits of civil government to the citizens . . . of the western counties, until such time as they might be separated with advantage and convenience to themselves." The act invited the western counties to elect and send their representatives to the General Assembly of North Carolina. It assured them that all who returned their allegiance to the mother state would be forgiven.[28] The westerners were not ready to be forgiven, however, and they held to their separate course.

One of the first acts of the government of Franklin had been to deal with the Cherokee for additional land. In June, 1785, Governor Sevier "for and in behalf of the white people, and for and in behalf of the state or government, or the United States," negotiated the Treaty of Dumplin Creek with the Cherokee. It permitted settlement south of the French Broad River as far as the ridge dividing the Little Tennessee River from Little River. The treaty did not address the question of which white government would have sovereignty and jurisdiction over the area. That question became moot in November of the same year when the United States sponsored the Treaty of Hopewell, repudiated the Treaty of Dumplin Creek, contracted the boundaries claimed by Franklin, and accepted the Avery line that left Greeneville, the capital of Franklin, in Indian country. In August, 1786, the Franklinites forced the Cherokee, under duress, to sign a new treaty at Coyatee that permitted settlers to take up land as far south as the Little Tennessee River. Of no validity as far as the United States was concerned, the Coyatee treaty satisfied the land hungry already in the area and others who soon joined them.[29]

The state of Franklin's first response to Indian raids was prompted when renegade Cherokee massacred eleven members of the family of John Kirk, Sr., about fifteen miles below the mouth of the French Broad River. Hotheads called for retaliation, and Governor Sevier led a militia expedition against the Cherokee towns along the Hiwassee River, burning

---

27. Corlew, *Tennessee, A Short History,* pp. 76-77; Williams, *The Lost State of Franklin,* p. 65.

28. J.G.M. Ramsey, *The Annals of Tennessee to the End of the Eighteenth Century* (1853; reprint, Kingsport: East Tennessee Historical Society, 1967), pp. 337-38.

29. Williams, *The Lost State of Franklin,* pp. 77-78, 99, 103.

them one by one. When he stopped at the Little Tennessee to rest his men, a group of Cherokee chiefs came into camp under a flag of truce to negotiate peace. While they slept they were tomahawked to death by one of Sevier's men, the lone survivor of the Kirk family, John, Jr., who had not been at home when the massacre occurred.

News of the slaying of the chiefs spread quickly and resulted in unsought notoriety for Franklin among the states it sought to join. The Cherokee waged a general war against the settlements in the disputed areas, and people living south of the French Broad survived by the narrowest of margins.[30]

Governor Sevier was stern but diplomatic in his dealings with North Carolina as he continually pleaded for that state to recognize that the westerners wanted to be "separated in government" but "united in friendship." Although the Franklin folk certainly were not of one mind about separation, Sevier worked tirelessly to hold the support of a majority.[31]

North Carolina regained the loyalty of many of the westerners in 1787 when the general assembly voted to forgive taxes assessed against them since 1784. Even Colonel John Tipton of Washington County, an early advocate of separation, recanted and declared his allegiance to North Carolina.[32]

During the early months of the year, Sevier corresponded with the governor of the old state, but he would not be driven from his commitment to separate statehood. Governor Richard Caswell wrote that his general assembly would accept separation "whenever your wealth and number increase as to make a separation necessary." Pleading with Sevier to refrain from "civil war," he promised that the next session of the general assembly would do what is "just and right" about the issue.[33]

The governor's concern about possible civil strife between the Franklinites and those loyal to North Carolina was shared by many. One of them was the senator from Sumner County who, while returning

---

30. Haywood, *The Civil and Political History of the State of Tennessee*, p. 197; Corlew, *Tennessee, A Short History*, pp. 87-88; Clark, ed., *The State Records of North Carolina*, Vol. 21, Part 1, p. 501; Williams, *The Lost State of Franklin*, pp. 211-13.
31. Ramsey, *The Annals of Tennessee*, pp. 348-49.
32. Clark, ed., *The State Records of North Carolina*, Vol. 22, Part 2, p. 673; Ramsey, *The Annals of Tennessee*, p. 356.
33. Ramsey, *The Annals of Tennessee*, pp. 367-68.

from a meeting of the North Carolina legislature, had attended deliberations of the Franklin assembly where he heard some governmental leaders "wish the period of the commencement of hostilities." To Senator Anthony Bledsoe, it was "a dread thought" but a likely possibility unless North Carolina forcibly intervened to protect loyal citizens. Governor Caswell agreed that the government would not "supinely look on" and see the two factions cutting each other's throats "without interfering and exerting her power to reduce the disobedient." General Evan Shelby, North Carolina brigadier general for Sullivan County, asked the governor to send one thousand troops to forestall "an effusion of blood" in hostilities between the partisans.[34]

If a majority of the Holston people really wanted a separate state, the law prescribed many ways by law to achieve it, Governor Caswell reminded them. The first step was to come again under the government of North Carolina, and the second was to petition the general assembly for cession. Optimistic for the future of the transmontane people, Caswell expressed the hope that his "life and health and strength" would last long enough for him to take up residence among them in the western country.[35]

Support for the Franklin government had so eroded by midyear 1787 that no elections were held for seats in its assembly. When the governor's term expired in March, 1788, and no elections were proposed to fill the office, the era of the separate state of Franklin came to an end.[36]

Before Franklin collapsed, Governor Sevier had made overtures to Spain to assist the fledgling state. Although more recently some have accused him of making that contact primarily to advance his own land speculation near Muscle Shoals of the Tennessee, his actions accurately conveyed the settlers' frustration over their failure to get protection from North Carolina and the federal government. Sevier understood, also, the implications of Spain's control of the Mississippi River: virtually all goods shipped from Franklin to eastern or foreign markets had to pass through Spanish hands and were subject to export fees and duties. That affected his people significantly and, of itself, could have justified an effort to improve relations with Spain. In the opinion of Thomas Jefferson, free navigation of the Mississippi was so important to the

---

34. Clark, ed., *The State Records of North Carolina*, Vol. 22, Part 2, pp. 681-84, 686.
35. Ibid., p. 673.
36. Ramsey, *The Annals of Tennessee*, pp. 388-89, 392, 401, 414, 433.

westerners that the United States should back them in achieving it or lose them altogether.[37]

Would Sevier have wanted to see Franklin become a Spanish colony? That is highly unlikely, although at one point he was represented to have said that the people of Franklin "wished to place themselves under the protection of the King [of Spain]." Sevier and Don Estevan Miro, the Spanish governor of New Orleans, corresponded extensively during 1786 and briefly in 1788, but no specific agreements resulted.[38] The discussions with Spain stood as an implicit threat to the United States. A defection by the small western state to Spain would have opened the possibility of additional Spanish influence—even ownership—in the eastern Mississippi Valley. The young nation was too busy with other problems to pay any serious attention to the Franklin threat, however.

As the state of Franklin passed from the scene in 1788, its internal struggles seem to have degenerated into a personal feud between Sevier and John Tipton, who had become strongly identified with North Carolina. The feud reached its climax when Sevier, seeking revenge for Tipton's sending the Washington County sheriff to seize some of his slaves to satisfy a court judgment, recruited fifty men and marched to attack him at his home. Tipton refused a demand for surrender unless Sevier agreed to abide by the laws of North Carolina, and a siege followed. During the night, a large number of Tipton's friends reinforced him. They attacked Sevier's camp at daylight and broke it up; the besiegers retreated. Two men died in the skirmishing. Several were wounded including Washington County Sheriff Jonathan Pugh who died a week later. Ill will existed between the principals for the remainder of their lives, although it did not result in further bloodshed.[39]

Unable to let the Franklin rebellion pass without at least symbolically chastising its leaders, North Carolina ordered the arrest of John Sevier and charged him with high treason. Briefly jailed at Morganton, he was released on bond, and the case was never brought to trial. In fact, the state administration courted his friends and supported his election to the general assembly in the autumn of 1788. To clear the

---

37. Williams, *The Lost State of Franklin,* p. 120.
38. Arthur P. Whitaker, "The Muscle Shoals Speculation," *Mississippi Valley Historical Review,* Vol. 13 (1926), pp. 379, 381; D.C. Corbitt and Roberta Corbitt, eds., "Papers From the Spanish Archives Relating to Tennessee and the Old Southwest," East Tennessee Historical Society *Publications,* No. 18 (1946), p. 144; Williams, *The Lost State of Franklin,* pp. 124, 235-44.
39. Williams, *The Lost State of Franklin,* p. 202.

way for his future service to the state, the general assembly passed a bill on November 30 pardoning Sevier for his role in the Franklin venture. He was restored, also, to his pre-Franklin position as commander of the militia of Washington District with the rank of brigadier general.[40]

During the existence of Franklin, its leaders little heeded the Cumberland settlements, and the Cumberlanders paid little attention to them. Apparently neither saw meaning in a union of Franklin and Cumberland. The mountain wilderness separating them was a barrier that suggested Franklin would have more in common with the residents of Virginia in the area between Cumberland Gap and Abingdon. As early as 1782, the prominent Virginian Arthur Campbell had advocated creating a new western state called Frankland stretching from Abingdon south to the French Broad River. Although Thomas Jefferson embodied the concept in his 1784 plan to develop several new states from western lands, the proposal made no headway.[41] Cumberland folk, similarly, had more in common with the Virginia settlers in the bluegrass area around Harrodsburg and Lexington, but politically nothing came of it.[42]

---

40. Ibid., pp. 97-98, 99-100.
41. The concept of Frankland as a southern mountain state is explained in detail by James W. Hagy in "Frankland: The Dream of Southern Appalachian Statehood, 1769-1786" (Piney Flats, Tennessee: Friends of Rocky Mount, 1989).
42. Corlew, *Tennessee, A Short History*, pp. 72-73.

CHAPTER II

WESTERNERS UNITE FOR CESSION

Although explorers and hunters had roamed the valley of the Cumberland River south of the Virginia-North Carolina boundary since the early 1760s, the first family settlements were not made there until the winter of 1779-80. Responding to the promotion of the inveterate frontier land speculator Richard Henderson, several families from the Holston Valley of North Carolina and others from Fort Blackmore on the upper Clinch River in Virginia met at French Lick, since that time the site of Nashville. Their new homeland was in the heart of the Indian hunting ground jointly held by the Cherokee, Chickasaw, and Shawnee.

The settlers were led to the Cumberland by James Robertson, an original Wataugan, and John Donelson of Pittsylvania County, Virginia. Robertson, agent to the Cherokee for both North Carolina and Virginia from 1776 to 1779, organized and guided a party of approximately two hundred men overland by the Wilderness Road.[1] Donelson assembled a flotilla of riverboats to transport the women, children, and remaining men. The overland journey, though strenuous, was the easier of the two expeditions. Robertson's caravan of men and horses set out from Watauga in October and reached the frozen Cumberland River at French Lick safely on December 25. Leaving Fort Patrick Henry on December 22, 1779, Donelson escorted the boats downstream to the confluence of the Holston and Clinch rivers. There they were joined by fellow travelers who had brought their boats down the Clinch from Fort Blackmore. The further voyage claimed the lives of some of the company as it passed with agonizing slowness down the Tennessee River, through Indian country, and up the Ohio and Cumberland rivers to reach French Lick on April 24, 1780.[2]

In what was becoming characteristic of southwestern settlers, they

---

1. The party followed the Wilderness Road as it led northwestward from the Holston Valley through Southwest Virginia and Cumberland Gap. After crossing the Kentucky country to a point about sixty miles northeast of their destination, the travelers turned southward, reentered North Carolina, and reached the Cumberland two or three days later. Robert L. Kincaid, "The Wilderness Road in Tennessee," East Tennessee Historical Society *Publications,* No. 20 (1948), pp. 37, 43.

2. The settlement at French Lick was first called Nashborough but in 1784 became Nashville. The Cumberland Compact, Tennessee Historical Society, TSLA.

did not wait for the state to extend the services of government to them. Their leaders drew up the Cumberland Compact to govern the new settlements, possibly even before the actual migration.[3] It included a plan of settlement predicated on the location of eight forts or stations at predetermined points along thirty-six miles of the 'valley of the Cumberland River from French Lick eastward to Bledsoe's Lick. The forts were considered to be centers of local settlement; each was apportioned representation on the tribunal of twelve "notables" or general arbitrators who administered the functions of government.[4]

Devised to serve until "the full and proper exercise of the laws of our country can be in use," the compact included a statement of principles and a commitment from each of the 256 male signers. They promised to cooperate to enforce the rules of the association and the rulings of its tribunal, by force if necessary. The compact provided, also, for a militia composed of all men above the age of sixteen.[5]

Signers of the compact acknowledged Richard Henderson's claim to all of the land in the settlement area with the provision that no pay was due to him from them until he could convey "a satisfactory and indisputable title." That time never came as his Transylvania purchase of western lands in Virginia and North Carolina had been ruled invalid by both governments, and the latter state recognized only its own vestment of title in the lands he claimed.[6]

Indian resistance to the Cumberland settlements was so fierce that the settlers were preoccupied with defense and survival from the beginning. Consequently, the operations of government were virtually suspended during 1780, 1781, and 1782 before they were resumed in 1783. Then the Cumberlanders petitioned North Carolina for official recognition, and the general assembly responded by making the entire Cumberland country into one large political division: Davidson County, the fourth county of the state created west of the Appalachians.

The creation of Davidson County ended government under the

---

3. Authorship of the compact is usually attributed to Richard Henderson, but he surely drew on the knowledge and experience of the long hunter-explorers in the group: Kasper Mansker, James Robertson, Isaac and Anthony Bledsoe, and others. Archibald Henderson, "Richard Henderson: The Authorship of the Cumberland Compact and the Founding of Nashville," *Tennessee Historical Magazine*, Vol. 2 (September 1916), pp. 171-72.
4. The Cumberland Compact, Tennessee Historical Society, TSLA; Corlew, *Tennessee, A Short History*, p. 53.
5. Ibid., pp. 53-54.
6. Henderson, "Richard Henderson: The Authorship of the Cumberland Compact and the Founding of Nashville," pp. 170-72.

Cumberland Compact. Magistrates were appointed to sit on a typical North Carolina county court, a local body that held judicial, legislative, and executive powers. As one of its first acts, the court elected James Robertson and Anthony Bledsoe, formerly a member of Virginia's house of delegates, to represent the new county in the house and senate of the general assembly at Raleigh, six hundred miles away.[7]

When they attended the next general assembly, Robertson and Bledsoe presented a memorial from their constituents asking "to have government established among us in all its different branches." Favorable action on their request would enable them to "avoid the evils" they had experienced by living virtually in a state of anarchy, they argued. Through the memorial they pledged unswerving loyalty to North Carolina and made it clear they considered themselves dutiful and responsible citizens, entitled to the protection of government.[8]

Although the general assembly could provide little immediate assistance to the settlers in their remote location, it took an important step toward increasing immigration to the area. A land reserve to benefit North Carolina soldiers of the American Revolution who had been paid in land warrants was established in an area one hundred miles east to west and fifty-five miles north to south that blanketed the Cumberland settlements and the entire Cumberland River Valley south of Virginia. After the commissioners and surveyors had received land in payment for their services, the original settlers were given preemption rights; then the remaining acreage was held for the war veterans. Immigration resumed quickly.[9]

The Military Reservation opened the way for land speculation in the watershed of the lower Cumberland on a grand scale. Since the land warrants could be traded freely, many soldiers elected to remain east of the Appalachians and sold their warrants for nominal sums. As privates received 640 acres and soldiers and officers of higher rank received correspondingly larger amounts,[10] speculators could often

---

7. Corlew, *Tennessee, A Short History*, pp. 54-55.
8. North Carolina Legislature and Gubernatorial Papers Relating to Tennessee, TSLA.
9. Corlew, *Tennessee, A Short History*, p. 155.
10. A noncommissioned officer received 1,000 acres; a subaltern officer, 2,560; a captain, 3,840; a major, 4,800; a lieutenant colonel, 5,760; a lieutenant colonel commandant, 7,200; a colonel, 7,800; a brigadier general, 12,000; a chaplain, 7,200; a surgeon, 4,800; a surgeon's mate, 2,560. Alice Barnwell Keith, ed., *The John Gray Blount Papers*, Vol. II (Raleigh, North Carolina: State Department of Archives and History, 1952), p. 486.

assemble huge tracts. For the next twenty years, two of the most active of them were William Blount, a prominent North Carolina business and political figure then living east of the mountains who would become the first and only governor of the Southwest Territory, and John Sevier, a highly visible leader in the Holston country destined to become the first governor of the state of Tennessee.[11]

Along with passage of the Military Reservation Act, John Gray Blount, legislator, businessman, land speculator, and brother of William, pushed through the general assembly the "land grab" act of 1783. Further spurring speculation, the law offered for sale almost all of the western lands not included in the Cherokee country and the Military Reservation area at the price of ten pounds per one hundred acres. Entries for purchases under the act were made at the office of John Armstrong, entry taker for the state.[12]

In 1786 North Carolina subdivided Davidson County and created from it Sumner County, the fifth county west of the mountains. In 1788 Tennessee County was created from portions of Davidson and Sumner. The three counties were then combined for the holding of "superior courts of law and equity" in what was designated the Mero District, a misspelled tribute to Don Estevan Miro, Spanish governor of New Orleans.[13]

After three years of relative quiet on the Cumberland, Indians renewed their raids in 1787. The outlying settlements at and near Bledsoe's Lick, supplemented by the arrivals of new families, nonetheless were struck frequently. On June 3, 1787, Indians killed young James Hall, son of Major William and Thankful Doak Hall, near Greenfield station and, in a return attack two months later, killed Major Hall, his eldest son, and another man.[14]

Fear pervaded the settlements. Hendricks's, a new fort on Station Camp Creek in Sumner County, was attacked in the summer of 1787, and several scalpings and deaths were reported in its neighborhood. Spanish traders among the Chickamauga, a Cherokee faction living in the five lower towns near the twentieth-century city of Chattanooga, had offered rewards for American scalps, and reports persisted that the Indians were planning to destroy the Cumberland settlements before

---

11. Corlew, *Tennessee, A Short History*, p. 155.
12. Lucile Deaderick, ed., *Heart of the Valley, A History of Knoxville, Tennessee* (Knoxville: East Tennessee Historical Society, 1976), p. 2.
13. Ibid., p. 62.
14. Ibid., pp. 89, 91-92.

autumn. A man in Sumner, hearing of attacks on Nashville, went into the town to join in its defense. Within a few hours of his arrival, a messenger brought news that "only twelve hours after his leaving home, his own house had been broken into [by Indians] and his young wife and three babies slaughtered."[15]

At the relentless prodding of Anthony Bledsoe and James Robertson, the North Carolina General Assembly authorized the raising of two hundred troops from the eastern districts in November, 1786. They were to defend the frontiers and cut a road from the lower end of Clinch Mountain through the wilderness to the Cumberland settlements. Conducted halfheartedly, recruitment of the soldiers was slow. After receiving many protests because of the delay that had extended into the summer of 1787, the governor on August 13 ordered Major Thomas Evans, commander of the authorized troops, to ignore his prior orders to cut a road but to "proceed directly to the Cumberland River." Evans's battalion, at half strength, finally set out on September 10.[16]

The preceding June, Bledsoe had been unsuccessful in gaining permission to organize an expedition against the Chickamauga. When the governor denied Bledsoe's request, he promised him that if the transgressors in the Cumberland country could be certainly identified as Chickamauga, he would immediately send an expedition to challenge them. On August 5 Bledsoe called upon the governor to honor his pledge. He told Caswell that, in concert with the Creek, the Chickamauga had done the settlements "very great spoil by murdering numbers of our peaceful inhabitants, stealing our horses, killing our cattle and hogs, and burning our buildings through wantonness, cutting down our corn, etc."[17] The governor authorized no expedition, however.

In the meantime, flaunting the governor's refusal to assist them, a mixed group of 130 militia and volunteers launched an unauthorized assault on Coldwater, an Indian village located at the mouth of Coldwater Creek on the south bank of the Tennessee River near Muscle Shoals. Led by General James Robertson, commander of the Mero Militia, they followed the fresh tracks of an Indian party returning from a raid on the Cumberland settlements. Surprised by their attackers, the

---

15. Ibid., pp. 88-89; James Roberts Gilmore, *The Advanced Guard of Western Civilization* (New York: D. Appleton and Company, 1888), p. 217.
16. Durham, *The Great Leap Westward*, p. 94.
17. Ibid., pp. 88, 93-94.

outnumbered Indians, most of whom were Creek, fought back but were no match for the well-armed frontiersmen. At least twenty-six of them died in the fighting, and the rest fled. After burning the town, the expeditionary force returned to the Bluffs with the loss of only one soldier, slain from ambush while transporting supplies.[18]

The Coldwater attack provided only temporary relief for the Cumberland settlers. When the Indians resumed their raids, they hit frequently and hard. On occasion, the war parties were as large as two hundred men. Even stepped-up scouting and patrolling by militia did little to deter them.[19] On their way home from the general assembly meeting in December, 1787, Bledsoe and Robertson learned that during their absence, Creek Indians had killed seven inhabitants and "wounded sundry others." They wrote at once to Governor Samuel Johnston asking that he intercede with the Spanish minister then at Congress to use his influence with his allies, the Creek, to "prevent further effusions of blood." It seemed to be their only hope as the general assembly had listened to their protestations "unfeelingly."[20]

There was little to encourage the Cumberland people, however. Some discussed moving to a safer haven. In 1788, many felt especially desperate when they heard that a party of Creek had mortally wounded Anthony Bledsoe at his brother Isaac's fort on July 20. Bledsoe, colonel commandant of the Sumner Militia, died the next day leaving a void in the leadership ranks of the West. He had been one of the few stalwarts rallying the doubtful to remain in the settlements.[21]

During the late summer and autumn, Indian raiders continued to plunder and kill. They struck Mayfield's and Brown's stations on the west fork of Mill Creek in Davidson, killed several of the defenders, and drove the remainder to Rains's station nearby. Later James Robertson's son Charles was killed by Creek raiders. Reporting the names of the dead to the governor and the secretary of war became a regular ritual as the settlers begged for protection.[22]

The new year, 1789, brought no change in the pattern of raids. Several inhabitants were killed near Bledsoe's Lick, although scouts patrolled known trails leading from Indian country. At least one group of raiders

---

18. Haywood, *The Civil and Political History of the State of Tennessee*, pp. 230-35.
19. Ibid., pp. 237-41.
20. Clark, ed., *The State Records of North Carolina*, Vol. 21, Part 1, p, 437.
21. Durham, *The Great Leap Westward*, pp. 99-101.
22. Haywood, *The Civil and Political History of the State of Tennessee*, pp. 248-49, 254.

was routed by scouts, led by Colonel James Winchester, who found them by following a trail that threaded through the Cumberland foothills into the area that became DeKalb County in 1837. There were raids with the accompanying loss of several lives in Tennessee County on the Sulphur Fork of Red River, and near Nashville, James Robertson was wounded when raiders attacked his station. Two men were slain from ambush and another killed and scalped in separate incidents nearby.[23]

Although their relations with the Cherokee, Chickamauga, and Creek were violently antagonistic, the Cumberland folk enjoyed friendly support from the Chickasaw. The chief Piomingo, leader of the largest faction in the nation, was a constant, dependable ally of the Cumberlanders. There were no hostilities between the Chickasaw and the settlers, and on many occasions, the Chickasaw alerted Robertson, Smith, and other Mero leaders to the treacherous intentions of the other tribes.

Their friendship was vital to the survival of the settlements, a fact recognized even by the state government. When the Creek assassinated the Chickasaw chief Long Hair and his son while they were en route to the French Broad River to attend a treaty between North Carolina and the Cherokee, the general assembly voted funds to purchase presents to be acquired and delivered by Daniel Smith to the chief's family. The gifts were made "to conciliate their affections to this state, and mitigate their sorrows for the loss of their murdered friends."[24]

The persistence of attacks by the southern Indians and the inability of North Carolina to provide protection on the frontiers[25] caused Mero District leaders to turn to Spain for aid. It was an article of faith among the settlers that agents of that nation were encouraging the southern tribes to break up the Cumberland settlements because of the threat they posed to Spanish interests along the Mississippi River and in the country south and west of the Tennessee River. Andrew Jackson, Daniel Smith, and James Robertson were only three of many who advocated establishing

---

23. Durham, *The Great Leap Westward*, pp. 102-3; Clark, ed., *The State Records of North Carolina*, Vol. 22, Part 2, pp. 790-91; Haywood, *The Civil and Political History of the State of Tennessee*, pp. 255-57.

24. Clark, ed., *The State Records of North Carolina*, Vol. 21, Part 2, p. 709.

25. Governor Samuel Johnston explained to Elijah Robertson at Nashville that he understood the settlers' need for protection but could not provide it because of "your distant situation, the exhausted state of the treasury, and the impracticability of raising and marching any considerable number of men." Clark, ed., *The State Records of North Carolina*, Vol. 21, Part 1, p. 442.

direct relations with the Spanish governor of New Orleans as the most likely way to obtain peace with the Indians.[26]

In 1789 Daniel Smith, a former Virginian and newly appointed commanding general of the Mero District Militia, initiated a correspondence with Miro that resulted in carefully phrased exchanges about the possibility of improved relations between the parties. Spanish restraint of the Creek Indians and open navigation of the Mississippi River were the subjects first broached. The couriers who delivered Smith's letters were less circumspect. They told Miro that the western settlers were seeking independence from their mother state and that, once it was granted, they would look with favor upon sending representatives to discuss putting themselves under the King of Spain.[27]

James Robertson wrote to Miro, also, confirming Smith's invitation to improved relations on the frontier. The governor responded by inviting the settlers to relocate to Spanish territory where he would grant free of charge to each family, based on its size, a tract of land from 200 to 800 acres.[28]

Dr. James White, United States Superintendent of Indian Affairs in the Southern Department from 1786 to 1788, recognized the desire of the Holston and Cumberland people for better ties with Spain. His interest was not entirely unselfish. After resigning his federal office in 1788, he became a special agent for the Spanish emissary Don Diego Gardoqui. In that position he was charged with winning the settlements for Spain, either as subjects or as allies. At first enthusiastic in his new role, White told Gardoqui a few months later that the inhabitants of North Carolina's western lands were ready to become Spanish citizens. Such was not the case, however, nor was Spain prepared to deal with that possibility until after they "achieved separation from the United States."[29]

In the meantime Governor Miro reassured the Cumberland folk that he had induced the Creek leader McGillivray to make peace with all of North Carolina. He promised to let the chief know he was concerned

---

26. Walter T. Durham, *Daniel Smith, Frontier Statesman* (Gallatin, Tennessee: Sumner County Library Board, 1976), pp. 103-4.
27. Ibid., p. 105; John Allison, "The 'Mero' District," *Tennessee Old and New,* Vol. I (Nashville: Tennessee Historical Commission and Tennessee Historical Society, 1946), p. 149.
28. D.C. Corbitt and Roberta Corbitt, eds., "Papers from the Spanish Archives Relating to Tennessee and the Old Southwest," East Tennessee Historical Society *Publications,* No. 21 (1949), pp. 89-92.
29. A.V. Goodpasture, "Dr. James White, Pioneer, Politician, Lawyer," *Tennessee Historical Magazine,* Vol. 1, (December 1915), pp. 262-66.

that the peace should be kept by all parties. Belatedly, on September 15, Miro offered to open the Mississippi River for shipment of goods from Cumberland, but he advised Smith that duties of 15 percent would be imposed on cargo. In an obvious effort to curry favor with the general and James Robertson, the governor offered to reduce duty charges for their "own private accounts" to 6 percent.[30]

Before Miro offered to open the river, General Smith had abandoned all hope of negotiating "effectual protection" from Spain, and by the end of the year, he would terminate his cautious flirtation with Governor Miro. He and Robertson were convinced that the future of the western country depended on cession by the state of its lands west of the Appalachians. They believed that territorial status was the only way to obtain protection against their Indian neighbors. They desperately hoped the central government would act without the interminable delays they had experienced from the government of North Carolina.[31]

A common need prompted the Cumberland and Holston settlements, whose relationships had been less than cordial during the Franklin years, to join forces in 1789 to push the general assembly to cede the western lands. They understood that the idea of cession had been made more palatable to the mother state by the undisciplined acts of disorderly settlers who ignored the governor's orders at will and were especially contemptuous of him in matters relating to the Indians.[32] It was not unreasonable for them to expect, also, that North Carolina would follow the example of Virginia, Massachusetts, Connecticut, and South Carolina, each of whom had ceded substantially all of its western lands.[33] After all, Congress had been asking for cession of the "backlands" since 1780. It had called on North Carolina in 1785 to reconsider its repeal of the cession of 1784 and made separate attempts to persuade the state to cede the area in 1786, 1787, and 1788.[34]

Meeting at the Greene County Courthouse on January 12, 1789, to discuss mutual defense against the Indians, Holston Valley folk agreed

---

30. Corbitt and Corbitt, eds., "Papers from the Spanish Archives," No. 21 (1949), pp. 89, 91.
31. Ibid., pp. 105-18; Clark ed., *The State Records of North Carolina*, Vol. 22, Part 2, pp. 791, 792.
32. Clark, ed., *The State Records of North Carolina*, Vol. 21, Part 2, p. 546; Part 1, p. 515.
33. Virginia had put her grant in "acceptable form" in 1783, Massachusetts in 1784, Connecticut in 1786, and South Carolina in 1787. Nevins, *The American States During and After the Revolution, 1775-1789*, pp. 596, 671; Jack Ericson Eblen, *The First and Second United States Empires, Governors, and Territorial Government, 1784-1912* (Pittsburgh: University of Pittsburgh Press, 1968), p. 20.
34. Eblen, *The First and Second United States Empires*, p. 20; Clark, ed., *The State Records of North Carolina*, Vol. 21, Part 1, pp. 503-4.

to recommend "to the people to petition the next assembly to divide the state at the Appalachian Mountains, or cede the territory west of said mountains to Congress." They voted, also, to raise a fund to pay the expense of a representative to appear at the first meeting of Congress under the "new Constitution" to explain the dangerous predicament of the frontier people, and "to express our earnest desire to be admitted into the Union as soon as possible." To coordinate their actions with similar undertakings in Mero, they requested Joseph Hardin "to wait on Cumberland settlement with our plan of safety and redress of grievances."[35]

Cumberland people, meeting at Nashville in August, 1789, voted to petition North Carolina for cession of its western lands to the United States. James Robertson, observing that he and his neighbors could not help wishing for "a more interesting connection" than territorial status, reported the results of the meeting to Miro on September 2. Lamenting the failure of the central government to protect the frontier settlements, Robertson acknowledged, "For my own part I conceive highly of the advantages of your government." His remarks were intended by indirection for the elected officials of North Carolina and the United States as a warning to act with dispatch or expect the westerners again to look to Spain for help. In fact, Daniel Smith had told Governor Johnston on July 24 that many settlers would agree to place themselves under the government of Spain if such an opportunity were presented. The Cumberland leaders were desperate.[36] Their situation was distinctly different from that represented in extracts made by the New York *Daily Advertiser* from a letter boosting immigration to the area. The writer had ebulliently portrayed the Cumberland country as a western paradise attracting immigrants by the thousands.[37]

As the late autumn session of the general assembly approached, it seemed apparent to the leadership in the western counties that a cession act would be passed. Daniel Smith, in Fayetteville as a delegate to the concurrent convention to ratify the federal Constitution, again made the case for cession in private conversations with Governor Johnston. Senator William Blount labored incessantly with his colleagues

---

35. Clark, ed., *The State Records of North Carolina*, Vol. 22, Part 2, pp. 722-25.
36. Arthur P. Whitaker, *The Spanish-American Frontier, 1783-1795* (Boston and New York: Houghton Mifflin Company, 1927), p. 115; Archibald Henderson, *The Conquest of the Old Southwest* (New York: The Century Co., 1920), p. 346; Clark, ed., *The State Records of North Carolina*, Vol. 21, Part 2, pp. 558-59.
37. February 17, 1789.

to win their support for ceding the western lands. John Sevier, also a state senator, worked tirelessly to advance their common cause. Senator James Robertson had remained at Nashville, however, because he believed that his presence was necessary to prevent some of the war-weary settlers from abandoning their homes.[38]

Ending a year outside the Union, North Carolina in convention ratified the new federal Constitution, including the Bill of Rights amendments, on November 21, 1789. The exclusion of the state from the Union had been self-inflicted by its refusal to approve the Constitution as drafted in 1787, even though the three North Carolina delegates, one of whom was William Blount, had participated in the drafting and had signed the final document. Having rejoined the Union, the state could then act on the question of cession.[39]

The senate and the house of the North Carolina General Assembly voted to cede the lands west of the Appalachians to Congress on December 11 and 12, 1789. In the senate, the vote was 30 to 13; in the house, 68 to 30. The cession included all North Carolina lands west of a line beginning at the top of Stone's Mountain, "where the Virginia line intersects it," and running southwestwardly from mountaintop to mountaintop: Iron Mountain, Bald Mountain, Painted Rock, the Great Iron Mountain, Unaka Mountain and along its ridge to the southern boundary of the state. Apparently there was discussion of ceding the lands to their inhabitants, but that possibility was shunned because the westerners sought federal protection, a benefit they could enjoy only as a territory or state of the Union.[40]

Both houses adopted a resolution on December 16, offered by Senator William Blount, that directed the governor to send "without delay" an authenticated copy of "the act for the purpose of ceding to the United States certain western lands therein described" to the senators from North Carolina in the Congress. The resolution instructed the senators "to use their endeavors to obtain as early as possible an acceptance" of the cession.[41]

Each state cession of western lands had distinctive features, and North

---

38. Durham, *Daniel Smith, Frontier Statesman*, p. 119; Driver, *John Sevier, Pioneer of the Old Southwest*, pp. 100-101; Masterson, *William Blount*, pp. 166-67.
39. Corlew, *Tennessee, A Short History*, p. 85.
40. Clark, ed., *The State Records of North Carolina*, Vol. 25, Part 1, p. 4.
41. Ibid., Vol. 21, Part 2, p. 697; Durham, *Daniel Smith, Frontier Statesman*, p. 119; Williams, *The Lost State of Franklin*, p. 250; Driver, *John Sevier, Pioneer of the Old Southwest*, pp. 100-101.

Carolina's was no exception. The preamble to the act set out two reasons for deeding the area to Congress. First, the United States Congress had "repeatedly and earnestly recommended to the respective states in the Union" who owned or claimed western lands "to make cessions of part of the same, as a further means, as well of hastening the extinguishment of the debts as of establishing the harmony of the United States." The other reason, of equal importance, was the desire of the inhabitants of the western territory that "such cession should be made, in order to obtain a more ample protection" than they had received previously.

The body of the act was divided into ten paragraphs protecting the rights of North Carolina and the rights of property owners and land claimants in the territory. The first specified that neither the inhabitants nor the lands in the cession should be estimated "in the ascertaining the proportion of this state with the United States in the common expense occasioned by the late war." The second protected the titles and claims of soldiers and officers in the Military Reservation and provided that if the area should not contain sufficient land to satisfy their claims, additional land would be made available in the territory, "not already appropriated." It guaranteed, also, the rights of those who had made legal entries for land but who had not yet perfected title by grant or otherwise. Specific protection for those who had made entries in John Armstrong's office only to find their survey already taken by others was made by providing similar sites from vacant lands elsewhere. The proceeds from the sale of unappropriated lands in the ceded territory were considered a "common fund" for the United States of America, including North Carolina, "according to their respective and usual proportion in the general charge and expenditure," and could be used for no other purpose.

Of especial interest to the western leaders was the paragraph that dealt with forming the territory "into a state or states," although it was somewhat ambiguous. Specifying that as soon as Congress accepted the cession, the area would be governed by the United States of America under the terms of the Ordinance of 1787, the act stipulated that the national government "shall protect the inhabitants against enemies, and shall never bar or deprive them . . . of privileges which the people northwest of the Ohio enjoy." Contrary to the provisions of the Northwest Ordinance, however, slavery was sanctioned and emancipation outlawed: "No regulations made or to be made by Congress, shall tend to emancipate slaves."

Inhabitants of the territory would be liable to pay their just portion of the debt of the United States and "the arrears of the requisition of the Congress on this state." Any who were in debt to the state of North Carolina were deemed "liable to pay such debt or debts . . . as if this Act had never been passed."

The seventh paragraph gave Congress a maximum of eighteen months to accept the cession or it would become of "no force or effect whatsoever," and the eighth continued the laws of North Carolina in effect until they were "repealed or otherwise altered by the legislative authority of the . . . territory."

The handiwork of Senator William Blount, who with his brothers had vast landholdings in the territory, appeared in the provision that the lands of nonresident proprietors would "not be taxed higher than the lands of residents." John Sevier was probably responsible for the tenth paragraph that guaranteed preemption rights for the settlers "residing south of the French Broad, between the rivers Tennessee and Pigeon." The statute reminded all and sundry that North Carolina would maintain "sovereignty and jurisdiction" over the territory and its people until Congress "shall accept the cession."[42]

The cession act brought joy to the westerners and a certain amount of relief to the mother state. A prominent public figure of Wilmington, North Carolina, spoke for many east of the mountains when he wrote to a friend, "The cession of the western territory is at last completed, so we are rid of a people who were a pest and a burthen to us."[43]

Before the cession act was placed before Congress, James Robertson wrote politely to Governor Miro thanking him for his apparent intercession with the Creek as the Cumberland settlements had "received little or no injury from them for some time past." Robertson solicited a continuation of their correspondence, although he was only then answering letters from Miro written in April and September of the prior year. Acknowledging the governor's "exceedingly liberal" invitation to Cumberland folk to settle in Spanish territory, he predicted it would "draw most of the people into Louisiana" unless "a better policy is

---

42. Clark, ed., *The State Records of North Carolina*, Vol. 25, Part 1, pp. 4-6.
43. A. Maclaine to James Iredell, December 22, 1789, Griffith J. McRee, *Life and Correspondence of James Iredell, One of the Associate Justices of the Supreme Court of the United States*, Vol. II (1857; reprint, New York: Peter Smith, 1949), p. 274.

adopted by our states respecting the western country than at present prevails."[44]

Thousands of miles from the ceded lands and far from the minds of many on the frontier, the French Revolution had developed an irresistible momentum. Reported in American newspapers, the exciting events were followed with interest by those in leadership roles on the frontier. The news was electrifying. The Third Estate seceded and created the national assembly on June 17; six weeks later a mob stormed the Bastille. Leaders of the revolution signed the newly drafted Rights of Man on August 26, and early in October, Parisians attacked the palace at Versailles, bringing the Royal family to Paris. The ongoing drama of the revolution and the six year life of the Southwest Territory would be played out concurrently.[45]

---

44. Robertson to Miro, January 13, 1790, Corbitt and Corbitt, eds., "Papers From the Spanish Archives," East Tennessee Historical Society *Publications*, No. 22 (1950), p. 131.
45. *The New Encyclopaedia Britannica*, Vol.4 (Chicago: Encyclopaedia Britannica, Inc., 1988), p. 978.

CHAPTER III

THE TERRITORY OF THE UNITED STATES SOUTH OF THE RIVER OHIO
1790

The North Carolina act of cession cleared the way for Congress, then meeting in New York, to accept the territory and establish government over it. On February 1, during the second session of the first Congress under the Constitution, President Washington sent copies of the cession act to both houses. When the Senate committee recommended acceptance and made it conditional upon the delivery of a duly executed deed to the ceded territory, North Carolina Senators Samuel Johnston and Benjamin Hawkins, acting with the authority of their state, signed and delivered the instrument on February 25.

There was little debate. After exchanging amendments to clarify bills proposed in each chamber, the Senate and House agreed on *An Act to Accept a Cession of the Claims of the State of North Carolina to a Certain District of Western Territory*. It was signed into law by the President on April 2, 1790.[1]

Congress next provided a name and a form of government for the newly ceded lands. On May 26, President Washington signed *An Act for the Government of the Territory of the United States, South of the River Ohio*, adopted by the Senate and House of Representatives a few days earlier. The House had sought to substitute the word *Southeast* for *South* in the name, but agreed to let South stand when the Senate objected to the change.[2] This awkward, ambiguous name was to remain unchanged until the new government was later converted into a state of the Union.[3]

---

1. Linda Grant De Pauw, ed., *Documentary History of the First Federal Congress of the United States of America, March 4, 1789-March 3, 1791*, Vol. VI, *Legislative Histories* (Baltimore: Johns Hopkins University Press, 1986), pp. 1544-51.

2. *Journal of the House of Representatives of the United States, Being the Second Session of the First Congress, Begun and Held at the City of New York, January 4, 1790* (Washington, D.C.: Gales and Seaton, 1826), pp. 204, 209.

3. Carter, ed., *Territorial Papers, SWT*, IV, p. 18.

Declaring that the territorial government was by its nature temporary, the Congress established it as a single district. The act provided that the inhabitants should enjoy "all the privileges, benefits and advantages" set forth in the Ordinance of 1787 for the Territory Northwest of the River Ohio. It mandated that the government of the newer territory would be similar to that of the older except as otherwise provided in the act to accept the cession. In addition, the office of governor would be united with that of the Superintendent of Indian Affairs in the Southern Department. The officers of the territory, including the governor, the secretary, three judges, and generals of militia, would be nominated and appointed by the President with the advice and consent of the Senate.[4]

As the President evaluated potential appointees to fill the offices of the territorial government, he received advice from many, especially members of the North Carolina congressional delegation. That group, which included Hugh Williamson, Timothy Bloodworth, John B. Ashe, and Benjamin Hawkins, advocated the selection of William Blount as governor.[5] Significant support for Blount, a prominent North Carolina Federalist with prowestern sympathies, had been developed by Mero District Militia General Daniel Smith. The general had lobbied his Virginia friends in Congress with good results, notwithstanding Patrick Henry's offering General Joseph Martin of Virginia for the office. Blount seems to have been the choice of Secretary of State Thomas Jefferson, also.[6] He was known to the President as a soldier in the American Revolution, a former member of Congress, and a delegate to the convention that framed the federal Constitution in 1787. In 1790 William Blount was at the pinnacle of his political career, and he enjoyed great popularity throughout North Carolina. He was associated with his brothers Thomas and John Gray Blount in various commercial and shipping enterprises, and as a land speculator he claimed more than a million acres.[7] As early as 1782 he had favored the cession of the state's western lands, and in 1787 he had helped Mero District leaders James Robertson

---

4. Carter, ed., *Territorial Papers, SWT*, IV, pp. 18-19.
5. William H. Masterson, "William Blount and the Establishment of the Southwest Territory," East Tennessee Historical Society *Publications*, No. 23 (1951), p. 4; Carter, ed., *Territorial Papers, SWT*, IV, pp. 19-24.
6. Carter, ed., *Territorial Papers, SWT*, IV, pp. 21n, 23-24, 37.
7. Corlew, *Tennessee, A Short History*, p. 88; Alice Barnwell Keith, "Letters From Major James Cole Mountflorence to Members of the Blount Family (William, John Gray, and Thomas) From on Shipboard, Spain, France, Switzerland, England, and America, January 22, 1792—July 21, 1796," *North Carolina Historical Review*, Vol. XIV, (July 1937), pp. 251-52; A.V. Goodpasture, "William Blount and the Old Southwest Territory," *American Historical Magazine*, Vol. 8, (January 1903), p. 3.

and David Hays draft a memorial to the general assembly asking for cession of the western territory to the federal government as a means of obtaining protection for the frontier people.[8]

Blount actively sought the office of governor, mobilizing key political personalities in his support wherever he could. By March 31 he was looking upon himself already "as an officer of distinction under the Federal Government, being assured...that he will be appointed governor of the western territory," an acquaintance at Wilmington learned.[9] Public office was not a new experience for Blount. He had been a member of the North Carolina House of Commons four times and its speaker once; he was for two terms a state senator in North Carolina. A member of Congress in 1786, he had opposed ratification of the Treaty of Hopewell concluded in November of the prior year. The stand won many friends for him in the West.

The President was aware of the enthusiasm in the Holston country for John Sevier. A convention had been held at Greeneville, and those present unanimously "urged in strong terms" that the former governor of the state of Franklin be appointed governor of the territory.[10] Sevier had little support elsewhere, however.

On June 8 President Washington appointed Blount to a three-year term as governor of the territory and superintendent of Indian affairs for the southeastern United States. On the same day he selected Daniel Smith of Mero District to be secretary of the territory and later appointed John McNairy, David Campbell, and Joseph Anderson to be judges.[11]

Gratified by his selection as governor, Blount confided to a friend

---

8. St. George L. Sioussat, "The North Carolina Cession of 1784 in its Federal Aspects," *Proceedings of the Mississippi Valley Historical Association, 1908-1909*, Vol. II (Cedar Rapids, Iowa: The Torch Press, 1910), p. 44; Goodpasture, "William Blount and the Old Southwest Territory," p. 4.

9. McRee, *Life and Correspondence of James Iredell*, Vol. II, pp. 285-86.

10. Samuel C. Williams, *Phases of Southwest Territory History* (Johnson City, Tennessee: The Watauga Press, 1940), p. 2.

11. John McNairy was admitted to the bar of the Superior Court of Washington District at Jonesborough in 1788. In the same year he was appointed judge of the Superior Court of North Carolina for Davidson and Sumner counties and was continued when the Mero District Court became its successor. He became a delegate from Davidson County to the Tennessee Constitutional Convention of 1796. Carter, ed., *Territorial Papers, SWT*, IV, pp. 22n, 25-26, 27-29. David Campbell, a major in the Continental Army during the Revolution, was licensed to practice law in 1780 in Washington County, Virginia. Later he settled in the Holston country and became chief judge of the state of Franklin. Williams, *The Lost State of Franklin*, pp. 291-92. Joseph Anderson, also a Revolutionary War major, was, in Blount's words, "a good citizen, a gentleman, a learned judge and a very agreeable and open companion." He and his wife Patience Outlaw lived on a large tract of land on the Nolichucky River when he was named a judge. Fay E. McMillan, "A Biographical Sketch of Joseph Anderson (1757-1837)," East Tennessee Historical Society *Publications*, No. 2 (1930), pp. 84-85.

that the appointment was more important to him than "any other gift of the President could have been." His presence in the western country would "secure" his landholdings and increase their value, he said. Indeed, he saw in the whole territory a series of unmatched opportunities to trade in land, even though his appointment required him to enforce treaties that would slow the opening of the lands to settlement.[12]

Although Congress had reenacted the Ordinance of 1787 at its first session in 1789 and was familiar with its contents, the specific provisions of the statute were virtually unknown in North Carolina. Blount could not locate a copy within the state and delayed his departure for the West until after the text could be sent to him from Philadelphia. In the interim the laws of North Carolina remained in force.[13]

From his copy of the Ordinance of 1787, Blount learned that it provided for the establishment of a temporary government that would be terminated when the population of specific areas reached the minimum levels required for statehood. The ordinance was in two parts. The first set forth the form of government to be organized, and the second outlined in six articles a "compact" or solemn agreement between the people of the states and those of the territory.

The form of government was designed to provide an evolutionary process of development from territory to full statehood in three stages. By devising a method for rising above an initially subordinate status, it successfully addressed the problem *"how to govern a dependency"* that the British had been unable to solve in North America. Territories or parts of territories could finally be admitted to the Union *"on a basis of equality with the existing states."* If sufficiently populated, no territory could avoid movement toward and achievement of statehood.[14]

In the first stage, all political control was vested in the federally appointed governor, who exercised supreme executive power, and the three judges, who wielded ultimate judicial authority. Jointly those four persons constituted a general assembly in which legislative authority resided. At that level, there was no provision for self-government, and the officials "were answerable solely to the President and Congress of the

---

12. Blount to John Steele of North Carolina, July 10, 1790, H.M. Wagstaff, ed., *The Papers of John Steele*, Vol. I (Raleigh, North Carolina: Publications of the North Carolina Historical Commission, 1924), pp. 67-68, 69; Masterson, "William Blount and the Establishment of the Southwest Territory," p. 14.

13. Eblen, *The First and Second United States Empires*, p. 48n; Carter, ed., *Territorial Papers, SWT*, IV, pp. 32, 36.

14. Harlow Lindley, Norris F. Schneider, and Milo M. Quaife, *History of the Ordinance of 1787 and the Old Northwest Territory* (Marietta, Ohio: Northwest Territory Celebration Commission, 1937), pp. 77-78.

United States." There was a secretary who kept the records of the territory and who served, also, as acting governor when the governor was absent or otherwise unable to fulfill his duties. The five ranking officials had to meet property ownership qualifications: the governor must own at least one thousand acres in the territory; the secretary and the judges (and in the second stage, the councillors) must have five hundred acres each.[15]

Settlers could choose to move to the second stage of government when there were five thousand free adult male inhabitants in that area of the territory looking to statehood. At that point a general assembly of two houses would be organized with the members of one house selected by the voters and the members of the other chosen by a procedure involving both the voters and the national government. The governor, secretary, and judges would continue to function as federal appointees. The assembly could elect a delegate to Congress who had the right to speak on the floor about matters pertaining to the territory but had no right to vote.

The third stage was reached when the prospective state achieved a minimum population of sixty thousand free inhabitants. The voters could then petition Congress to be admitted to the Union "on equal footing with the original states in all respects whatever." At the same time it was necessary to adopt a constitution and organize a state government that Congress would find to be suitably democratic.[16]

Although the compact contained certain articles dealing with the maximum and minimum number of states and their boundaries that could be created from the territory, there were others of more far-reaching effect. For example, the first article guaranteed complete freedom of religious belief and worship. Other articles addressed additional basic rights such as guaranteeing the sanctity of private contracts, a provision copied into the United States Constitution. A third article abolished the law of primogeniture, dashing the age-old practice of the eldest son alone inheriting the estate of his father. Yet another spoke eloquently—and ahead of its time—for education and schools: "Religion, morality, and knowledge, being necessary to good government and the

---

15. Eblen, *The First and Second United States Empires,* pp. 35, 36.
16. Lindley, Schneider, and Quaife, *History of the Ordinance of 1787 and the Old Northwest Territory,* pp. 77, 80.

happiness of mankind, schools and means of education shall forever be encouraged."[17]

Recognizing the importance of navigation on the waterways of the Mississippi and St. Lawrence river systems, the compact proclaimed that the navigable streams leading into the two great rivers were to be "common highways, 'forever free' to the people of the United States." This provision was close to the hearts of the Southwest Territory folk who needed river transportation to get their produce to market.[18]

Blount, a slave owner, paid no attention to the article prohibiting slavery and involuntary servitude in the territory. That provision had been made inapplicable to the Southwest Territory by act of Congress when it accepted the North Carolina cession law forbidding the passage of any law or laws that interfered with the practice of slavery.

The governor must surely have nodded his head skeptically when he read the compact's rules for dealing with the northern Indians, who, as their counterparts in the Southwest, were determined to prevent further settlement. Could the Golden Rule be applied? Would it work? The ordinance insisted that the Indians should be treated with good faith and their liberties respected. It required the frontier people to enact "laws founded in justice and humanity" to preserve peace and friendship with them.[19]

A reading of the Ordinance of 1787 must have been politically reassuring to settlers in the Holston and Cumberland valleys. Its language opened a step-by-step path from wilderness territory to statehood, avoiding any inclination that might have been harbored by some to accept traditional colonial or dependency status. This and other territories would not become the exploited partners in colonial empire but instead would be divided into new states when their population was sufficient. And always the new states would have the same rights and privileges as the original thirteen.[20]

President Washington's selection of Blount as governor of the territory placed "the archetype of the 'powerful speculators' of our history"

---

17. Ibid., pp. 81-82.
18. Ibid., p. 83.
19. Ibid.
20. James W. Livingood, "The Tennessee Country at the Birth of a Nation," *Chattanews,* Vol. XVIII (December 1987), p. 11; Robert F. Berkhofer, Jr., "The Northwest Ordinance and the Principle of Territorial Evolution," *The American Territorial System,* ed. John Porter Bloom, National Archives Conferences, Vol. V (Athens: Ohio University Press, 1973), pp. 45, 46.

in an even more powerful position. Nevertheless, the speculator had much in common with the settlers. Both needed a greater population in the West, Blount for land sales and the citizens for security. Both were on the side of local law and order, with the exception of dealings with the Indians; both coveted river transportation rights. They easily agreed that Indian resistance to settlement must be broken, and they were committed to democracy, especially in land ownership. Neither would tolerate old-world practices or other forms of elitism in the selection of buyers for land. Although the speculator and the frontier citizens did not always agree, they often recognized that the mutuality of their interests was compelling.[21]

At Washington, North Carolina, on August 18, Governor Blount received copies of the congressional acts establishing the territory, and six days later he started back across the mountains to take the reins of government. During a stopover at Hillsborough, he persuaded George Roulstone, editor of the Fayetteville *Gazette,* and his partner, the printer Robert Ferguson, to relocate to the territory and become editor-publishers of its first newspaper.[22] Aware of the importance of the press to communicate his acts and opinions to the settlers, Blount probably promised the newspapermen that he would subsidize them by placing the printing business of the territorial government in their shop.[23]

Later Blount stopped at Governor Alexander Martin's in Guilford County where he "met some unexpected information" that impelled him to redirect his journey to include a visit to President Washington. Before leaving Martin, he acquired a proclamation from the North Carolina governor confirming the acceptance by Congress of the cession, a document that would be valuable to him in setting up the new government. He took with him, also, some grants for lands in the territory, signed by Governor Martin.[24]

As Blount left Guilford County on September 6 for Alexandria, Virginia, he dispatched a trusted aide, Major George Farragut, to Mero District to deliver the President's commission to General Smith as secretary of the territory. By letter he promised Smith that he would

---

21. William H. Masterson, "The Land Speculator and the West—The Role of William Blount," East Tennessee Historical Society *Publications,* No. 27 (1955), pp. 3-6.
22. Masterson, *William Blount,* pp. 181-82.
23. Keith, ed., *The John Gray Blount Papers,* Vol. II, pp. 116-17.
24. Carter, ed., *Territorial Papers, SWT,* IV, pp. 35-36; Goodpasture, "William Blount and the Old Southwest Territory," p. 5; Masterson, *William Blount,* p. 182.

join him in the West as soon as possible. He warned that the administration of the laws of North Carolina should go on "as if no cession had been made or accepted" until the governor arrived, published all facts pertaining to the change, and organized the government of the territory. Farragut carried a manuscript copy of the Northwest Ordinance of 1787 to be passed to Judge John McNairy to acquaint him with the primary laws by which the territory would be governed.[25]

On September 17, 1790, Blount reached Alexandria, and he spent the next day and night in consultation with President Washington at Mount Vernon. On September 20, Blount took the oath of his office before Justice James Iredell of the United States Supreme Court. He visited the President again on September 21, and on the next day he set out for the ceded territory.[26]

Although no records of Blount's exchanges with the President have been discovered, it must be assumed they discussed the duties of the governor and reviewed federal policy toward the Indian tribes of the southern department over which Blount was superintendent. The President's proclamation of August 26, 1790, warning citizens against violating the terms of the 1786 Treaty of Hopewell with the Choctaw and Chickasaw and requiring all officers of government to enforce it, surely received their attention. It is equally certain that Washington briefed Blount on both the United States treaty with the Creek that had just been concluded in New York and the prospects of war between Spain and Great Britain.[27]

Perhaps at that time Blount began to understand the extent of the numerous powers conferred upon him as territorial governor. Never before had he exercised such far-reaching political control.[28] The appointive power alone was extraordinary; the governor was charged with appointing all county officeholders and all militia officers below the rank of general. He was to recommend candidates for general officers to the President for appointment by him.

The governor held authority in many other areas of government. As commander of the regular army and the militia in his territory, he could requisition regular troops and/or militia from neighboring states, and

---

25. Carter, ed., *Territorial Papers, SWT,* IV, pp. 35-36.
26. Masterson, "William Blount and the Establishment of the Southwest Territory," p. 12; Keith, ed., *The John Gray Blount Papers,* Vol. II, p. 120.
27. Carter, ed., *Territorial Papers, SWT,* IV, pp. 32, 34, 37.
28. Masterson, "William Blount and the Establishment of the Southwest Territory," p. 12.

as superintendent of Indian affairs, he could treat with the Indians. He could decree ordinances and with the three judges could propose and enact laws. Not only could he make laws, but he possessed a veto over them and was their enforcer. He also licensed lawyers. He could create towns and counties, locate seats of government, and change boundaries within the territory. Even his salary, set and paid by Congress, was secure from local tampering. He was essentially an autocrat, remaining responsible only to the President and Congress until the territorial general assembly was convened in 1794.[29]

Eventually Blount reached the ceded territory on October 10 and stopped at the residence of William Yancey just south of the twentieth-century city of Bristol, Tennessee. From Yancey's he reported his presence to distant Mero District, telling Smith and Robertson that he would first organize government on the east side of the Cumberland Mountains and subsequently proceed to the Cumberland settlements to "fill the commissions for civil officers" there.[30]

Within the next ten days, Blount traveled a short distance southeastward to the home of William Cobb in Washington County. There, near the Watauga River, he established residence with the Cobbs in their nine-room, two-story house built of white oak logs. It became at once the seat of the territorial government and remained so until the spring of 1792 when the governor would move to Knoxville, a town yet to be laid out near James White's fort, 105 miles to the southwest.

Although the house, which became known as Rocky Mount, was probably built by Cobb in the early 1770s, it was spacious and comfortable.[31] The governor was delighted to find it had glass windows, rare on the frontier, and several fireplaces, one of which warmed the room assigned to him.[32]

Cobb, one-time close associate of Richard Caswell, late governor of

---

29. Carter, ed., *Territorial Papers, NWT*, II, pp. 42-45; Eblen, *The First and Second United States Empires*, p. 49; Masterson, *William Blount*, p. 184.
30. Carter, ed., *Territorial Papers, SWT*, IV, pp. 37-38.
31. Research to determine the date of the original construction of the William Cobb house led Liz M. Johnson to entertain serious doubts that the building standing at the end of the twentieth century was built before the early part of the nineteenth century. Her report, "Construction Analysis of Rocky Mount," Typescript, Rocky Mount Historical Association, January, 1981, Tennessee Historical Commission, is well reasoned, but depends almost wholly on preservation science, a discipline then in its infancy.
32. Pauline Massengill De Friece and Frank B. William, Jr., "Rocky Mount: The Cobb-Massengill Home, First Capitol of the Territory South of the River Ohio," *Tennessee Historical Quarterly*, Vol. XXV (Summer 1966), pp. 119, 120-21; P.L. Cobb, "William Cobb—Host to Governor William Blount," *Tennessee Historical Magazine*, Vol. IX (January 1926), pp. 258-59.

North Carolina, was an admirable choice to be host to the governor and supplier of the seat of government. Although he may not have been the wealthy planter depicted by some nineteenth-century historians, he bought and sold land and was of comfortable means, a land trader rather than a land speculator. Cobb had no political scars. He had been loyal to North Carolina during the life of the state of Franklin and had successfully avoided alignment with either principal in the Tipton-Sevier feud. Respectfully regarded by his neighbors, he had been one of the commissioners to lay out the town of Jonesborough and was a member of the Washington County Quarterly Court.[33]

Why did Blount choose Rocky Mount as the first capital of the new territory? He left no written explanation. It appears to have been chosen because it was accessible to most of the settled areas of the Holston country and was a site from which the seat of government could be relocated without offending the civic pride of the town left behind. For example, Blount did not locate in nearby Jonesborough or in Rogersville, the most advanced towns in the area. He was thinking ahead to a location farther down the Holston, nearer the Cherokee Nation. Probably he was envisioning a place that could serve well as a trading post and/or as a base for further settlement in areas to be acquired from the Cherokee.

Although he had not selected such a site, he was inclined to a location "about the mouth of Clinch" on land he owned on Emory River. Such a choice would be agreeable to the citizens of the district, but Blount knew that he could not make a final decision until after he held a treaty with the Cherokee and until he could determine from the secretary of war "how many and on what part of the Tennessee the continental troops" were to be stationed. The advantages of his land on Emory River included its central location between the districts of Washington and Mero, its attractiveness to prospective settlers, and its nearness to the territory of the southern Indian tribes. A garrison there would prevent the Indians from crossing the Tennessee into the territory and guarantee safe passage to and from Mero. With the seat of government settled, it would be possible to compel the "Indian traders generally to trade there" with the result that the "greater part of the Indian trade

---

33. Masterson, *William Blount*, p. 184; Cobb, "William Cobb—Host to Governor William Blount," pp. 255-56; De Friece and Williams, "Rocky Mount: The Cobb-Massengill Home," pp. 121-23.

might be drawn to that spot." Public discussion of the Emory site had doubled its value.[34]

Ever the consummate politician, Blount was planning to use the name Knoxville for the permanent capital city of the territory. The name would honor Secretary of War Henry Knox whose favorable interest was crucial to the welfare of the frontier people. In fact, when Roulstone and Ferguson began publishing the territory newspaper in 1791 at Rogersville, its name was the Knoxville *Gazette*. It may have been the first time in America that a newspaper had appeared with the name of the town on its masthead before the town existed.

There seems to have been little opposition to Blount's choice of Rocky Mount as the first capital of the territory. Although the trip from Mero District to Washington County was long and difficult for Secretary Daniel Smith, even he understood that the seat of government had to be where the population was concentrated. Some in the Cumberland settlements, so far removed from the prior seat of government east of the Appalachians, hoped that the capital would be located at Nashville. The French-born attorney, teacher, and land speculator James C. Mountflorence was one of these, but they had no reason to expect that Mero District would be selected to furnish the territorial capital. They had made the point of their distance from Washington County, however, and Blount was well aware of it.[35]

The conversion of local government to territorial status was begun on October 22 when the governor ordained that the county of Washington, North Carolina, created in 1777, would be known thereafter as "Washington County in the Territory of the United States of America South of the River Ohio." On the next day at the courthouse, Blount convened all the officeholders of Washington County who held their appointments or elections under the authority of North Carolina, gave them official notice of the cession, its acceptance, and the creation of the territory. He produced his credentials as governor and administered the oath of office to Judge David Campbell. From the leadership elite of the county, he then appointed the justices of the peace, the sheriff and deputies, the constables, and the register. The last appointments he made were for the militia officers and their commander, Lieutenant

---

34. Keith, ed., *The John Gray Blount Papers,* Vol. II, pp. 136-37.
35. Durham, *Daniel Smith, Frontier Statesman,* p. 124; Keith, ed., *The John Gray Blount Papers,* Vol. II, p. 137.

Colonel Landon Carter. In most instances in this and the other counties, he made it a policy to reappoint those holding office under the authority of North Carolina.[36]

Blount deliberately dodged the reappointment of Sevier's enemy, John Tipton, as militia commander by offering him the county's first "Commission of the Peace." When Tipton refused to accept it on the grounds that he was too old to act as a justice of the peace, the governor extended his logic to include the more demanding office of militia commander and selected Carter in his place. Even though he had thought it necessary to reduce Tipton's level of prominence in government, the governor made face-saving appointments to the other three field officers of the county, all of whom "leaned toward" Tipton's faction.[37]

On October 25 the governor brought Sullivan County, created in 1779, into the territory, following the same procedure employed in Washington County. Greene County, since 1783, was next on November 1; Hawkins, 1786, followed two days later. The office of lieutenant colonel commandant of militia went to Gilbert Christian in Sullivan, Daniel Kennedy in Greene, and Stockley Donelson in Hawkins counties. Blount changed Washington District, North Carolina, containing the counties of Washington, Sullivan, Greene, and Hawkins, into Washington District in the territory and appointed Francis Alexander Ramsey court clerk for the district superior court of law and Andrew Russell clerk and master for the district court of equity. He made Jonesborough the seat of the superior courts. Also, he commissioned the officers in the district cavalry, appointing Thomas King as lieutenant colonel commandant.[38]

Considering the distance between the districts, the governor acceded to the North Carolina practice of having a commanding general of the militia in each. On November 26 he recommended to the secretary of war that John Sevier be appointed brigadier general, commander of the Washington District Militia, and James Robertson, brigadier general, commander of the Mero District Militia. Sevier had previously served as commander under North Carolina, but Robertson would be assuming a new responsibility, succeeding General Daniel Smith who had resigned the office to become secretary of the territory. Both Sevier

---

36. *The Blount Journal, 1790-1796* (Nashville: Tennessee Historical Commission, 1955), pp. 1-31; Keith, ed., *The John Gray Blount Papers,* Vol. II, p. 126.

37. Keith, ed., *The John Gray Blount Papers,* Vol. II, p. 136.

38. *The Blount Journal, 1790-1796,* pp. 31-39; Williams, *Phases of Southwest Territory History,* pp. 8, 16.

and Robertson were recommended by the President and later elected by Congress.[39]

The new government was well received by the settlers in the Holston country. The "officers and inhabitants of Greene County" drafted statements of welcome to Blount and Judge Campbell and assured them that the territorial government would be respected and supported. After establishing the territorial government in the four counties of Washington District, Blount was optimistic. He wrote to John Gray Blount: "Everybody appears to be perfectly pleased with the change and if I may judge from the attention shown me and honors paid me...as their governor—I could not wish for more and less would have been more agreeable—I will venture to say that the militia...are equal if not superior to any other four counties in the world."[40]

Blount had hoped to avoid going to Cumberland until spring, but he could conceive of no way to activate the territorial government there except by his own hand and presence. He had moved freely about Washington District without concern for his safety, but a journey to Mero would require a company large enough to fend off Indian attacks. Raiding parties had recently killed twelve travelers on the Kentucky Road and four or five hunters in Powell's Valley. Blount thought that ten guards would be adequate to accompany him, but at John Sevier's recommendation, he raised the number to twenty-five and added four or five friendly Indians. When he left Cobb's on November 27 with snow on the ground and more in prospect, some forty or fifty other travelers bound for Mero joined the party making it of such size that it made the passage without challenge.[41]

Holston folk looked forward to the governor's return and a report on the situation in Mero District. Many were anxious to relocate farther south and west; perhaps 70 percent were awaiting improved security in the West before relocating, but some were impatient and ventured westward to Cumberland.[42]

With the government of the most heavily populated part of the territory

---

39. Linda Grant De Pauw, ed., *Documentary History of the First Federal Congress of the United States of America, March 4, 1789-March 3, 1791*, Vol. II, *Senate Executive Journal and Related Documents* (Baltimore: Johns Hopkins University Press, 1972), pp. 475-77.
40. Carter, ed., *Territorial Papers, SWT*, IV, pp. 39-40; Keith, ed., *The John Gray Blount Papers*, Vol. II, pp. 131-32.
41. Keith, ed., *The John Gray Blount Papers*, Vol. II, pp. 138, 148-49.
42. Ibid., p. 140.

restructured and its ranking military commander identified, Governor Blount was ready to introduce the new government to the Cumberland country. First, he assembled at Nashville all of the county officials and militia officers of the counties of Davidson, Sumner, and Tennessee, and the court and militia officers of the Mero District. Explaining the origins of the new territory to them, he reconstituted the three counties under the authority of the Territory of the United States South of the River Ohio. Then the governor bound them together anew in the reorganized Mero District.

Two of the principal officeholders of the territory and all officials and militia officers of the three counties were recognized. John McNairy took his oath of office as one of the three judges provided in the Ordinance of 1787. Daniel Smith, secretary of the territory, presented his appointment from the President and subscribed the oath of office. The governor next appointed justices of the peace, sheriffs, registers, county court clerks, stray masters, solicitors, coroners, and constables for Davidson, Sumner, and Tennessee counties. He appointed the various militia officers including the lieutenant colonel commandant for each county: James Robertson, Davidson; James Winchester, Sumner; and James Ford, Tennessee. He made Robert Hays lieutenant colonel commandant of the Mero cavalry and appointed David Allison clerk of the district superior court of law and Joseph Sitgreaves clerk and master in the district courts of equity.[43]

Assuming his duties as secretary of the territory, Smith took over the keeping of Blount's journal, a record of the principal actions taken by the governor. He reconstructed it to include all of the governor's earlier official acts and appointments in Washington District and added, in order, the record of his meetings at Nashville. Smith would continue to be keeper of the journal throughout the lifetime of the territory, periodically sending transcriptions from it as the governor's report to the secretary of state.[44]

The Mero men were impressed by the well-dressed, dignified governor, but hardly had time to make an assessment of him during the eight days he was in Nashville. To be sure, he heard their petitions for aid to stop Indian attacks on the settlements, but after hearing them, he turned

---

43. *The Blount Journal, 1790-1796*, pp. 39-46.
44. Durham, *Daniel Smith, Frontier Statesman*, pp. 125-26.

his party eastward. After a slow crossing of the Cumberland Mountains, they arrived at Rocky Mount on December 29.[45]

Blount and the territory faced several difficult issues as they entered the new year. First, Virginia wanted to argue about the exact location of the state line separating that state from the territory. North Carolina seemed determined to continue to issue land grants in Indian territory south of French Broad causing friction there. Only two of the judges selected by the President were on the job as William Perry had declined to serve, and Judge Anderson had not yet been appointed in his place. Most vexing of all, the governor, under orders from the President to treat with the Cherokee for cession of the lands occupied by white settlers south of French Broad, was limited to negotiate within the framework of the Treaty of Hopewell. That order carried with it the mandate to block proposed white settlements at Muscle Shoals on the Tennessee.[46]

The organization of the territorial government was uppermost in the minds of many, yet some found time to plan financial speculations. John Sevier, Edmond Williams, and Landon Carter seized upon an opportunity with an unusually high potential for success. By virtue of the appointment of the latter two as state auditors and the former their secretary in 1783, they still held accounts and vouchers for which they could issue certificates of debt qualifying for assumption by the national government. Providing for interest for the seven years since the accounts were deposited and predating the certificates as if issued at that time, Sevier and associates produced the paper secretly and held it until the governor's brother could send money to make the purchase for speculative resale. Sevier and the Blounts would share the profits on about three-fourths of the value of the transaction. Carter and Williams would share the remaining one-fourth.

There were other opportunities. Sevier proposed "a scheme of old warrants." He had in hand warrants for about thirty thousand acres, already entered, that could be "levied on lands south of the French Broad" that would bring a twentyfold profit over their cost, payable in cattle. The warrants would not guarantee that a grant would be issued by North Carolina, but with Blount's behind the scenes help, Sevier

---

45. Keith, ed., *The John Gray Blount Papers*, Vol. II, p. 163; Masterson, *William Blount*, pp. 193-95.
46. Masterson, *William Blount*, p. 195; Carter, ed., *Territorial Papers, SWT*, IV. pp. 33, 40.

expected that the governor and secretary of state would honor them as they had honored others. Sevier and Blount believed that they could handle the sales without Blount's name ever appearing in connection with the transactions.[47]

---

47. Keith, ed., *The John Gray Blount Papers,* Vol. II, pp. 138-39.

CHAPTER IV

INDIAN NEIGHBORS AND THE TREATY OF HOLSTON

1791

Satisfied that government was established and the governor had taken up residence among them, the inhabitants of the territory were yet anxious about relations with their Indian neighbors. Although most believed that they could live at peace only if the Indians were overcome by force of arms, President Washington and the Congress were unanimous in their determination to avoid open war with the southern tribes. The northern Indians, encouraged by the British, were already at war with the United States in the Northwest Territory, and the young republic was in no position to fight wars on two fronts.

In neither territory were the settlers agents of peace. Both areas had been organized to accommodate and promote the immigration of settlers. Settlement, in turn, required additional land, and that meant whites would continually seek Indian holdings. The commitment to aggressive acquisition of land eliminated all possibilities of peaceful coexistence and, instead, cast the prospects of peace in the form of conquest where the victor takes all.

The settlers had reason to be encouraged when the duties of the governor and those of the superintendent of Indian affairs in the southern department[1] were combined and made the responsibility of William Blount. Blount understood that westward migration was fueled by the availability of land and that real estate could be supplied only by acquiring it from the Indians through negotiation or force or a combination of the two.

In 1790 uneasy relations existed between the westerners and the tribes living in or adjacent to the territory, except the Chickasaw who had a long-standing record as friends of the westernmost settlers. The largest Indian population in the southern department was claimed by the Creek whose hostility to non-Indian settlers had been demonstrated convincingly

---

1. In the southern department were the four tribes: Cherokee, Creek, Choctaw, and Chickasaw. They lived in the Southwest Territory and parts of the states of Virginia, North Carolina, South Carolina, Georgia, and Kentucky. Eblen, *The First and Second United States Empires*, p. 240.

in the Cumberland country. Backed by Spain, the Creek were regarded as such a threat to the United States that President Washington invited Chief Alexander McGillivray and representatives of the tribe to meet with him in New York.[2]

The result of Washington's meeting with the Creek chief was the conclusion of the Treaty of New York between the United States and the Creek Nation, signed on August 7, 1790. The Creek acknowledged themselves to be under the protection of the United States of America "and of no other sovereign whosoever." They agreed that they would not hold "any treaty" with another government or with any individual or group of individuals and that they would deliver to the proper authorities all prisoners then held in their nation. The United States guaranteed all Creek lands south and west of certain lines established by the treaty and agreed that any citizens of the United States who attempted to settle on any of the Creek's land would forfeit the protection of the United States and could be punished by the Indians as they saw fit.

Both sides agreed to refrain from reprisal or retaliation when an untoward act was committed against any person or persons until "satisfaction shall have been demanded and refused." The Creek promised to pass to the United States any information they might receive relative to any other tribe having hostile designs on any of the states or territories. In return, the United States promised to assist the Creek "to become herdsmen and cultivators" by furnishing "domestic animals and implements of husbandry." By a secret article to the treaty, McGillivray was commissioned brigadier general, U.S.A., with corresponding salary "and the understanding that he would act as agent of the United States among his people."[3]

Next-door neighbors to the inhabitants of Washington District, the Cherokee deeply resented the government's failure to enforce the Treaty of Hopewell. The most glaring violations of the treaty were the penetration of thousands of whites into an area south of the French Broad River and the establishment of the counties of Greene and Hawkins below the treaty line. Whites had strayed across treaty lines at other places

---

2. D.C. Corbitt, "Exploring the Southwest Territory in the Spanish Archives," *East Tennessee Historical Society Publications,* No. 38 (1966), p. 111.

3. *ASP, II, Indian Affairs,* Vol. I, pp. 81-82; D.C. Corbitt, "Exploring the Southwest Territory in the Spanish Archives," p. 110.

and had built homes west of the Holston and Tennessee rivers on lands guaranteed to the Indians.[4] Although in 1788 the United States had issued a proclamation forbidding "all such unwarrantable intrusions" and explicitly ordering all intruders to depart with their families without delay, the settlers had not complied. In fact, intrusions had continued.

Four days after McGillivray signed the Treaty of New York, the Senate authorized the President to enforce the Treaty of Hopewell or to renegotiate it with the Cherokee "for such further cession of territory... as the tranquility and interest of the United States may require." The Senate limited the size of any land acquisition by specifying that the government's annual payment for it to the Cherokee should not exceed one thousand dollars. Such a treaty could legitimatize the intrusions by purchasing the settled lands and relocating boundaries appropriately.[5]

A few months later, the War Department revealed a plan to prevent the usurpation of Indian lands along the lower Tennessee River targeted by speculators for settlement. Once its combat duties in the Northwest had ended, the army would send an expedition to erect a military post at Occochappo or Bear Creek, just below Muscle Shoals. Governor Blount was instructed to render the Cherokee Nation "cordial" to a United States military presence at the shoals.[6] A representative from the War Department who visited the Bear Creek site noted that maintenance of a post there would depend on the goodwill of the Creek and Cherokee since it was remote from the settlements and all access was controlled by the Indians. He doubted that the Cherokee would accept the post: "They are already so hemmed in and encroached upon by the Franklin and Cumberland people that the Tennessee is their only outlet, in case of misfortune... a post [there]... must shut this door against them."[7]

Responding to the President's order to treat with the Cherokee, Blount sent a message to their leading chiefs soon after January 1, 1791, inviting them to meet with him on the last day of May to discuss a revision

---

4. Corlew, *Tennessee, A Short History*, p. 90; *ASP, II, Indian Affairs*, Vol. I, p. 83.

5. *ASP, II, Indian Affairs*, Vol. I, p. 83.

6. A second post for the same purpose was proposed for the eastern bank of the Mississippi River on a site yet to be acquired from Spain by negotiation. Randolph C. Downs, "Indian Affairs in the Southwest Territory, 1790-1796," *Tennessee Historical Magazine*, Series II, Vol. III (January 1937), p. 240.

7. Colton Storm, ed., "Up the Tennessee in 1790: The Report of Major John Doughty to the Secretary of War," East Tennessee Historical Society *Publications*, No. 17 (1945), p. 126.

of the Treaty of Hopewell.[8] Friends of the territory rallied to support the conference. Arthur Campbell, a leader in neighboring Southwest Virginia, urged Cherokee Chief John Watts to accept Blount's invitation. Reminding Watts that President Washington loved all men, "red people as well as whites," Campbell advised the Cherokee to follow the Creek in making "a lasting peace." Even Creek Chief McGillivray, when asked by the Cherokee, advised them to treat with the Americans.[9]

As the summer approached, enemies of the governor interceded with the Cherokee. Andrew Pickens of South Carolina, an adversary of Blount's since they were on the opposite sides of most issues negotiated at the Treaty of Hopewell, warned the Indians that the governor coveted their land and would have it unless they were careful. Indian traders, fearing that Blount's lieutenants would preempt their livelihood, circulated rumors that he was leading the chiefs into a trap where they would be massacred. To assure the Cherokee of his benevolent intentions, Blount sent James Robertson to counsel with them. Robertson's good reputation, earned during prior years when he was agent to their nation, offset the work of the governor's detractors and guaranteed the presence of the important chiefs at the treaty grounds.[10]

The prospects for a willing gathering of the Cherokee chiefs had been threatened, also, by the antics of Zachariah Cox and members of the Tennessee Company. Holding a grant from the state of Georgia for 3.5 million acres in the great bend of the Tennessee River, Cox and his principal partners John Strother and Thomas Gilbert had advertised their lands extensively. They promised bounty grants of 500 acres to each settler family and 250 acres to every single man.[11]

Although prospective purchasers or "adventurers" had been notified to gather at the confluence of the Holston and French Broad on January 10, 1791, to begin the trip to the great bend, few appeared. After waiting nearly three months, Cox recognized he would be leading no armada down the Holston. Finally, on March 26, he, Strother, and Gilbert set

---

8. Keith, ed., *The John Gray Blount Papers,* Vol. II, p. 163.

9. Campbell to Watts, February 11, 1791, in Knoxville *Gazette,* January 28, 1792; *Dunlap's American Daily Advertiser,* June 21, 1791.

10. Masterson, *William Blount,* p. 198; Craig Symonds, "The Failure of America's Indian Policy on the Southwestern Frontier, 1785-1793," *Tennessee Historical Quarterly,* Vol. XXXV (Spring 1976), p. 30.

11. Philip M. Hamer, ed., "Letters of Governor William Blount," East Tennessee Historical Society *Publications,* No. 4 (1932), pp. 123-24; Isaac Joslin Cox and Reginald McGrane, eds., "Documents Relating to Zachariah Cox," *Quarterly Publication of the Historical and Philosophical Society of Ohio,* Vol. VIII, Nos. 2 and 3 (combined issue; April-June, July-September 1913), pp. 31-33.

out with twenty-nine other armed men by boat to visit their prize near Muscle Shoals. When members of the small party reached their destination, they hesitated to proceed with their project because Indian opposition was so unyielding. They quickly abandoned the undertaking when a messenger arrived bringing a warning from Blount that if they did not return, the Indians would be free to treat them as they might think proper without offense to the United States. The governor advised them that even if the Indians should permit them to settle at Muscle Shoals, the United States would not.[12]

The government's stern treatment of the land grabbers seemed partially to nullify the effects of their blatant violation of Indian territory. The Tennessee Company's attempted settlement of the "Bent" discouraged the attendance of local Cherokee at the upcoming treaty talks at Holston but prompted them to be alert to any proposals regarding settlements in their area.

Although Cox's colonization plan had been frustrated, the attempt confirmed the Creek's darkest suspicions about the land-hungry westerners. McGillivray had warned Miro in June, 1790, of potential land grabs by speculators styled the Virginia Yazoo Company, the South Carolina Yazoo Company, and the Tennessee Company. All posed threats to the Creek and to Spain, he reasoned.[13]

The Indians could not help observing that when the territorial government sought to have Cox indicted by the grand jury at the next term of the Washington District Superior Court, the efforts came to naught. His peers would not indict him. The grand jury's decision gave Cox a "sort of triumph" over government "in the eyes of ignorant people," Blount said. But, he warned, the government would halt him or anyone else who attempted a settlement on Indian lands. Never having totally abandoned his earlier designs to acquire and develop the bend of the Tennessee, Blount was pleased to thwart the plans of his competitors by loyally implementing the policies of the federal government.[14]

While the governor was preparing to meet the Cherokee, the Creek treaty of the prior summer came under destructive pressure created by

---

12. Kentucky *Gazette*, January 15, 1791; Cox and McGrane, eds., "Documents Relating to Zachariah Cox," p. 33; *ASP, II, Indian Affairs*, Vol. I, p. 115.
13. Holmes, "Spanish-American Rivalry Over the Chickasaw Bluffs," p. 33.
14. Carter, ed., *Territorial Papers, SWT*, IV, p. 79; Ramsey, *The Annals of Tennessee*, p. 551; Masterson, *William Blount*, p. 213.

William Augustus Bowles, brazen leader of a Bahama Islands group seeking to secure the Indian trade then controlled by Panton, Leslie and Company. After escorting several Creek and Cherokee chiefs to London, England, in 1790, Bowles had returned to represent himself falsely as the British agent to the Creek. He promised them not only war stuffs and other merchandise in trade, but the support of the British army against the United States if necessary. He succeeded in casting doubt on McGillivray's loyalty to his own people and made it impossible for the chief to win tribal support for the Treaty of New York. What had appeared to have been a salutary treaty for the people of the frontier, as it promised restraint by the Creek, suddenly became worthless.[15]

The national government in 1790 and 1791 was principally concerned with keeping the peace and consolidating its holdings. The Indians in the Northwest would have no peace, however, and the settlers in the Southwest would have peace only on their own terms and those cordially unacceptable to the Cherokee and Creek.[16]

While awaiting the midsummer convocation with the Cherokee, the sparsely manned territorial government had other tasks to perform. Probably the most pressing was a response to the congressional demand for an estimate of "the quantity and situation of the lands in the territory not claimed by the Indians, nor granted to, nor claimed by any of the citizens of the United States." After adding acreages represented by the Indian claims, the North Carolina Military Reservation, those grants and titles to grants vested in individuals by the laws of North Carolina, entries made in Washington and Sullivan counties for which grants had not been issued, and entries made in John Armstrong's office under the "land grab" act of 1783, about three hundred thousand acres remained open to disposal by the United States.[17]

Hundreds of thousands of acres entered in Armstrong's office were in tracts interspersed across the territory, with concentrations along the lower waters of the Tennessee and Cumberland rivers and the eastern banks of the Mississippi River. A great many entries were for lands still in possession of the Cherokee and Chickasaw.[18]

---

15. Philip M. Hamer, "The British in Canada and the Southern Indians," *East Tennessee Historical Society Publications*, No. 2 (1930), pp. 107-8.
16. Symonds, "The Failure of America's Indian Policy on the Southwestern Frontier, 1785-1793," p. 29.
17. Carter, ed., *Territorial Papers, SWT,* IV, pp. 48, 70, 93.
18. Ibid., p. 58.

Compiling data about specific land areas was further complicated by the fact that no one could walk with certainty the boundary between the territory and North Carolina because no map of the ceded area existed. Landmarks that anchored the line had been pointed out in the cession act, but the connecting lines had not been run nor had anyone laid down "on any regular chart" the distances between the stations, the directions of the water courses, and the lay of the land.[19]

The federal government also wanted to know the population of the Southwest Territory. Although the act of Congress calling for a national census to be made in 1791 did not include the territory, Secretary of State Jefferson requested Blount to have the enumeration made by assigning the duty to each county sheriff. He acknowledged that, as the act had not included the territory among the political subdivisions to be counted, there were no funds available for expenses.[20]

Even before he received Jefferson's letter about the census, Blount had notified the militia lieutenant-colonels that they should make "an actual enumeration" of the people in each county. He proposed that each militia captain of infantry would be responsible for his own district and that the counting should include "every person of every rank, sex, and color."[21]

The governor's census was necessary to determine if there were five thousand "free male inhabitants of full age" in the territory,[22] a minimum requirement for holding elections for representatives to a general assembly. Such elections would raise the new government to its second stage and give voters their first chance to participate in it.

On September 19, 1791, the Southwest Territory submitted a census of 35,691 persons; 7,042 were reported from Mero District and 28,649 from Washington District. Significantly, there were 6,271 white males twenty-one years of age and older, a total that made it legally possible for the governor to call for elections for members of a house of representatives. The report revealed the presence of 3,417 slaves, 361 free persons of color, and a near equality in the number of white males and females: 16,548 to 15,365. That the population was a young one was indicated by this statistic: 10,277 white males were under twenty-one

---

19. Ibid.
20. Ibid., pp. 52-53.
21. Ibid., pp. 49-50.
22. Carter, ed., *Territorial Papers, NWT,* II, p. 44.

years of age. The survey did not elicit the age of "free white females."

The population was reported by county, and the largest of the seven counties was Greene with 7,741 persons. In declining order the other counties were Hawkins, 6,970; Washington, 5,872; Sullivan, 4,447; Davidson, 3,459; Sumner, 2,196; and Tennessee, 1,387. In addition, the report included the area south of the French Broad where 3,619 persons had settled on Cherokee lands. Only five militia captains failed to report their totals in time to have them included in the report; one from Davidson, one from south of the French Broad, and three from Greene.[23] Blount estimated the "deficiency" to be "as high as one thousand five hundred souls." He believed, also, that the totals reported were somewhat understated because heads of households, "fearing a General Assembly would shortly be the consequence," were reluctant to turn in all family members. Blount used his interpretation of the census to delay the advent of a popularly elected assembly; he made no move toward holding elections.[24]

From mid-February, 1791, Secretary Smith had been at Rocky Mount, working with the governor on various problems facing the territory. Smith understood that the first object of the territorial government was "to render our country populous," and with that ever in mind, he watched carefully as Congress considered a tax bill on distilled spirits of domestic origin. Should the territory be made exempt, the result would be to "excite migrations" to it, he believed. When the law passed, its provisions exempted both territories, and Smith's expectations were soon fulfilled.[25]

In his first full year in the territory, Blount was more interested in promoting immigration than he was in making laws. Although the governor and the judges, acting together, had the authority to pass laws, none were passed during 1791. Governed by the Ordinance of 1787, the cession act, and the laws of North Carolina, the territory had a body of law adequate to meet its immediate needs. The first territorial statutes would not be adopted until June 11, 1792.[26]

---

23. *Enumeration of 1791*, p. 52.
24. Carter, ed., *Territorial Papers, SWT*, IV, p. 80; Masterson, *William Blount*, pp. 209, 242; Eblen, *The First and Second United States Empires*, p. 66.
25. Carter, ed., *Territorial Papers, SWT*, IV, p. 47; Hamer, ed., "Letters of Governor William Blount," p. 124.
26. *Laws of the State of Tennessee* including *Acts and Ordinances of the Governor and Judges of the Territory of the United States South of the River Ohio, 1792 and 1793, and Acts of the Territorial General Assembly, 1794 and 1795* (Knoxville: Printed and Published by George Roulstone, 1803), p. v (hereinafter cited as *Laws*).

The governor might have delayed his first venture into territorial lawmaking because he did not have a full complement of judges. The third judgeship had not been filled until the summer of 1791 when the President appointed Joseph Anderson to fill the position declined by William Perry. Anderson, a native of Pennsylvania who had studied law and attained the rank of major in the Revolutionary Army, was cordially received by Governor Blount. Filling the vacant judgeship contributed to the even flow of territorial justice as no superior court could be held without the presence of at least two of the three. Justice was served further by the requirement that the judges reside within the territory so that they could be reasonably prompt in meeting the schedules of the courts.[27]

To represent the government in the courts, Blount appointed attorneys general for both districts. He selected William Cocke for Washington District and Andrew Jackson for Mero.[28]

While Blount was dividing his time between government and business, the frontier public listened carefully for developments in Congress in regard to opening a new land office to dispose of the federal lands, probably at the rate of thirty cents per acre. Many land claimants in the territory seemed to have expected additional Indian areas to be opened at once for locating grants. At the end of 1790, warrants for 3,736,493 acres had been issued for the entire territory; grants had been issued for only 1,762,660 acres. In Washington County alone, there were entries made for 746,362 acres in 1791, but 531,812 acres had not been granted. Holders of those warrants were waiting for Indian lines to be pushed back so that better land could be had.[29] There was clearly plenty of work ahead for surveyors who would locate the entries, make surveys of them, draw plats, and prepare legal descriptions that became documentation for the grants.[30]

Early in 1791, leaders of the territory expected that new counties would be laid off after the signing of the Treaty of Holston with the Cherokee.

---

27. Carter, ed., *Territorial Papers, SWT*, IV, pp. 33, 40, 79; *The Blount Journal, 1790-1796*, p. 53; Durham, *Daniel Smith, Frontier Statesman*, p. 126.
28. *The Blount Journal, 1790-1796*, p. 46.
29. John Sevier to Daniel Smith, January 10, 1791, "Pioneer Letters," *American Historical Magazine*, Vol. II (January 1897), p. 93; Driver, *John Sevier, Pioneer of the Old Southwest*, pp. 107-8.
30. The surveyors typically were paid in land, approximately one-fourth of the acreage surveyed and platted. J. Glasgow and W. Williams to Colonel Martin Armstrong and Colonel Anthony Bledsoe, November 8, 1784, John Overton Papers, Murdock Collection, Tennessee Historical Society, TSLA.

Many were probably as excited as Stockley Donelson, Lieutenant Colonel Commandant, Hawkins County Militia, when he wrote to Martin Armstrong of Stokes County, North Carolina, on January 15, 1791.

> There is now the greatest prospect that there ever has been for selling lands down Holston and Clinch. The seat of government is and will be fixed at or near that place and the encouragement Governor Blount has given for a settlement in that quarter that lands in that part I am certain will command anything but cash. I think I could recommend it to you to come over and assist me in selling.[31]

Other desirable lands were far to the west of the Holston and Clinch. During his December trip to the Mero District, Blount had been greatly impressed by the quality of the land there. "The Cumberland lands do really exceed in richness of soil any description I ever heard given of them," he exuded to Governor Alexander Martin of North Carolina.[32]

But many land questions could not be answered until a dependable map of the territory could be produced. Probably in pursuit of that goal, Daniel Smith left Cobb's about March 10 on a surveying trip to the Chickasaw lands along the eastern bank of the Mississippi River between parallels of latitude 35 and 36 1/2 degrees. On that outing Smith recorded the surveys of streams flowing westward into the river that appeared on his first map of the territory published in 1794. Prior to that time, he had accumulated several surveys of the eastern and middle divisions of the territory. While in the Chickasaw Nation, Smith was shown a small fort erected by Spanish soldiers at Walnut Hills ostensibly in response to the abortive attempt by Zachariah Cox and associates to plant a settlement at Muscle Shoals.[33]

In one of the first treaty negotiations with Indians since the new Constitution had shifted that authority from the states to the federal government, William Blount and his aides met representatives of the Cherokee in the early summer of 1791. The governor had chosen to locate the treaty grounds on the banks of the Holston River about four miles below the mouth of French Broad near White's fort. Although Blount had

---

31. Ibid.
32. Keith, ed., *The John Gray Blount Papers,* Vol. II, p. 164.
33. Durham, *Daniel Smith, Frontier Statesman,* p. 128; Masterson, *William Blount,* p. 209.

invited the Cherokee to meet on May 31, they did not have full representation until the latter part of June.[34]

Outside the territory there were great expectations. The conference was represented to many as "the largest and most general treaty" that had been held with the Cherokee since the American Revolution. A Philadelphia newspaper regarded Blount as "very industrious," a man who would leave "no stone unturned" to achieve a new treaty.[35]

Blount came to the treaty grounds on May 31[36] and remained there until July 13, eleven days after the treaty was signed. He had Captain Hugh Beard's company of militia on hand throughout the proceedings.[37] Awaiting the Cherokee, the governor attended to administrative chores and made several appointments to both civil and militia offices in Davidson, Sumner, Sullivan, Hawkins, and Tennessee counties. Most vacancies had occurred when the incumbent was promoted or when he relocated elsewhere.[38]

Operating the government with a minimum of overhead expense, Blount found that his powers as governor were more restricted by the federal budget than by statute. He had virtually no funds at his disposal. The federal budget for 1791 allocated a total of $4,500.00 for the Southwest Territory. There were only four items in it:

Governor for his salary as such, and for discharging the duties of superintendent of Indian affairs,

Southern Department	2,000.00
Secretary of said district	750.00
For stationery, office rent, etc.	150.00
Two judges at $800. per annum	1,600.00
	$ 4,500.00

The Northwest Territory budget was set at $5,500.00, most of the

---

34. Prior to the treaty, the War Department had paid into Congressman John Sevier's hands the sum of $1,529.90 to be delivered to Governor Blount for defraying the expenses of the treaty deliberations. Of that amount, $250.00 was designated for other contingencies "of the Indian Department." John Sevier Papers, McClung Collection, Knoxville Public Library.

35. *Dunlap's American Daily Advertiser,* June 21, 1791.

36. Carter, ed., *Territorial Papers, SWT,* IV, p. 70.

37. Including the captain, the company was seventy-seven men strong. Most of them were on duty from June 1 to July 18. "Compiled Service Records of Volunteer Soldiers Who Served from 1784 to 1811, Territory South of the River Ohio," National Archives, Record Group 94, M-905, Roll 26.

38. *The Blount Journal, 1790-1796,* pp. 50-52.

difference occasioned by there being three judges on the payroll instead of two.[39]

As late as June 6, James Robertson was still in the Cherokee Nation at Hanging Maw's, trying to encourage John Watts, Bloody Fellow, and his host to go to the treaty grounds. The reason for their delay was the death of an Indian at the hands of a Mero District scouting party led by Colonel James Winchester. Robertson explained to the chiefs that the attack by Winchester occurred when the scouts, tracking a raiding party, had become confused and mistook a camp of friendly hunters for their quarry.[40]

Accepting Robertson's explanation, Double Head, Bloody Fellow, John Watts, Hanging Maw, and thirty-seven other Cherokee chiefs eventually reached the treaty grounds. They were accompanied by interpreters James Carey and John Thompson and approximately twelve hundred of their people, among whom were women, children, and a large number of braves. The latter were decorated with eagle feathers on their heads and with other insignia but were unarmed.[41]

Blount was attended by an official party that included two representatives from both the state of Georgia and the future state of Kentucky, and one each from Virginia and North Carolina. When the last of the chiefs arrived, Secretary Smith was present as were James Robertson representing Mero District; John Chisholm, Washington District; and Robert King and Thomas Gregg, at large. Inquisitive settlers wandered in and out of the grounds, eagerly anticipating the results of the conference.[42]

As the convocation had been called by the United States, the Indians approached it with understandable apprehension. They let Blount take the lead as they waited to see what he wanted.

Well aware of the Indians' appreciation of ceremony, Blount appeared in full military dress, complete with sword and cockaded hat. He took his seat under a marquee erected for his use and received the forty-one

---

39. *Dunlap's American Daily Advertiser*, January 11, 1791. The salary for the third judge of the Southwest Territory was not included as he was not sworn in until July, 1791. Masterson, *William Blount*, p. 209.
40. Carter, ed., *Territorial Papers, SWT*, IV, p. 59.
41. Ramsey, *The Annals of Tennessee*, p. 555.
42. Carter, ed., *Territorial Papers, SWT*, IV, pp. 65-67; Kentucky *Gazette*, March 19, 1791. Created from Virginia's western lands by act of Congress on February 4, 1791, Kentucky was accepted into the Union on June 1, 1792. *Journal of the House of Representatives of the United States, Being the Third Session of the First Congress, Begun and Held at the City of Philadelphia, December 6, 1790* (Washington, D.C.: Gales and Seaton, 1834), pp. 353, 377.

chiefs one by one. Serving as the governor's chief of protocol, James Armstrong[43] introduced each chief by his aboriginal name. During the introductions, Blount's aides contributed to the dignity of the occasion by standing near him with their heads respectfully uncovered.[44]

After the formalities were concluded, Blount led the Indians through his agenda, following a format similar to that of the Creek treaty signed the year before at New York.[45] He opened the talks by trying to prepare the Cherokee for a federal presence near Muscle Shoals. He told them that earlier he had purchased lands at the shoals from the state of Georgia and now he wanted to make a "fuller purchase" from them. It was his purpose, he said, to erect storehouses from which the Cherokee could be supplied with goods and smith shops, where their guns could be repaired. Speaking for the Indians, Bloody Fellow explained that the lands in question were not exclusively the property of his people but were a jointly held hunting ground of "the four nations." His explanation, though unsatisfactory to the governor, was not further challenged.[46]

Blount next questioned the Cherokee about recent raids into the Cumberland settlements. The chiefs responded that the Creek were the principal perpetrators but admitted that some of their own young men were probably with them.[47] Wondering at the same time if he could control intruding settlers, Blount undoubtedly demanded that the Indians restrain their young braves.

The chiefs insisted for the first few days of the talks that they would agree only to a truce for a period of twelve months and that further agreements should wait until the truce was tested. At length, however, they agreed that there should be "perpetual peace and friendship between all citizens of the United States and all individual Cherokees," and acknowledged that all parts of their nation were under the sole protection of the United States. They promised that their nation would not "hold any treaty with any foreign power, individual state, or with individuals of any state." Each nation consented to restore to the other all of the prisoners of the other then in captivity.[48]

---

43. Often called "Trooper" Armstrong, James had been trained in military protocol in Europe. Ramsey, *The Annals of Tennessee*, p. 555.
44. Ibid., pp. 555-56.
45. Keith, ed., *The John Gray Blount Papers*, Vol. II, pp. 170-71.
46. *ASP, II, Indian Affairs*, Vol. I, p. 204.
47. Carter, ed., *Territorial Papers, SWT*, IV, pp. 72-73.
48. Ibid., pp. 60-61; *Dunlap's American Daily Advertiser*, August 11, 1791.

The greatest difficulty faced by the negotiators was agreeing on a new boundary line that would recognize the territory's acquisition of most of the areas where white settlement had overflowed onto Indian lands.[49] The Indians asserted that they were completely surprised by the proposed cession of land by them. They had come to treat on the question of friendship, Chief Bloody Fellow argued. Blount remained adamant in his demands, and John Watts conceded that it was hopeless for the Indians to contend for the present boundary because Blount was one of the headstrong North Carolina people who would have their own way even if it meant ignoring the orders of Congress. He said, "Whenever you North Carolinians make a line, you tell us it shall be a standing one; but you are always encroaching upon it . . . we cannot depend upon what you say." At one point the discussion became so acrimonious that the governor asserted, contrary to official policy, that all of the disputed lands had belonged to the United States by right of conquest since the signing of the peace treaty of 1783 that ended the American Revolution.[50]

The Cherokee continued to resist the boundary proposal but, concluding that they had little choice, at last reluctantly accepted it. Their decision may have been hastened by warnings delivered by the Kentucky representatives who accused the Indians of inflicting such injury on their people that only the prospects of the peace treaty had prevented an army marching for the destruction of the Chickamauga towns.[51]

By their agreement, which came after they had endured seven days of pleas, arguments, and threats, they confirmed the Transylvania Purchase of the Cumberland area and conveyed lands between the Holston and Clinch rivers south to an east-west line running from near the mouth of Clinch to the North Carolina border. The Cherokee accepted Blount's proposal for the United States to have "free and unmolested use of a road from Washington District to Mero District" and to have free navigation of the Tennessee River. They agreed, also, for the United States to have the exclusive right of regulating their trade.[52]

The treaty did not give Blount the southern boundary line he wanted, however. He had proposed the ridge dividing the waters of the Tennessee

---

49. *ASP, II, Indian Affairs,* Vol. I, pp. 628-29.
50. Ibid., p. 204.
51. Hamer, ed., "Letters of Governor William Blount," p. 126.
52. Carter, ed., *Territorial Papers, SWT,* IV, pp. 60-65; *ASP, II, Indian Affairs,* Vol. I, p. 204.

from those of Little River, but the chiefs would not budge from their position that the line should be a straight one, running approximately east and west but anchored at the point where the ridge between the two rivers strikes the Holston. The accepted line left all of the settlers south of the ridge in Indian territory.[53]

Both sides agreed to have the new boundary line surveyed and marked "to preclude forever all disputes" about its location. A party of six, three chosen by the Cherokee and three by the United States, would locate and mark it at a later date.[54]

For the land, the United States agreed to pay an annuity of one thousand dollars, a sum Bloody Fellow aptly decried as not being enough "to buy a breech clout" for each of his nation. Blount assured the chiefs that the United States would protect the Cherokee in their trade, furnish them implements of husbandry and instructions for their use, and guarantee the boundaries of their remaining lands. He then delivered "certain valuable goods" to the chiefs and braves for the use of their nation. The treaty was concluded after several articles establishing procedures for dealing with law violators of both parties were adopted.[55]

Although Blount had gotten most of what he wanted, he was disappointed that he was unable to extend the boundary in every respect as far as he had "wished and hoped." Nonetheless, it included "all the settlers on the North Carolina grants," and that pleased him greatly.[56]

There was little in the treaty to please the Indians. Even as its terms were being concluded, white settlers were crossing into Indian lands that the United States had just guaranteed to protect to them. In fact, the concessions extracted from them later caused the Cherokee leadership to split into two factions. Bloody Fellow would lead those who still believed that they could treat successfully with the whites; Double Head, the war faction.[57]

On July 2, 1791, the assembled chiefs and Blount signed the Treaty of Holston. Four months later, on November 11, 1791, the treaty was

---

53. *Letter From the Secretary at War Accompanying His Report Relative to the Running of a Line of Experiment From Clinch River to Chilhowee Mountain...* (Philadelphia: Printed by Order of the House of Representatives, 1798), pp. 4-5.
54. Carter, ed., *Territorial Papers, SWT*, IV, p. 62.
55. Ibid., pp. 60-65; *ASP, II, Indian Affairs*, Vol. I, p. 204.
56. *ASP, II, Indian Affairs*, Vol. I, p. 629; Keith, ed., *The John Gray Blount Papers*, Vol. II, p. 171.
57. Symonds, "The Failure of America's Indian Policy on the Southwestern Frontier, 1785-1793," pp. 31-32.

ratified by the United States Senate and proclaimed as law of the land by President Washington.[58]

After the signing of the treaty, Double Head requested of Blount and was granted a written permit to hunt on the waters of the Cumberland River. It was an example of the many attempts— before and since—to win Indian support for government policies by granting special privileges to their leaders. That form of bribery would have little influence on the chief in his later dealings with the United States.[59]

With the Treaty of Holston successfully completed, Governor Blount obtained a two-month leave of absence from his official duties to attend to business in North Carolina and to move his family from that state to the territory. He would be gone from September 15 to November 20. Before he left, however, he announced the treaty to the frontier leadership as federal law that must be obeyed.

> The treaties with Indians must be observed inviolate and it is the duty of every officer so to speak and act for they have sworn to support the Constitution. Let the officers support the government and the government will support them. All treaties made or to be made are the supreme law of the land. Hence all treaties with Indians are the law of the land.[60]

In his absence, the responsibilities of the governor rested on the shoulders of Daniel Smith, secretary of the territory.

Although the Treaty of Holston restrained some of the Cherokee, there was no ascertainable relief from Indian harassment in the Mero District. There on August 1, civil and militia officers adopted a memorial to President Washington outlining the plight of their people. Acknowledging that by the treaty Blount had done "everything that a man could do to restore peace to the territory," they reported that raiding parties of Cherokee and Creek had killed nine settlers and stolen fifty or sixty horses since June 1.[61]

What could be done to protect the Cumberland frontier? The secretary of war wrestled with the question. Agreeing that the depredations of the Indians must be "immediately and effectually checked," he admitted the national government could do little to help. Blount's government

---

58. Carter, ed., *Territorial Papers, SWT*, IV, pp. 65-68.
59. *ASP, II, Indian Affairs*, Vol. I, p. 275.
60. Carter, ed., *Territorial Papers, SWT*, IV, pp. 71, 79.
61. Ibid., pp. 72-73.

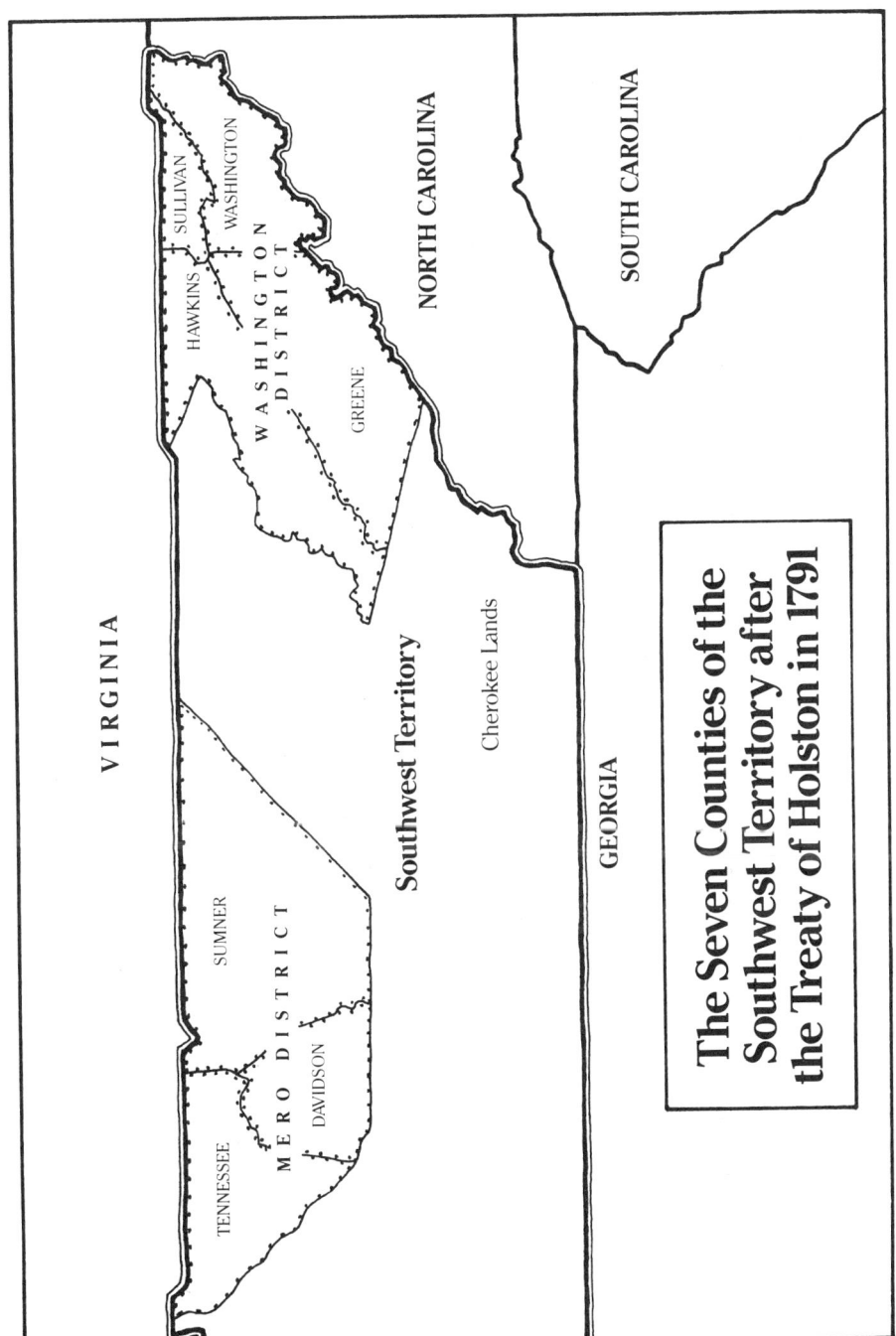

had suggested establishing military posts in the area and manning them with federal soldiers, but Knox dismissed the posts as too expensive and said that not even one company of federal troops could be spared until the end of the Indian war in the Northwest. He won authorization from the President for the governor to call out any territorial militia that he might need, but cautioned against using them too freely. He hoped that two companies would be sufficient for the task.[62]

The President continued to follow his policy of pursuing peace by negotiation and talks. He directed the governor to send some "discreet person" to the tribes to which the offending raiders belonged in order to persuade the leaders to punish their guilty young men. The tribes should be told that the United States would not continue to suffer the depredations "of any part of the Indian tribes with whom we have treaties."[63]

Recognizing that the Indians could not be blamed for all of the difficulties between them and the settlers, Judge David Campbell advised President Washington to make it the *ex officio* duty of the district attorneys general to commence prosecutions against violators of treaties "that they may be bound to answer in the Supreme Court of the United States." He insisted that government could not depend on the people at large to take to court those of their number who had injured Indians. Believing that the frontier electorate would obey only those laws that it found acceptable, he concluded that the territorial government should be continued in its first stage, "at least until the people are taught to obey the law and pay due respect to treaties."[64]

In the early part of 1791, prior to the Treaty of Holston, the national government had asked the Southwest Territory and neighboring states to supply militia to assist United States forces[65] opposing the Indians in the Northwest. To raise the quota for the territory, Governor Blount

---

62. Ibid., pp. 76-77.
63. Ibid., p. 77.
64. Ibid., p. 101.
65. Available regular army forces were incredibly small. In 1790 Congress had authorized the President to enlist a maximum of 1,216 regular troops. That number was supplemented on March 3, 1791, when Congress authorized an additional 2,000 "levees," enrolled for terms of six months. The next year a basic militia law was passed that called for the enrollment of "every able-bodied white male citizen between the ages of 18 and 45." Militia units were directly commanded by the respective governors of the states and territories, however, and they were called out by the President only in times of national emergency. "Compiled Service Records of Volunteer Soldiers Who Served from 1784 to 1811, Territory South of the River Ohio," National Archives, Record Group 94, M-905, Rolls 26-32.

called upon John Sevier, commanding general of the Washington District Militia. Sevier, who was in Philadelphia still representing western North Carolina in Congress, sent word to his command to enroll a battalion of three hundred men. The governor had excluded the Mero District Militia from the call as it was busily engaged in defending its area against Indian raids from the south.

While the volunteers were being enrolled, Sevier started homeward with $3,438.00, the sum sent by the War Department to supply and transport the battalion. Stricken ill at Richmond, Virginia, he was unable to recover and reach home in time to go with the force to the Northwest Territory.

Acting in Sevier's place and under his orders, Major Matthew Rhea failed to fill the quota, but raised approximately two hundred soldiers who were members of three companies, one from each of the counties of Sullivan, Washington, and Greene. About July 1, Rhea marched his volunteer battalion, one of only six raised nationwide, from Jonesborough through Cumberland Gap to Fort Washington, near the site of the twentieth-century city of Cincinnati, Ohio.

The secretary of war had invited the volunteers to equip themselves with good rifles, for which a nominal rental would be paid, and promised them that clothing would be acquired and forwarded as soon as possible. He had instructed Sevier to supply the men with camp equipment and to keep the records necessary for them to be paid. Although Knox had ordered Sevier to fill the companies by draft if volunteers were not forthcoming, the response was deemed adequate, and a draft was not employed.[66]

Rhea and his men reached Fort Washington on July 19 and reported to General Arthur St. Clair, commander of United States forces in the Northwest. Only 126 of those who left Jonesborough remained with the battalion when it arrived as both sickness and desertion had taken a heavy toll on them. It was the first time that the new territorial government had been called upon to furnish troops for duty outside its boundaries, and it responded affirmatively even though its own borders were not secure.

On November 4, when United States forces finally engaged the Indians

---

66. Knox to Sevier, March 23, 1791, "War Department Collection of Post Revolutionary War Manuscripts, Territory Southwest of Ohio River," National Archives, Record Group 94, M-904, Roll 4.

on a small tributary of the Wabash River near the later location of the Ohio-Indiana state line, the battalion from Washington District was thrown into the heat of the action. The battle raged for four hours and the Indians were victorious.[67] Rhea's battalion sufferd several casualties including the death of Captain Jacob Tipton of Washington County.[68]

The defeat of General St. Clair's troops was distressing to the people of the Southwest Territory, not only because of the losses of some of her finest young men, but because the victory of the northern Indians might stimulate the southern tribes to even greater resistance. It had shown anew that Indians could defeat a white army in battle; it suggested there might be a limit to just how far the whites could penetrate into Indian country. In addition, it meant that the secretary of war would hold a tight rein on whites in frontier areas, and would insist that Governor Blount maintain peace with the southern Indians at all costs. The prospect of the territory's receiving the aid of federal troops, fresh from victory in the Northwest, receded abruptly. There had been no victory, and there were no troops to spare.[69]

Even as reports of the defeat of St. Clair's troops trickled in, the filibustering speculator Zachariah Cox renewed his efforts to colonize an area at Muscle Shoals. Falsely advertising in Virginia that his party had established a settlement at the shoals, Cox invited prospective settlers to assemble in Washington District at the mouth of French Broad in November. From there he would lead them by boat to the new settlement. He hoped to capitalize on the refusal of the Washington District Superior Court Grand Jury to indict him when his illegal land speculations had been brought to its attention in August by Judge David Campbell. For a brief period, it appeared that at least "a few of the inhabitants" of the territory believed that they could not be punished by law for settling

---

67. John Sevier Papers, McClung Collection; Hamer, ed., "Letters of Governor William Blount," p. 127; Knoxville *Gazette*, December 3, 1791; Philip M. hamer, ed., "A Muster Roll of Captain Jacob Tipton's Company in St. Clair's Campaign," East Tennessee Historical Society *Publications*, No. 3 (January 1931), p. 150; Williams, *Phases of Southwest Territory History*, pp. 21-23.

68. In Tipton's company, Lieutenant John Lyle and Ensign Ethelred Cobb, son of William Cobb whose home was the seat of government for the territory, were wounded and several privates either killed or wounded. Casualties suffered by the two other companies have not been ascertained. Samuel Cole Williams, "The Southwest Territory to the Aid of the Northwest Territory, 1791," *Indiana Magazine of History*, Vol. XXXVII (June 1941), p. 155.

69. Eblen, *The First and Second United States Empires*, pp. 243-44; Downs, "Indian Affairs in the Southwest Territory, 1790-1796," p. 243.

at the shoals and, consequently, gave serious consideration to the opportunity.

The speculator-led expedition met its match in acting governor Daniel Smith who, about October 1, published a proclamation forbidding its members from proceeding through the territory. He enjoined citizens to abstain from associating with or joining "these adventurers" and informed them that "should they be so injudicious they would subject themselves . . . to answer their conduct before the federal court." Smith agreed with Judge Campbell: "It is not oppression to control unjustifiable and lawless speculations. [Let us] show the citizens of other states that this territory will not be an asylum for lawless and disorderly men." The secretary's firm hand in dealing with Cox and others seeking to settle on Indian lands won high praise from Secretary of State Jefferson.[70]

During Blount's absence from the territory, the President appointed the three commissioners to run the Cherokee line as stipulated in the Treaty of Holston. As a gesture of good faith, he chose men who were not known for their speculations in land: Colonel Landon Carter, Judge David Campbell, and Secretary Daniel Smith.[71] The President wanted to have the line run by "gentlemen who can have no inducement to infringe in any degree upon the boundary truly meant and intended." Soon afterward those good intentions were overridden by circumstances in the Northwest, which caused the central government to seek participation by the southern Indians on the side of the United States in its war against the northern Indians. Fearing that running the line might renew old points of controversy between the Cherokee and the whites, the secretary of war suggested the undertaking be postponed until the Northwest Territory could be pacified.[72]

Further uncertainty about the behavior of the southern Indians was generated by the retirement of Governor Miro and the assumption of his office on December 30, 1791, by Luis Francisco Hector-Baron de Carondelet. Reasserting Spain's determination to defend Louisiana against the encroachment of western American settlers, the new governor stated he would build new forts at points guarding the approaches to Louisiana, expand the Spanish naval squadron on the Mississippi River,

---

70. Carter, ed., *Territorial Papers, SWT*, IV, pp. 83, 106; Knoxville *Gazette*, December 31, 1791.
71. Carter, ed., *Territorial Papers, SWT*, IV, pp. 103-4.
72. *Letter From the Secretary at War Accompanying His Report Relative to the Running of a Line of Experiment from Clinch River to Chilhowee Mountain...*, pp. 6, 7.

and organize the major tribes of southern Indians into a military alliance under the protection of Spain.[73] To territory leaders, the baron's proclaimed defensive posture had the potential to turn offensive at a moment's notice, especially when the Indians were well armed and encouraged to harass the settlements.

---

73. Holmes, "Spanish-American Rivalry Over the Chickasaw Bluffs, 1780-1795," p. 37.

CHAPTER V

BEYOND TREATIES

1791-92

Convening at Estanaula in the autumn of 1791 before Governor Blount returned from leave in North Carolina, the people of the Cherokee Nation had heard many of their own denounce the provisions of the Treaty of Holston. After deliberating at length, the Cherokee decided to send a delegation of chiefs to Philadelphia to confer with President Washington. The delegation not only would represent the views of its own tribes but would deliver a message from the Creek and a joint communication from the Chickasaw and Choctaw to the President.[1]

As Blount was absent from the territory, the Indians' efforts to communicate their plans to him were fruitless, and they seem to have made no effort to talk to acting governor Smith. Nonetheless, the chiefs and their delegation traveled to Charleston, South Carolina, and there took a ship bound for Philadelphia. They reached the capital city on December 28, 1791, to the complete surprise of the national government. The five chiefs, Bloody Fellow, King Fisher, The Northward, The Disturber, and The Prince, were accompanied by interpreter James Carey and George Miller, a young Cherokee who was to assist Carey and be a witness to the meetings.[2]

The delegation was received hospitably, and after introductions to President Washington on January 4, 1792, the chiefs met with the secretary of war periodically for several days. Recalling details of the treaty negotiations with Blount, they emphasized their reluctance to part with the lands they had surrendered. It was important, they said, to complete their business at Philadelphia quickly so that they could return to the nation with a message from the President that they hoped would restrain the young warriors. Specifically, the chiefs requested payment of an additional five hundred dollars per year for the lands conveyed in the treaty and the removal of white settlers who had intruded on

---

1. *ASP, II, Indian Affairs,* Vol. I, pp. 204-5.
2. Ibid., p. 203; *Letter From the Secretary at War Accompanying His Report Relative to the Running of a Line of Experiment From Clinch River to Chilhowee Mountain...,* p. 8.

Cherokee lands. They asked for the appointment of an agent of the United States to reside in their territory and serve as their "counsellor and protector." They insisted that the projected settlement of the Tennessee Company at Muscle Shoals be prevented and asked that their annual allowance of goods along with implements of husbandry be made available to take back with them. Finally, they wanted James Carey "and any such other person as the nation shall hereafter choose" appointed interpreters.[3]

The President and Congress, then in session, responded sympathetically. The annual payment for land under the Treaty of Holston was increased from one thousand to fifteen hundred dollars, and a payment was made to them. A promise to punish white settlers who should encroach on their grounds was given, and a deputy agent to live in the Cherokee Nation, Leonard S. Shaw, was authorized to return with the chiefs. James Carey was appointed interpreter, and the Indians were assured that the government was firmly opposed to white settlements at Muscle Shoals.[4]

On February 17 the secretary of war responded to the talks of the Creek, Choctaw, and Chickasaw delivered by the Cherokee chiefs. Answering the Creek's brief talk that questioned the credentials of the interloper Bowles, Knox stated bluntly that the man was an impostor "and deserved to be driven out of your nation immediately." To the Choctaw and Chickasaw who asked only that the government refrain from appointing North Carolina people to hold talks with Indians, "as they always asked for land," he reassured them of the peaceful intentions of the government. Sending suits of clothing with silver ornaments to the chiefs of both, he invited them to send warriors the next summer to fight alongside United States troops against the northern Indians. He invited the Choctaw and Chickasaw each to send four of their principal chiefs to visit him at Philadelphia after the next campaign. After thanking the Chickasaw for having provided warriors the prior year to fight north of the Ohio, Knox designated medals to be given their chiefs and ordered presents to be sent from Fort Washington to the Chickasaw nation generally.[5]

News that the President and Congress had amended the Treaty of

---

3. *ASP, II, Indian Affairs*, Vol. I, pp. 205, 245.
4. Ibid., pp. 245, 246; Carter, ed., *Territorial Papers, SWT*, IV, pp. 120-21.
5. *ASP, II, Indian Affairs*, Vol. I, pp. 205, 248-49.

Holston reached the territory in the latter part of February, although no mention of it was made in the Knoxville *Gazette* at that time. Governor Blount learned of the chiefs' visit and the government's response in a letter from Secretary Knox written January 31. Lest Blount be disturbed because the changes had been made without his knowledge or consent, the secretary pledged to him that it was handled in such a way as "to induce a more perfect confidence on the part of the Indians" in his character.[6]

Two weeks later Knox gave Blount the responsibility for shielding the returning chiefs from "all insult or injury" on that part of their overland journey from Staunton, Virginia, to Holston. Knox considered their safety so essential that he directed Blount to do everything possible "to render the protection perfect." The governor was also to furnish boats to take the chiefs and their goods down the Holston and Tennessee rivers to the Cherokee country.[7]

Although the only newspaper in the territory reported nothing about either the purpose or the results of the chiefs' visit to the seat of national government,[8] their journey must have been general knowledge on the frontier after Hanging Maw, John Watts, and John Taylor met with Blount in early March. Those Cherokee chiefs, who had not gone to Philadelphia, went to Knoxville to give the governor their "strongest assurance of the peaceful disposition of their nation," and undoubtedly told him about the trip of the other chiefs to the capital.[9]

Hanging Maw met the party of returning chiefs at Knoxville on April 22. As they arrived with the annual payment to the nation in the bulky form of goods and as their young Cherokee interpreter, George Miller, was accompanied by a white woman from Philadelphia, there is no doubt that accounts of their trip circulated by word of mouth throughout the territory. Even though the editors of the *Gazette* ignored the political results of the trip, they twice called attention with chaste alarm to the white "Lady" companion of the Cherokee Miller. They first suggested her expulsion from the territory, but later relented when they were

---

6. Ibid., p. 245.
7. Ibid., pp. 246-47.
8. The only reference to the chiefs' presence in Philadelphia made by the *Gazette* was a brief note in its issue of April 21; on May 5 it barely mentioned their return.
9. Knoxville *Gazette*, March 10, 1792.

advised that she would make her home with Miller in the Cherokee Nation.[10]

On the occasion of the chiefs' arrival at Knoxville, Blount was fully briefed about their negotiations in Philadelphia by Leonard Shaw, the newly appointed deputy agent to the Cherokee. Although the national government strongly supported the governor, its policy toward the southern Indians had not changed; war with them was to be avoided. Attributing Indian hostility to the wanton action of white intruders, the secretary of state observed that he preferred to send an armed force to make war against the intruders, a course he deemed "more just and less expensive."[11]

Sometime later a book containing transcriptions of the talks at Philadelphia was brought to the governor who, after reading it, charged that the chiefs had "egregiously lied" about his role and manner in the treaty negotiations. He promised to reply to it in justice to himself.[12]

Even before the returning chiefs had reached Knoxville, there were ominous signs that the five lower Cherokee towns, whose residents constituted the Chickamauga faction, were about to join the Shawnee and Creek in hostilities against the United States. The towns—Running-water, Nickajack, Long Island Villages, Crow Town, and Lookout Mountain—lay on the south bank of the Tennessee or close to it, separated from the rest of the Cherokee Nation by the Chattanooga mountains. Many of their warriors were Cherokee or Creek renegades. The natural barriers and the congregation of young renegades in the towns made it almost impossible for Little Turkey, the principal chief of the Cherokee, to control them. He had become so incensed by the conduct of the towns that he ordered the rest of the nation to discontinue "all intercourse and society with them."[13]

Reporting these developments to the secretary of war, Blount suggested that the rest of the Cherokee Nation would remain neutral if the United States attempted to punish or destroy the five towns. He believed, however, that if the renegades were not challenged by the government, they would be much slower to ally with the Shawnee and Creek. Yet the Cumberland settlements desperately needed protection against

---

10. Ibid., May 5, 19, 1792.
11. Carter, ed., *Territorial Papers, SWT,* IV, pp. 131, 132.
12. Ibid., p. 144.
13. Knoxville *Gazette,* March 24, 1792; Carter, ed., *Territorial Papers, SWT,* IV, pp. 129-30.

raiders from those towns, and he proposed to supply it by activating militia companies to defend them. The President authorized Blount to call up two companies of militia unless there was an indispensable need for more, but warned him to keep even that force at a minimum level and in service for the shortest possible time. Since the first of the year Blount had been planning to raise a guard to be stationed at key points along the frontier. One of these was the future site of Fort Blount at the crossing of the Cumberland on the road from Knoxville to Mero District. The President's authorization did not enable him to fulfill his plans, but it opened the way for further militia calls in greater strength.[14]

Differences between the various chiefs over relations with the United States after amendments had been made to the Treaty of Holston probably were responsible for an invitation to Blount to meet with some of them May 17 at Coyatee, a Cherokee village on the banks of the Tennessee River. The Cherokee were gathering there to divide the goods they received for the first annual payment under the treaty. Eager for an opportunity to reassert his authority as superintendent of Indian affairs in the southern department, Blount agreed to attend. He even promised twenty head of cattle and a quantity of meal for provisions. When the shooting deaths of three settlers on May 16 were attributed to Indians, Blount delayed his departure from Knoxville, but the chiefs repeated their invitation and he went to Coyatee on May 20.[15]

The governor must have been worried, also, about the "definitely pro-Cherokee turn" taken by Spanish imperial policy since the first of the year. The new Spanish governor of Louisiana, Carondelet, was eager to bring the Cherokee into the "family of protectorates" that served as a buffer between his empire and the United States. In that connection he had made overtures to their chiefs. At the same time, Panton, Leslie and Company, holding the supply concession from Spain, was planning to expand its services into the Cherokee country.[16]

Blount was aware, also, that the Shawnee, victorious over General St. Clair, were actively soliciting the southern tribes to join the northern Indian confederacy. He knew, too, that the impostor William Augustus Bowles was having some success in spreading his plan to create an

---

14. Carter, ed., *Territorial Papers, SWT,* IV, pp. 109, 129-32.
15. *ASP, II, Indian Affairs,* Vol. I, pp. 267, 268; Hamer, ed., "Letters of Governor William Blount," p. 128.
16. Downs, "Indian Affairs in the Southwest Territory, 1790-1796," p. 245.

independent state embracing the Creek, Cherokee, Choctaw, and Chickasaw, to be sustained by trade with Great Britain.[17]

The governor was received at Coyatee with great ceremony. He and his escort were led through the entire assemblage of about two thousand Indians who had been formed in two parallel lines. As they made their way, muskets were fired and "shouts of joy" rose from the crowd. Blount reported to Knox that he had never seen Indians behave with such cheer and good humor.[18]

The celebration continued for two days featuring ball play, eating, and drinking. Blount was able to talk privately with most of the chiefs, and on Wednesday he addressed the whole group, still about two thousand strong. Among the leaders present were Bloody Fellow, titled and commissioned General Eskaqua by President Washington at Philadelphia; Head Man of Hiwassee; John Watts; Nontuaka; Hanging Maw; Kittagiska; Tuskigatahee; Richard Justice of the Look-Out; The Cabin; The Breath of Nickajack; The Broom; and Charley and Will of Running-water.[19]

Blount explained to the Indians that he had made no misrepresentations to them at the treaty grounds and that always he spoke to them with the authority of the President. Endorsing the amendments made at Philadelphia, he emphasized that the President was a person of great goodness, full of love for them and their nation.

Nonetheless, dangerous clouds were hanging over relations between them and the people of the territory, he observed. The Indians had killed and wounded numerous settlers, primarily in the Mero District, since the treaty was signed last summer. That kind of behavior endangered the peace, he argued, acknowledging that other Indians—probably Creek—had been coparticipants in the raids. Warning them that militia units had been deployed to guard the frontiers of the settlements, he emphasized that they had been ordered out only for defensive purposes. He extended the chiefs a standing welcome at his house and gave them directions for a safe route to travel whenever they should come into Knoxville.[20]

---

17. Ibid. Bowles overplayed his hand, however. By the end of April he had been expelled by the Creek who, at the same time, reinstated McGillivray as the principal chief of their nation. Later Bowles was executed by order of the Spanish government. Knoxville *Gazette*, May 5, 19, 1792.
18. *ASP, II, Indian Affairs*, Vol. I, p. 267; Knoxville *Gazette*, June 2, 1792.
19. *ASP, II, Indian Affairs*, Vol. I, pp. 267, 268.
20. Ibid., pp. 268, 269.

Responses to Blount's remarks were generally conciliatory. The most encouraging comment came from The Breath of Nickajack who admitted that the people of the lower towns had been deaf to Blount's talks on prior occasions, but were at last ready to listen. Hanging Maw announced that the council of all the tribes would meet June 23 at Estanaula, and John Watts promised that all of the talks held there would be made available to Blount if he would have Captain Chisholm attend to bring them to him.[21]

The governor believed that prospects for peace were much improved. Mistakenly concluding that the five lower towns had opted for peace, he characterized John Watts and Bloody Fellow to Secretary Knox as "champions for peace."[22]

When the Grand Cherokee National Council convened June 26 through June 30 at the council town of Estanaula, neither John Watts nor Bloody Fellow was present. While both offered explanations for their absences, it was believed that the latter avoided the meeting because he feared the council would take a hostile stance toward the United States. John Watts was away because he had accepted an invitation to Pensacola extended by the Spanish through the Indian trader William Panton.[23]

Notwithstanding the absence of those two, the council professed friendship for the government in spite of the Cherokee's unallayed concern about the exact location of the boundary line and their fury over the continued intrusion of settlers into their territory. Little Turkey, the most influential chief of those present, lamented that free navigation of the Tennessee had been guaranteed by the Indians in the Treaty of Holston because it was "disagreeable" to the entire nation. To the prospect of a settlement at Muscle Shoals or a station at the mouth of Bear Creek, he responded that the Cherokee could accept neither because both were located in the common hunting ground of the four nations.

Although the chiefs had trouble controlling their young warriors during the early sessions, harmony was restored before the council adjourned.

---

21. Ibid., p. 269.
22. Masterson, *William Blount*, p. 224; Carter, ed., *Territorial Papers, SWT*, IV, p. 160; Knoxville *Gazette*, June 2, 1792.
23. *ASP, II, Indian Affairs*, Vol. I, p. 270; Knoxville *Gazette*, August 25, 1792. William Panton was a partner of Robert Leslie in the trading firm of Panton, Leslie and Company, the largest mercantile house in east Florida. Since 1786 the partners had worked closely with the Spanish government to purchase and supply British goods to the southern Indians to combat the influence of the United States in the area. Whitaker, *The Spanish-American Frontier, 1783-1795*, pp. 38 *et seq.*

The cooperation of the young men made it possible to agree to return all horses stolen from the settlers. When John Chisholm turned over to them a young Indian boy who had been held prisoner in the territory and reminded them of the treaty agreement to exchange prisoners, some of the chiefs agreed to deliver prisoners held by their tribes. In response to a request from the governor, it was agreed to send a detachment of braves and chiefs to meet and escort the boats transporting goods down the Tennessee for the upcoming conference at Nashville with the Choctaw and Chickasaw. Three of the chiefs who escorted the goods would remain to attend the conference as Blount had invited Cherokee participation.[24]

Honoring invitations sent by Blount in April, "a large representation of the Chickasaws and [a smaller group of] Choctaws... well disposed toward the United States" gathered at Nashville for talks with him during the last few days of July. The goods to be distributed at the conference arrived on time in riverboats commanded by the experienced western waters pilot Alexander Moore. Escorting the shipment was the Cherokee delegation promised at Estanaula, but Bloody Fellow and John Watts, personally invited by the governor, did not appear. Blount and General Andrew Pickens of South Carolina, sent by the President to be commander of the Indians that he hoped would join the United States in its war against the northern tribes, arrived about the same time. They had been escorted through the wilderness by a Washington District "troop of cavalry" called out for a three-month tour of duty "for the protection of the frontiers."[25]

The secretary of war and the governor agreed that the purpose of the conference was to cultivate the good friendship then existing between the two tribes and the settlers, to attach both nations firmly and cordially to the interests of the United States, and to solicit warriors from both for the campaign above the Ohio against the northern Indians. Blount hoped that the Cherokee chiefs would be sufficiently impressed by the Chickasaw and Choctaw commitments of friendship that they would support strengthening their own nation's uncertain alliance with the United States. The conference was somewhat undercut by Spanish pressure on the Choctaw to avoid it, however. That tribe,

---

24. Carter, ed., *Territorial Papers, SWT*, IV, p. 160; *ASP, II, Indian Affairs*, Vol. I, pp. 270-73.
25. *ASP, II, Indian Affairs*, Vol. I, pp. 270, 275; Knoxville *Gazette*, August 25, 1792; Carter, ed., *Territorial Papers, SWT*, IV, pp. 147, 157.

weakened by hunger and virtually unarmed, yielded by reducing the size of its delegation.[26]

Prior to the Nashville talks, the secretary of war briefed Governor Blount on current United States policy toward the southern Indians. First, he pleased the governor by telling him that the President had consented to recognize James Robertson as temporary agent for the Chickasaw and suggested that he be sworn to duty at once. Robertson was to perform his duties, the reconciliation of the Choctaw, Chickasaw, and others, at Blount's command. Restating that the overall policy continued to be peace through negotiation, Knox said that it must be established "on such pure principles of justice and moderation, as will enforce the approbation of the dispassionate and enlightened part of mankind." The Indians should be told repeatedly that the United States demanded no more of their land, but instead would bury past differences to celebrate friendship and peace. He instructed Blount to impress upon the conferees the government's desire for peace and its resolution to deal with the intractably hostile by decisive force of arms.[27]

Knox warned Blount that the outbreak of a general Indian war would be considered by the citizens of the middle and eastern states as "an insupportable evil." He concluded, "Everything depends upon your exertions to avert the event of a war, that will be reluctantly entered into, and at best illy supported... You will leave no reasonable expedient unattempted, to effect a general tranquility... Your efforts to preserve peace must... be rendered conspicuous."[28]

The War Department's view was influenced in no small part by the erroneous assessment of Indian attitudes by James Seagrove, agent to the Creek, who continued to regard the Creek and Cherokee as peacefully inclined friends of the United States. In addition, Seagrove entertained serious doubts about the "insatiable rage which our frontier brethren have for extending their limits." In a statement ill-calculated to make friends in the West he wrote, "The United States, like most other countries, is unfortunate in having the worst class of people on her frontiers,

---

26. *ASP, II, Indian Affairs*, Vol. I, pp. 250-52; Carter, ed., *Territorial Papers, SWT*, IV, p. 173.
27. *ASP, II, Indian Affairs*, Vol. I, pp. 252-53.
28. Ibid., p. 258.

where there is least energy to be expected in her civil government."[29]

When Blount convened the meeting at Nashville on August 7, Piomingo and eighteen other Chickasaw chiefs were present; only three were absent. The popular John Pitchlyn and twenty-two other Choctaw chiefs were in attendance, although their total retinue was much smaller than that of the Chickasaw. The Cherokee were represented by the three chiefs who had accompanied the Indian goods to Nashville. Blount was attended by Daniel Smith who had furnished at the governor's request two hogsheads of tobacco for smoking by those assembled.[30]

Blount opened the talks by explaining that the purpose of the conference was to strengthen the Indians' friendship with the United States based on the Treaty of Hopewell. To further this, he asked them to accept a quantity of goods as proof of the sincere friendship of the United States. He said, also, that he wished publicly to thank Piomingo, the Colberts, and their followers who had fought side by side with American troops against their enemies in 1791 by presenting each with a rifle. Assuring them that the United States wanted none of their land, he declared, "The United States have land enough." Blount promised that President Washington would soon open a trading post to serve them at Bear Creek in line with terms agreed to at Hopewell. He called attention to a hostile Cherokee camp or settlement on the south side of the Tennessee River in an area near the line between the Choctaw and Chickasaw and asked the two nations to mark their boundaries clearly and make them known to the United States.[31]

The Indians were greatly relieved to hear that the United States sought no additional land from them. The influential Chickasaw chief Wolf's Friend expressed his gratitude for that assurance and requested that "if ever the President calls us together again," land may "never more be mentioned." Wolf's Friend was joined by Piomingo in seeking cancellation of the plans for a trading post at Bear Creek because they believed it had the potential for creating unnecessary bloodshed. The former even

---

29. Seagrove to Henry Knox, October 28, 1792, "Territorial Papers of the United States Senate, 1789-1873, Territory of the United States South of the River Ohio, 1789-1808," National Archives, Record Group 46, M-200, Roll 2.

30. *ASP, II, Indian Affairs*, Vol. I, pp. 284-85; Carter, ed., *Territorial Papers, SWT*, IV, p. 173; Hamer, ed., "Letters of Governor William Blount," p. 131.

31. *ASP, II, Indian Affairs*, Vol. I, p. 285.

suggested that trade might be carried on successfully from Nashville without the risk inherent at Bear Creek. Blount agreed to hold the Bear Creek post in abeyance "for a time."[32]

Pursuing the boundary question, Piomingo argued for a map with Chickasaw boundaries marked clearly to protect their land. He accused the Cherokee of wanting Chickasaw land to sell or replace other of their lands sold to the whites. He said he feared Cherokee presence on Chickasaw lands because of their hostility to the whites and the likelihood that the whites would seize the land to curb Cherokee raids.[33]

Piomingo noted the useful implements of husbandry given by the United States to the Creek and Cherokee and expressed hope that his people would be supplied, also. Responding that such a commitment was beyond his authority, Blount said that he would make the request known to the President who would be happy to hear that they preferred cultivating the land to hunting.[34]

The Choctaw chiefs spoke of friendship for the United States and gratitude to the Chickasaw for insisting that they attend the meeting. On specific issues they deferred to the Chickasaw.

Blount reminded both Choctaw and Chickasaw that they had received letters inviting delegations of chiefs to visit the President at Philadelphia. If they should accept, he recommended that they travel by way of Nashville and Knoxville where they would be aided on the journey by General Robertson and himself. On the last day, Piomingo caused a string of white beads to be delivered to Blount for forwarding to the President as a token of his plan to go to Philadelphia the next spring.[35]

Blount and Pickens did not ask for Indian warriors to go north the next summer, although they carefully sounded out the Indian leaders on the strength of their commitments to the United States. The Chickasaw and Choctaw would fight as allies with the states in a war against the Cherokee or Creek, but their concern for that likelihood seemed to preclude their promising to send troops northward. At any event, the inability of the Choctaw to withstand pressure from Spain probably would have kept their warriors at home.[36]

---

32. Ibid., pp. 285, 287.
33. Ibid., p. 286.
34. Ibid., p. 287.
35. Ibid., pp. 287-88.
36. Carter, ed., *Territorial Papers, SWT*, IV, pp. 173, 174, 180.

The conference at Nashville ended when medals and ornamented clothing were awarded to the chiefs and presents given to all from both nations. Before they left, the Indians who had brought firearms to be repaired collected them; Blount had authorized local gunsmiths to repair the arms at government expense.[37]

Although Governor Blount spent much of 1792 preparing for and conducting talks with the Indians, he had to deal with many Indian raids into the settlements, especially in the Mero District. Citizens on the frontier, distressed by the central government's refusal to strike the enemy on his own grounds, doubted anew that peace could be achieved through negotiation.

The citizens of Tennessee County petitioned General Robertson for relief on February 1 citing Indian attacks and Spain's closing of the Mississippi River to shipments from the territory. In the absence of an expedition that would strike the Indians at home, they predicted that the frontiers would "break" and the land would be abandoned.[38]

Washington District was an occasional target of Indian marauders in 1792, but raids occurred in Mero almost every week. The usual goal was to steal horses, but the raiders, most of whom were Chickamauga from the lower five towns, wielded their tomahawks recklessly when challenged. Sometimes entire families were slaughtered, as on February 28 when they killed James Thompson, his wife, and two children about five miles from Nashville. On March 5 another party killed four young boys when it attacked Brown's station about eight miles from Nashville, and on the day following, raiders burned Dunham's station, its barn, and corn cribs.[39] Infrequently the Indians took prisoners, usually women, children, or slaves.

The pace of killings seemed to pick up. On March 12, Indians killed a man named McMurray on his place near the mouth of Stone's River and on April 5 killed Mrs. Harper Radcliff and three children about twenty miles from Hawkins Court House in Washington District. Three days later raiders wiped out Benjamin Wilson and his entire family of eight persons at their place on Station Camp Creek in Sumner County. On April 16 two boys were slain about twelve miles from Knoxville,

---

37. *ASP, II, Indian Affairs,* Vol. I, p. 283.
38. William R. Garrett, ed., "Correspondence of General James Robertson," *American Historical Magazine,* Vol. I (January 1896), p. 284.
39. *ASP, II, Indian Affairs,* Vol. I, pp. 263, 268, 330-31.

and on the next day, a man traveling with Judge Campbell from Nashville to Knoxville was fatally shot. During the same period, other travelers to and from Nashville suffered heavily. Even the veteran frontiersman General James Robertson and his son were wounded at their plantation by shots fired from raiders' guns. A young woman was tomahawked to death near Nashville on May 13, and on May 15 a man was killed and scalped in his front yard as his family watched in Hinde's valley, twelve miles from Knoxville.[40]

In what was perhaps the most devastating raid of the summer, Zeigler's station, about two miles from Bledsoe's Lick in Sumner County, was besieged and burned June 26. Four defenders were killed and one burned to death, thirteen made prisoner, four wounded but escaped, and three escaped unhurt. Later nine of the captives were ransomed and returned to their families. They had been taken to Running-water Town.[41]

The Mero District was greatly alarmed. A citizen there wrote to a friend in Knoxville on July 16:

> This is the boldest stroke ever made by Indians in this quarter, and has spread a more general alarm than has heretofore been felt. The inhabitants began to complain loudly that they were neglected, and even at most to despair of the protection of government; but Governor Blount, since his arrival, has ordered three hundred militia into actual service, under the command of Major Sharpe.[42]

When news of the raid on Zeigler's reached Philadelphia, President Washington, regarding the attackers to be an alliance of renegades, briefly considered a strike at them. "If the banditti," he said, "...could be come at without involving disagreeable consequences with the tribes to which they belong, an attempt to cut them off ought by all means to be encouraged." He concluded, "An enterprise judiciously concerted, and spiritedly executed, would be less expensive to the government, than keeping up guards of militia, which will always be eluded in the attack, and never be overtaken in a pursuit."[43] It was soon evident, however, that the raiders represented more than bandits; to strike them would risk the wider war Washington was trying to avoid.

---

40. Ibid., pp. 268, 270, 276; Knoxville *Gazette*, April 21, May 5, June 2, 1792; Symonds, "The Failure of America's Indian Policy on the Southwestern Frontier, 1785-1793," p. 33.
41. *ASP, II, Indian Affairs*, Vol. I, p. 276; Knoxville *Gazette*, August 25, 1792.
42. Knoxville *Gazette*, August 25, 1792.
43. Jared Sparks, *The Writings of George Washington*, Vol. X (Boston: American Stationers' Company, 1836), pp. 262-63.

The government's policy of restraint caused shared frustration throughout the settlements. In the Mero District, the inhabitants were incredulous when General Robertson stopped Captain John Edmiston from leading a party of volunteers on a retaliatory strike against Indian raiders on July 10. A citizen of Mero District wrote Robertson that he was surprised by the general's action. "But, hearing it generally reported... that it has always been your endeavor to stop all those that wish to do good to this country, and damage to the Indians, I must join with the rest of my countrymen, and wish Edmiston great success, and you gone from hence, and a better in your room."[44]

The wrath of the Indians was felt less frequently throughout the territory in July, August, and September, although they continued to "take hair and steal horses." Governor Blount's incomplete count showed nine whites killed, two wounded, and two taken prisoner.[45]

A raiding party of fifteen Creek tried to burn Captain John Morgan's house near Bledsoe's Lick on August 27, but failed when Captain Joseph Lusk's militia company drove it away. On the following night the same raiders opened the stables of James Douglass and took his horses, but a neighbor, Samuel Wilson, overtook them the next day, wounded one warrior, put the rest to flight, and recaptured the animals.[46]

Indian hostility to the settlers could not be attributed entirely to intrusions by the latter. Probably speaking for the governor, who seemed constantly to whip up public opinion against the Indians only to stifle it by invoking the more conciliatory policy measures of the United States, the editor of the Knoxville *Gazette* accused the Cherokee and Creek of grossly violating their treaties with the United States.

> A too general opinion prevails in the interior parts of the country that the murders and robberies committed by the Indians on the frontier settlers are provoked by their intrusions on the Indian lands. This was too true previous to the treaties of New York and Holston, with the Creeks and Cherokees, but by no means since; for no intrusion whatever has been made on their lands; and it is to be observed, the Creeks, from whose hands the frontier people of this country are made to bleed

---

44. Albigence W. Putnam, *History of Middle Tennessee or Life and Times of General James Robertson* (Nashville: N.p., 1859), p. 388.
45. Knoxville *Gazette*, August 25, 1792; *ASP, II, Indian Affairs*, Vol. I, pp. 330-31.
46. Knoxville *Gazette*, September 22, 1792.

at every pore, never had a claim to any lands in the limits of the southwestern territory, nor even to any north of the Tennessee.

A thirst for blood, the desire for making the defenseless frontier people slaves, and the fondness of riding fine stolen horses, must now be their justification, if they have any.[47]

The editor might have mentioned Spain's success in winning McGillivray and the Creek back into their camp and the Indians' zestful responsiveness to Spanish suggestions that they obliterate the settlements, especially those on the Cumberland.[48]

On September 7 or 8 the five lower towns declared war on the United States, and before the end of the month, some of their warriors marched with John Watts on the Mero District, notwithstanding assurances given by Bloody Fellow and The Glass on September 10 and 14 that they had dissuaded their tribesmen from war and wanted only peace with the settlers. Blount responded by announcing that he would erect "a number of block houses" on both the Mero and eastern frontiers "and put at them a number of men . . . for the protection of the frontiers." He warned the Cherokee to keep their good people away from the installations lest they be mistaken for "bad ones."[49]

Blount sent nine additional companies to join the five militia companies that he had called up in March and June. His action drew prompt criticism from the secretary of war who, agreeing that the increased calls for troops might have been justified by appearances at that time, directed him to reduce their number as quickly as possible. Even the inhabitants of Mero District complained. They were furious that militia companies from Washington District were never integrated with the local command but were responsible only to their own commanders; neither the commanding general nor any other officer of Mero had authority to give orders to the visiting militia. Whatever the protocol, the net result was less efficient protection of the frontiers.[50]

An attack on September 30 by a force of 500 Creek, 197 Cherokee, and 30 Shawnee might have obliterated Nashville but for a last-minute

---

47. Ibid.
48. Ibid., August 25, 1792.
49. Connecticut *Courant* (Hartford), October 29, 1792; *ASP, II, Indian Affairs*, Vol. I, pp. 280-81.
50. Downs, "Indian Affairs in the Southwest Territory, 1790-1796," pp. 247-50; Putnam, *History of Middle Tennessee*, p. 390.

disagreement between the two chiefs leading the advance. Cherokee Chief John Watts insisted that they attack John Buchanan's station on the outskirts before they assaulted the town itself. Chief Osalotiska of the lower Creek held the opposite view. After a long discussion, it was agreed that Watts and his warriors would attack Buchanan's while most of the Creek and Shawnee waited, ready to join their allies in sacking the town.

Warned by lookouts that a war party was on its way, the defenders of the stockaded station prepared to protect the families gathered there. Soon after the Indians attacked, telling fire from inside Buchanan's seriously wounded John Watts and six others and killed three including the Creek chief known as the Shawanese Warrior and an unidentified Creek chief. With the two chiefs dead and Watts disabled, the attackers became disorganized and withdrew. They were soon in full retreat. No casualties were reported within the station, but two neighbors, Jonathan Gee and Seward Clayton sent out as scouts, had been killed by the Indians' advance guard on Taylor's Trace.[51]

On October 3 five Cherokee and five Creek attacked Black's blockhouse at the head of Crooked Creek, a tributary of Little River. They killed one and wounded three before withdrawing. The house was defended by a sergeant's command of Captain John Crawford's militia company.[52]

Concurrent with the attacks on Buchanan's and Black's, the principal Cherokee chiefs gave notice that all of their people, except the five lower towns, were peaceably disposed toward the United States; the inhabitants of those towns, wooed anew by the Spanish, favored war against the settlers, and the settlers were well aware of it.[53]

Throughout October in the Mero District, small parties of Indians riding through the settlements were seen frequently. They killed one man, William Smart, and fired ineffectively at others. Readers' credulity was strained to the breaking point by a territory newspaper report that John Cotton had escaped unscathed when fourteen of a hail of Indian bullets pierced his clothing but not one touched his skin. The alleged incident occurred near Cotton's home on Station Camp Creek. That

---

51. *ASP, II, Indian Affairs*, Vol. I, p. 331; Knoxville *Gazette*, October 6, 20, November 17, 1792; Connecticut *Courant* (Hartford), December 3, 1792.
52. Knoxville *Gazette*, October 6, 1792.
53. Ibid.; *ASP, II, Indian Affairs*, Vol. I, pp. 288-93.

the raiders meant serious business was evident to all who saw the smoldering ashes after they burned three houses on Sycamore Creek, demolished a quantity of valuable household furniture, shot and killed several hogs, and destroyed a large amount of corn. They burned Obadiah Roberts's residence on Brushy Creek of Red River and stole horses from him, from Major Josiah Ramsey in Tennessee County, and from one Suggs on White's Creek.[54]

The raids occurred along the extended frontiers of Mero despite the presence of guards from local militia companies and one company of mounted infantry and two of foot from the Washington District. Captain Hugh Beard commanded the mounted men and Captains Joseph Lusk and Jacob Brown the infantrymen. The governor called up additional companies of militia, and the individual soldiers this time "responded with unusual alacrity."[55]

On October 6 fifty Cherokee warriors led by Chief Talotiska attacked travelers from Kentucky in the wilderness, killing two and mortally wounding a third. They slew two others on Cumberland Mountain.[56]

How could the frontier folk fight back when they were restricted to defensive operations within their own border? In a letter to the Knoxville *Gazette,* William Cocke spoke for many when he wrote, "Fear is the best and only assurance of the friendship of an Indian. The idea of signing treaties and purchasing peace of the Cherokee Indians is as absurd to me as the fabulous story of the goat treating with the wolf for the security of her kids."

Cocke demanded that the Cherokee Nation be held accountable for the depredations committed by their people. The only way to have peace with the Cherokee was to "make a sudden, indiscriminate well-directed attack" upon them, he insisted. He hinted that if Governor Blount did not have the legal power to punish such offenders, volunteers might undertake it without authorization.[57]

Cocke's letter was answered by a "talk" printed in the Knoxville *Gazette* of October 20, purportedly submitted by Hanging Maw. Asserting that Cocke knew nothing about treaties, the chief chided him for suggesting that all Cherokee should be killed because "some of them

---

54. Knoxville *Gazette*, October 20, 1792.
55. Ibid.; *ASP, II, Indian Affairs,* Vol. I, p. 292.
56. Knoxville *Gazette*, October 20, November 17, 1792.
57. Ibid., October 6, 1792.

are bad men and go to war." President Washington would pay no attention to Cocke's suggestions, he said. Cocke "talked like a squaw," and was "not a man and a warrior," but only one who puts his talks "on paper."

Responding to the attacks on Zeigler's and Buchanan's stations and the declared hostility of the lower Cherokee towns, the governor ordered General Sevier to muster a brigade of militia. By November 3 a troop of horse, commanded by Captain James Richardson, and "several companies of foot" had reported to Sevier at Knoxville. The editor of the Knoxville *Gazette* took note of them, thinly veiling his hope for a decisive strike against the enemy.

> The orderly and regular behavior of these troops...has gained them the highest honor; and we have every reason to hope...that our bleeding country will be well supported and defended, and perhaps entirely relieved from the bloody, barbarous, and unrelenting hands of merciless savages.[58]

To friends outside the territory, Governor Blount regularly made the case for attacking the Cherokee and Creek and openly sought the participation of fighting men from whatever source he could tap. In October, Blount had written to the governor of North Carolina expressing the belief that the time was at hand for the Creek and Cherokee to "be chastised and restrained by the strong hand of Government." Assuming that North Carolina would play an important part in the chastising, Blount expected to see the frontier citizens of that state engaged in an expedition against the Indians. He wrote, "I anticipate the pleasure of seeing them return victorious crowned with laurels from the field of battle."[59]

Blount's North Carolina friend, John Steele, learned of the governor's assessment of the Indian problem in a letter written November 8. Blount wrote, "Now it is essential that Congress should . . . declare war. The Creeks must be scourged and well, too, and the Cherokees deserve it." Unlike the war in the Northwest, destruction of the two nations would be "only a party of pleasure," he said.[60]

The plan of those who favored launching a preemptive strike was vindicated in large part by reports that the Cherokee, with assistance

---

58. Ibid., November 3, 1792.
59. Keith, ed., *The John Gray Blount Papers,* Vol. II, p. 212.
60. Wagstaff, ed., *The Papers of John Steele,* Vol. I, pp. 85-86.

from the Creek, were about to erect stockade forts with blockhouses at three strategic locations. One was to be at the confluence of the Clinch and the Tennessee, a second at the Running-water Town on the Tennessee, and the third at the Creek crossing of the Tennessee near Muscle Shoals. The forts were to provide bases for raiding parties.[61]

Even as Sevier mustered the militia, the Knoxville newspaper printed an address "to the inhabitants of the South-Western frontiers of the United States" signed "Observer" but probably written or inspired by Governor Blount in response to Cocke. Congratulating the citizens for their strict observance of the Treaty of Holston with the Cherokee and the Treaty of New York with the Creek, "Observer" acknowledged that the Indians had violated the treaties by wholesale killing, laying waste the countryside, and stealing horses in great number. Nonetheless, observing the treaties as laws of the United States was yet the best course to follow, he said.

> Congress is equally bound to protect every citizen of the Union, as much you who live in poverty on the extreme frontier, as those who live in luxury and ease, in the large and opulent cities, and no doubt will.[62]

In the same issue, the *Gazette* presented a short piece addressed to Hanging Maw and signed "Red Bird." It was critical of both Cocke and the chief. The writer, probably Blount or an agent, charged that Cocke was a coward, referring to him as "the white man...[who] talks very strong and runs very fast." Red Bird twitted Hanging Maw for his response to Cocke's letter printed October 6: "You should give out big talks; make the people believe you are a great man and a warrior; may be their hearts will become soft, and send you to the big council, the place where some of the white pretended warriors want to go."[63]

A few weeks later, William Cocke appeared in print again, lambasting the letters of "Observer" and "Red Bird." Agreeing that only Congress could declare war, Cocke contended that states invaded by an enemy had the right to engage in war and that Congress was "bound to support" them. He insisted that peace could be achieved only when the upper towns of the Cherokee are attacked and their warriors defeated.

Berating all efforts to negotiate peace with the Indians, Cocke wryly

---

61. Knoxville *Gazette*, November 3, 1792.
62. Ibid.
63. Ibid.

suggested that some person of authority had purloined an Indian name to conceal his true identity in the "Red Bird" letter.

> But perhaps I shall be told again that the Great Man did not bid me speak, and some senseless animal, for want of reason to point out my errors, may purloin another Indian name, and chatter with as much insolence as the two Jack Daws under the patronage of Hanging Maw and Red Bird.[64]

When a party of five Creek stole horses on Little River about twenty miles from Knoxville, no one wrote to the *Gazette*. Instead, nervous neighbors rallied fifty-two men to go on a mission to destroy the towns of Chilhowee and Tellassee. Although the armed men had begun their march, they turned back when General Sevier ordered them to disperse. Their response to Sevier was applauded by supporters of federal Indian policy, including the Knoxville newspaper. Knoxville area settlers were disturbed anew, however, when a report reached them through the Cherokee that Spain had ordered the Creek to go to war against the United States and had supplied them arms and ammunition.[65]

In the meantime, after rendezvousing at Knoxville, General Sevier's brigade had moved down to Southwest Point at the confluence of the Holston and Clinch rivers. At that time the soldiers probably began construction of the blockhouse that later was expanded into a stockaded fort.

The general's reputation and the size of his force were not lost on the Indians; there were no depredations committed in the Washington District during the first fifteen days of November. However, in the last week of October, Indians had killed and scalped two men riding express from Knoxville to Nashville to pick up and deliver a number of military warrants and the surveyors' plats so that "the grants might issue thereon, within the time limited by the act of cession."[66]

Although there was quiet in Washington District, a party of Indians ambushed Captain Samuel Henley and forty men of the Washington County Militia on November 25, the second day of their crossing from Southwest Point to go to the assistance of Mero District. Henley and eight soldiers were captured when "the major part" of his detachment

---

64. Ibid., December 29, 1792.
65. Knoxville *Gazette*, November 17, 1792.
66. Ibid., December 14, 1792.

"shamefully deserted him" and returned to Southwest Point. They estimated the Indian force to be from 160 to 200 strong.[67]

Indians resumed raids into Washington District in mid-December to steal horses, and on the twenty-second, three women and two children died in an undefended house in Jefferson County on Little Pigeon River. The victims were attacked with tomahawks and a war club after their assailants had lain in wait until the only male in the house had departed. On the next day Indians, attempting to steal horses, were driven off.[68]

Apparently unaware of the tragedy in Jefferson County, Hanging Maw and twelve Cherokee came to Knoxville on Christmas Day to deliver peace talks from John Watts. News of their mission was "particularly pleasing to the unhappy frontier inhabitants."[69] Although many settlers must have doubted Watts's sudden friendship, even they were glad to hear talks of peace.

The "actual causes" of the violent conduct of the Indians may not have been understood in Philadelphia, but Governor Blount had his theories and he kept the secretary of war well advised of them. The officers administering the Spanish government of Louisiana and "their instrument" the trader Panton relentlessly encouraged the Indians to war against the settlements and, at times, supplied them for that purpose, Blount explained. The ready use of violence, he held, was deeply rooted in tribal traditions as a method of acquiring national honors.[70]

Indians were being manipulated by "the greatest of all rascals," white people living among the Creek and Cherokee, Blount declared. As most were traders, they had promoted the stealing of horses from the settlers by furnishing a ready market for them. The traders, in turn, sold them to whites in an area of the frontier remote from that in which they had been stolen.

The tribal practice of "taking satisfaction" for all injuries inflicted on its members could not be eliminated by treaties nor could retaliation be stopped when a member was killed, the governor said. Tribal custom would not permit the chiefs to interfere with those long-established practices, he argued.[71]

---

67. Ibid., December 1, 1792.
68. Ibid., December 29, 1792.
69. Ibid.,
70. *ASP, II, Indian Affairs*, Vol. I, p. 325.
71. Ibid.

Blount discredited claims that Indian hostility was a natural response to whites encroaching on their lands. He maintained that the Cherokee had sold their claims to the lands on Cumberland to Richard Henderson while the Creek had never had "the color of claim" to land on the north side of the Tennessee. While steadfastly denying that the settlers were engaged in any violation of the treaties then in force with the Creek and Cherokee, Blount admitted to the commissioners charged to run the Cherokee line that he was concerned about whether there were settlers "residing on the Indian lands or not."[72]

Backing the governor's defense of the behavior of territory settlers, Daniel Smith wrote to Secretary of State Thomas Jefferson to assure him that Indians in areas of the territory contiguous to portions settled by whites had been treated fairly since the treaties of New York and Holston. Spain persistently incited them to war against the settlers and supplied guns and ammunition for the purpose, he said, explaining that the highest achievements recognized by Indians are reached only in acts of war. He recommended "a well directed war against the hostile parties" as a merciful treatment for all.[73]

The survey to locate the boundary line separating the Cherokee Nation from federal lands in the area south of French Broad was postponed throughout the year. At first the national government delayed it. Later, on June 4, when Governor Blount invited the Cherokee to name their commissioners to meet October 8 for the joint survey, the Indians balked, smarting under their reconsideration of the Treaty of Holston. On November 15 the Cherokee sent Blount a letter expressing their hope that by the spring of the next year, "everything will be settled according to the treaty, to each other's satisfaction, and the line shall be run."[74]

Ignoring the Cherokee foot-dragging, Blount had dispatched his commissioners, instructed by the President to be liberal in trying to make the location satisfactory to the Indians, to meet their representatives on October 8. When the Cherokee failed to appear at the appointed place, the United States commissioners implemented contingent instructions from the governor. They examined the location of the ridge dividing

---

72. Ibid., pp. 325, 332.
73. Durham, *Daniel Smith, Frontier Statesman*, pp. 138-39.
74. *Letter from the Secretary at War Accompanying His Report Relative to the Running of a Line of Experiment From Clinch River to Chilhowee Mountain...*, pp. 10, 11.

the waters of the Tennessee and Little rivers and found that its point "strikes the Holston at the mouth," farther downstream than the Indians had expected. They then ran experimental lines from which they concluded that the most equitable and easily identifiable boundary would be a line run from the ridge point south 60 degrees east to Chilhowee Mountain and from that point north 60 degrees west to the Clinch River. According to this line, very few white families would be found living on Indian lands.[75]

As if establishing the Cherokee boundary were not line problem enough, Blount was suddenly caught in a cross fire between Virginia, North Carolina, and Kentucky over the correct location of the northern boundary of the territory as it adjoined North Carolina on the east and the other two states along their southern reaches. The controversy had originated in the initial survey of the line begun in 1779 by commissioners representing Virginia and North Carolina. When a dispute arose among them about the exact location of the line, the North Carolina representatives, claiming that the Virginians had pushed the line two miles too far to the south, abandoned the survey. The Virginians completed the survey as far west as the north-flowing Tennessee River before calculating and plotting the remaining distance to the Mississippi River. Their line was called Walker's line, and the North Carolina claim, a roughly parallel line two miles to the north, was referred to as Henderson's line.[76]

In 1780 the issue was settled in the view of the Virginians when the North Carolina commissioner Henderson told Daniel Smith at the future site of Nashville that North Carolina was going to accept Walker's line. Henderson's prediction did not materialize, however, and North Carolina later laid claim to land within Henderson's line. Interpreting the cession act to establish Henderson's line as the territory's northern boundary, Blount took possession of the land in question. Virginia had not passed an official act declaring Walker's line to be the official boundary until after the cession. With that chronology of events, Blount would not accept Walker's line because by so doing he said he would be giving away federal territory without authorization. President Washington

---

75. Ibid., pp. 12-16.
76. The lines were named for Dr. Thomas Walker, leading the Virginia commissioners, and Richard Henderson, head of the North Carolina commissioners.

recommended that Congress settle the dispute, but it languished until long after the territory became a state of the Union.[77]

Beginning with the issue of November 5, 1791, the Knoxville *Gazette* kept its readers abreast of the major events of the French Revolution for the next four years. During the latter weeks of 1791 and the early months of 1792, the *Gazette* reprinted serially the text of the Rights of Man with comments by the American writer Thomas Paine and others. Territory news rarely received the prominent display usually reserved for reports from France.

---

77. William Blount to the governor of Virginia, September 2, 1792, "Territorial Papers of the United States Senate, 1789-1873, Territory of the United States South of the River Ohio, 1789-1808," National Archives, Record Group 46, M-200, Roll 2; *Journal of the Senate of the United States of America, Being the Second Session of the Second Congress, Begun and Held at the City of Philadelphia, November 5, 1792* (Philadelphia: Printed by John Fenno, in Fifth Street, 1792), p. 13; Knoxville *Gazette*, June 2, 1792; Draper Manuscripts, 7ZZ51, 46J18, the Collection of Lyman C. Draper held by the State Historical Society of Wisconsin, Madison; William Waller Hening, ed., *The Statutes at Large; Being a Collection of all the Laws of Virginia, from the First Session of the Legislature in the Year 1619*, Vol. IX (Richmond: Printed by and for Samuel Pleasants, Jr., Printer to the Commonwealth, 1821), p. 564.

CHAPTER VI

CONQUERING THE FRONTIER

1790-92

Peace with the Indians had been a high priority with almost every frontier inhabitant since before the territorial government was created. In the minds of most, there was no more certain way to achieve it than by increasing the numbers of settlers until their combined strength would be overwhelming to the natives. A strong, well-located town to be the capital of the territory was likely to reassure prospective immigrants that civilization was rising in the West in a way that guaranteed Indian opposition would recede before it.

Prior to the Cox challenge, the location of a permanent capital for the Southwest Territory had been settled by Governor Blount. He made the decision sometime during his six or seven weeks at the treaty grounds. Impressed with its elevated location on the north bank of the Holston River about four miles below the mouth of French Broad and its proximity to White's fort, he chose the site to be the seat of the territorial government. From the beginning he had planned judiciously to name the capital Knoxville in honor of Henry Knox, secretary of war.[1]

Other geographic and strategic factors recommended Blount's selection. The site was 205 miles east of Nashville, 638 miles from Philadelphia, 543 miles from Baltimore, and 458 miles from Richmond with a wagon road connecting it to the latter three. It was 25 miles from the ''Beloved Town of Chota'' of the Cherokee and was ''the most eligible spot in the possession of the United States for a repository of goods for supplying the Cherokees, Chickasaws, Choctaws, and perhaps the Creeks.'' It presented an opportunity for United States traders, using the Holston and Tennessee rivers, to supplant the British merchants in Pensacola and the Spanish traders in both East and West Florida.[2]

The entire site was on undeveloped lands in Hawkins County owned by James White of White's fort. White, as proprietor, had the town

---

1. Blount to John Steele, July 22, 1791, Wagstaff, ed., *The Papers of John Steele,* Vol. I, p. 80.
2. Knoxville *Gazette,* February 11, 1792.

laid out into sixty-four lots, each containing one-half acre and having access to spacious common areas. By October 3 he had appointed three commissioners to conduct a lottery, superintend the drawing of tickets for the lots, and "regulate all matters respecting the...town" until an act of assembly should be passed to provide rules and regulations. When the lottery was held, all sixty-four lots were purchased. Among the buyers were William Blount, Judge Campbell, Judge Anderson, George Roulstone, John Chisholm, and John Stone. With this auspicious beginning for the new capital, Blount and others who owned surrounding lands could anticipate increased land values and sizeable profits.[3]

Placing the capital city on the second largest eastern tributary of the Mississippi River called further attention to the importance of free navigation throughout its system. There was even talk in the territory of straightening the meandering curves of the Mississippi not only to shorten the distance between New Orleans and the mouth of the Ohio but to enhance the use of sails on upstream boats.[4]

Almost everyone realized that settlement in the territory without the free navigation of the Mississippi was of doubtful value and uncertain future. Those already in the area would not remain silent while they were denied free use of the river to take their products to market. Recognizing that free navigation of the Mississippi was vital to their interests, Secretary Smith later explained: "The western people consider the navigation of the Mississippi as the light of the sun, a birthright that cannot be alienated."[5]

The development of the new town of Knoxville as a trade center and as seat of the territorial government was begun in earnest in 1792. Its well-chosen location would support a future growth inconceivable at that time.[6]

Governor Blount contributed to its development by beginning construction of a commodious home to serve simultaneously the needs of his family and the ceremonial needs of his office. He located his residence and a separate working office in its back yard at the corner of Hill and State streets on a lot that sloped steeply to the rear toward Front Street and the Holston River.

---

3. Ibid., December 17, 1791; Masterson, *William Blount*, pp. 207-8.
4. [Smith], *A Short Description of the Tennassee Government*, p. 13.
5. Ibid., pp. 14-17.
6. Knoxville *Gazette*, February 11, 1792.

Construction of the Blount residence was probably started in the latter part of 1791 as it was in an unfinished state in January, 1792, when the governor wrote to General Sevier asking for his assistance in forwarding to Knoxville a box of window glass ordered from Richmond. By that time Mrs. Blount and two of their sons had arrived at William Cobb's where they awaited completion of the house in Knoxville. After living through the winter months at Cobb's, they moved to Knoxville in March and took temporary lodging. A few weeks later they moved into the new house where they were joined by their two daughters who had been left at Tarborough, North Carolina, with their aunt Mary Sumner Blount, wife of Thomas Blount.[7]

One of the first two-story wood frame buildings erected west of the Appalachian Mountains, the house had on the first floor two large rooms separated by a hall that connected to a kitchen ell. The entire second floor was one large room reached by a steep, narrow stairway. Seven years later, the east wing of a single story consisting of one large room was added. Below its floor, a room was built that could be reached by raising a trap door and descending a concealed staircase.[8]

Three chimneys, built of brick burned at the site, served the original fireplaces. Another was built when the east wing was added.

Wood was the principal building material. All structural members—beams, joists, studs, and rafters—were of yellow pine. The roof was covered with hand-split cedar shakes, and the exterior walls sided with poplar clapboard. The floors, interior walls, and ceilings were made of clear heart yellow pine as were the windows, doors, and all trim items. The many lights of glass in the multipaned windows on both the front and the rear elevations of the house so entranced Indian visitors that the building was known to them at first as the "house of many eyes."[9]

Most of the early buildings in Knoxville were clustered on or near the lower ends of streets leading to the river—Central, State, and Gay—and along Front and Hill streets that paralleled the river. A vacant lot, dedicated by James White for the purpose, waited for a public house

---

7. Stanley J. Folmsbee and Susan Hill Dillon, "The Blount Mansion," *Tennessee Historical Quarterly*, Vol. XXII (June 1963), p. 106; Goodpasture, "William Blount and the Old Southwest Territory," p. 8.

8. Roberta Seawell Brandau, ed., *History of Homes and Gardens of Tennessee* (Nashville: Parthenon Press, 1936), pp. 65-67.

9. Ibid.; Folmsbee and Dillon, "The Blount Mansion," p. 107.

of worship to be built, but twenty years would pass before such a structure was raised.[10]

At the rear of the residence, a small one-story house facing State Street was used as Governor Blount's office. It was built of the same materials as the residence.

Diagonally across the block from the governor's place at the corner of Front and Gay streets, John Chisholm erected a tavern. A roomy wood frame building of three levels, it was almost as essential to the territorial government as Blount's office and residence. The tavern provided room and board for overnight guests, a meeting room for officials of the territory, and a center for the gathering of those from near and far who had special interests in the affairs of government. Much of the revenue generated by the tavern came directly from those sources. Chisholm was closely associated with Blount, serving him in both private and public business matters. When Knox County was created, the governor appointed him a justice of the peace. On other occasions he employed Chisholm as an emissary to the Indians and as special express to Mero District and to the War Department in Philadelphia.[11]

Another location of significance was the house of John Stone, on the southwest corner of Gay and Cumberland streets. The site of the first meeting of the Knox County Quarterly Court on July 16, 1792, Stone's house was often used for meetings and other requirements of the territorial government.[12]

Surely prompted by the governor, the editor of the *Gazette* raised the prospect of Knoxville's becoming a center for extending trade to the southern Indians and breaking the Spanish and British trade monopoly that had been so injurious to the United States. He declared that Knoxville was by far the best possible location in the country for a depot to supply the needs of the southern Indians. It was an opportunity that

---

10. Folmsbee and Dillon, "The Blount Mansion," p. 106; Transcript of W. Russell Briscoe address at 175th Anniversary Ceremonies, October 29, 1967, First Presbyterian Church Records, 1792-1967, Knoxville, Tennessee, Church Records—Presbyterian, TSLA.

11. Kate White, "John Chisholm, A Soldier of Fortune," East Tennessee Historical Society *Publications*, No. 1 (1929), pp. 61, 62.

12. *History of Tennessee, From the Earliest Times to the Present: Together with an Historical and a Biographical Sketch of the County of Knox and the City of Knoxville, Besides a Valuable Fund of Notes, Original Observations, Reminiscences, etc., etc.* (Easley, South Carolina: Southern Historical Press, 1982; reprint of portions of a volume originally published at Nashville: Goodspeed Publishing Co., 1887), p. 809 (hereinafter cited as Goodspeed, *History of Knox County*).

should not be overlooked.[13]

The presence of a newspaper at Knoxville in 1792 was another indication that settlers were overcoming at least some of the obstacles to civilization found on the frontier. The capability of producing and distributing the printed word from within the territory had been realized when the first issue of the Knoxville *Gazette* came off the press at Rogersville on November 5, 1791. George Roulstone and Robert Ferguson, fulfilling their prior commitment to Governor Blount, had brought their printing equipment from North Carolina and had set up a printing office at Rogersville. They issued the paper there while awaiting the governor's selection of a site for the permanent capital of the territory that he planned to call Knoxville.[14]

The building for the printing shop of the *Gazette* was readied at Knoxville during the early autumn of 1792, and Roulstone and Ferguson occupied it with their equipment about October 1. Apparently they had moved their presses by boat down the Holston from Rogersville. The first edition actually printed at Knoxville was issued October 10, 1792, four days after its regular biweekly publication date.[15]

Those participating directly in the development of the new capital probably had little time to think about the growth throughout the territory itself. Prior to Knoxville, towns had been established at Jonesborough, 1779; Nashville, 1784; Greeneville, 1784; Clarksville, 1785; and Rogersville, 1789. Blountville followed Knoxville in 1792.[16]

Growth was the watchword in the states of the Union as well. Between 1775 and 1791 their population had doubled, and in April, 1791, at Philadelphia alone "the foundations of 400 houses" had been laid since the prior October.[17]

In the towns and countryside of the territory, the most obvious evidence of growth was in the number and kinds of buildings erected. The number of frontier houses, nearly all of log wall construction, increased from a few dozen in the early settlements to a few thousand in 1792.

---

13. Knoxville *Gazette*, February 11, 1792.
14. Ibid., November 5, 1791.
15. George F. Bentley, "Printers and Printing in the Southwest Territory, 1790-1796," *Tennessee Historical Quarterly*, Vol. VIII (December 1949), p. 335; Knoxville *Gazette*, October 6, 1792.
16. James Patrick, *Architecture in Tennessee, 1768-1897* (Knoxville: University of Tennessee Press, 1981), p. 59.
17. *The Gentleman's Magazine for April, 1791*, Vol. LXI, No. 1, Part I (London: Printed by John Nichols for David Henry, 1791), p. 372.

Residences of stone, brick, and wood frame appeared. The first stone houses were primitive, but promised permanence. Typical of those were Thomas Amis's house near Rogersville, c. 1780; the George Gillespie house at Limestone, c. 1783; Jeremiah Dungan's house on Brushy Creek, c. 1785; Thomas McClain's in Powell's Valley, c. 1785; the Thomas Embree house at Telford in Washington County, c. 1791; and Daniel Smith's Rock Castle, under construction in 1792 in the Mero District. The houses of brick built in the late 1780s had more of permanence than style, also. Examples were Stony Point near Surgoinsville and the William Bowen and John Bearden houses in Sumner County. A premier wood frame house near twentieth century Elizabethton was erected by John Carter, probably about 1772. Still standing over two hundred years later, the house is known for its sophisticated design and the excellent craftsmanship of its wood mantels and paneling.[18]

Structures to house commercial establishments sprang up. Retail merchants, warehouses, and hostelries known variously as inns, taverns, or houses of entertainment were the usual occupants. Yancey's tavern was located on Island Road north of the Long Island of Holston, and Thomas Amis kept a tavern at Rogersville. David Hamblen at Rogersville and John Chisholm with partners Alex Carmichael, John Wood, and Pete McNamee at Knoxville advertised houses of entertainment.[19]

Water-powered mills to produce flour and meal and even to saw lumber dotted the countryside, although they were not as numerous as distilleries. A cotton factory, operated by John Hague at Nashville, was producing thread and cloth in 1791, and Robert Love opened a fulling mill in Knox County near Campbell's station in 1792.[20]

Some of the most ambitious undertakings were the ironworks. Probably the most extensive, belonging to the Virginia businessman David Ross, was set up near the west end of the Long Island of Holston between the North Fork and Reedy Creek. Among others were Nicholas Tate Perkins's ironworks near Bull's Gap in Greene County and James

---

18. Kincaid, "The Wilderness Road in Tennessee," p. 44; Patrick, *Architecture in Tennessee, 1768-1897,* pp. 23, 25, 61, 71.

19. Knoxville *Gazette,* January 14, December 14, 1792.

20. Samuel Cole Williams, "The South's First Cotton Factory," *Tennessee Historical Quarterly,* Vol. V (September 1946), pp. 212, 216-17, 219; Knoxville *Gazette,* November 5, 1791; August 11, 1792.

King's works in Sullivan County. In 1792 Landon Carter was planning the construction of iron forges.[21]

Bountiful supplies of lead ore were extracted from William Colyer's mine in Bumpass Cove, Washington County. The ore was said to be so rich that it could easily be reduced over an open wood fire and moulded directly into bullets.[22]

The trade of merchandise and supplies for products of the frontier was generally done from stores scattered throughout the territory. Most merchants like John Summerville who had a store on German Creek would trade for "good linsey, seven hundred linen,[23] bees-wax, bear skins, deer skins, fur skins of all kinds, rye, corn and oats." Merchant James Miller of Rogersville, who also had stores at John Adair's in Grassy Valley, at Peter Morrison's on the North Fork of Holston, and at Knoxville, would accept skins from the bear, deer, otter, wildcat, muskrat, mink, fox, and raccoon, "and all kinds of fur whatever," as well as beeswax, linsey, and seven hundred linen. Almost anything for which there was a market in Baltimore, Philadelphia, or New Orleans and which could be transported satisfactorily could be swapped for dry goods, hardware, groceries, liquors, and other staples of frontier living.[24]

Advertisements by merchants appeared regularly in the Knoxville *Gazette*, usually announcing the arrival or the impending arrival of new goods. Some of the advertisers, in addition to Summerville and Miller, were A. Nelson and Company, Rogersville; Francis Bird, Flat Creek; James Guthery near Colonel Thomas King's mills; David Deaderick, Greeneville and Jonesborough; John Shelby, Jr., Sullivan Court House; Nathaniel and Samuel Cowan, Jonesborough and Knoxville; Ambrose Yancey and Patrick Nenney at Bear Creek; and Stephen Duncan and Company and Charles McClung, Knoxville. The *Gazette* printed, also, an announcement by George Bean, gunsmith, that he had expanded his

---

21. Patrick, *Architecture in Tennessee, 1768-1897*, pp. 25, 26; Samuel Cole Williams, "Early Iron Works in the Tennessee Country," *Tennessee Historical Quarterly*, Vol. VI (March 1947), pp. 39-40, 41, 43; W. Calvin Dickinson, "Frontier Splendor: The Carter Mansion at Sycamore Shoals," *Tennessee Historical Quarterly*, Vol. XLI (Winter 1982), p. 319.

22. Paul M. Fink, "The Bumpass Cove Mines and Embreeville," *East Tennessee Historical Society Publications*, No. 16 (1944), pp. 48-49.

23. Seven hundred linen was a relatively coarse cloth containing seven hundred "warp threads to the inch in a fabric." Mary Brooks Picken, *The Fashion Dictionary; Fabric, Sewing and Dress as Expressed in the Language of Fashion* (New York: Funk and Wagnalls Company, 1957), p. 312; Harriet Simpson Arnow, *Flowering of the Cumberland* (New York: The Macmillan Company, 1963), pp. 251-52.

24. Knoxville *Gazette*, November 5, 1791; January 14, March 10, December 14, 1792.

services to include a goldsmith's and jeweler's business at his house near Bean's Station on German Creek, Hawkins County.[25]

Additional noncommercial structures such as courthouses, jails, meetinghouses, and schools appeared during the early years of the territory, but usually one was indistinguishable from another. Practically all were of log construction with stone chimneys. Their designs were purely functional, devoid of architectural ornamentation. In fact, the buildings looked much like the log houses used for family living.[26]

No standing structures marked two important frontier services. Individual proprietors offered their ferryboats to lessen the usually hazardous river crossings. Two of these were R. Dodson, who kept one such ferry at Dodson's Ford of the Holston, and Samuel Doak, who kept another at his plantation on the Holston, six miles north of Knoxville. Doak's was represented to afford the "nearest way" from Knoxville to Perkins's ironworks and Jefferson Court House.[27]

The second much-needed service was transportation of the mail. John Chisholm of Knoxville offered the first post route in the autumn of 1792. Promising that the route would be ridden in its entirety every twenty-one days, Chisholm planned it to extend from Knoxville through Greene Court House and Jonesborough to Abingdon, Virginia, the southern terminus of a post road from Richmond. The return route was by way of Sullivan Court House and Hawkins Court House to Knoxville. Chisholm's venture did not last long, however. He abandoned it a few weeks later when the postmaster general announced that a post office had been established in the territory at Hawkins Court House with regular mail connections west to Danville, Kentucky, and northeast to Richmond.[28]

New construction and expanded commerce were obvious signs of growth, but the key to continued expansion was the successful marketing and acquisition of land. The large transactions were still in land, which meant ultimately the Indians would be forced to give up their holdings and retreat before the westward movement. No settler was more deeply involved in land speculation than Governor Blount, but he was only

---

25. November 5, 1791; January 14, February 11, March 10, 24, May 19, June 2, 16, July 14, 28, August 11, October 6, December 1, 14, 1792.
26. Knoxville *Gazette*, December 1, 1792; Patrick, *Architecture in Tennessee, 1768-1897*, p. 103.
27. Knoxville *Gazette*, September 8, December 29, 1792.
28. Ibid., October 20, December 1, 1792.

one of many. Land grants located in the Chickasaw country, made earlier by North Carolina, were bought and sold without hesitation. A certain Robinson Munford registered grant Number 306 to five thousand acres on the north side of the Big Hatchie River. It adjoined another tract of his of like size. James Robertson of Nashville bought and sold lands in Chickasaw country, as did scores of others. The governor's brothers, John Gray and Thomas, had extensive holdings in the area.[29]

The autumn of 1792 witnessed a rush of surveys and land descriptions to the North Carolina secretary of state's office as purchasers hastened to convert military warrants into land grants before the deadline of December 22. The Blount brothers, acting through James Robertson in the Mero District, were especially anxious to have their surveys completed and the supporting documents sent to North Carolina. The governor warned Robertson not to miss the deadline.[30]

Most inhabitants of the territory lived on lands they had purchased with cash or had earned by military duty or by their service to government in capacities such as guards, surveyors, or boundary line commissioners. In the Mero District several lived on tracts of 640 acres that had been granted to them because they were among the original Cumberland settlers in 1779-80 or were their heirs.

A large majority of frontier families engaged in agriculture with the men and boys doing a considerable amount of hunting and trapping. Corn seemed always to be the first crop to be made, but other row crops, notably tobacco and cotton, soon followed. Corn was the most versatile product of the three, however. Furnishing meal and food grain for both man and beast, corn was easily distilled into spirits for which there were ready markets. Corn shucks could be fed to hungry cows or used to make mud mats, horse collars, dolls, and shuck ticks to go between bed ropes and feather beds.

The labor was hard, and the few slaves must surely have done more than their share of it. There was work for all members of settler families, and most participated in it. At first it was virtually all handwork, but by the 1790s plows could be had. As the plows were pulled by horses,

---

29. Shelby County Grant Book 1, pp. 110-75; Davidson County, Tennessee, Records, Deed Book B, Microfilm, Roll 1, TSLA, pp. 97, 98, 99, 100; Deed Book C, p. 72 (Davidson County Records on microfilm at TSLA are hereinafter cited as DCR).

30. William R. Garrett, ed., "Correspondence of General James Robertson," *American Historical Magazine*, Vol. I (October 1896), pp. 392-93.

mules, or oxen, there was apparently no thought of following the lingering European practice of using peasants for that purpose. Research into the practice has produced no record of any human being, black or white, having pulled a plow in the Southwest Territory.[31]

Settlers were quick to recognize that slave labor could assist them materially, especially in farming the bottomlands of Mero District. The number of slaves in Davidson County increased 50 percent from 659 in 1790 to 992 in 1795 while the white population increased a bare 5 percent from 3,459 to 3,613. John Donelson, coleader with James Robertson of the 1780 settlement that became Nashville, brought thirty slaves with his family at that time. By the 1790s, it was still the largest group that had been taken across the mountains by a single owner.[32]

Little is known of individual blacks in the Southwest Territory. They were usually anonymous, achieving notoriety only when in trouble, typically as runaways. One of those who appeared in print was "a Negro Fellow named Natt, about 5 feet 9 inches high, about 22 years of age" who had been committed to jail in Washington County. Claiming to be the property of "a certain Joseph Phillips of Cumberland, Mero District," the runaway said that, when jailed by Sheriff George Gillespie, he was on the way to see his wife and children living near Tarborough, North Carolina. "The owner is desired to come and prove his property, pay charges and take him away," the sheriff advertised.[33]

Sometimes the names of others were recorded when they were engaged in Indian warfare fighting alongside the whites. Abraham, a servant of Anthony Bledsoe, shot and killed the Cherokee chief Mad Dog; Sam, James Bosley's "good wagoner and active plantation Negro," was taken away by the Creek. Robert, James Robertson's servant who had come to the Cumberland with his owner in 1780, died defending Freeland's station in an Indian attack the following year.[34]

Repeated Indian raids made it necessary for farm laborers black or white to work under the watchful eye of a guard or guards. Even with

---

31. Harriet Simpson Arnow, "The Pioneer Farmer and his Crops in the Cumberland Region," *Tennessee Historical Quarterly*, Vol. XIX (December 1960), pp. 291, 295.
32. Anita Goodstein, "Black History on the Nashville Frontier, 1780-1810," *Tennessee Historical Quarterly*, Vol. XXXVII (Winter 1979), pp. 401, 403.
33. Knoxville *Gazette*, December 1, 1792.
34. Goodstein, "Black History on the Nashville Frontier," p. 402.

this precaution, several farmers were shot to death in their fields.[35]

Settlers often had milk cows and chickens and sometimes hogs, beef cattle, and sheep. Many had mules, oxen, or horses, the latter the most coveted animal possession of all.

The practice of breeding horses to improve blood lines was widespread, and the territory newspaper displayed frequent notices of fine stallions at stud. William Shelton of German Creek advertised his stud Leadall; A. Nelson offered the services of Mountain Leader; James Ore, Piomingo; John Adair and Robert Christian, Young Northumberland; and James Manasco, Young St. George.[36]

Horse racing had been popular in the area since the time of the Watauga settlements. Race courses, designed for the sport, existed as early as 1791, and betting was the rule of the day.[37]

The influx of settlers to take up the essentially virgin lands of the territory was a migration of neighbors and families. The resettlement of neighbors—sometimes an entire community— resulted in the organization of new churches, the construction of meetinghouses, the development of cemeteries adjacent to the places of worship, and the presence of a local preacher.

Families included children, and that called for schools and teachers. Few schools existed in the period 1790-92, but two prominent exceptions were Martin Academy in Washington County, incorporated by North Carolina in 1783, and Davidson Academy, chartered in 1785, whose classes were taught in Thomas Craighead's meetinghouse near Nashville. Both were started by Presbyterian ministers, Samuel Doak the former and Thomas Craighead the latter. In addition to them, another minister, Samuel C. Carrick, announced in 1792 that beginning in January of the following year he would open a "Seminary" at his home near Knoxville. In each school the conventions of the period were followed. After basic instruction in the "3 R's," students undertook heavy assignments in the classics, with emphasis on Latin and Greek. When there was time, they were exposed to courses in some or all of the following: geography, logic, natural and moral philosophy, astronomy, and rhetoric.

---

35. Arnow, "The Pioneer Farmer and his Crops in the Cumberland Region," p. 297.
36. Knoxville *Gazette*, April 7, June 2, 1792.
37. Lucy K. Gump, "Possessions and Patterns of Living in Washington County: The 20 Years Before Tennessee Statehood, 1777-1796," Thesis, East Tennessee State University, 1989, pp. 94-96.

Most schools or classes were taught in the teacher's home and some in the homes of students, although meetinghouses sometimes doubled as schoolhouses. At first, teaching was done by anyone who would undertake the task. Later, schoolmasters were sought out and brought into communities by the promise of opportunity and good pay. They always found the opportunity, but they rarely realized the pay because of widespread default on their tuition bills. The result was that many teachers became itinerant, rarely staying in the same community more than a year or two.[38]

Although the need for schooling was recognized, indifference to religion was widespread. Yet by 1791 the inhabitants of the territory were attended by several Protestant ministers, most of whom represented the Presbyterian, Baptist, and Methodist churches. The congregations they served first appeared in the small communities of the countryside and were much slower to form in the towns.

Presbyterian ministers, educated in the East, had come into the territory soon after the first settlers. Samuel Doak, who came to the Watauga settlements in 1777 and moved to Jonesborough in 1780, is regarded generally as the most noted of the early Presbyterian ministers. He is due much of the credit for the twenty-six Presbyterian congregations that would be spread throughout the Holston Valley by 1797.[39]

Samuel C. Carrick, another Presbyterian, was also a prominent minister in the eastern part of the territory. About 1790 he preached to a large gathering at the Indian mound located in the fork of the Holston and French Broad and later organized a church there: Lebanon in the Fork. Thomas Craighead, like Doak and Carrick a preacher and teacher, ministered to the earliest Presbyterian congregations in the Nashville area. His Spring Hill Meetinghouse, located about six miles northeast of town, housed Davidson Academy for which he was the schoolmaster.[40]

Baptist preachers, free from the responsibilities of the schoolmaster that weighed heavily on the Presbyterians, were usually farmers or

---

38. Harriet Simpson Arnow, "Education and Professions in the Cumberland Region," *Tennessee Historical Quarterly*, Vol. XX (June 1961), pp. 134-38.

39. Corlew, *Tennessee, A Short History*, pp. 120-21.

40. Transcript of W. Russell Briscoe address at 175th Anniversary Ceremonies, October 29, 1967, p. 4; John B. McFerrin, *History of Methodism in Tennessee*, Vol. I (Nashville: A.H. Redford, Agent, Methodist Episcopal Church South, 1875), p. 37.

traders who labored during the week and preached on Sundays. Although relatively uneducated, they worked untiringly at their ministry, and by 1792 there were about eighteen churches in the Holston Association and five in the Mero District. The Baptists attracted a cross section of frontier folk, but their message was received enthusiastically among the unlettered ones who "felt more at home with the uneducated preachers than with the learned Presbyterian divines." The early work of ministers Matthew Talbot, Jonathan Mulkey, and Tidence Lane was especially effective. Baptist congregations in the territory had about nine hundred members by 1792, all white.

Methodist preachers participated in a traveling ministry, a practice that set them apart somewhat from their colleagues in the other two Protestant churches. Among them were both the lettered and the untutored. The itinerant minister Jeremiah Lambert, assigned to the Holston country in 1783, traveled up and down the river and its valley, usually meeting in the homes of Methodists to organize societies to further their work. Benjamin Ogden undertook a similar duty in the Cumberland settlements, and despite the infrequent appearances of the itinerant preachers, the church grew.[41]

The Methodist Church admitted both free and slave to membership while it opposed slavery and, at times, invoked a provision in its *Discipline* that forbade slaveholders from becoming or remaining members of its fellowship. In 1792, the reported membership of the church in the territory included 819 whites and 78 slave blacks.[42]

The most awesome Methodist personage on the frontier of the 1790s was Bishop Francis Asbury. Traveling mostly on horseback but sometimes on foot, the bishop made sixty-two trips across the Appalachians. Seeking the comfort of an occasional tavern along his route, Asbury rarely missed a chance to talk to its proprietor about his soul and his obligation to hold to high moral standards in his earthly conduct. While at Thomas Amis's tavern near Rogersville on April 13, 1790, he wrote of his host:

> He is highly offended that we prayed so loud in his house. He is a distiller of whiskey, and boasts of gaining 300 pounds [sterling] per annum by the brewing

---

41. Corlew, *Tennessee, A Short History,* pp. 119-22; McFerrin, *History of Methodism in Tennessee,* Vol. I, p. 36.
42. Robert L. Kincaid, ed., "History of the Southwest Territory, 1790-1796, by Samuel Cole Williams," Typescript (Nashville: Tennessee Historical Commission, 1960), p. 164.

of his poison. We talked very plainly; and I told him that it was of necessity, and not of choice, we were there—that I feared the face of no man. He said he did not desire me to trouble myself about his soul.— Perhaps the greatest offense was given by my speaking against distilling and slave holding.[43]

Before his visit to Amis's, Asbury had stopped overnight with a family in whose crude house a man had recently been killed by "savages," he was told. He noted of the unfortunate family in his journal, "They are but one remove from savages themselves."[44]

In the early 1790s it was not customary for territory folk to extend bed and board to a preacher—even a bishop—on a complimentary basis. Such was the usual practice in parts of Virginia and North Carolina, but not so in Holston. There the attitudes were more "practical," Bishop Asbury said, and the traveler paid for his accommodation.[45]

Other faiths were represented on the frontier, notably the Catholic and the Quaker. No Catholic churches were established in the early years of the territory, but Quaker meetings in the settlement along the Nolichucky River began in 1792. At first the congregation was called Nolichucky and, later, New Hope.[46]

Concurrent with the establishment of churches was the appearance of fraternal orders. Two lodges of the 1790s were the Freemasons, who sometimes met at the residence of T. Arthur on Little Pigeon River, and Lodge Number 20, Western District, which met at the North Fork of the Holston.[47]

The professional services most in demand and most lucrative during the territory years were those of the land surveyors. When land was taken up initially, surveyors had first to survey and plot all acreage in any land grant before it could be issued. In addition there were on-going requirements for subdividing large tracts into smaller ones, laying out towns, and running boundary lines.[48]

---

43. Francis Asbury, *The Journal of the Rev. Francis Asbury, Bishop of the Methodist Episcopal Church, From August 7, 1771, to December 7, 1815*, Vol. II (New York: Published by the Methodist Episcopal Church, 1821), p. 71.
44. Ibid., pp. 70-71.
45. Ibid.
46. Stephen B. Weeks, *Southern Quakers and Slavery, A Study in Institutional History* (Baltimore: The Johns Hopkins Press, 1896), Appendix III, p. 340.
47. Knoxville *Gazette*, August 25, 1792.
48. Arnow, "Education and Professions in the Cumberland Region," p. 139.

Daniel Smith, secretary of the territory, was probably the most highly regarded surveyor of the period. He had participated in the westward extension of the Virginia-North Carolina state line in 1779-80 after having practiced the profession in Southwest Virginia about ten years. Between 1780 and 1792, he had completed extensive surveys in the Holston and Cumberland valleys that would be incorporated into the first printed map of the territory.[49]

Although physicians of the time had limited training and few skills, representatives of their profession seemed slow to arrive on the western waters. The hardy settlers must have had confidence in their own ability to maintain the health of their families as there seems to have been no outcry for professional medical services. One student of frontier life in the territory commented, "Every household was both hospital and doctor's office, and homemade remedies as well as patent medicine had long been a part of life." The medicinal properties of herbs, cultivated and tended in family gardens, were well known. For mothers in labor, midwives were indispensable, and a bottle of whiskey was basic to every home medicine chest. For those who survived after their scalps had been removed, General Robertson— and perhaps others—could provide treatment. Robertson had learned the procedure when he lived in the Watauga settlement from a Dr. Patrick Vance.[50]

The supply of lawyers was as excessively large as the supply of doctors was excessively small. For example, ten licensed attorneys practiced in 1790 in Nashville, to serve Davidson County's combined slave and free population of approximately 4,136. In 1792, seven attorneys in Knoxville served a comparable population.[51]

Among the frontier people were some who tested the bounds of the law and the patience of its enforcement officers. Punishment for offenders was often swift, sometimes final. Found guilty of burglary by the Superior Court of Washington District on April 15, Absalom Morris and Welcome Hodge were hanged at Jonesborough a week later.[52]

---

49. Durham, *Daniel Smith, Frontier Statesman*, pp. 179-80.

50. Arnow, "Education and Professions in the Cumberland Region," pp. 143-44, 146; Margaret Burr Deschamps, "Early Days in the Cumberland Country," *Tennessee Historical Quarterly*, Vol. VI (September 1947), p. 215.

51. *The Blount Journal, 1790-1796*, p. 43; Knox County, Tennessee, Records, Minutes of the Court of Pleas and Quarter Sessions, 1792-1795, Book O, Microfilm, Roll 139, TSLA, p. 4 (Knox County Records on microfilm at TSLA are hereinafter cited as KCR; minutes of the Court of Pleas and Quarter Sessions of any county are hereinafter cited as Quarterly Court Minutes).

52. Knoxville *Gazette*, August 25, 1792.

While court dockets were cluttered with suits alleging paternity out of wedlock, slander, trespass, larceny, assault and battery, Sabbath breaking, and profane swearing, most litigation involved personal property, the collection of debts, and the settlement of misunderstandings arising out of contracts loosely made. Although runaway wives were advertised by their husbands left behind, such matters rarely came to court. If there were runaway husbands, wives must have considered them good riddance; no advertisements for runaway husbands have been discovered.[53]

In their legislative capacities, county courts directed such internal improvements as could be accomplished by neighbors working together with little or no financial support from government. They authorized the laying out and clearing of public roads, named overseers of the roads, and granted permits to operate ferries and to locate mill seats. They levied taxes and sometimes set tavern rates for drink, board, bed, and stable.[54] The courts, in their judicial capacities, impaneled grand and trial juries, licensed attorneys, received the reports of county officeholders, and administered probate matters.

Local militia companies from fifty to one hundred men strong, paid with federal funds when called to duty, played important roles in government beyond their primary purpose of defending the settlements. Militia duty was required of every free male and indentured male servant between the ages of eighteen and forty-five years. Slaves were exempted from service as were ministers, judges, justices of the peace, ferrymen, post officers, iron furnace workers, and veteran officers with three years of duty during the American Revolution. Each company was commanded by a captain, elected by his men, all of whom were residents of a common section of their county.

Company duties were various, but sometimes included preparing tax lists, working on roads, taking the census, and communicating information to other citizens. Each company was mustered at least once every three months, a practice that provided time for military instruction but also afforded opportunities for political discussions, exchange of news,

---

53. Ibid., March 24, 1791; Deschamps, "Early Days in the Cumberland Country," p. 225; KCR, Quarterly Court Minutes, Book O, p. 8.

54. Washington County, Tennessee, Records, Quarterly Court Minutes, 1778-1809, Microfilm, Roll 129, TSLA, pp. 453, 455, 459, 460, 461, 462, 463, 470, 473, 482, 483, 494, 541 (Washington County Records on microfilm at TSLA are hereinafter cited as WCR).

and eating and drinking together.[55]

Increasingly the workings of the territorial government became matters of popular concern. Some of Blount's decisions were questioned. Thus far the governor had enjoyed the support of the inhabitants despite their disappointment in the failure of the national government to protect them from the southern Indians. He had endeavored to involve the frontier leadership in his plans for the territory and had especially tried to head off factional rivalries.

Before moving his family from Rocky Mount to Knoxville, Governor Blount sought to reduce the disruptive personal tensions between Colonel John Tipton and General Sevier, and he achieved a measure of success. The two rivals for political power had led separate, hostile factions since the days of the state of Franklin, but when the governor visited Tipton on March 6, 1792, he was received kindly. His host was cooperative, and Blount believed that he had achieved his goals: "Conciliation and public happiness." In the governor's presence, Tipton burned a petition that had been circulated to discredit Sevier.[56]

The Tipton-Sevier feud was nothing compared to the political discussions set off on November 20, 1792, when the governor and two judges passed an act authorizing the county courts to levy and collect taxes. Essentially free from taxation for two years, the frontier folk looked askance at their heads of government. Although the taxes could apply only to polls and land and rates could not exceed fifty cents per poll or more than seventeen cents for each one hundred acres of land, there was widespread discontent. Most probably agreed that they must pay for the courthouses, jails, and stocks, and for jurors at the superior courts as provided in the act. They rebelled, however, at the provision that taxes could be collected to "defray the contingent charges of said counties." One rebel was Henry Bradford of Mero, a neighbor of Daniel Smith, who claimed that the public was confused by the act and that it constituted taxation without representation. An elected general assembly could do no worse.[57]

The creation of an elected general assembly had been advocated earlier in the year by the citizen who sent letters to the *Gazette* using the pen name Trenk. "The congregating of men for the good of society is a

---

55. Deschamps, "Early Days in the Cumberland Country," p. 223.
56. Hamer, ed., "Letters of Governor William Blount," p. 127.
57. Durham, *Daniel Smith, Frontier Statesman*, pp. 143-44; *Laws*, p. v.

good device," he said as he upheld the principle of making laws by duly elected representatives instead of by an appointed governor and judges. During the prior December, Trenk, reminding his fellow citizens that they had "no hand in the conducting of this government," had challenged them to call for the election of a representative general assembly.[58]

The editor, probably taking his cue from the governor, took the position that the public needed knowledge more than representatives. Like many before and since who have tried to stop the advance of representative government, he counseled caution and advocated that a government of stability should first be achieved. *The Rights of Man* and the *Gazette* should be read and pondered, he suggested, and "all the different classes of citizens" should cooperate "with the utmost spirit and vigor" to attain a government of stability and principle.[59]

Predictably Blount's confidence that the public was not yet ready to elect a general assembly was shaken. Only twelve days before adopting the tax ordinance he had written to a friend, "The People of the Territory and myself are unanimous in agreeing to have no General Assembly."[60]

There had been virtually no complaint a few months earlier when the governor and judges created two new counties in the eastern part of the territory. Organizing local government over the lands to which the Cherokee claim had been extinguished by the Treaty of Holston, they laid out the counties of Knox and Jefferson on June 11, giving them the names of the secretaries of war and state. They located the new counties below a line that circumscribed the boundaries of Hawkins and Greene. They also provided for a court of pleas and quarter sessions for each county; the Knox County Court would meet at Knoxville and the Jefferson County Court at the house of Jeremiah Matthews in that county.[61]

---

58. Knoxville *Gazette*, December 17, 1791; March 10, 1792.
59. Ibid., March 10, 1792.
60. Wagstaff, ed., *The Papers of John Steele,* Vol. I, p. 85.
61. Knoxville *Gazette*, June 30, 1792.

CHAPTER VII

IS PEACE POSSIBLE?

1793

Achieving peace between the Cherokee and the Americans during 1793 was rendered the more difficult by the inability of the Indians to agree on a policy toward the invaders and by their failure to have a single chief or ruling body firmly in control. While the upper towns seemed inclined toward peaceful coexistence, the lower towns sent raiders without let up.[1]

A similar situation existed with the Creek. After the death of McGillivray on February 17, 1793, the chiefs of that nation held widely divergent views toward the Americans. Their differences were exacerbated by the impetuosity of the young warriors who struck frequently into Mero District and, less often, visited the eastern part of the territory.

Residents of the Mero District could not free themselves from their attackers who came in groups as small as three or as large as a few hundred warriors. During a ten-day period beginning January 16, 1793, the district experienced numerous murders and depredations.

On the sixteenth on the north side of Cumberland near Clarksville, Indians seriously wounded Colonel Hugh Tinnan. Two days later raiders killed Major Evan Shelby, brother of Governor Isaac Shelby of Kentucky, James Harris, and an unidentified Negro slave of Moses Shelby, near the same place. On January 22, Captain William Overall and a certain Burnet were slain on the track from Kentucky to Cumberland at the Dripping Spring. The flesh was cut from the bones of Overall and carried off.

Within forty-eight hours, an Indian party ambushed a salt boat and a French pirogue on the Cumberland at the mouth of Half Pone. Shots from the shore killed Malachia Gaskins and David Crow, mortally wounded St. Clair Pruet, and seriously wounded John McLugen and Robert Wells in the salt boat. In the pirogue, two were killed and one mortally wounded.

---

1. *ASP, II, Indian Affairs,* Vol. I, p. 436.

On January 26, raiders felled Thomas Heaton and Anthony Bledsoe, son of Colonel Anthony Bledsoe, on the north side of Cumberland. Although both were shot through the body, they survived.[2]

Information reaching Governor Blount indicated that a general war by the Creek and lower Cherokee towns against the territory might break out at any minute. He was told that the lower towns had received a war club from the Creek and had promised to "take hold of it, join the Creeks in war...[and] take it with them to Cumberland."[3]

At the same time, the Cherokee Nation had been invited to hold council with the Shawnee to plan "a general war against the United States," a proposition said to have been strongly supported by the lower towns and the young warriors. The initial blow was proposed to fall on the Cumberland settlers in April. Simultaneously, the Shawnee would settle scores with the Chickasaw by assaulting that nation for having supplied warriors for St. Clair's army. Although an agreement between the two nations was not reached, the Shawnee continued to promote a general Indian war against the settlers. When they failed to receive an affirmative response, they demanded a war against the Mero District, at least.[4]

A new dimension to Indian-white relations was introduced February 13 with the outbreak of hostilities between the Creek and the Chickasaw. The development was encouraging to Blount and the Cumberlanders who hoped that the Creek would be too busily engaged in the conflict to continue incursions into Mero District. The Indian war might even change life in the district where the inhabitants had been "so apprehensive of hourly receiving death" from the Creek that they ventured "out of doors [only] with great caution."[5]

The Cherokee, suddenly invited by both principals to take sides in the Chickasaw-Creek conflict, made no response while John Watts assured Governor Blount that they would not become allies of the Creek. In spite of the chief's assurances, the territory people doubted he could control the warriors in the lower towns.[6]

The Chickasaw had asked the governor for aid against the Creek the

---

2. Ibid., pp. 436-37.
3. Ibid., p. 438.
4. Ibid., pp. 438, 454; *Dunlap's American Daily Advertiser*, February 9, 1793; Knoxville *Gazette*, January 12, March 23, 1793.
5. Knoxville *Gazette*, March 9, April 6, 1793; *ASP, II, Indian Affairs*, Vol. I, pp. 441, 452.
6. *ASP, II, Indian Affairs*, Vol. I, pp. 439, 451, 454.

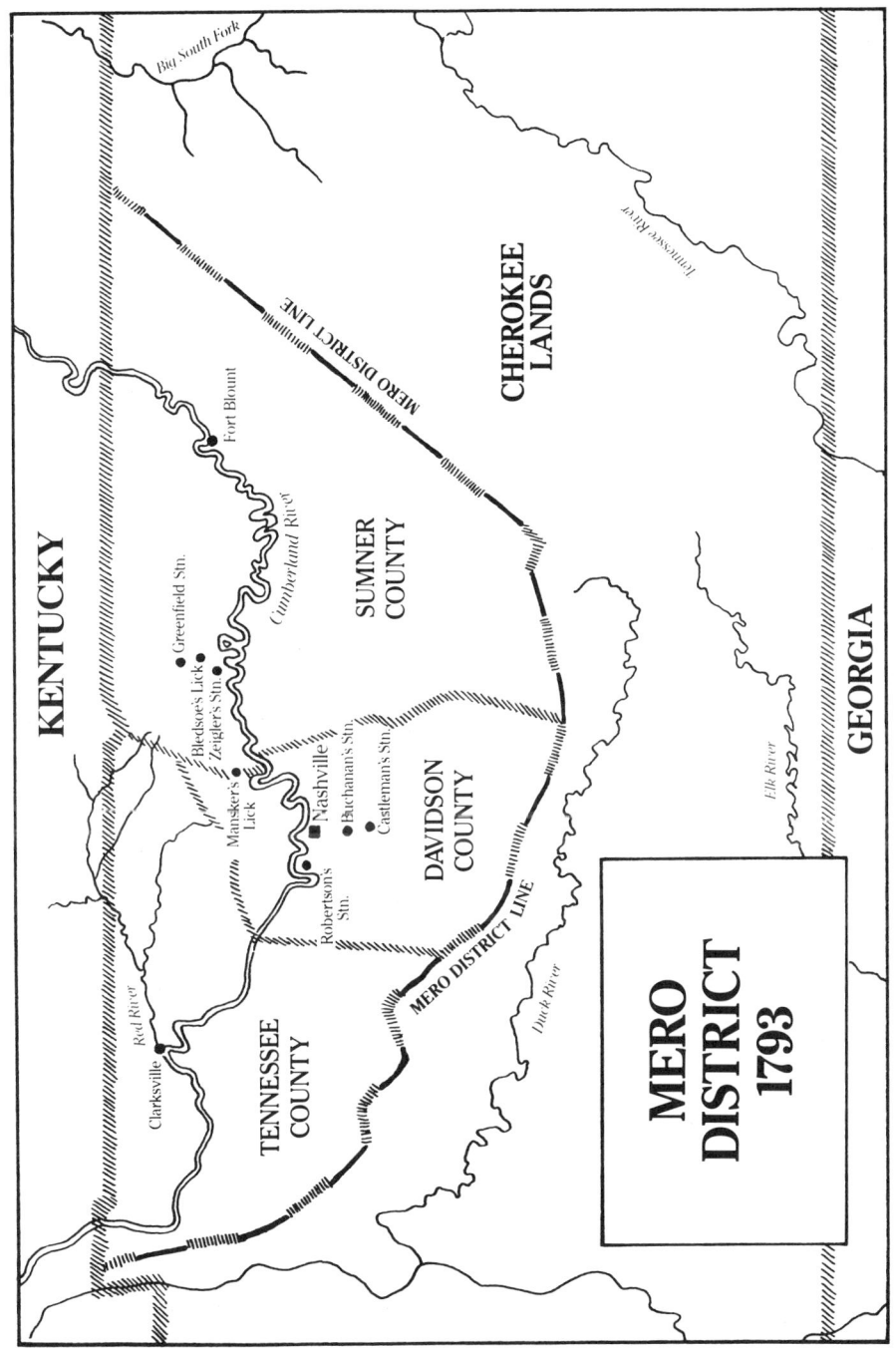

minute hostilities began. In their need they enjoyed the allegiance of James Robertson and the Mero folk, and by June 1 that support was transformed into specific assistance from the United States. The War Department ordered General Anthony Wayne to ship to the Chickasaw Bluffs by river from Fort Washington 500 stands of arms, ammunition for them, 1,500 bushels of corn, 100 bushels of salt, and 100 gallons of whiskey. From Nashville, General Robertson sent "one swivel and three blunderbusses," 40 gallons of whiskey, a quantity of corn, and other items of supply.[7]

Concurrent with the dispatch of military aid, Secretary of State Jefferson warned the court of Spain that the United States was contemplating war with the Creek. Declaring that it was impossible for his government "to submit with folded arms, to be butchered by these savages," Jefferson said that the United States would be forced to more vigorous measures against the Creek if the moderate ones then being pursued should fail.[8]

The Creek looked to Spain for their implements of warfare and expected, not without reason, that Great Britain would aid their cause, also. They hoped that Spanish opposition to the growing settlement of the Cumberland area would translate into substantial assistance against Cumberland's staunch friends, the Chickasaw. In the lower Creek country, their leaders promised agent James Seagrove that their nation sought nothing but peace with the United States.[9]

Their conflict with the Chickasaw was probably the reason the Creek registered little interest in the Shawnee's effort to mobilize a general war against the United States. Regarding the inhabitants of Mero District as allies of the Chickasaw, the Creek kept up their attacks in the Cumberland area. They believed they could better rely on aid promised by Spain than on a grandiose alliance with the Shawnee.[10]

Even as the settlers hoped to use the Chickasaw-Creek war as an occasion to negotiate peace with the entire Cherokee Nation, Governor Blount learned that a volunteer army was being assembled in Kentucky to march on the lower Cherokee towns. The governor quickly denounced the adventure. "Such a measure would be totally destructive of the

---

7. Ibid., pp. 430, 442, 443; Carter, ed., *Territorial Papers, SWT*, IV, p. 248.
8. Downs, "Indian Affairs in the Southwest Territory, 1790-1796," p. 254.
9. *ASP, II, Indian Affairs*, Vol. I, p. 439; Knoxville *Gazette*, April 20, 1793.
10. Knoxville *Gazette*, March 23, 1793.

plans...of the President, and would destroy the hopes of returning peace," he wrote to General Robertson. He ordered Robertson to command the Kentuckians, who were expected to pass through Nashville, to remain north of the Tennessee River and to desist from their planned attack. He wrote the governor of Kentucky asking his cooperation to abort the volunteers' plans.[11]

During the six weeks from February 1 to March 12, only six murders by Indians were reported in Mero. Heavy flooding along the Cumberland River and its tributaries was probably responsible for the respite.[12]

After the rains, the Creek resumed their visits to the Cumberland country. It was almost impossible to determine whether their forays constituted warfare against the United States or were multiple but unrelated acts of larceny. Certainly raids to steal horses provided in their execution a chance for impetuous young braves to demonstrate their manhood by spilling blood and taking scalps. Whatever the motive, the murders and thefts were real, and Blount responded by pledging he would send from 160 to 500 mounted infantry from the eastern districts "as soon as possible."[13]

During the latter half of March and the month of April, seventeen deaths were reported at the hands of Indians in Mero. Perhaps the most noteworthy victim was Isaac Bledsoe, killed April 9 while working in a field near his stockaded fort at Bledsoe's Lick. At the time he was lieutenant colonel commandant of the Sumner County Militia. About twenty Indians were in the attacking party.[14]

Approximately two hundred warriors assaulted the station at Greenfield, two miles from Bledsoe's fort, on April 27, but were driven off after they killed two of the defenders and suffered two dead and several wounded among their own. The attack was frustrated by the bravery of three young frontiersmen whose families already had paid a high price for defending their homes. Previously William Hall and William Neely had each lost a father and two brothers to the Indians and William Wilson a brother. A witness to the "bloody scenes" in Mero addressed the editor of the Knoxville *Gazette,* "Where will these mischiefs end?

---

11. *ASP, II, Indian Affairs,* Vol. I, p. 452.
12. Ibid., p. 443.
13. Ibid., p. 452.
14. Knoxville *Gazette,* May 18, 1793.

What are the blessings of government to us? Are we to hope for protection?"[15]

On April 24 the governor dispatched Major Hugh Beard from Southwest Point with 125 militia to relieve the people of Mero District from an anticipated "powerful invasion by the Creeks." Directing Beard to proceed across the southern or upper waters of Caney Fork River to the paths that Creek parties followed when approaching Mero, Blount instructed him to "consider all Indians found on the waters of the Cumberland River as Creeks and enemies, and treat them as such." If they encountered identifiable Cherokee, Choctaw, or Chickasaw, they should consider them friends. Relief for the Cumberland settlements could best be achieved, Blount advised, by "falling on and destroying the principal camps of the Creeks on Caney Fork and the other southern waters of the Cumberland River, and by intercepting or pursuing...incursive parties."[16]

Following orders, Beard destroyed many abandoned Creek camps, both on his trip to Nashville and on the return journey that brought him back to Knoxville on June 3. The few small parties of Indians that were in his path escaped ahead of his scouts.[17]

From the latest intelligence reports, Governor Blount noted that between April 1 and May 18, a total of 560 Creek in groups of all sizes had crossed the Tennessee River to attack Mero District. There were so many parties of Indians in the vicinity of Nashville that planters were obliged to post sentinels "whilst others are at work in the fields." In a somewhat exaggerated claim, the Kentucky *Gazette* at Lexington reported that the Cumberland settlements were breaking up and that those remaining behind were huddled together in the stockaded forts.[18]

General Robertson added to the credibility of the *Gazette*'s claim when he reported that the collapse of the Cumberland settlements was imminent unless peace with the Indians could be restored. Catherine Montgomery Bledsoe, widowed eight days before when Indians killed her husband Isaac, underlined the plight of those living at the outside limits of the settlements as she begged for protection. In a letter written April 17 to Secretary Smith, a friend of long-standing, she asked for troops to

---

15. Ibid.
16. *ASP, II, Indian Affairs,* Vol. I, p. 453.
17. Ibid., p. 455.
18. Knoxville *Gazette,* May 18, June 3, 15, 1793; *ASP, II, Indian Affairs,* Vol. I, p. 467.

man the frontier posts left unattended when Major Anthony Sharpe's battalion was withdrawn. "This settlement cannot possibly stand [without them]," she wrote.[19]

While Blount contemplated the fate of his western district, he was advised by the Cherokee chiefs Little Turkey and John Watts that, without doubt, the Creek were at war with the settlers. Declaring that their people were "determined to be at peace," the chiefs warned territory officials not to blame them for injury or damages inflicted by others. The Creek threat to Mero was so ominous that Governor Blount wrote to Governor Isaac Shelby of Kentucky to warn him that some of the invaders might "bend their force against the southern frontier" of that state.[20]

By June 1 it was reported that "many parties of Creeks" had returned to cross the Tennessee at the lower Cherokee towns "on their way home from Kentucky and Cumberland with many scalps and valuable horses." The story was becoming a familiar one; scalps proved bravery and patriotism, and horses meant money. The editor of the Knoxville *Gazette* could hold back no longer. "The Creek nation must be destroyed," he cried. "*Delenda est Carthago.*"[21]

On May 14 the secretary of war, prompted by correspondence between the President and Congressman Hugh Williamson of North Carolina, suggested establishing a post at the crossing of Cumberland in Mero as a base for patrolling that district's eastern frontier and for guaranteeing its communications with the nation's capital. Soon afterward he expressed the hope that it might be garrisoned by a company of federal troops that he expected to make available to the territory. General Robertson announced at once that he would build a blockhouse on the river bank "as a beginning stand" for the regulars.[22]

From mid-May until the end of August, Indian raids in Mero District continued unabated. At least twenty-five settlers were killed, and more were wounded.[23]

Hostile Indian activity in the district declined significantly after General

---

19. *ASP, II, Indian Affairs*, Vol. I, p. 465; Draper Manuscripts, 7ZZ36; *Dunlap's American Daily Advertiser*, April 8, 1793.
20. *ASP, II, Indian Affairs*, Vol. I, p. 457; William Blount Letters, Special Collections, Hoskins Library, University of Tennessee, Knoxville.
21. June 1, 1793; *ASP, II, Indian Affairs*, Vol. I, p. 446.
22. Carter, ed., *Territorial Papers, SWT*, IV, pp. 243, 257; *ASP, II, Indian Affairs*, Vol. I, pp. 464, 467.
23. *ASP, II, Indian Affairs*, Vol. I, pp. 466, 468; Knoxville *Gazette*, August 13, 1793.

Robertson sent Captain George D. Blackmore's troop of cavalry to flush out any raiders encamped east of Bledsoe's Lick along the several trails leading into the settlement. Recommended by James Winchester, lieutenant colonel commandant of the Sumner County Militia, the August excursion turned up no Indians in force, but the cavalry's presence and demonstrated mobility were probably responsible for the relative peace the area enjoyed during September and October.[24]

The peaceful interlude ended abruptly on November 5 when Lieutenant William Snoddy, with thirty Sumner militiamen, broke up a camp of Indian horse thieves near the Rock Island ford of Caney Fork River. Snoddy lost two men, and three others were wounded. Comparable damage was inflicted on the Indians who in flight left a large cache of supplies behind.[25]

By that time it was obvious that Creek aggressions against the Cumberland country were incited not only by the Spanish government but also by white traders among the Creek. The traders' latest ploy was to represent to the Indians that the territory had been "thrown away" by Congress and, thus, could be violated with impunity. Their motive was clear; they wanted a continuing supply of stolen horses that they could purchase from the Indians and resell in other white markets.[26]

Though vulnerable in its remote location, the Mero District was not the only target for the Creek and lower Cherokee. The eastern part of the territory, although more heavily populated and lying contiguous to the states of North Carolina, Virginia, and Kentucky, was the scene of murder and horse stealing.

A raid in January brought death to one John Pates who lived on Crooked Creek, sixteen miles from Knoxville. On March 9, the brothers James and Thompson Nelson were killed and scalped by Indians on Little Pigeon River about twenty-five miles from the capital. A party of nine Cherokee from the upper towns killed and scalped two young men by the name of Clements on March 18 about sixteen miles below Knoxville. Two days later Indians slew one Taylor in Jefferson County. They fired so many shots from ambush that those within hearing thought a nearby station had been attacked in force. Earlier in the month, a man and a woman had been struck down on the Kentucky Road. Those

---

24. *ASP, II, Indian Affairs*, Vol. I, pp. 466, 467; Knoxville *Gazette*, November 23, 1793.
25. Knoxville *Gazette*, December 7, 1793; Draper Manuscripts, 32S490.
26. Philadelphia *Gazette of the United States*, July 17, 1793.

attacks and other reports of Indians scouting, stealing horses, and planning additional scalpings resulted in the governor's calling out rangers for the protection of the frontiers of Jefferson and Knox counties. The rangers had hardly been mustered when Indians killed William Massey and Adam Green on March 31 at the gap of Powell's Mountain on the Clinch River about twenty-six miles from Hawkins Court House.[27]

To afford easier access to superior courts for the citizens, Governor Blount established by ordinance a third district in the territory on March 13. He included in its domain the two counties of Knox and Jefferson and called it Hamilton District to honor the secretary of the treasury of the United States. A few months later, the Hamilton District Superior Court was organized by Judge Campbell to sit at Knoxville. He appointed Francis A. Ramsey clerk of the law court and Samuel Mitchell clerk and master of the chancery court.[28]

Indifferent to changes on the settlers' political map of the eastern region, neighboring Indians increased the intensity of their raids. On March 26 eighteen Indians, led by a renegade white man, attacked a party of nine men and ten women and children from the territory near the Hazel Patch in Kentucky. Five of the men were missing and presumed killed; three were wounded. The women and children were unharmed. The leader of the Indians was killed in the contest, and several of his followers were wounded.[29]

The range of the raiders seemed almost limitless. Some Creek braves burned two houses six miles apart on the Holston on April 8 and 11, and on April 18 unidentified Indians killed two men and wounded a third on the east fork of Little Pigeon River in Jefferson County. Travelers arriving at German Creek from Kentucky reported on April 18 that shortly before their departure, a neighboring station had been attacked by Indians who took the lives of three of the inhabitants before eighteen others surrendered to them. The eighteen were marched into the woods and slain.[30]

Hostile incursions into the eastern part of the territory caused families to collect at stations for protection. During extended periods, living

---

27. Knoxville *Gazette*, January 26, March 23, 1793; *ASP, II, Indian Affairs*, Vol. I, pp. 436, 438, 440, 444; Kentucky *Gazette*, March 25, 1793.
28. Knoxville *Gazette*, March 23, 1793; *Laws*, p. vi; Goodspeed, *History of Knox County*, p. 815.
29. Knoxville *Gazette*, April 20, 1793.
30. Ibid.; *ASP, II, Indian Affairs*, Vol. I, p. 450.

conditions became intolerable. At John Craig's station there were 280 people, "men, women, and children, living in a miserable manner in small huts," on April 11.[31]

By midyear some marauders were bold enough to challenge militia units. On July 31 when a party of horsemen commanded by Lieutenant Telford was returning from reconnoitering a wooded area near Wells's station, Indians fired on them, wounding two and destroying one of their mounts. A few days before at the head of Pistol Creek, Ensign Joel Wallace escaped when Indians fired at him, one ball harmlessly striking a large knife in his belt.[32]

The unsuspecting were the easiest targets. On August 11 a party of twenty Indians killed Jonathan Cunningham in his father's field near M'Tear's station, fifteen miles from Knoxville. Neighbors arrived too late to save him but in time to slay one of his attackers. On the same day, a certain Walker was killed and two men wounded by a party of eighteen Indians on Little Pigeon River, twenty miles from Knoxville, and on the day before, one Reed fell to raiders on Muddy Creek above Little Pigeon.[33] Abraham Wells was ambushed and mortally wounded by Indians on the path between Wells's and Kelly's stations on August 17.

Death at the hands of marauders often meant that the victims' bodies would be treated with utter contempt. Indians killed two children and wounded a third at Cloyd's plantation on the south side of Nolichucky River about eleven miles from Greene Court House on June 29. Then they "carried off the wife of Mr. Cloyd about half a mile, where they put her to death, with the tomahawk, stripped her, ripped open her bowels, and otherwise mangled her in a manner too shocking to relate."[34]

There were other examples. Braves attacked Henry's station August 29. Nearby they captured Lieutenant George Tedford and Samuel Jackson and put them to death "in a most cruel manner." On the next day two Indians appeared at the house of Sebastian Hetler, on the south side of Nolichucky in Washington County, about fifteen miles from Jonesborough. They "wounded and scalped his wife in a most inhuman manner, and killed his daughter, 12 years old, cut off her head, carried

---

31. *ASP, II, Indian Affairs*, Vol. I, p. 448.
32. Knoxville *Gazette*, July 13, August 13, 1793.
33. Ibid., August 13, 1793.
34. Ibid., July 13, 1793.

it some distance, and skinned it." Where was Hetler? "Mr. Hetler and a Negro [slave] were in the barn but could not afford any assistance," the Knoxville *Gazette* reported.[35]

On September 3 about fifteen Indians beset the home of Zephaniah Woolsey on the south side of Nolichucky ten miles from Greene Court House. In the ensuing melee they shot Mrs. Woolsey through the head, shot a young woman through the thigh, scalped a small girl, and shot Woolsey through the breast and hand. All of the victims attained unlikely recoveries.[36]

Knoxville is thought to have been the destination of an army of seven hundred Cherokee and two hundred Creek that crossed the Tennessee thirty miles below the capital on September 25. Slowed when the two chiefs John Watts and Double Head could not agree on a strategy to assault Knoxville, the Indians were eight miles short of it the next morning. There they laid siege to the blockhouse of Alexander Cavet where he and his family, thirteen persons in all, men, women, and children, had barricaded themselves. Among them there were only three gunmen, but they killed two of the attackers and wounded three others before the besieged family accepted an offer to surrender with the promise of being exchanged for Indian prisoners held by the whites. As they emerged from the house, a party led by Double Head fell upon them and slaughtered all, except one son saved by the intervention of John Watts. The half-white Bob Benge, who had offered the terms of surrender, tried in vain to save the victims, but Double Head's warriors would not be stayed. They burned the house and destroyed Cavet's cattle, sheep, and hogs. The Knoxville newspaper observed: "The cruelty and obscenity practiced in the killing, and upon the bodies of this unfortunate family . . . equal if not surpass whatever has before been seen or the imagination can conceive." Nearby they burned the house and stacks of grain belonging to Luke Lea and then abandoned the expedition.[37]

A week later a young woman and a boy were killed on a public road on the south side of French Broad near Dandridge in Jefferson County. Their assailants had lain in ambush for them. On the next day, a young man named Cunningham, on his way to assist in burying the victims,

---

35. Kentucky *Gazette*, October 16, 1793; Knoxville *Gazette*, September 14, 1793.
36. Knoxville *Gazette*, September 14, 1793.
37. Ibid., October 12, 1793; February 13, 1794.

was killed within half a mile of the same place.[38]

On October 13 a party of twenty-eight Indians struck twenty miles from Jonesborough in Greasy Cove on the frontiers of Washington County, an area regarded as a safe haven for settlers. They took the lives of Mrs. William Lewis and her five children and burned their dwelling and other houses in the cove.[39]

Wells's station, a series of blockhouses, was the scene of an ambuscade on December 23. Indians "way-laid a path" to Wells's and fired upon "a party of citizens conveying a wagon load of corn from a neighboring plantation to the station." Two men, Roger Oates and Nicholas Ball, were slain, and "a mulatto boy" was made prisoner by the attackers, believed to be Creek.[40]

Reports of horse stealing by Indians were received almost daily by the governor's office. From the eastern part of the territory, twenty animals were taken on May 25 in Raccoon Valley.[41] On June 19 a large party of Indians raided Wear's Cove in Jefferson County where they stole ten horses, killed two cows and three hogs, took seven bags of corn meal, cut down a large stand of corn, and extensively damaged Wear's mill. Two nights later, raiders took ten horses at Gamble's station on Little River, four from John Craig's, and four from Bird's station on the Holston, twelve miles below Knoxville. On June 23 Indians took six horses from David Craig's station and left a trail indicating they had fled to Chilhowee, one of the upper towns of the Cherokee. During the last week of July and the first week of August, about eighteen horses were taken from the vicinity of Wells's station and seven from Low's. The practice contnued throughout the autumn.[42]

Horse stealing was equally prevalent in Mero District, although there were fewer reports because the settlers had offered to ignore the property losses if the national government would protect their lives. Nonetheless, the theft of Mero horses threatened to become a point of contention between that district and the eastern districts. Some people in Mero believed that the horses stolen by the Indians were resold in the Holston region. In the eyes of David Wilson of Sumner County,

---

38. Ibid., October 12, 1793.
39. *ASP, II, Indian Affairs,* Vol. I, p. 469; Knoxville *Gazette,* November 23, 1793.
40. *ASP, II, Indian Affairs,* Vol. I, p. 474.
41. Ibid., p. 455.
42. Knoxville *Gazette,* June 29, August 13, October 12, 1793.

there was something amiss. On July 23 he complained to Secretary Smith: "They must certainly be men of consequence that are concerned in this business or they could not carry it on under the very eye of government with impunity."[43]

As superintendent of Indian affairs in the southern department, Blount had entered the year 1793 with orders from the President to negotiate and maintain peace with the native Americans. At the same time, as governor of the territory he was under intense pressure from the settlers to permit a decisive strike against the Indian towns that harbored the raiding parties. Blount's response was to cultivate friendships with key chiefs and to encourage territory folk to join him in demanding that the federal government extend military protection to the southwestern frontiers.

From time to time the governor's balancing act seemed to be working. Blount accepted at face value promises from John Watts and Hanging Maw that they could be counted in the camps of the peaceful. On January 6, 1793, Blount received delegations of Cherokee from Estanaula and Chota who had come to Knoxville to confirm further the sincerity of Watts's overtures for peace. Two weeks later interpreter John Thompson and Arthur Coody, formerly a British interpreter, assured Blount that "the heads of the Cherokee generally are using their endeavors to induce the young warriors to desist from the commission of depredations on the citizens of the United States."[44]

Blount was encouraged by the unsolicited visits. He was further heartened when the Cherokee safely returned Captain Samuel Henley, who had been captured on Cumberland Mountain when his small detachment of militia, en route to Mero District, was surprised by the Cherokee on November 23, 1792. Henley was escorted to Knoxville in January, 1793, by Middle Striker, a Cherokee chief who had signed the Treaty of Holston. The freed prisoner believed that Watts's interest in peace did not extend to the Cumberland settlements and that small parties of Creeks and Cherokees would continue "to infest that district." Nonetheless, Blount had "the most sanguine hopes" that the measures he had taken in the past and those he planned for the future would bring

---

43. "Papers of General Daniel Smith," *American Historical Magazine,* Vol. VI, No. 3 (July 1901), pp. 225-26.
44. Knoxville *Gazette,* January 12, 26, 1793.

about peace with the Cherokee.[45]

Under instructions from Philadelphia, Blount met with John Watts, Hanging Maw, Double Head, and a large gathering of Cherokee at Henry's station on February 6. He delivered an invitation from President Washington to send representatives to meet with him in Philadelphia on April 17 and offered to accompany them on the journey. The President expected that the result of the meeting "would have a powerful tendency to remove all causes of hostility" between the Indians and the whites.[46]

Hanging Maw was willing to go; however, after consultation, Watts spoke for the group and stated that they would respond in three weeks after a council of all the chiefs at Running-water Town. He said he wanted to see peace among the southern tribes before meeting the President and warned Blount that there was no certainty they would accept the invitation. Watts did not tell the governor that the resident agent in the Cherokee Nation, Leonard Shaw, was counseling the Indians privately that they should avoid Blount and approach President Washington directly. He held out hopes to them that the President might restore lands they had signed over to Blount at the Treaty of Holston.[47]

In other discussions at Henry's station, Blount admitted Cherokee claims to lands on the north side of the Tennessee, but recommended to them "to forbear to carry arms on that part which lay above the mouth of Clinch" until the treaty line should be run. He told the Cherokee that if their people had business in Knoxville, they should approach it unarmed by paths leading directly from their towns. Blount explained that the rangers the Cherokee might see along the frontiers were on duty to defend the territory from the Creek.[48]

Almost always a defender of the governor's positions—if not a spokesman for him—the editor of the Knoxville *Gazette* agreed that there were good prospects for peace with the Cherokee. He wrote, "The Cherokees have given many proofs of their disapprobation of the conduct of the Creeks. They appear sincerely disposed for peace. John Watts...was explicit and clear on that head."[49]

---

45. *ASP, II, Indian Affairs*, Vol. I, p. 434.
46. Ibid., p. 429.
47. Ibid., pp. 429, 447-48; Carter, ed., *Territorial Papers, SWT*, IV, pp. 246-47.
48. Knoxville *Gazette*, April 20, 1793.
49. Ibid.

A month later Hanging Maw's friendly disposition toward the government was further cultivated when he visited the Knoxville encampment of a company of federal troops that had arrived February 27 from Salisbury, North Carolina. The soldiers, under the command of Lieutenant William Rickard, formed and fired a "federal salute" to the chief.[50]

The military bearing of the regulars impressed the Indians and the citizens as well. It was not long, however, before the federal infantry lost strength through desertions. From New Boston, the camp on the Holston near Knoxville, Rickard published notice of a reward of ten dollars for Francis Holmes, a deserter, in the *Gazette* of March 23. On April 20, Rickard advertised for three more deserters, and on May 4, another. Two others deserted from the company on July 1 and yet another on November 29. When Captain Joseph Kerr led a second federal infantry company into the territory, he experienced desertions at once. On July 9, six of his men fled in canoes downriver from the garrison at Southwest Point. Before the year was out, the soldiers would be selling articles of their equipment such as axes and even the "regimentals" they wore.[51]

Aware that the federal soldiers' presence was important primarily because of its symbolism, Blount continued to curry friendship with the Cherokee chiefs. Earlier he had detailed John McKee, a long-time friend and acquaintance of Watts, to "stay with and about him, in order to use his influence to the establishment of peace." McKee was highly regarded by the chiefs in the lower towns as well as by the whites generally. He accepted his mission and left Knoxville loaded with presents that he would give to indicate the personal esteem in which he held Watts and other key figures of the nation.[52]

McKee's close attention to Watts did not achieve the desired results, however. By March 28 the Cherokee chiefs had declined the invitation to visit the President. Blount communicated their decision to Secretary Knox. He added that he would set out early in April for Philadelphia to confer with the secretary and the President as soon as Daniel Smith arrived at Knoxville from Mero to assume the governor's duties during his absence from the territory. Blount promised to show them

---

50. Ibid., March 9, 1793.
51. Ibid., April 20, May 4, July 13, August 13, December 19, 1793; January 2, 1794.
52. *ASP, II, Indian Affairs*, Vol. I, p. 435.

convincing proof of the hostile disposition of the Creek.[53]

While Blount had awaited a reply from Watts, it became evident that there was little hope of peace between the Creek and the territory. All information reaching Knoxville indicated that the Creek were unrelenting in their commitment against the Cumberland settlements and that pleas of peace from the Cherokee would at best "retard their operation for...perhaps a moon or two."[54]

The outlook for peace with the Creek[55] brightened momentarily in July when the Cumberlanders sent "artillery" and pledged volunteers to assist the Chickasaw against their mutual enemy. Promising to put a total stop to their young people going against Cumberland and Kentucky, the Creek begged President Washington to intervene with Blount to restrain his people. The government of Spain complained about Robertson's aiding the Chickasaw and observed that it was in the interest of both that government and the United States to keep the Indian nations at peace among themselves. Such a belief prompted Spain to refuse aid sought by the Cherokee and, instead, to counsel them to "stop every hostility against the Cumberland settlement," the Baron de Carondelet stated.[56]

Blount, with the cooperation of Secretary Smith, demonstrated government's desire for peace by trying to curb retaliatory acts. On January 23 the governor learned that friends of one Pate, recently killed by the Indians, were planning to recruit a force to attack the upper Cherokee towns. He dispatched Lieutenant Colonel Kelly at once to the distressed neighborhood with orders to prohibit any "citizen or citizens" from crossing the Tennessee River or entering any Indian town.[57]

Five days later the governor issued a proclamation forbidding the irate settlers from taking satisfaction in the Cherokee Nation. Characterizing them as "disorderly, ill-disposed persons," he commanded them to "desist...disperse, and retire peaceably...within one hour from the moment of the promulgation of this proclamation." Directing all officers "civil and military" to enforce the terms of the Treaty of Holston,

---

53. Ibid., p. 443; Knoxville *Gazette*, April 6, 1793.
54. *ASP, II, Indian Affairs*, Vol. I, p. 443.
55. Certain Cherokee chiefs had advised Governor Blount in early April that the Creek would never make peace with the Cumberland folk because they had never given up their claim to the hunting ground in the Cumberland basin that they held jointly with other tribes. Ibid., pp. 439, 449.
56. Ibid., p. 408; Carondelet to Robertson, May 21, 1793, James Robertson Papers, TSLA.
57. *ASP, II, Indian Affairs*, Vol. I, p. 435.

he warned citizens that the treaty was the law of the land and its violators placed themselves in grave jeopardy. He wondered aloud about establishing a tribunal solely to try treaty violators.[58]

On the same day, Lieutenant Colonel James White read the proclamation to "from eighty to one hundred" persons collected at Gamble's station with arms and provisions. Although they protested that they were unprotected by the federal government yet not themselves permitted to exact retribution, they agreed to disperse the next morning and did so. White reported to the governor that the greater part of the crowd had assembled "upon a mistaken zeal to serve their country," not foreseeing the consequences of such conduct. The crowd's willingness to cooperate probably resulted from the governor's sending out some rangers to patrol the near frontier and calling a company of militia to enforce the terms of his proclamation.[59]

The governor again warned his impatient constituents that they must avoid actions that would bring on a general war, especially when he had no force in the field, "and when there is not provision to be had to support one." He reminded his officers that justice would not be served by attacking the Cherokee towns; "it would be punishing the innocent for the guilty."[60]

Somewhere in the territory, resentment against the Indians was almost always at the boiling point. In Washington County, John Tipton, lieutenant colonel commandant of militia, set out to raise a large party to rendezvous March 10 at Jonesborough where he boasted they would be joined by at least nine hundred, all with the common purpose: destruction of the Cherokee towns. Coming at a time when the county was relatively free of raiders, Tipton's effort was a failure. Only five men responded. With proof in hand that Tipton intended to disturb "the peace and order of government," the judges issued warrants to arrest him and "several other turbulent characters...engaged with him."[61]

James Winchester, like many of his fellow citizens in the Cumberland country, did not believe that the national government understood their desperate situation. With Blount's approval, Winchester preceded the governor to Philadelphia where he arrived March 1 to present a memorial

---

58. Ibid., pp. 434, 435.
59. Ibid., p. 435.
60. Ibid.
61. Ibid., p. 436.

from the inhabitants of Mero District seeking federal protection against the southern Indians. Although the national government offered little help, Winchester was able to convince Secretary Knox that aid must be supplied from some quarter. Accordingly, on May 14, Knox authorized Blount to send militia from other districts of the territory to aid Mero and raised the possibility that Captain Kerr's company of regulars might properly be sent there.[62] The authorization rekindled the settlers' hope that they would be able to protect themselves yet avoid all-out war with the southern Indians.

One of the most challenging obstacles facing the frontier people was determining friend from foe among the Indians. In fact, most of the time it was extremely difficult to identify the tribe of a person or a party from appearances.

There were many incidents when a settler was so uncertain as to an identity that he resolved it by assuming that the Indian was an enemy. At dusk on March 15, rangers near Knoxville spied a lone Indian off the path with a gun, mistook him for a Creek, and killed him. The unfortunate victim was Noon-day, a Cherokee from one of the upper towns, who was highly regarded in Knoxville. The killing caused an immediate crisis with the Cherokee and threatened to cancel their plans for sending a delegation of chiefs to meet with the President. Watts claimed that he would hold back those who sought immediate satisfaction and stated that he wanted to see peace made quickly. Blount apologized for the murder, explaining that it occurred because of mistaken identity. He offered to give satisfaction in goods to Noon-day's friends if they would be content to forego further bloodletting.[63]

Two months later on May 23, John Morris, a Chickasaw Indian, was killed by an unknown white who fled the scene with the Indian's horses. Unarmed, Morris and his brother James Anderson, who had fought in General St. Clair's army against the northern Indians, and a Cherokee were attending to their horses near the governor's house when they were attacked. Anderson and the Cherokee barely escaped. The victim, who spoke English well, had been a visitor at the governor's house repeatedly, and was well known and respected in town. Blount offered a reward of one hundred dollars for the killer; it was never claimed.[64]

---

62. Ibid., p. 429.
63. Ibid., p. 450.
64. Ibid., pp. 454-55; Knoxville *Gazette*, June 1, 1793.

Convinced that John Morris and his associates had been mistakenly identified by their attacker as Cherokee, Blount explained again to Secretary Knox the feelings of his people toward that nation. In the eastern district "[they] believe that every murder is committed by Cherokees, commit it who will," he said. On the other hand, throughout the territory his people were very friendly to the Chickasaw.[65]

The Knoxville editor commented, "Every good man must detest the horrid act, every friend to government must feel the insult offered it, and himself thereby personally injured.

"The law is the rule and guide for all free men...all violators of it should be brought forth and punished according to their offenses."[66]

In justice to the victim and to show due respect to his nation, Blount ordered an unusual display of public ceremony for his burial.

> John Morris, the Chickasaw who was inhumanly murdered on the 23rd instant, by the base hand of some unknown assassin, to be buried this afternoon, at the usual burial ground of the white people, with the military honors due to a warrior of his friendly nation. — The procession to commence in the street near the magazine at four o'clock.
>
> Order of Procession
> Sergeant, Corporal and twelve privates to precede the corpse.
> The governor and brother of the deceased as chief mourners.
> The Chickasaws two and two.
> The civil and military officers two and two.
> Private citizens two and two.

A large crowd from town and the surrounding countryside attended the procession and burial.[67]

After the funeral, Governor Blount prepared to set out for Philadelphia to consult with the President and the secretary of war. His departure was accompanied by an uncommonly solicitous exchange between the governor and the people of Knoxville. In "An address of the Inhabitants of Knoxville and its vicinity to His Excellency Governor Blount," his close companions James White, Joseph Greer, and John Stone heaped praises upon him, "for and in behalf, and at the request of the other inhabitants." They praised Blount's judgment and propriety in the

---

65. *ASP, II, Indian Affairs*, Vol. I. p. 455.
66. Knoxville *Gazette*, June 1, 1793.
67. Ibid.

administration of government and expressed the hope that he would be reappointed by the President for a second term of office.

Promising to continue to exert his very best efforts to secure peace and happiness for the territory, Blount answered that his visit to the President would be devoted to accomplishing those objectives. He complimented the settlers, most of whom had exercised admirable restraint in response to Indian raids. He hoped that "more efficient means," such as a strike into Indian territory by government-sponsored forces, might be authorized soon.[68]

---

68. Ibid., June 29, 1793.

CHAPTER VIII

A TRYING SCENE

1793

Acting as governor in Blount's absence, Secretary Daniel Smith was left to reap the whirlwind of settler determination to retaliate against the Cherokee in their towns and villages. Speaking for the overwhelming majority, an unidentified citizen of the territory made the case for retaliation in an eloquent letter written from Richmond, Virginia, on April 26, 1793.

> The yeomanry of this territory are among the best disposed citizens in the world, and evidence a greater degree of patience and fortitude than government has (in my opinion) a right to expect. It is a trying scene to see our children, parents and relations daily killed before our eyes, and forbear to retaliate, because Congress have said, we shall not act offensively, till they give permission, at the distance of 650 miles.[1]

Before leaving for Philadelphia on June 7, the governor had ordered Captain John Beard to lead a company of mounted infantry in pursuit of the Indian party responsible for "the late murders and depredations on Bull's Run and Flat Creek" with the warning that he should not cross the Tennessee into Cherokee territory. Angered that for the past year Indian raiders had escaped each time they had been pursued by militia, Blount wanted blood: "I repeat...my order to you to well scour the mountain in pursuit and search of them. Your chastising them by which I mean your killing of them will afford me great pleasure."

James White, lieutenant colonel commandant of Knox County, heartily agreed with Blount. He wrote to Beard: "A spirited pursuit, for the present, may in future give us as much rest and ease...I hope, sir, you will have success and kill your enemies with cheerfulness."[2]

Ignoring the governor's warning, Beard and his fifty-six men crossed

---
1. *Dunlap's American Daily Advertiser,* May 3, 1793.
2. James White to Beard, May 27, June 2, 1793; Blount to Beard, May 31, 1793, "War Department Collection of Post Revolutionary War Manuscripts, Territory Southwest of Ohio River," National Archives, Record Group 94, M-904, Roll 4.

into Cherokee territory and attacked a number of Indians who had gathered at Hanging Maw's to discuss plans to go to Philadelphia in the autumn to see the President. Their consultation was prompted by Blount's recent request for them to consider a later date as he could delay his own trip no longer.[3] At the time of the attack, the Cherokee's leading chief, Little Turkey, had gone to the Creek to tell them of his plans to take a delegation of headmen from his nation to confer with President Washington.

Totally surprised by the daybreak attack on June 12, the Indians offered little resistance. Hanging Maw's wife Betty, Scantee, Fool Charley, and eight or nine others were killed. Hanging Maw suffered bullet wounds in an arm, and Betty, the daughter of Nancy Ward, was wounded. The carnage was stopped only after two of Blount's agents, Major King and David Carmichael who were on the scene when the troops arrived, begged the soldiers to spare the rest of Hanging Maw's family and his house from burning.[4]

The agents rushed to Knoxville where they reported the tragic event to Smith on the evening of the twelfth. They warned him that the Indian deaths would be attended with "fatal consequences" and the certainty of retaliation. On their way to Knoxville, King and Carmichael had informed settlers of Beard's acts. They told Smith, "[The settlers] are much alarmed, blame the perpetrators, expect the utmost hostility of the Indians, and are crying out for assistance on the frontiers."[5]

Outraged, Smith dispatched a letter to the secretary of war reporting Beard's attack, "as inhuman an act as was ever committed." The captain would be tried by court-martial for violation of the eleventh article of the Treaty of Holston, he said. Although the acting governor was not altogether surprised by the outburst of settler rage that Beard's killings represented, he said it surpassed anything that "could have been supposed." Preparing to defend against expected Indian retaliation, he admonished General Sevier to stand at the ready to lead a large contingent of Washington District Militia to the defense of the frontiers and ordered more than one-half of the Knox County Militia "to take post at the most proper places on the frontiers."[6]

---

3. *ASP, II, Indian Affairs,* Vol. I, p. 457.
4. Knoxville *Gazette,* June 15, 1793; *ASP, II, Indian Affairs,* Vol. I, pp. 459, 460.
5. *ASP, II, Indian Affairs,* Vol. I, p. 459.
6. Ibid.

Smith immediately sent letters of apology and explanation to the Indians. He told Hanging Maw that he was ashamed and that he despised the perpetrators of the violent deed "for their act was horrid and unmanly." The chiefs should not let the dastardly act deter them from accepting the President's invitation to go to Philadelphia where they could negotiate a peace that would bring a halt to excesses committed by either side, Smith advised. He asked them to forbear taking satisfaction for the deaths but to "let us punish them for you" as the Treaty of Holston provided.[7]

Hanging Maw responded by chiding Smith for his inability to control the settlers in Blount's absence. "Surely they are making their fun of you," he wrote. "Surely you are no head-man nor warrior."[8]

Double Head demanded satisfaction for the lives taken by Beard's men and wanted to know how and when it would be provided. He said that he was delaying a journey to tell Little Turkey of the tragedy until he received certain assurances the territory people would take satisfaction for the Indians.[9]

Bold Hunter said that he was willing to wait for a talk from the President because Smith had promised satisfaction would be given. To Smith, he wrote, "We shall look to you to see it done; and not for our young warriors to say that you told them lies."[10]

Smith won Cherokee agreement to delay taking satisfaction until they could hear from the President. Their constraint was dictated in part by the scarcity of provisions in the nation and the need to tend their crops. They were not ready for a general war. Smith correctly doubted that the chiefs could control "all small parties" and believed that invasions by such groups were likely. He was equally concerned about the whites whose animosity toward the Cherokee continued to be fed by every report of horse thefts. Ill will toward the Indians was so widespread that any attempt to punish John Beard by law was "out of the question."[11]

Hurrying off separate letters to Edward Adair, John Watts, John Thompson, and "the Chiefs of the Cherokees," Smith tried desperately to maintain the status quo ante until the President could

---

7. Ibid., pp. 459, 460.
8. Ibid., p. 460.
9. Ibid.
10. Ibid., p. 462.
11. Ibid., p. 460.

communicate with the Indians on the Beard atrocity. In response to a plea from Tickagiskee, he sent provisions by Major King including whiskey and "a little of the white people's tobacco, to promote good thoughts as you smoke." Answering John Thompson's contention that the Indians favored peace "if the whites will let them alone," Smith countered that repeated Indian depredations on the frontiers had so incensed the settlers that "their reason seemed to be laid waste." He said that he could control the whites if the Indians would refrain from "stealing horses and doing acts of violence."[12]

Many in the territory viewed with alarm the slaughter at Hanging Maw's. One of them, "A fellow sufferer," made a public statement through the columns of the *Gazette*. Branding Captain Beard's conduct as "imprudent and unwarrantable," the writer declared there were no principles in the laws of God, nature, or man that would sanction it. Acknowledging that he, as a frontiersman, had shared the pain suffered by his fellows when Indian raiders took precious lives, he reminded his readers that abandoning their own law and act for "savage satisfaction" invited cruel retaliation. To have killed men and women "who had convened under an assurance of peace and safety" from the national government was a violation of good faith and deserved the condemnation of all, he said.[13]

Equally alarmed but for altogether different reasons was the friendly Chickasaw chief Piomingo. He was unable to understand why the whites treated with tribes at war with them. Writing on that subject to General Robertson, Piomingo warned that the Creek and Cherokee would continue to war upon the whites "until you whip them." He noted, "Surely . . . if you knew how lightly and despisingly they speak of you and your friends, you could not bear it as you do."[14]

In addition to Piomingo, Beard had other defenders. The national government should be blamed, one unidentified friend argued, because of its insistence that the settlers contain their defensive operations within the bounds established by treaty. It was urgently necessary, he said, to pursue the Indians across the line into their sanctuaries to punish and disarm them. The authority to make preemptive strikes against the hostile tribes was an essential part of self-defense, he explained, but national

---

12. Ibid., pp. 461, 462, 463.
13. Knoxville *Gazette*, June 15, 1793.
14. *ASP, II, Indian Affairs*, Vol. I, p. 466.

policy did not allow it. He said that Beard had acted correctly in taking Indian lives, no matter what the circumstance, to offset the many lives of settlers lost during the prior year. He demanded destruction of the whole Cherokee Nation unless the perpetrators were delivered to territory authorities.[15]

Referring to the governor, Beard's apologist said: "We wish not so worthy a man to suffer. We have taken advantage of his absence. We have pursued the murderers into their own country. If it is a crime, let the charge fall on us in a body."[16]

Reaction in Philadelphia to Beard's excursion was swift. President Washington expressed his "highest indignation," and Secretary of War Knox ordered Blount to bring "the perpetrators of that wicked affair to full punishment." Knox admonished the settlers that the United States would not support "a war brought on the frontiers by the wanton, blood thirsty disposition of our own people." Nothing would be more satisfactory to the national government than "peace with the Indian tribes, founded in humanity and justice."[17]

Peace with the southern Indians was vital for another reason. Secretary of State Jefferson believed that, notwithstanding its professed willingness to try to keep the Indians friendly to both governments, Spain was trying to pick a quarrel with the United States that would lead to hostilities. The President's cabinet expected war with Spain, although the administration was making every effort to avoid it.[18]

While Beard's attack on the helpless Indians at Hanging Maw's was still the centerpiece of public conversation, the brash captain led yet another unauthorized expedition into Cherokee territory. Gathering at Blackburn's plantation, two or three miles below Campbell's station, Beard and about 130 men resisted the acting governor's efforts to dissuade them from their course: the wholesale destruction of the Cherokee and their towns. After talking with many of the men face-to-face, Smith issued an order to Captain Beard:

> As the court martial has not yet proceeded to judgment on your former conduct, you are yet to be considered an officer subject to the order of government, and

---

15. Knoxville *Gazette*, August 13, 1793.
16. Ibid.
17. *ASP, II, Indian Affairs*, Vol. I, p. 431.
18. McMurry, "The Indian Policy of the Federal Government and the Economic Development of the Southwest, 1789-1801," p. 27; Holmes, "Spanish-American Rivalry Over the Chickasaw Bluffs, 1780-1795," pp. 40-41.

I now call upon you, requiring you to desist from your unwarrantable conduct, to disband your men, and send them to their respective homes.[19]

Beard ignored the order and rode with his mounted volunteers into Cherokee territory on July 17 heading for the towns along the Hiwassee River. At the first town they killed five or six Indians. At the old Hiwassee town they were turned back when their attack on some strong houses was heavily resisted. Indian fire killed one of the men and wounded another. The rest of Beard's volunteers "came off in confusion." The men were back in the territory on July 23, and Smith was able to report that the outing had done "less damage than could have been supposed."[20]

Hoping to avert another strike into Indian territory, Smith summoned General Sevier to confer on the latter's plan to lead an expedition down the north side of the Tennessee as far as the lower Cherokee towns. Such an authorized outing in force should calm the nerves of those wanting action against the Indians and could determine the extent of Indian movements of size or importance in the area.[21]

Soon after Beard's first expedition, settlers in the Wear's Cove area replied to an Indian raid into their neighborhood on June 19 by sending about thirty men in pursuit of the raiders. Before the pursuing party had been mustered, seven volunteers had raced after some of the raiders separated from the main body. They overtook the Indians, killed two of them in a fire fight, and recovered several horses they had stolen. Led at first by Lieutenant William Henderson, who soon yielded command to Samuel Wear, the pursuing party headed for the town of Tellassee. Before they reached their destination, they came upon a group of Indians on the north bank of the Tennessee. After an exchange of fire, the Indians tried to escape by jumping into the river and swimming to safety. That only made them easier targets, however. Fifteen Indian men and one woman died; four women were taken prisoner. None of Wear's men was hurt, but they had taken retribution on the wrong persons. It was discovered afterward that the raiders had crossed the

---

19. *ASP, II, Indian Affairs*, Vol. I, p. 464.
20. Knoxville *Gazette*, July 27, 1793; *ASP, II, Indian Affairs*, Vol. I, p. 464.
21. "This spirit of war against Indians, pervades people of all ranks so far, that no order of government can stop them," Smith wrote to the secretary of war. *ASP, II, Indian Affairs*, Vol. I, pp. 463-64.

river prior to that time with the horses and plunder taken at Wear's Cove.[22]

Ninety-one volunteers from the neighborhood came forward quickly to retaliate for the June 29 murder of a woman and two children on the Nolichucky River. Raised by Lieutenant Colonel John McNabb without the knowledge of the governor's office, the party went to a small Indian village on the Tuckasegee River where they killed a man and a woman. Most of the Indians had fled when some of McNabb's men raised the war whoop before they reached the town. Unable to agree on a course for further action, the volunteers returned home.[23]

The "violent and lawless inroads" into Cherokee territory by the whites caused President Washington "extreme concern." He called for the governor to use his "highest exertions" to bring the agents of the "disgraceful outrages" to trial, to be punished in "an exemplary manner." Failure to control the frontiersmen would mean that treaties would be scuttled, violence and injustice would become "the arbiters of all frontier disputes between the whites and neighboring tribes of Indians," and innocent blood would be spilled repeatedly, the President believed.[24]

The Cherokee towns were becoming regular targets for the agitated settlers. An unauthorized contingent of approximately 180 men from Knox and Jefferson counties, assembled by Lieutenant Colonel George Doherty at Gamble's station on Little River, crossed the Tennessee River into Cherokee territory on Sunday, August 4. At Big Tellico, on the following day, the whites killed three Indians. Crossing the mountain Tuesday to Tynoila on the Hiwassee River, they wounded two defenders, burned the town, and destroyed a large quantity of growing corn. On Wednesday the volunteers marched to Big Valley Town, burning villages and destroying corn crops while en route. While making their way over a mountain pass on Thursday, Doherty's men were attacked from ambush, but they recovered quickly, suffering only a few wounds. They killed three Indians and wounded several others in the skirmish. On Friday the volunteers killed five of a small party of Indians following them. The trailing party attacked the volunteers in camp the next day and wounded three of them before withdrawing without losses. Doherty brought his force back to the settlements by way of Big Pigeon in

---

22. Knoxville *Gazette*, July 13, 1793; *ASP, II, Indian Affairs*, Vol. I, pp. 460-61, 463.
23. *ASP, II, Indian Affairs*, Vol. I, p. 464; Knoxville *Gazette*, July 27, 1793.
24. *ASP, II, Indian Affairs*, Vol. I, p. 430.

Jefferson County, arriving on August 11. On the eight-day march they had taken the lives of nine Indian men and "by mistake, two squaws." They brought in fifteen warriors and seven women and children as prisoners and had burned twenty towns and villages.[25]

After those excursions against the Cherokee, the volunteer spirit of the frontiersmen of the eastern districts was dampened temporarily by their fatigue and by governmental opposition. No one doubted that the spirit could be rejuvenated by a call from the governor or other authorized government official. In the meantime most settlers again had gathered in neighborhood forts for their mutual protection against expected Indian responses to the invasions.[26]

Retaliation for the murders of members of his Nashville family was the motivation for Abraham Castleman's leading some volunteers across the Tennessee River to Will's Town in mid-August. Although most of his men, obeying General Robertson's order to stay north of the Tennessee, remained behind, Castleman and four others pushed ahead until they came upon a camp where thirty or forty Indians were at breakfast. A round of fire from the volunteers' rifles sent the surprised Indians into hurried flight. But the attackers, realizing they were badly outnumbered, beat a quick retreat to Nashville. Castleman was certain that those Indians were on the march for war against the Cumberland settlements as they were painted black and had large bundles with them but no women or horses.[27]

A few days prior to Castleman's raid, Captains John Rains and John Gordon had led an authorized pursuit of the Creek party that killed Samuel Miller at Joslin's station near Nashville. Overtaking the Indians about seven miles below the Duck River, they killed five and took a sixth prisoner.[28]

Able neither to restrain his own people nor to keep his Indian neighbors satisfied, the acting governor must have welcomed the diversion provided by friendly Indian chiefs walking into his office. On their way to visit the President at the governor's prior invitation, Piomingo and four other Chickasaw chiefs, escorted by a guard of thirty, arrived at Knoxville on September 25. As they passed the Knoxville garrison, they

---

25. Knoxville *Gazette*, August 27, 1793; *Dunlap's American Daily Advertiser*, September 9, 1793.
26. *Dunlap's American Daily Advertiser*, September 9, 1793.
27. Knoxville *Gazette*, September 14, 1793.
28. Ibid.

had been given a salute of fifteen guns by members of Lieutenant Rickard's federal company.

After replenishing supplies, the Chickasaw, accompanied by Captain John Chisholm of Knoxville, journeyed north to Abingdon, Virginia. There they met Governor Blount, then on his return trip from the capital. When the governor told the chiefs of an epidemic raging in Philadelphia that was taking the lives of fifty to sixty persons each day, they abandoned their plans to see the President and instead turned homeward.[29]

At Abingdon the governor had been met, also, by several friends from the territory who had come to learn the results of his mission and to escort him back to Knoxville. To most, the news was disappointing. Blount had been unable to convince the President and the secretary of war that a disabling blow against the Creek was a prerequisite to lasting peace with them. The national policy toward the southern Indians was unchanged: Blount should seek peace through negotiations and goodwill while restricting the settlers to defensive measures within the bounds of the territory.

Washington and Knox had listened at length to Blount and General Andrew Pickens as they made a strong case for war against the Creek. Drawing on his considerable experience on the southeastern frontiers, Pickens averred that "a demonstration of the power of the United States to punish the Creeks" was the only measure that would halt their vicious raids. The President asked for details about mounting and supplying such a "demonstration." There was talk of strategy, timetables, and troop strength, but the consultations came to naught, casualties to two unexpected developments far from Philadelphia. First, restless territory folk had made their strike into Cherokee country on June 12 without authorization, and from the West came news that negotiations to end the war in the Northwest had broken down during early August.[30]

The governor had been greatly displeased to find that a war against the Indians required a recommendation of war by the President and a declaration of war by Congress. Disappointed that Congress, in its first session under the Constitution, had not provided enough "latitude" for the President to protect the frontiers, he wrote to his brother John Gray, "May the approaching Congress be guillotined if they do not declare

---

29. Knoxville *Gazette*, October 12, 1793; *ASP, II, Indian Affairs*, Vol. I, p. 458.
30. Downs, "Indian Affairs in the Southwest Territory, 1790-1796," pp. 254-55.

war [against the southern Indians]...and proceed to the most vigorous execution."[31] William Blount's language reflected his knowledge of the bloody violence of the French Revolution as manifested in the use of the guillotine to behead Louis XVI on January 21.

Riding back to Knoxville, Blount's friends learned from him that he had been in error when he believed his appointment was for a term of three years and that it was, in fact, "co-existent with the temporary government." They would be surprised to discover a year later that the President did not agree with the governor's interpretation of his term of office. Nonetheless, in accordance wih the provisions of the Ordinance of 1787, Washington reappointed Blount to a three-year term beginning December 10, 1794.[32]

The governor's friends did not learn that he had spent an immense amount of time on his journey attending to personal business, including extensive consultations with Hugh Williamson and others about private land deals. It is not known whether they properly appreciated that the governor had arranged to be absent from the territory at a very explosive time, thus avoiding direct blame for settler excesses that he knew were imminent.[33]

Blount, accompanied by Colonel David Henley, David Allison, and those who joined him at Abingdon, arrived in Knoxville on October 10. They, too, were greeted by a salute of guns by the federal detachment. Seeking to minimize public disappointment at his failure to win the support of the national government for a tougher policy toward the southern Indians, the governor had timed his return to cast himself as Smith's savior. "My popularity," Blount confided, "has ebbed and flowed several times...I believe it is now as high as ever it was."[34]

Just as Captain Beard had been en route to the Cherokee Nation without authorization when the governor departed for Philadelphia, General Sevier with perhaps 600 men was inside the bounds of that nation on orders of the acting governor when Blount returned to Knoxville. Sevier's expedition, which crossed into Indian country on September 25, had been authorized to pursue a force of approximately one thousand Cherokee reported to be moving on Knoxville. The Indians turned back,

---

31. Keith, ed., *The John Gray Blount Papers,* Vol. II, p. 315.
32. Carter, ed., *Territorial Papers, SWT,* IV, pp. 302, 374.
33. Masterson, *William Blount,* pp. 244, 245.
34. Knoxville *Gazette,* October 12, 1793; Keith, ed., *The John Gray Blount Papers,* Vol. II, p. 325.

however, after stopping at the residence of Alexander Cavet, eight miles short of their destination. There they killed all thirteen members of the Cavet family.[35]

The general had been marshaling militia at Ish's mill since the early part of September. Not all came readily. When the Greene County Militia appeared at half strength, Sevier sent a sizzling message to Daniel Kennedy, colonel commandant at Greeneville. He was pained, he wrote, to see the men of Greene County "so slack at a time of such imminent danger." Reminding Kennedy of the "urgent necessity for their being at this time on the frontiers which appear liable to be overrun and totally destroyed by the enemy," Sevier ordered him to send the remainder of the number he had requisitioned previously.[36]

Smith had ordered Sevier into Cherokee territory because he thought that the territorial government could wait no longer to answer their challenge decisively. Reports reaching him indicated that the territory was "infested" with Indians. Their presence had been reported "from opposite Greene Court House, round by Ish's, and up Clinch on the northwestern frontier, a distance of at least 200 miles."[37]

In what became known as the Etowah campaign, Sevier and his mounted troops had left their camp at Ish's mill and ranged southward through the Cherokee Nation as far as Etowah, a Creek town on the Hightower River near its junction with the Coosa River.[38] Leaving death and destruction in their wake, they razed a number of Cherokee and Creek towns, killed livestock, and burned crops still in the fields. On several occasions Indians harassed their camps, especially at night, but there was only one full-scale engagement, the attack on Etowah. In that battle Sevier's men crossed the Hightower River to be met by strong resistance from a mixed force of Creek and Cherokee. Three whites were killed, but the Indians, soon routed, left several dead on the field as they fled, taking an undetermined number of dead and wounded with them. Lieutenant Colonel Gilbert Christian of Sullivan County became Sevier's fourth casualty when he died a few days after returning home of a fever contracted on the march. The general reported that the warriors

---

35. *ASP, II, Indian Affairs*, Vol. I, pp. 458, 468; Knoxville *Gazette*, October 12, 1793.
36. *ASP, II, Indian Affairs*, Vol. I, p. 466; Richard H. Doughty, *Greeneville, One Hundred Year Portrait, 1775-1875* (Greeneville, Tennessee: Published for the author, 1975), p. 8.
37. *ASP, II, Indian Affairs*, Vol. I, p. 468.
38. Durham, *Daniel Smith, Frontier Statesman*, p. 165; Knoxville *Gazette*, December 7, 1793.

he bested at Etowah had been a part of the group that massacred the Cavet family.[39]

After the Etowah campaign, the Creek and Cherokee did not kill a single settler in the eastern part of the territory for about six weeks. Small raiding parties stole horses and personal property but refrained from violence during the "unexpected cessation of hostilities." In Blount's opinion, the Indians' peaceful behavior was prompted by a fear of another visit from General Sevier's militia.[40]

Before he knew the results of Sevier's campaign, Blount had advised the secretary of war that territorial militia had crossed the Tennessee into the Cherokee Nation in pursuit of a large body of invaders. "The long sufferings, and the present spirit of the people, required such a measure," he explained. Blount despaired of reconciliation with the Cherokee "until a general pacification with all the nations" could take place, but he acknowledged that it was his duty to "make every effort."[41]

The leaders of government at Philadelphia held to their belief that much of the Indian hostility was provoked by the settlers. Secretary Knox could envision no permanent peace "unless an effectual mode can be devised to punish the violators of it on both sides." He noted, "It will be with an ill grace that the United States demand the punishment of banditti Indians, when, at the same time, the guilty whites escape with impunity."[42]

Distressed by the national government's policies, the inhabitants of the territory began to focus their wrath on Governor Blount early in 1793. He and the judges, who constituted the general assembly, were criticized widely for usurping power. There was population enough to have an elected house of representatives, but the governor had not chosen to call elections. The Sumner County Grand Jury reported the lack of elected representation as an abuse, and doubt was expressed by more than one that the true condition of the frontiers had ever been communicated to the President.[43]

Some hinted that independence from the federal government should be sought when the territory had grown sufficiently in population and

---

39. *ASP, II, Indian Affairs*, Vol. I, pp. 469-70; Ramsey, *The Annals of Tennessee*, pp. 587-88; Knoxville *Gazette*, November 23, 1793.
40. *ASP, II, Indian Affairs*, Vol. I, pp. 469, 470, 474.
41. Ibid., p. 458.
42. Ibid., p. 363.
43. Masterson, *William Blount*, p. 242; Knoxville *Gazette*, April 6, 1793.

wealth. But the frontier people depended on the United States and had no feasible alternative but to follow the national policy limiting them to defensive measures within the territory, a correspondent of the Knoxville *Gazette* wrote. "Although they might think themselves ill-treated in not being allowed to carry on a war, they have only to be contented until they have men, money, and provisions to stand for themselves," he concluded.[44]

The settlers were not the only ones contemplating a possible course of independence for the Southwest Territory. Many at the highest levels of the French government believed that the trans-Appalachian West would not long remain part of the United States. The French, seeking to protect their vast holdings west of the Mississippi River, pushed relentlessly until they later obtained control of New Orleans from Spain. By controlling the river at that point, they planned also to control the "fierce inhabitants of the [American] West."[45]

In the meantime, some inhabitants of Mero, unwilling further to hazard their chances with the southern Indians, began to migrate down the Mississippi into Spanish territory or northward into Kentucky. The result was "a daily increase of population to the Spanish government" and to the state of Kentucky. The Cumberland settlements were declining at a rate that alarmed many people, including Andrew Jackson.[46]

Meanwhile those loyal to the Union cautioned their neighbors about "dissensions taking place . . . and a spirit of opposition to the government." The proper course, they said, was one of patience. Congress should be given time to act because "great plans" could not be matured "in an hour nor in a few days." If everyone will "act like good citizens of a great republic . . . things will be better ordered than if our narrow schemes had taken place."[47]

Another observer cautiously suggested that a representative general assembly should be elected and convened. Primarily to show the need for such an assembly, the unidentified citizen drafted an elaborate proposal for "a system of common defense and contingent warfare." The

---

44. Knoxville *Gazette*, January 12, 1793.
45. Frederick Jackson Turner, "The Policy of France Toward the Mississippi Valley in the Period of Washington and Adams," *American Historical Review*, Vol. X (1905), pp. 266, 269.
46. Sam B. Smith and Harriet Chappell Owsley, eds., *The Papers of Andrew Jackson, 1770-1803*, Vol. I (Knoxville: University of Tennessee Press, 1980), pp. 48-49; Durham, *The Great Leap Westward*, p. 107; Knoxville *Gazette*, August 13, 1793.
47. Knoxville *Gazette*, April 6, 1793.

only innovative suggestion in the lengthy manuscript was his proposition to create committees of correspondence in each county that would elect representatives to a territory convention. He probably chose the indirect approach to avoid the appearance of being critical of the governor.[48] But the message was there: the people needed to meet, consult, and act through duly elected representatives.

Public hostility to the existing government increased in mid-March when the governor and judges adopted an ordinance requiring local officials to remit annually to the secretary of the territory most monies collected and/or held by them. Revenues arising from fines and forfeitures and from taxes on the proceedings at law and equity, on the probate of deeds, the registering of land grants, and the issuing of marriage and ordinary licenses were designated for the territorial coffers. Responsible officials were required to account for the monies handled and to post bond for their performance. Secretary Smith was to hold the funds "subject to the future appropriation of government,"[49] a provision suggesting the governor and judges would determine when and where the money was spent.

Typical of the reception the act enjoyed was the response of Sumner County reported to Secretary Daniel Smith on July 23 by Major David Wilson.

> Our court paid no regard to the acts of the governor or judges as they refused to take bond of the clerk and register agreeable to said acts; the Federal Constitution says no capitation or direct tax shall be laid only agreeably to the general census; if then the governor's power does not originate in the General Government from whence is it.[50]

Having earlier objected to tax laws passed without elected representation, local citizens made a "bustle . . . at several of the county courts" about the tax on proceedings at law. The governor responded by stating that the contention could only "sow an impolitic and unwise degree of dissatisfaction among the unthinking but well meaning part of the people." He promised John Sevier that the tax revenues were for "the common benefit of the people at large" and would be "appropriated

---

48. Ibid.
49. Ibid., May 4, 1793; Carter, ed., *Territorial Papers, SWT,* IV, pp. 242-43.
50. Carter, ed., *Territorial Papers, SWT,* IV, p. 265n.

by a legislature whenever that event takes place and not till then."[51]

Although Blount had been pleased to conduct government without having to deal with an independent general assembly, he realized by late spring that it was time to talk in positive terms about the election of such a body. On May 31 he told Sevier that he had always favored having an assembly whenever the people "believe it will be for their benefit." He added, "It is my wish that the question should be considered as yet open for their determination."[52]

The Ordinance of 1787 came under attack by the advocates for representation. Acknowledging that the ordinance was less than desirable as a constitution for the territory, Blount urged its detractors to take comfort in the fact that it was "temporary not permanent." Its provisions were not all bad, however. Explaining that the expenses of the territorial government and the militia were paid by the national government, he noted: "If certain liberties are given up temporarily, temporary benefits are given in lieu, that is the expense of government, of which the people bear no part, not even the tax of an excise, for it is borne by the federal government."[53]

By June 1, the governor had sent out directions to each county commandant of militia to poll the eligible voters on the question of holding an election to select representatives to a general assembly. To friends, Blount declared it was his "earnest wish" that the people would vote in favor of an assembly, but he did not feel himself "at liberty" to call one if they determined against it. In fact, he believed that most of the political agitation had been caused for the benefit of "designing persons" who did not have the public good at heart. "I hope these disturbers will be disappointed of their object if an assembly does take place," he told Sevier.[54]

Before he could have heard the results of the militia polls, Blount left Knoxville for his trip to Philadelphia. Traveling northward through the territory, he was confronted by insistent demands to call an election for a representative general assembly. A single representative elected from each county was preferred by many who talked to him, and at one point he concurred with that view. Although he wrote hastily to

---

51. Ibid., p. 265
52. Ibid., pp. 264-65.
53. Ibid., p. 266.
54. Ibid., p. 267.

Daniel Smith before reaching Jonesborough that he expected to issue writs of election when he arrived there, Blount abandoned the idea just as quickly.[55] He would not risk loss of political control by permitting an election of such importance to be held in his absence.

To calm the uneasy public, the governor asked Sevier to enlist the aid of friends of his and Blount's "to quiet the minds of the people." He recommended their attendance at the next session of Washington District Superior Court where a large crowd was customarily present.

Concerned, also, that local militia might be converted into vigilantes overnight, Blount selected George Roulstone to cultivate a public perception that orders for a campaign against the Indians were in hand and would be published at an uncertain but proper future time. He hoped the tactic would be reassuring to all and would lessen the likelihood of unauthorized strikes across the Tennessee River. He wanted the public to believe that government was going to respond and not stand idly by. He seemed to believe that the game could be played for several weeks, if necessary, while he sought federal support to go to war.[56]

Although debate about the assembly continued during the governor's absence, the public mind was preoccupied with stopping Indian excesses. Familiar demands to strike decisively into Indian country were only occasionally countered by thoughtful discussions of government and respect for the law. A memorial to President Washington from Mero District indicated that the inhabitants were impatient to take control of their destinies. If the national government could not offer further assistance, the Mero people asked for permission to do themselves "justice," to retaliate to whatever extent they deemed necessary. They despaired that failure to take a firm stand would threaten the entire dissolution of the settlements.[57]

When Governor Blount returned to Knoxville in early October, he was urged to proceed with electing an assembly. On October 17, the grand jury of Hamilton District adopted an address to Blount declaring that the citizens of the territory were ready to exercise their right to elect a legislature. Recalling the provisions of the Ordinance of 1787 that "secured to the people...a legislature" as soon as their numbers amounted to five thousand free males, the grand jury asked him to issue

---

55. "Papers of General Daniel Smith," p. 222.
56. Hamer, ed., "Letters of Governor William Blount," pp. 133-34.
57. Knoxville *Gazette*, June 1, July 13, August 13, 1793.

writs of election. An opportunity to vote would have the "happy tendency to promote the tranquility of this government."[58]

Apparently convinced that the citizens strongly favored an election for the territorial general assembly, Blount made no effort to conduct a referendum on the subject, but on October 19 called for the elections. They would represent the first ballots ever cast in the United States for members of a territorial general assembly, and the body elected would be the first such representative body to function in a territory. The Northwest Territory would not elect its first house of representatives until 1799.[59]

Publishing an ordinance that gave "authority for the election of representatives to represent the people in General Assembly," the governor set the election to be held on the third Friday and Saturday in December. "Free male inhabitants of full age" would be permitted to vote, and a total of thirteen representatives would be elected. Each of the counties of Washington, Hawkins, Jefferson, and Knox would have two representatives; similarly, Davidson, Sullivan, Greene, Sumner, and Tennessee would have one. The ordinance required the sheriff of each county to conduct the elections and to report the names of those elected to Secretary Smith as early as possible.[60]

To remind prospective candidates and electors of the minimum qualifications for office, the governor prepared an extract from the Ordinance of 1787. The ownership of land was a prerequisite in both cases.

> No person to be eligible or qualified to act as a representative, unless he shall have been a citizen of one of the United States three years, and be a resident in the district; or unless he shall have resided in the district three years; and in either case shall hold in his own right, in fee simple two hundred acres of land within the same: Provided, that a free-hold of fifty acres of land in the district, having been a citizen of one of the States and being a resident in the district, or the like free-hold and two years residence in the district, shall be necessary to qualify a man as an elector of a representative.[61]

While the governor had been delaying elections to avoid dilution of

---

58. Ibid., November 23, 1793.
59. Lindley, Schneider, and Quaife, *History of the Ordinance of 1787 and the Old Northwest Territory*, p. 49.
60. Knoxville *Gazette*, November 23, 1793; Carter, ed., *Territorial Papers, SWT*, IV, p. 309.
61. Carter, ed., *Territorial Papers, SWT*, IV, pp. 309-10; Knoxville *Gazette*, November 23, 1793.

his political power, he had been giving serious consideration to increasing the size of the territory. He maintained his dream for settling the lands in "the Bent of Tennessee," the area that sprawled north of the southernmost stretch of the Tennessee River but below the southern boundary of the Southwest Territory. He had a substantial interest there that, under the right circumstances, could be perfected to great advantage, although he cautioned his brother John Gray to delete his name from the deed "as it were by mistake...as I am now an official man." In a published description of the territory, Daniel Smith predicted that the area north of the great bend would soon be joined to the North Carolina cession. He also suggested that it would not be unreasonable to establish the latitude of the southernmost reach of the bend as "our southern boundary for the purpose of settlement."[62]

The settlers' confidence in their ability to survive the rigors of frontier life and war with the Indians was challenged again in December. Thomas Jefferson, a long-time supporter of the development and settlement of the western lands, resigned as secretary of state.[63]

The increased use of militia for defense in 1793 cast paymaster David Allison in a prominent public role. Although the militia was under the governor's command and was both called to duty and dismissed by him, the soldiers received their pay from the federal government. Payroll records were kept for each company, and the company captain's responsibility was to see that they were promptly and properly submitted to the government for approval. When Allison received monies for payrolls from Philadelphia, he advertised the dates and places for payday and the names of the captains who should appear for their companies.[64]

While the governor was at Philadelphia, Secretary Knox appointed David Henley, earlier a troubleshooter in the Northwest Territory,[65] to be agent for the War Department in the Southwest Territory. The position was created without prior consultation with Blount to attempt to control expenses that had been "considerably multiplied by recent occurrences in the territory." Henley was instructed "in all cases to

---

62. Keith, ed., *The John Gray Blount Papers*, Vol. II, p. 313; [Smith], *A Short Description of the Tennassee Government*, p. 19.
63. Whitaker, *The Spanish-American Frontier, 1783-1795*, p. 188.
64. Knoxville *Gazette*, March 9, October 12, 1793.
65. Samuel Cole Williams, "Colonel David Henley," East Tennessee Historical Society *Publications*, No. 8 (1946), p. 9.

Rocky Mount, the residence of William Cobb, was the original seat of government for the Territory of the United States South of the River Ohio from 1790 to 1792. From this house, since regarded as the first capitol of the territory, Governor William Blount and Secretary Daniel Smith administered the affairs of government. Located eight miles north of Johnson City, Tennessee, it was acquired in 1959 by the state of Tennessee as a historic site.

Clothed in period dress, interpreters cook before the large kitchen fireplace at William Cobb's Rocky Mount. Outside another interpreter finishes a split oak shingle for use on the roof of one of the buildings. The site is open daily with living portrayals of the 1790 period.

An ACT for the Government of the Territory of the United States, South of the River Ohio.

SEC. 1. BE it enacted by the Senate and House of Representatives of the United States of America, in Congress assembled, That the territory of the United States, south of the river Ohio, for the purposes of temporary government, shall be one district; the inhabitants of which shall enjoy all the privileges, benefits and advantages, set forth in the Ordinance of the late Congress, for the government of the territory of the United States, north-west of the river Ohio; and the government of the said territory, south of the Ohio, shall be similar to that which is now exercised in the territory north-west of the Ohio; except so far as is otherwise provided in the conditions expressed in an Act of Congress of the present Session, entitled, " An Act to accept a cession of the claims of the State of North-Carolina, to a certain district of western territory."

SEC. 2. *And be it further enacted,* That the salaries of the officers, which the President of the United States shall nominate, and with the advice and consent of the Senate, appoint by virtue of this Act, shall be the same as those, by law established, of similar officers in the government north-west of the river Ohio.—And the powers, duties, and emoluments of a Superintendant of Indian affairs for the southern department, shall be united with those of the Governor.

PRINTED BY JOHN FENNO.

The Territory of the United States South of the River Ohio was created by an act of Congress, signed by President Washington on May 26, 1790. The act is shown above in its original printing.

In the top row, left to right, are William Blount, James Winchester, and John Sevier; middle row, Andrew Jackson, William Cocke, and James Robertson; bottom row, Archibald Roane, John Overton, and Samuel Doak.

In 1792 Governor Blount relocated the territorial capital to the new town of Knoxville and there built this house for his family on a site overlooking the Holston River. The handsome structure has since been known as the Blount Mansion.

Governor Blount erected this small office building a few steps from his home. Both the office and residence were used by him and Secretary Smith to conduct the business of the territorial government. The interior view shows the room as it was furnished during the governor's tenure.

Chisholm's tavern, a short distance from the Blount Mansion, furnished food, drink, and lodging for travelers, especially those having business to discuss with the governor or secretary. When meetings of state could not be accommodated in the governor's residence and office, they were often held at the tavern. This photograph was made circa *1916.*

William Bowen, a long-standing friend and adviser to Secretary Smith, built this sturdy brick house near Mansker's Fort in 1787. Its permanent type construction was a compelling indication that early Mero District settlers had come to stay. Known in the twentieth century as the Bowen-Campbell House, it is located in Goodlettsville, Tennessee.

Although begun in the 1780s, the construction of Rock Castle, Daniel Smith's home, was not completed until 1796. The slow pace of the undertaking was occasioned in no small part by Smith's frequent absences to attend to business of the territory. The house, a state-owned historic site, is located at Hendersonville.

Federal troops occupied the palisaded blockhouse barracks at Knoxville depicted by the artist Lloyd Branson. Erected in 1794, the barracks was used also to store goods received for the annual payment to the Cherokee Nation.

One of the busiest places on the Mero District frontier was Mansker's Fort, a stopping place for travelers from the Holston country and Kentucky. The above reconstruction of the original complex was erected at Goodlettsville, Tennessee, in 1987.

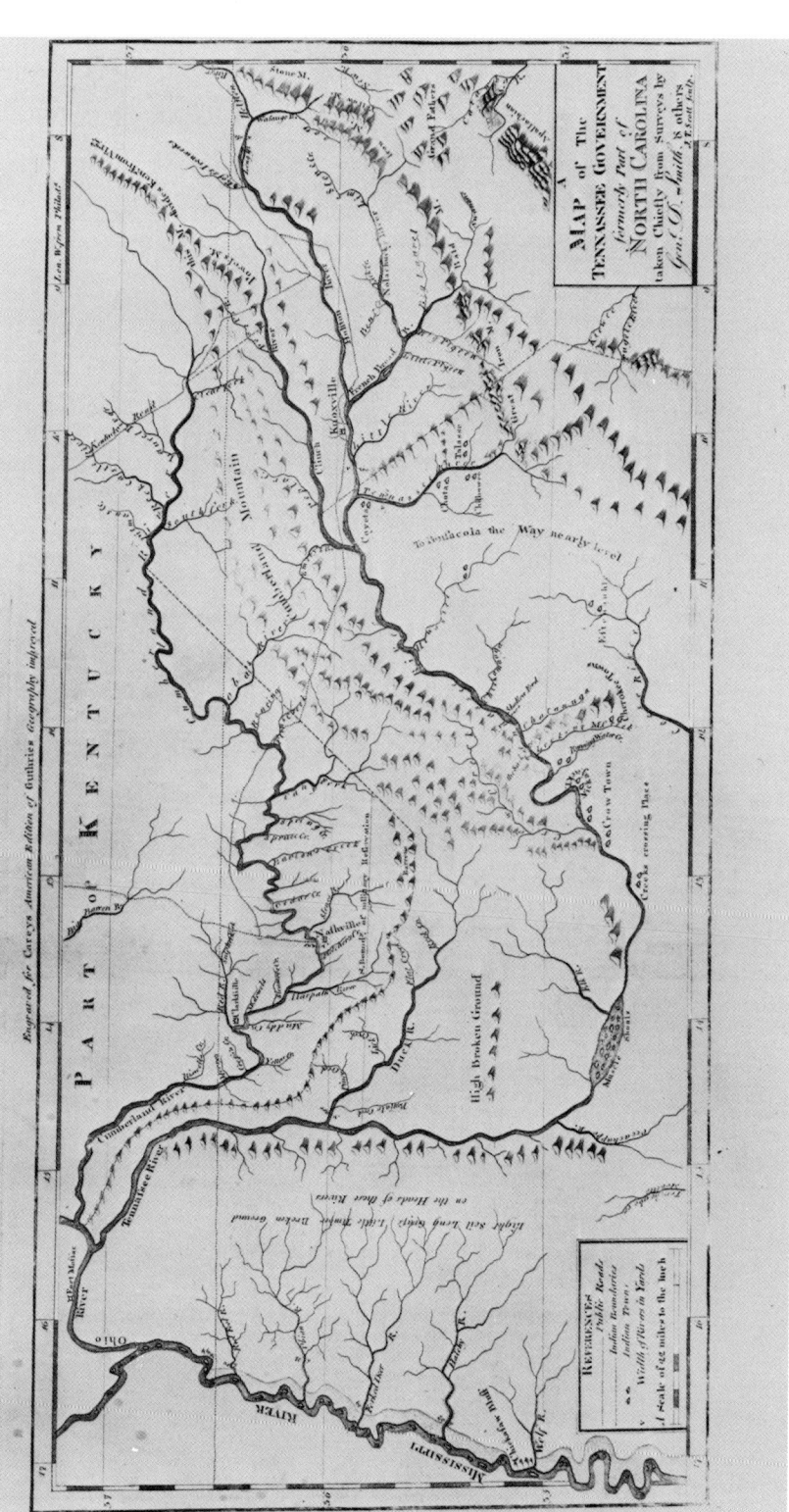

Identifying the area as the Tennassee Government, this first map of the Southwest Territory was published in 1794 by Mathew Carey of Philadelphia. It was based on surveys made by Daniel Smith. Included in Carey's American Edition of Guthrie's Geography Improved, it was advertised for sale separately in the Philadelphia Independent Gazetteer, January 29, 1794.

The eighteenth century button, buckles, and Spanish coins were found in Sumner County at the site of Isaac Bledsoe's fort by Bernard D. and Brenda K. Drake of Madison, Tennessee, while conducting archaeological explorations there in 1985-86. With the Spanish milled dollar of 1793 are pieces of eight, each used as coin worth one-eighth the value of the dollar. The larger buckle is of iron and the smaller of brass. Made in London, the button was gold gilt.

The Nashville Inn was the most impressive facility of its kind in the territory when opened to the public in 1796 by William T. Lewis. It was located on the north side of the Nashville public square. This lithograph was made circa 1840.

No. 167. Dollars 339.

William Blount Governor in and over the Territory of the United States south of the river Ohio.

To David Henley Esquire Agent for the Department of War

Pay to William Pickard pay-Master pro tem, to the Troops in the Territory aforesaid three hundred and thirty nine dollars, out of the money in your hands appropriated, for the defensive protection of the frontiers for the pay of a company of infantry on the frontiers of Mero District commanded by Captain Thomas Murray from the twenty second of October to the twenty second of November 1793, agreeably to pay-roll and your report thereon of this date, for which this shall be your warrant — Given at Knoxville under my hand and seal this 3rd day of December 1794

Wm Blount

By the Governor
Willie Blount Pro Secretary

Registered in the Secretary's Office
Knoxville December 3rd 1794
Willie Blount

This warrant signed by Governor Blount authorized the War Department to pay militia for services on the frontiers of Mero District.

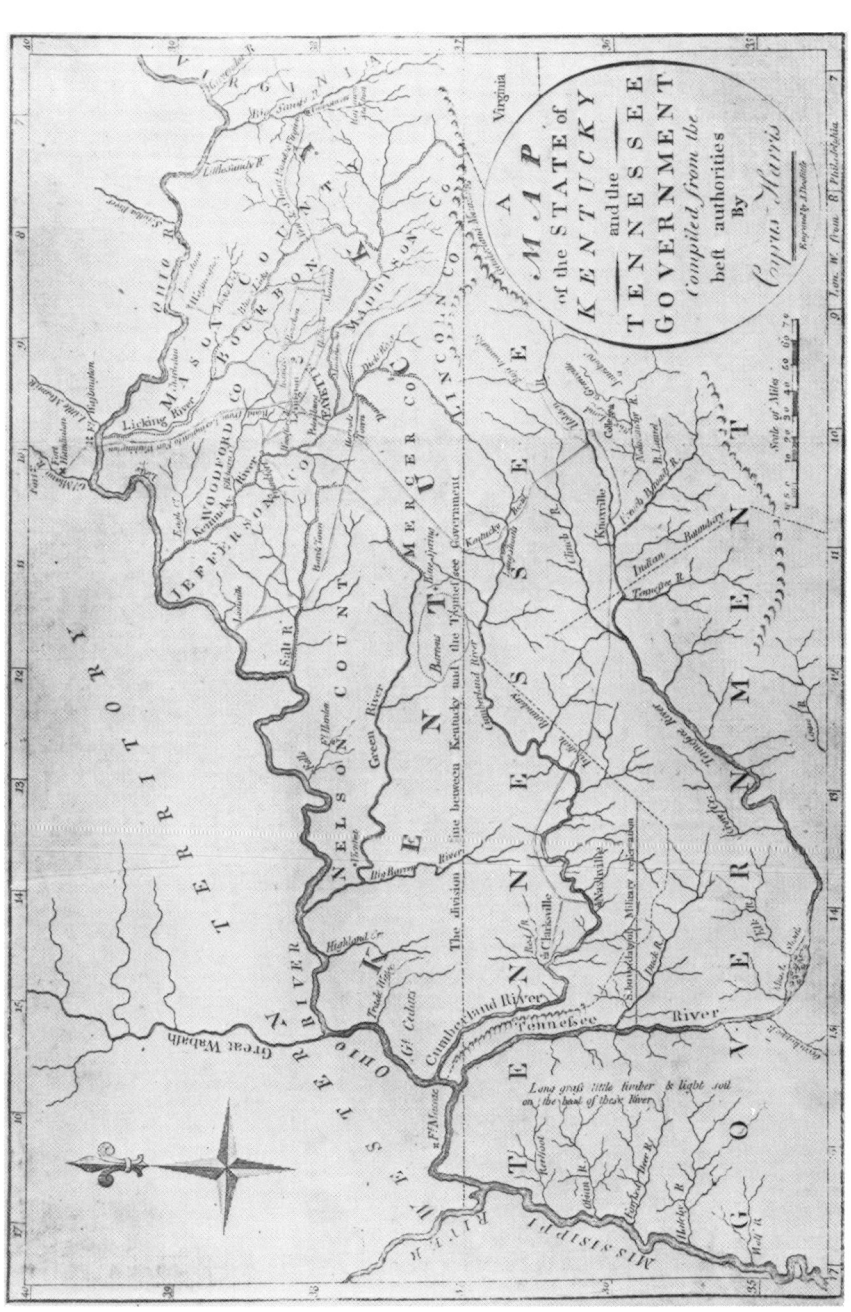

This map of Kentucky and the Tennessee Government was published in 1796 by Thomas & Andrews, Boston, for Jedidiah Morse's The American Universal Geography, 3rd. ed., 1796.

We the People of the Territory of the United States south of the River Ohio having the right of admission into the General Government as a member State thereof, consistent with the Constitution of the United States and the act of Cession of the State of North Carolina, recognizing the Ordinance for the Government of the Territory of the United States Northwest of the River Ohio, do ordain and establish the following Constitution or form of Government, and do mutually agree with each other to form ourselves into a free and Independant State, by the name of the State of Tennessee.

Article 1st

Section 1st. The Legislative Authority of this State shall be vested in a General Assembly which shall consist of a Senate and House of Representatives both dependant on the People.

One of the original transcriptions of the constitution written and adopted in 1796 for the new State of Tennessee is preserved in the Tennessee State Library and Archives at Nashville.

use the highest vigilance to prevent all abuse or injury to the public interests which may arise from negligence or design." Allison was made his deputy but with special responsibility for processing and paying such payrolls, invoices, and claims as might be ordered by warrant of Governor Blount.[66]

Henley's appointment was hastened by frontier discontent with the slow response of the federal government to any claims for payment, whether payroll or otherwise. The Mero District Militia was forced to send to Knoxville for its pay when it finally arrived. David Wilson of Sumner County complained to his neighbor Secretary Smith, "This district considers it a great grievance that the paymaster of the territory does not attend to pay the militia for their services. Sir, the people look up to you for redress of this grievance."[67]

Even before he had been vested with his duty as agent for the War Department, Henley had been chosen by the Treasury Department as the government representative to receive bids at Knoxville on October 15 for rations required for militia and regular troops at various stations in the territory. Busy representing the interests of both departments, Henley was not at first a political threat to Blount. His presence probably freed additional time for the governor to spend on his speculations.[68]

---

66. Henry Knox to David Henley, August 31, 1793, David Henley Letters, MS 736, Special Collections, Hoskins Library, University of Tennessee, Knoxville.
67. "Pioneer Letters," p. 94.
68. Knoxville *Gazette*, October 12, 1793.

CHAPTER IX

REPRESENTATIVE GOVERNMENT

1794

On January 1, 1794, Governor Blount issued a call for the thirteen members-elect of the territorial house of representatives to convene at Knoxville on February 24. Although a majority of them had campaigned proclaiming their opposition to him, he was ready to join them in advancing the cause of statehood. Prior to the opening of the first session of the newly elected house, the Congress had upheld the validity of an act passed by Blount and the three judges functioning as a general assembly under the terms of the Ordinance of 1787 and three ordinances enacted by Blount alone.[1] The legislation had been questioned in the territory, but the decision of Congress effectively answered the critics who had alleged that the governor and the judges had usurped power not properly theirs.

When the organizational meeting of the house of representatives was convened on February 24, the members present were Leroy Taylor and John Tipton, Washington County; George Rutledge, Sullivan; Joseph Hardin, Greene; William Cocke and Joseph McMinn, Hawkins; Alexander Kelly and John Beard, Knox; Samuel Wear and George Doherty, Jefferson; Dr. James White, Davidson; James Ford, Tennessee; and David Wilson, Sumner. Their first action was to elect David Wilson of Sumner to be speaker of the house and Hopkins Lacy of Davidson, clerk.[2]

Following the provisions of the Ordinance of 1787, Blount advised the house to limit its action to selecting a panel of ten men from whom President Washington would appoint five to make up the legislative council, the companion body of the house. After the five had been appointed, the general assembly would be duly constituted and ready to undertake its duties.[3]

---

1. Carter, ed., *Territorial Papers, SWT*, IV, pp. 327-28; *Annals of the Congress of the United States, Third Congress-First Session*, Vol. IV (Washington, D.C.: Gales and Seaton, 1849), p. 41.
2. Carter, ed., *Territorial Papers, SWT*, IV, p. 329.
3. Ibid., pp. 319, 328.

On February 25 ten nominees for the council were chosen: James Winchester, William Fort, Stockley Donelson, John Sevier, Sr., Richard Gammon, David Russell, Adam Meek, John Adair, Griffith Rutherford, and Parmenas Taylor. Prior to selecting the councillors, members of the house had gone "in procession" to hear a sermon delivered by the Reverend Mr. Carrick.[4]

Ignoring the governor's reminder that the "objects" of their session were limited to nominating ten councillors, the first elected representative body of the territory did not adjourn until after it had filed with Blount a strong petition for additional protection from the Indians and prepared a memorial addressing the same concerns for delivery to Congress. It was the first opportunity that representatives from all counties had had to speak on that issue in one voice.[5]

Acknowledging to the governor that he did not have authority to conduct or condone offensive operations against the Indians, the petitioners suggested that military posts be erected to obstruct the "principal inroads of the Indians" into the settlements. They proposed one post in Washington County, two in Greene, four in Jefferson, twelve in Knox, two in Hawkins, three in Sumner, and unspecified numbers in Davidson and Tennessee counties to be determined respectively by General Robertson and Colonel Ford. The petitioners recommended, also, that each militiaman assigned to the posts serve a tour of duty limited to two months. Recognizing the danger facing the representatives about to return to Mero, they asked the governor for a guard to escort them.[6]

At the same time the house prepared the first memorial submitted to Congress by a representative body under the Ordinance of 1787. It offered reasons aplenty for a declaration of war against the Creek and Cherokee. Recalling the settlers' bloody experiences with those two nations since 1790, the memorial declared that citizens on the frontiers were subject to suffering that, in its extremity, might even drive them to attack the Indians as a matter of self-preservation. Yet the frontier people recognized that their needs were not the only call on the national government. Bidding for reciprocal support from the coastal states, they vowed their total support of "vigorous and decided measures for the protection...of our Atlantic fellow-citizens against the...enslaving

---

4. Knoxville *Gazette*, March 13, 1794; Carter, ed., *Territorial Papers, SWT*, IV, p. 328.
5. Knoxville *Gazette*, March 13, 1794.
6. Ibid.

hands of the Algerines," steps that Congress seemed prepared to take.[7]

The memorial, adopted February 26 by unanimous vote, argued persuasively that the citizens of the West were due by right the same protection afforded other citizens of the United States, wherever they lived. Needling the prosperous city dwellers along the East Coast, it declared: "Citizens who live in poverty on the extreme frontiers are as much entitled to be protected in their lives, their families, and their little property, as those who roll in luxury, ease, and affluence, in the great and opulent Atlantic cities."[8]

On March 1 Governor Blount prorogued the house of representatives until the fourth Monday in August and persuaded Dr. James White of Davidson County to deliver a record of the proceedings of the house to Congress and the President. He wanted to exploit White's personal acquaintances with officers of the national government arising from his tenure representing North Carolina in the Continental Congress, 1786-88. Blount expected that the doctor could so convince them of the territory's need for protection that they would take the measures long sought to "stay the savage hand."[9]

White's way was made easier by Secretary Daniel Smith who recommended him to his friend, Congressman Francis Walker of Virginia. Receiving White enthusiastically, Walker made his stay agreeable, "extend[ed] his acquaintance amongst the members of Congress," and assisted him to "promote the public object of his journey to Philadelphia." Dr. White was assisted, also, by the governor's brother Thomas Blount, then a first-term member of Congress from North Carolina.[10]

Dr. White was hardly out of sight before Governor Blount began assessing public reaction to the first session of the territorial house. Representatives returned home to tell of the first territory-wide memorial to Congress and of their petition to the governor; responses were favorable. Within a month Blount was so pleased by what he heard that

---

7. Ibid., March 27, 1794.
8. Ibid.
9. Carter, ed., *Territorial Papers, SWT,* IV, pp. 330, 331.
10. Walker to Daniel Smith, April 15, 1794, Miscellaneous Manuscript File, Tennessee Historical Society, TSLA; *Biographical Directory of the American Congress, 1774-1971* (Washington, D.C.: Government Printing Office, 1971), p. 605.

he wrote Daniel Smith that the convocation had "diffused general satisfaction to all ranks."[11]

The long-awaited election of representatives had not been held without controversy, however. Jefferson County provided an example. In the Knoxville *Gazette* of January 16, "A Friend to the Public" delivered a blistering attack on balloting practices in Jefferson County that he said were "contrary to the law and modes prescribed" for the conduct of an election.

The alleged law violations were various. "Friend" complained that paper ballots had been opened and inspected before they were admitted to the box and that from time to time before the close of the polls, ballots had been removed from the box and counted. Young men not yet twenty-one had been permitted to vote, and a "mercenary wretch," boasting that he had funds to buy votes, had been "very officious in purchasing suffrages," he said. If his charges were correct, he was justified in concluding that the whole was an "encroachment on that inestimable and unalienable blessing, liberty."[12]

His charges did not go unchallenged. On March 13 "An Enemy to Envious Fools" appeared in the *Gazette* to answer the allegations. Denying categorically that any votes had been purchased or that anyone had attempted to buy votes, the writer chided his adversary for demanding the ballot box be closed, a practice that would make it impossible, he said, to place ballots inside. He said that "Friend" criticized inspection of the ballots because by that practice one of his supposed friends was shown to have voted twice. "Enemy" suggested that "Friend" was an apologist for the Indians and was a "cringing, whining sycophant."[13]

County sheriffs, all appointed by Governor Blount, had supervised the balloting. Since Blount appointees were in control, most criticisms of the election were directed at the governor. He confidently answered the faultfinders by piously reasserting his commitment to representative government and, in so doing, redirected their attention to the opportunities ahead.

Prior to the meeting of the house of representatives at Knoxville, many on the frontier had looked with surprise at a proposal by the Minister

---

11. Carter, ed., *Territorial Papers, SWT*, IV, p. 333.
12. Knoxville *Gazette*, January 16, 1794.
13. Ibid., March 13, 1794.

of France to unite frontier volunteers with French Army regulars to attack Spanish positions along the Mississippi River and the Gulf Coast. The French plan, advertised by General George Rogers Clark who had joined as "commander in chief of the French Revolutionary Legions on the Mississippi River," would open the river to trade and give freedom to the inhabitants. Volunteers for the expedition would be paid one dollar per day or a lump sum grant of one thousand acres from the conquered lands. For the French, then at war with Spain, the venture held promise.[14]

Warned by the President that the United States was following a policy of neutrality in the war between France and Spain, few Americans volunteered. The proposal was scrapped in its entirety in the latter part of February when the French Minister Edmond C. Genet was removed and replaced. Blount was relieved that the Mississippi River plan, fostered by the "Jacobin incendiary Genet," had been thwarted by his own government. Talk of the plan may have been the reason that the Spanish governor at New Orleans promised to exert new pressure on the Creek to adopt a peaceful policy toward the United States.[15]

The memorial delivered to Congress by Dr. White evoked a sympathetic response from the committee of the anti-Federalist House to which it was referred. Declaring that the situation in the territory called for "the most energetic measures on the part of government," the committee made three specific recommendations to Congress. First, the President would be authorized to call out the militia in the territory in adequate number to conduct offensive operations against any Indians "that may continue hostile." Second, in cases when awaiting orders from the President would greatly "inconvenience" the settlers, Governor Blount would be empowered to order out the territorial militia in strength appropriate to the task. He would have, also, the authority to send militia forces to "repel, annoy and pursue" any body or nation of Indians contemplating invasion of the territory. Finally, the President would be authorized to establish military posts for "the permanent security of the frontier settlers" to be manned by regular troops.[16]

On May 29 the House passed a bill embodying those recommendations

---

14. Ibid., February 27, 1794; Keith, ed., *The John Gray Blount Papers*, Vol. II, p. 368.
15. Carter, ed., *Territorial Papers, SWT*, IV, pp. 324, 325, 333; Keith, ed., *The John Gray Blount Papers*, Vol. II, p. 369.
16. Carter, ed., *Territorial Papers, SWT*, IV, pp. 335-36.

but with the additional provision for presidential authority to call out up to ten thousand militia from the territory and the states of Virginia, North Carolina, South Carolina, and Georgia to carry on offensive operations against the Creek and Cherokee. The Federalist Senate so emasculated the bill by amendments that when it was later returned to the House, it was rejected.[17]

While the matter was yet before Congress, the secretary of war had met with Dr. White to work out a temporary plan of defense, but it amounted to very little. On April 14 Secretary Knox authorized Blount to make an "arrangement" in Mero District for guards. Some would be stationed at a post and garrison at the crossing of the Cumberland soon to be called Fort Blount, some at the confluence of the Red and Cumberland rivers, and others at unspecified places in Sumner and Davidson, although in the latter county the "chief post" was to be "in the front of Nashville." As the national government had no regular troops to spare, guards would be drawn from the militia of either or all of the three districts. To range as needed, an unassigned complement of two subalterns and thirty mounted militia was allowed for Mero. To impress the Indians who stood in awe of large artillery pieces, the secretary of war ordered six three-and-one-half-inch howitzers to be shipped by river to General Robertson at Nashville.[18]

Approaching the President through the secretary of state on April 16, Dr. White reminded him that prompt appointment of the five members of the legislative council of the territory was essential to the function and success of the first meeting of the general assembly called for August. Taking advantage of that and every other opportunity to mention the danger the frontier folk faced from hostile Indians, White warned that the meeting might be "frustrated by delay in notifying...the members of the council, for Mero District, their appointment; the savages rendering the communication from Knoxville through the wilderness precarious and infrequent."[19]

White relayed Speaker David Wilson's recommendations for men to fill the five seats on the council and stated that the same five had been

---

17. Ibid.; Knoxville *Gazette*, August 25, 1794; Downs, "Indian Affairs in the Southwest Territory, 1790-1796," pp. 258, 259; Masterson, *William Blount*, pp. 259-60.
18. Carter, ed., *Territorial Papers, SWT*, IV, pp. 336-39; Downs, "Indian Affairs in the Southwest Territory, 1790-1796," p. 259.
19. Carter, ed., *Territorial Papers, SWT*, IV, p. 342.

recommended to General Alexander Mebane, representative of North Carolina, from "another quarter," probably referring to the Blount brothers. Concurring with the recommendations, President Washington appointed James Winchester and Griffith Rutherford from Mero and John Sevier, Sr., Stockley Donelson, and Parmenas Taylor from Holston. The appointments seem to have given general satisfaction in the territory where Winchester, Rutherford, Sevier, and Donelson had been considered certain selections from the moment they were nominated. Blount professed to be "well pleased" with the five.[20]

During the early part of June, a delegation of Cherokee chiefs, invited by the President, arrived in Philadelphia. Led by Double Head, the Cherokee had come ostensibly to negotiate a reestablishment of peace and friendship between their nation and the United States, but in reality to renegotiate certain provisions of the Treaty of Holston.

The result of their visit was the addition of five articles of agreement to the Treaty of Holston. Agreeing that the original was in full force and binding upon them, they next concurred in a stipulation that the boundaries mentioned in the treaty should be run contingent upon the Cherokee receiving a ninety-day notice from the United States of the time and place at which the survey would be commenced. In the third article the United States agreed to raise the payment to the Cherokee for land relinquished under the treaties of Hopewell, 1785, and Holston, 1791, to goods in the amount of five thousand dollars annually. It was agreed in the fourth article that for every horse stolen from a white settler by a Cherokee and not returned within three months, the sum of fifty dollars would be deducted from the annual payment of five thousand dollars. The final article specified that the five articles would become a permanent part of the Treaty of Holston as soon as they were ratified by the President and Senate of the United States. The agreement was signed by thirteen Cherokee chiefs and by Secretary Knox.[21]

After concluding their business, the Cherokee chiefs left Philadelphia on the last Sunday in June on the brig *Fame* for Charleston, South Carolina. Thus they were able to report to their people the results of the negotiations with President Washington prior to the August 25

---

20. Ibid., pp. 342, 350-51; Knoxville *Gazette*, July 31, 1794; Keith, ed., *The John Gray Blount Papers*, Vol. II, p. 421.
21. Carter, ed., *Territorial Papers, SWT*, IV, pp. 346-47.

meeting of the territorial general assembly.[22]

The Chickasaw chief Piomingo, having turned back short of Philadelphia the year before when he learned of the epidemic there, retraced his steps but this time completed his journey without adverse developments. Escorted to Knoxville by General Robertson, Piomingo's party included the brothers George and William Colbert and several other chiefs. As proven friends of the settlers, the Chickasaw were greeted warmly along the way before reaching Knoxville on May 27. To equip Piomingo's entourage properly for the remainder of their journey to Philadelphia, Blount appropriated "sundry articles" from goods that had just arrived for the Cherokee. Replacing General Robertson as "conductor" of the party, the governor's dependable associate Captain John Chisholm escorted the chiefs to Philadelphia and returned with them to Knoxville.[23]

Welcomed by President Washington, the Chickasaw were treated with great respect in the capital. The President thanked them for the warriors that they had furnished to the Army of the Northwest in 1793, although he was apparently unaware that another contingent was then on its way to join General Wayne. Extending the hospitality of the government, Washington declared an annual gift of three thousand dollars to the nation and bestowed additional presents upon members of Piomingo's party and their families. He offered, also, to make arrangements for them to see the city of New York if they so desired. Expressing the hope that means could be devised to make "the blessings of civilized life" available to them, he offered to provide instructions to "read, write and manage a farm" to any of their young men who might be interested. The students would be instructed in Philadelphia at public expense and returned to their nation whenever their elders desired it. The visiting dignitaries were invited to consider themselves "at home and take comfort accordingly." In a ceremonial act impressive to the Indians, the President commissioned Chief William Colbert major general of militia and presented him an appropriate uniform.[24]

Homeward bound, Piomingo and his delegation arrived at Knoxville on August 18. They reported to the editor of the *Gazette* that they had

---

22. Knoxville *Gazette*, August 25, 1794.

23. Carter, ed., *Territorial Papers, SWT*, IV, p. 368; Knoxville *Gazette*, June 5, August 25, 1794.

24. Carter, ed., *Territorial Papers, SWT*, IV, pp. 349-50; Knoxville *Gazette*, June 5, 1794; Timothy Pickering to James Robertson, May 9, 1795, James Robertson Papers.

been "well pleased with their visit, and with the friendly treatment they received, not only from the President and other officers of government, but from people in general."[25]

Even as the leaders of the Cherokee and Chickasaw were feeling better about their relations with the government of the United States, the inhabitants of the Southwest Territory were beginning to feel better about themselves. The reason was clear: the first session of the complete general assembly of the territory was scheduled to begin August 25, and public discussion of the desirability of statehood was far advanced. The most appealing aspect of becoming a member state of the Union was that elected representatives in both House and Senate would have the right to vote on the question of war against the Creek. Few settlers needed the reminder offered in the *Gazette* that "not a month, rarely a week has elapsed for ten years past, without some defenceless frontier family having fallen victims to their savage barbarity."[26]

Popular interest in the prospective deliberations of the general assembly was at fever pitch. On August 22 approximately two hundred persons from Mero District, including the influential Nashville attorney John Overton, arrived at Knoxville. Among them were the members of both houses of the general assembly from Davidson, Sumner, and Tennessee counties. Others from the upper reaches of the Holston, also committed to having the voice of the people heard in the assembly, flooded into the city.[27]

At first all eyes were fixed on the legislative council meeting in the house of John Stone[28] as its members presented their credentials and took the necessary oath of office. On the second day of the session, August 26, Griffith Rutherford of Sumner County was elected president of the council. His election and the earlier choice of David Wilson as speaker of the house of representatives gave Sumner County and Mero District the privilege of supplying the presiding officers of both houses of the general assembly. The selections posed no immediate threat to

---

25. Knoxville *Gazette*, August 25, 1794.
26. Ibid.
27. Ibid.; Masterson, *William Blount*, p. 261; John Overton to Colonel Thomas Overton, August 24, 1794, Claybrooke and Overton Papers, Tennessee Historical Society, TSLA.
28. The house of representatives seems to have held some of its sessions at Carmichael's tavern and others in James White's courthouse. Some of the later meetings of the council may have been held in the courthouse as well. Masterson, *William Blount*, p. 263.

Blount as both were pleased by the election of a general assembly. George Roulstone was made clerk of the council.[29]

Meeting in James White's courthouse with thirteen representatives present, the house adopted strict rules of decorum on August 26. Some of them, surely designed to counter the often impetuous conduct of frontiersmen, invoked politeness in the extreme. When the speaker was in his seat, all members must be in theirs. Heads would be uncovered at all times except when members were in their seats. To have the privilege of the floor, a member should stand uncovered by his seat until recognized by the speaker. There would be no moving about the room while another member was speaking, and upon adjournment "no member shall presume to move until the Speaker arises and goes before."[30]

The call for formal conduct in the house was in stark contrast to what was occurring outside its walls. A reported advance of hostile Indians below the city on August 27 prompted the house to vote leaves of absence for Knox County representatives Alexander Kelly and John Beard so that they could join a force "to go on a scout" against the invaders.

The legislative council was not untouched by the threat of Indian raids. For most of the session only four members were present. Despite James Winchester's important role within it, the body granted his request for a leave of absence on September 8 to return to the Mero District, and he did not rejoin it until the next session. The reasons for Winchester's leave are not known with certainty, but his responsibilities as commandant of Sumner Militia were probably reasons enough. During the summer, his county, and especially the area near his home, had been a frequent target of raids.[31]

In a joint session a few days before, the council and the house had elected Dr. James White of Davidson County as territorial delegate in the Congress of the United States. Both Dr. White and William Cocke

---

29. *Journal of the Proceedings of the Legislative Council of the Territory of the United States of America, South of the River Ohio, Begun and Held at Knoxville, the 25th Day of August, 1794* (Knoxville: Printed by George Roulstone, Printer to the Territory, 1794), pp. 3, 33 (hereinafter cited as *Legislative Council, August 25, 1794*).

30. *Journal of the Proceedings of the House of Representatives of the Territory of the United States of America, South of the River Ohio, Begun and Held at Knoxville, the 25th Day of August, 1794* (Knoxville: Printed by George Roulstone, Printer to the Territory, 1794), p. 4 (hereinafter cited as *House of Representatives, August 25, 1794*); *Legislative Council, August 25, 1794*, p. 33.

31. Walter T. Durham, *James Winchester, Tennessee Pioneer* (Gallatin, Tennessee: Sumner County Library Board, 1979), p. 42.

were nominated, but White prevailed by a vote of 11 to 7.[32]

The house and the council faced a busy agenda. They repealed the act passed by the governor and judges in 1792 that authorized county courts to levy a tax for the building of courthouses, jails, and stocks and a contingency tax to fund the costs of county government. Before opponents of the measure, who criticized it as being taxation without representation, could celebrate its repeal, the representative house and the appointed council passed a new act for the identical purposes.[33]

Other tax matters were addressed. The most important was an act to determine what constituted taxable property, the rates on it, and the method of collection. Over that act the house and the council, in a rare disagreement, went to battle on September 29. The house proposal for a tax of 25 cents per one hundred acres faced a council recommendation for a rate of 12 1/2 cents. The two bodies exchanged amendments, pleas, and counterproposals throughout the day with the council first offering to go up to 18 cents and finally acceding to the house for the 25-cent rate. The act provided, also, for a tax of 25 cents on each white poll, 50 cents on each Negro poll, four dollars on every stud horse three years and older, and one dollar on each town lot. As the council position on the land tax had reflected Blount's wishes, the final version was something of a defeat for the governor.[34]

Much of the session was devoted to legislation treating the various courts of law. Territorial law for establishing courts and regulating their proceedings was adopted along with a separate act to "regulate and ascertain" the fees of the several court officers. Another act changed the schedules for holding the three superior courts. It also altered the schedules of the county courts of pleas and quarter session in the districts of Washington and Hamilton and in the county of Tennessee. The new county of Sevier was assigned to Hamilton District, and a new apportionment of jurors from each county to the district court was prescribed. To head off further confusion in land titles, an act was passed empowering executors, administrators, and sheriffs to make binding conveyances.[35]

---

32. Knoxville *Gazette*, September 6, 1794.
33. *Laws*, pp. 35-38.
34. *Legislative Council, August 25, 1794*, pp. 32-33; Masterson, *William Blount*, p. 265; Knoxville *Gazette*, October 11, 1794.
35. *Laws*, pp. 1-29, 33-35, 36, 39.

The legislators authorized construction of two courthouses for the use of judicial districts. One was for Washington District located at Jonesborough, and the other was for Mero District located at Nashville. The acts provided for a jail and stocks at both places. Construction of the Washington District courthouse and support facilities was to be financed by taxes levied in Washington County for a period of two years. The other counties in the district were not taxed, apparently because Washington County was expected to reap economic benefits in the form of growth and development that would outweigh the tax burden. The complex at Nashville was to be funded from the proceeds of a lottery to be held in the district.[36]

The general assembly established a treasury department. It not only assured the handling of revenues in a conventional manner, but by designating one treasurer to be located at Knoxville and another at Nashville, it generally assuaged the interest that both eastern and western parts of the territory expressed in keeping their money at home.[37]

George Roulstone, publisher of the Knoxville *Gazette,* was appointed public printer. He was to print the journals of the house and the council and other proclamations and public acts as required.[38]

Education was not ignored. Separate acts provided for the establishment of Greeneville College in Greene County and Blount College at Knoxville, both predecessors of twentieth-century institutions. Greeneville College survived as Tusculum College, and Blount as the University of Tennessee, Knoxville.[39]

Counties and towns received attention from the general assembly. Sevier County was created from a portion of Jefferson, and commissioners were appointed to run dividing lines between the counties of Hawkins and Sullivan and between Hawkins and Knox. The justices of Hawkins County were authorized to lay a tax to erect a courthouse, prison, and stocks for the county in Rogersville. The town of Knoxville was recognized and commissioners appointed to regulate it.[40]

In the first major internal improvement undertaken by the territorial government, the general assembly authorized raising a fund by lottery

---

36. Ibid., pp. 40-42, 47-48.
37. Ibid., pp. 36-37.
38. Ibid., pp. 42-43.
39. Ibid., pp. 43-45.
40. Ibid., pp. 38-40, 42.

to defray the cost of "cutting and clearing a wagon road from Southwest Point to the settlement on Cumberland River in Mero District." Colonel James White, Colonel James Winchester, Colonel Stockley Donelson, Captain David Campbell, Colonel William Cocke, and Colonel Robert Hays were appointed managers of the lottery. They were made commissioners to "let out, to the best advantage, the cutting and clearing out a good and sufficient wagon road from Southwest Point in Hamilton District, to Bledsoe's Lick, in Mero District."[41]

Considering two separate categories of problems, the assembly first passed an act introduced by John Sevier for the relief of those disabled by wounds or rendered incapable of providing for themselves and their families by virtue of their service in the militia. The statute provided, also, for the widows and orphans of men who had died while in the service of the militia. The second act promised relief to "such persons as have suffered or may suffer" by failure to have their deeds, grants, and mesne conveyances proved and registered within the time previously prescribed by law.[42]

Although Sevier's act was roundly applauded by militiamen, he was well aware that no funds were available to pay those who qualified for relief. The general's critics saw the action as a blatant play for popularity among the men of voting age.[43]

Working under the ever-present threat of Indian warfare, the general assembly adopted a memorial to Congress on September 15 informing the national government that since the petition of February 26 sent by the Territorial House of Representatives, the Creek and Cherokee, "with an unremitting hand," had continued to kill citizens of the territory and to pillage the country. A list of "murders and thefts" committed between February 26 and September 26, eleven days after the date of the memorial, included sixty-seven persons killed, ten wounded, twenty-five captured, and 374 horses stolen.

The remonstrance contended that the practices of making treaties, giving large presents, and paying annuities to the Indian nations were having an effect contrary to that intended. It stated, "Fear, not love, is the only means by which Indians can be governed...until they ...feel the horrors of war they will not know the value of peace, nor observe

---

41. Ibid., pp. 46-47; Knoxville *Gazette*, January 9, 1795.
42. *Laws*, pp. 48-50.
43. Kincaid, ed., "History of the Southwest Territory, 1790-1796, by Samuel Cole Williams," p. 189.

the treaties they may form with the United States."

The general assembly begged Congress to punish the hostile nations. The security of the persons and property of United States citizens resident in the territory could be achieved only when "those two faithless and bloodthirsty nations, the Creeks and Cherokees," were punished "according to the usage and custom of nations."[44]

In addition to pleading for protection, the general assembly petitioned Congress to grant preemption rights to settlers living in the area south of the French Broad River. Their rights would be restricted to perfecting titles to their "hard earned improvements and possessions."[45]

One of the most promising measures taken by the general assembly was passage of a resolution September 5 authorizing and requesting the governor to call for a new census to be made in July of the next year so that representation could "be apportioned to population in the respective election districts or counties." Of perhaps even greater portent was adoption of a resolution on September 29 requesting the governor, at the time of the census taking, to inquire into the extent of popular support for statehood.[46]

There were many hours of less stimulating deliberation. Both houses agreed to reaffirm the laws of North Carolina as prevailing in the territory except where superseded by acts of the territorial general assembly. Charged with estimating the expense of operating the territorial government for the year 1794, a committee chaired by Stockley Donelson reported an expense budget of $2,390. The assembly created a cavalry for Hamilton District with "the same privileges and immunities" enjoyed by the cavalry troops of Washington and Mero districts.[47]

On September 30 the governor prorogued the assembly until the first Monday in October, 1795, at which time members would reassemble at Knoxville. Late in the day the members of the assembly and the governor gathered at Chisholm's Tavern to celebrate the conclusion of their work over glasses of wine.[48]

Taking note of the end of the session, the editor of the *Gazette* hailed its good work and complimented "the great unanimity and good

---

44. Knoxville *Gazette*, October 11, 1794; *Legislative Council, August 25, 1794*, p. 28.
45. *House of Representatives, August 25, 1794*, p. 24.
46. *Legislative Council, August 25, 1794*, pp. 13, 33.
47. Ibid., pp. 16, 18, 33.
48. John H. DeWitt, ed., "Journal of Governor John Sevier, 1790-1815," *Tennessee Historical Magazine*, Vol. V (October 1919), p. 171.

understanding [that] prevailed between the Governor and the other two branches of the Legislature." Elated by the outcome, Governor Blount confided to his brother John Gray that he was "in full possession of more popularity" than he had ever enjoyed. Even the majority of the representatives, elected eleven months before as his opponents, had become his "warmest friends." The general assembly "by one side stroke or other" had restored public faith in the governor, curing doubts about his previous acts and making him secure in his powers for the future.[49]

Blount had entered the session convinced that statehood was the only way to win protection from Indian attacks. He emerged with the additional perception that the prospective state would provide a role for Sevier as governor and a role for himself in the United States Senate.[50]

Satisfied that Blount was trying to implement federal Indian policy, even under adverse circumstances, President Washington reappointed him governor of the Southwest Territory on December 10, 1794. It was the vote of confidence that would see him through to the creation of the new state.[51]

The exodus of members of the general assembly and the many curious who had streamed into Knoxville was followed a month later by the departure of Piomingo and his small party of Chickasaw. Encamped on the riverbank about four hundred yards below the city since August 18 when they had returned from their visit to Philadelphia, the Indians had patiently awaited the oft-delayed arrival of the goods given to their nation by President Washington. The last wagonload finally rolled in on November 3, and the entire shipment was loaded onto a riverboat provided by Governor Blount and commanded by David Moore. The large craft transported goods and Indians down the Holston and Tennessee to the mouth of Bear Creek where the cargo was transferred to a train of pack horses for the rest of the journey to the nation.[52]

---

49. Knoxville *Gazette*, October 11, 1794; Keith, ed., *The John Gray Blount Papers*, Vol. II, p. 449.
50. Masterson, *William Blount*, p. 266; Keith, ed., *The John Gray Blount Papers*, Vol. II, p. 449.
51. Carter, ed., *Territorial Papers, SWT*, IV, p. 374.
52. Ibid., pp. 363-64; Governor William Blount and David Moore of Knoxville, Articles of Agreement, October 12, 1794, Governors Papers, TSLA.

CHAPTER X

TERROR AND VIOLENCE EXCHANGED

1794

The organization of the general assembly of the territory in 1794, an important milestone on the road to statehood, nonetheless failed to overshadow the bitter differences persisting between the settlers and the Indians. Nor did Blount's belief at the beginning of the year that he had attained peace with the Cherokee prove valid. Although the agent to the Creek, James Seagrove, reported December 5, 1793, that the principal Creek chiefs were peaceably disposed and had agreed to reestablish peace with the United States, that, too, was suspect; the lesser chiefs and warriors showed little evidence of such a disposition.[1]

Raids into the settlements occurred throughout 1794. On January 1 a party of twenty-eight Creek fired upon the blockhouse at Bull Run, sixteen miles from Knoxville, and wounded one of Lieutenant Rickard's regulars. Captain John Beard led a part of his militia company in pursuit, but the raiders escaped. In Mero District on the same day, Indians wounded John Drake at his hunting camp, fired on his companions, and made off with all their baggage, their arms, and fifteen horses.[2]

On January 30 the Knoxville *Gazette* reported an incredible instance of near-miss marksmanship when, the week before, twenty Indians pursued a settler on the Clinch nearly a mile. They peppered him with shots, none of which touched him, although seven balls passed through his clothing. There were other reports of Indian bullets flying harmlessly close to defenders of the frontier, but the raiders more than compensated for any deficient marksmanship by the success of their horse stealing. They struck hard at the neighborhood around Pevahouse's station in early February, taking away several horses.[3]

The Pevahouse horse thieves did not escape without retaliation,

---

1. Hamer, ed., "Letters of Governor William Blount," p. 135.
2. Carter, ed., *Territorial Papers, SWT*, IV, p. 323; Knoxville *Gazette*, January 16, February 27, 1794; "War Department Collection of Post Revolutionary War Manuscripts, Territory Southwest of Ohio River," National Archives, Record Group 94, M-904, Roll 4, p. 85.
3. Knoxville *Gazette*, January 30, February 13, 1794.

however. Followed for eighty miles by twenty-one men of the Hawkins County Militia, they were finally overtaken. The militia detachment killed two of them and recaptured the stolen horses.[4]

In Mero District, Indians wounded Deliverance Gray January 3 near Nashville and killed John Dier and Benjamin Linsey near the mouth of Red River. On February 7 a party killed one Helen at the plantation of James Robertson; others mortally wounded James Gamble at Morgan's station.[5]

At every opportunity, settler parties pursued the raiders. Following the trail left by horses ridden by the killers of Oats and Ball on December 23, 1793, several pursuers were led to Hanging Maw's camp where they killed three men, and "forgetting the respect due to themselves," seven squaws. Another party commanded by Captain Nathaniel Evans of the Knox County Militia tracked a returning party of raiders through Tellico Plains and had a skirmish with them in a laurel thicket. The cavalrymen killed one raider and wounded several as they fled. The Indians left several scalps behind.[6]

Pursuit by Mero settlers resulted in even more bloodshed. Thomas Murray and his group chased the Creek who killed Helen, overtaking them 120 miles away on the bank of the Tennessee River. He exacted the lives of all eleven of the men and made prisoners of two women.[7]

Although the frontier folk were often successful in pursuing and punishing raiders, the raids continued without letup. During the month of February, every quarter of Mero District was "infested with their depredations, and almost every path and plantation marked with destruction." Few horses were left in the district. A long-time resident of the area stated that he had "not known a more general invasion from the savages for ten years past." Many dreaded the approach of summer.[8]

The attacks on Mero had resulted in "the butchery of thirteen... citizens." The acts of the Indians' "usual line of inhumanity...left the divided limbs of some of the sufferers scattered over the ground."[9]

In March, killings in the Washington and Hamilton districts were reported frequently. Samuel Martin was killed near Henry's station and

---

4. Ibid., February 27, 1794.
5. Ibid.
6. Ibid., January 16, 1794.
7. Ibid., March 13, 1794.
8. Kentucky *Gazette*, March 13, 22, 1794.
9. Knoxville *Gazette*, March 13, 1794.

James Ferguson between David's and John Craig's stations. Colonel Alexander Kelly and a detachment of the Knox County Militia pursued the killers of Martin and Ferguson but were unable to overtake them. They brought back nine stolen horses that they found at Tellassee, however. Cherokee and Creek Indians in ambuscade, led by Double Head, killed four men of a party of twelve traveling on the Kentucky Road near Middleton's station. Another group shot and seriously wounded John Wood near William Russell's place on Beaver Dam Creek. In those same neighborhoods, Indians were taking horses almost every day.[10]

Three Indians—a father and his two sons—seized a Negro slave at the ironworks on Slate Creek on March 26 and told him that they were going to take him to Detroit and sell him to the British. When they encamped the first night, the ironworker escaped into a nearby canebrake and later made his way back to Slate Creek.[11]

Indian depredations shared the columns of the Knoxville newspaper with news of the French Revolution, including in its March 27 issue an account of the death of the queen, Marie Antoinette. Indians and Jacobins were portrayed as equally bloody operatives. The editor was led to remark that Chief Double Head, a signer of the Treaty of Holston, had shed as much human blood with his own hands "as any man (not a Jacobin) of the age."[12]

On March 8 Governor Blount warned General Robertson that the Creek and Cherokee were "for war and not peace" and that he should plan the defense of Mero District accordingly. Seagrove's hopeful assessment of the Creek's attitude had been proved wanting in every respect, although he had renewed it February 10 and would renew it again on March 20 when he reported that thirty-seven Cherokee chiefs had assured him their nation would not injure the territory except in retaliation. Prophetically advising Robertson that Mero should expect frequent raids from small parties from the lower Cherokee and upper Creek towns, Blount nonetheless counseled close attention to economy. He suggested that from twenty-five to fifty mounted infantry would be adequate to chase parties of the size likely to be in the Cumberland settlements.[13]

---

10. Ibid., March 13, 27, 1794.
11. Ibid., April 24, 1794.
12. Ibid., March 13, 27, 1794.
13. Carter, ed., *Territorial Papers, SWT*, IV, pp. 331-32; Keith, ed., *The John Gray Blount Papers*, Vol. II, p. 368; Knoxville *Gazette*, April 24, 1794; Seagrove to Blount, February 10, 1794, James Robertson Papers.

Perhaps encouraged by the milder weather of April, Indian marauders brazenly appeared along the paths of the settlements. On April 1 an Indian party concealed beside the Cumberland road near Crab Orchard fired into a company of five travelers, killing the legendary Thomas Sharp Spencer of Sumner County. Another of the company was wounded, but the four returned to the blockhouse at Southwest Point where earlier the same day they had departed for Nashville. Approximately one thousand dollars in gold and other valuable articles in Spencer's possession were taken by the Indians.[14]

About twenty-five warriors mortally attacked William Green, a regular soldier, near the blockhouse at the mouth of Town Creek close to Knoxville. They rushed the house only to be repulsed with three wounded.[15]

Indians killed and scalped the two cousins Anthony Bledsoe, one a son of the late Isaac Bledsoe and the other a son of the late Anthony Bledsoe, near the home of Secretary Smith on Drake's Creek in Sumner County. At the time the young men were living at the Smiths' place in order to attend school nearby. Both of the fathers had been killed by Indians. A Negro slave, accompanying the boys, was taken away by the killers.[16]

The people of Hamilton District demanded retaliation when marauders killed William Casteel, his wife, and five children at their house on the south side of French Broad about eight miles from Knoxville on April 22. Lieutenant Colonel Kelly and the Knox Militia pursued the murderers and, after crossing the Tennessee near Tellassee, overtook them in camp. After a brisk exchange of shots in which one Indian was killed and another wounded, the remainder fled to "the almost inaccessible spurs of the mountain." Following persistently, the Knox Militia overtook them and killed five warriors while capturing several squaws and children. After the fighting ended, the soldiers freed their prisoners. Leaving the Indians' horses, corn, and other property undisturbed, the militia returned to Knoxville.[17]

Although the pursuers of the Casteel family's killers had drawn blood, there were renewed demands in the territory for a major assault on the

---

14. The life and exploits of Spencer are told in Walter T. Durham, "Thomas Sharp Spencer, Man or Legend," *Tennessee Historical Quarterly*, Vol. XXXI (1972).
15. Knoxville *Gazette*, April 10, 1794.
16. *Legislative Council, August 25, 1794*, p. 23.
17. Knoxville *Gazette*, April 24, May 8, 1794.

Indians. Upon his return May 19 from a visit to North Carolina, Governor Blount saw that his people nursed a renewed hostility toward the Cherokee. He confided to John Gray Blount, "The frontier people... have gone all wrong and have not yet got right."[18]

Chasing raiders who stole horses at Beaver Dam Creek, Captain Beard and a party of militia caught them after a pursuit of over one hundred miles. The frontiersmen killed three and wounded four of the Indians. They retook thirteen horses and brought in an assortment of guns, shot bags, and blankets, arriving at Knoxville on April 25.[19]

On May 5, Indians killed Peter Pearcifield near Wear's Cove in Jefferson County. Dressing and painting themselves like the enemy, four settlers from Wear's Cove attempted to pursue the killers but were unable to pick up their trail. Determined to exact retribution, they turned toward the towns on Big Tellico and were not long in finding a large encampment of warriors. They went into the camp under the cover of darkness and killed four men asleep on the ground. They returned safely to the settlements on May 21.[20]

The vigorous punishment of certain of the party who murdered the Casteels caused Hanging Maw to sue for peace. In a letter written May 25 to Blount, the chief stated that the Casteels were killed by "a fellow from Tallassee" to avenge the death of his mother at the hands of white men. Although whites had killed six Indians in retaliation for the Casteel murders including a relation of his, Hanging Maw and his people wished to consider the matter closed.

In a conciliatory gesture, Hanging Maw said that the Cherokee would have no more talks with the Spanish but were ready "to take the United States by the hand." Both Little Turkey and John Watts had reached the same conclusion and even the young men of the lower towns had changed their minds, he declared. "We have often told lies," he concluded, "but now you may depend on hearing the truth."[21]

In conversations with several chiefs gathered at Tuskeega, John McKee, who had just replaced Leonard Shaw as agent to the Cherokee, listened to their new commitment to peace. Hanging Maw was the principal spokesman for the group that included unidentified chiefs from

---

18. Keith, ed., *The John Gray Blount Papers,* Vol. II, p. 396.
19. Knoxville *Gazette,* May 8, 1794.
20. Ibid., May 22, June 5, 1794.
21. Ibid., June 5, 1794.

Will's Town, Chilhowee, Tellassee, and other towns up the Tennessee. Returning seven stolen horses to McKee, the Indians stated that they had taken steps to curb horse stealing by appointing persons in each town to whip and crop the "young fellows as may in future steal horses." In fact, two sets of thieves had been punished in that manner a few days before. McKee also learned that the return of Watts and Bloody Fellow, absent from the nation since the prior fall, was expected daily. Recently the peaceful disposition of the two chiefs toward the territory folk had been made known to the nation.[22]

Several frontier settlers attended McKee's exchanges with the Cherokee chiefs. Even the most extreme of them were reported well satisfied with Cherokee representations. One of them told McKee that he was going "to move out of the station to his own house immediately." Other settlers, long confined to Craig's and Henry's stations, expressed equal confidence in the Indians' expressed intentions.[23]

Better relations between the Cherokee and the eastern settlers could be fostered by the government's erecting a blockhouse and establishing a post at the mouth of Nine Mile Creek on the Tennessee River, Hanging Maw suggested to McKee. Such a development would contribute to "the better security of peace and intercourse" between the neighbors.[24]

Protestations of peace by the Cherokee did not convince Andrew Jackson, however. The murder of John McCoy in Mero District in early May, although probably committed by the Creek, caused Jackson to despair for the future of the settlements. He knew the settlers in Mero were so discouraged that many were moving to Kentucky. He wrote McKee that unless Congress came forward with "a more ample protection, this country will have at length to break or seek a protection from some other source than the present."[25]

During the first two weeks of June, the Cherokee's professed attitudes changed radically. At Tuskeega on June 15, Hanging Maw told John McKee that warriors from the lower towns were threatening to invade the settlements to kill the inhabitants and attribute the action to him.

---

22. Ibid.; William G. McLoughlin, *Cherokee Renascence in the New Republic* (Princeton, New Jersey: Princeton University Press, 1986), p. 42.
23. Knoxville *Gazette*, June 5, 1794.
24. Ibid.
25. Smith and Owsley, eds., *The Papers of Andrew Jackson, 1770-1803*, Vol. I. pp. 48-49.

They expected the whites to retaliate by taking his life and thus eliminate his influence for peace among the other chiefs. The spirit of war had been revived in the lower towns by the recent killing of the chief Bench, a relative of both John Watts and Talotiska, on the frontiers of Virginia. At that very moment, Talotiska and a party of warriors, bent on taking satisfaction for Bench's death, were awaiting Watts's arrival before setting out. Hanging Maw further advised McKee that he had sent messengers to intercede with a group of warriors from the valleys who had come to the Buffalo Town on their way to war but was doubtful that his counsel would be heeded. A few days later, Indians killed Stephen Jones on the east fork of Little Pigeon River.[26]

The war factions among the Cherokee had been encouraged during the same two-week period by a talk from the Creek delivered to the upper Cherokee towns. Suggesting that those Cherokee living close to the settlements might want to withdraw to a safer distance, the Creek declared that they were going to invade the territory and would begin by taking the post at Southwest Point. The Creek were on the warpath because they claimed that all but three of a party of thirty-three of their chiefs, en route to visit the Congress, were killed by whites in Georgia. While he would not vouch for the truth of the claim, Hanging Maw said it was so reported by the Creek and believed by his people.[27]

McKee told Blount that although Maw and his small circle at Tuskeega seemed genuinely to want peace with the United States, there was no longer reason to believe that prospects for peace with the larger number of that nation were favorable. To demonstrate his apprehension for the safety of the whites, Hanging Maw sent a special guard to escort McKee safely back to the settlements.[28]

A month later McKee, then at Tellico, implored the Cherokee chiefs of the lower towns to conduct themselves peaceably and to demand that their people quit killing the settlers and stealing their property. He threatened that unless the lower towns made peace immediately, "they would feel what war is before winter." Urging the chiefs to talk seriously of peace to the Creek, he pointed out that the Cherokee would "lose more by a war with the United States than with the Creeks."[29]

---

26. Knoxville *Gazette*, June 19, July 3, 1794.
27. Ibid., June 19, 1794. It was later learned that only one chief had been killed and three wounded. Ibid., July 3, 1794.
28. Ibid., June 19, 1794.
29. John McKee to Blount, July 14, 1794, James Robertson Papers.

Even as Indian attitudes hardened into new hostility, the national government refused to change its policy. Specifically denying the governor's request for permission to strike the Chickamauga towns, Secretary Knox wrote on July 26:

> With respect to destroying the lower towns, however rigorous such a measure might be, or whatever good consequences might result from it, I am instructed... by the President, to say, that he does not conceive himself authorized to direct any such measure, more especially, as the whole subject was before the last session of Congress, who did not think it proper to authorize or direct offensive operations.[30]

The pattern of incursions by small parties of Indians continued throughout the summer. During the latter part of May, they stole horses from several places in Sumner County, killed a man on Station Camp Creek, and wounded his wife. On June 11, a party of them killed a woman within four miles of Nashville. Captain John Gordon led a small detachment in pursuit for ninety miles, overtook the Indians, and killed one of them while losing one of his own men—Robert McRory. On June 16 another Indian party shot Hugh Webb to death and seriously wounded his companion Joseph McAdam near Dripping Spring in Mero District.[31]

Approximately fifteen Indians surprised and killed Isaac Mayfield July 6 about five miles from Nashville as he stood guard for his son-in-law who was working in a field of corn. A newspaper report, whether factual or designed to incite, stated that the attackers had fired eight balls into Mayfield's body before removing his scalp and driving a new British bayonet through his face. Mayfield was the sixth person of his "family and name" to have been killed or captured by Indians.[32]

About June 14, Indians massacred the entire white party of thirteen, including six men, four women, and three children, and made prisoners of their twenty-two Negro slaves on board a riverboat that had left Knoxville June 9 bound for "the Natches." The boat was loaded with "several tons of pots, kettles, cast iron ware and other valuable property." The iron castings were products of the ironworks in Washington District.

As the boat passed down the Tennessee River exercising the right

---

30. Downs, "Indian Affairs in the Southwest Territory, 1790-1796," p. 259.
31. Knoxville *Gazette*, July 3, 1794.
32. Ibid., July 17, 1794.

of free, unmolested passage guaranteed by the Treaty of Holston, it came under fire from the lower Cherokee at Running-water Town and at Long Island Villages. Although the shots from the riverbank were harmless, fire returned by the boatmen wounded two Indians and aroused such animosity that a party of about 150 assembled and followed the boat to Muscle Shoals. There the pursuers surrounded it, went on board, and massacred the whites. Three Indians lost their lives in the assault, and a fourth was wounded.[33]

On July 24 some Creek warriors killed John Ish at his plow in a field near his blockhouse, about eighteen miles below Knoxville. Ish's death left a widow and eight children, "the eldest not eleven years of age."[34]

Advised by John McKee of Ish's murder, Hanging Maw assured Governor Blount that the Cherokee would give satisfaction within ten to fifteen days or acknowledge the right of the United States to take it indiscriminately. On July 26 he sent Chief Boggs with eleven young warriors, accompanied by Major Robert King and Lieutenant James Cunningham, in search of the culprits. Two days later the search party returned to Tellico Blockhouse with a Creek, alleged to have been one of the murderers.

The large assemblage of Cherokee, relieved that the killer was not of their nation, cheered the prisoner's arrival. Middle Striker, a distinguished chief from Will's Town, seized the Creek and "dashed him with great violence on the ground." Hanging Maw wanted to scalp him alive, but settled for taking only the warlock. That act prompted a scalp dance that lasted all night. Before the celebration was over, however, the Cherokee understood that their role in capturing the Creek warrior might "draw the Creeks upon them." They quietly asked the governor what kind of support they might expect from the United States in that case.[35]

The Creek prisoner, Abongpohigo, was taken to Knoxville and there brought to trial August 1 under the terms of the Treaty of Holston. Judge Anderson, dutifully following the procedures of his court, first impaneled a grand jury that returned an indictment charging the Indian with the murder of John Ish. After selecting a trial jury and appointing an attorney

---

33. Ibid.
34. Ibid., August 4, 1794.
35. Ibid.

to defend Abongpohigo, Judge Anderson heard the case. Through an interpreter the defendant admitted that he had killed Ish, said the upper Creek towns had long since turned their backs on the provisions of the Treaty of New York, and bragged that he would never have been captured had not the perfidious Cherokee joined forces with the whites. He promised that there were plenty of warriors in his nation to avenge his death. The trial lasted the better part of one day and ended with a verdict of guilty. He was sentenced to die, and on August 4 he was executed by the sheriff of Knox County.[36] By the marked propriety of all procedures surrounding the trial and execution, the leaders of the territorial government hoped to show that they could be expected to honor the terms of the Creek treaty—and others, as well.

In the Mero District, mounted militia had been unsuccessful in their pursuit of the Indian party responsible for the death of George Winchester on July 9. Winchester, brother of James Winchester of the legislative council, was killed and scalped about nine o'clock in the morning near David Wilson's place in Sumner County. He was riding horseback along the public road that connected his house to Sumner Court House. A justice of the peace, he was on his way to attend a session of the quarterly court when he was struck down.[37]

The upper Cherokee became alert to the presence or passage of the Creek and passed information about their movements to the United States agent. When eight Creek were discovered about twenty-five miles below Hiwassee during the first week of August, Hanging Maw led a party of Cherokee to attempt to intercept them. Eluding the Cherokee, the small party was reported to be seeking out the Cherokee warrior who had captured the killer of Ish. At the same time news was received at Tellico Blockhouse that approximately one hundred Creek had crossed the Tennessee River near the mouth of Chickamauga Creek on their way to strike the frontiers of Hamilton District. The Cherokee responded by dispatching a number of their warriors, accompanied by Major King and three other militia officers.[38]

When the whereabouts of the smaller Creek party were reported on August 9, fifty-three Cherokee led by Hanging Maw's son Willioe and

---

36. Ibid.; Goodspeed, *History of Knox County*, pp. 815-16.
37. Knoxville *Gazette*, August 4, 1794.
38. William Blount to David Henley, October 24, 1794, Henley Papers, William R. Perkins Library, Duke University, Durham, North Carolina; Knoxville *Gazette*, August 25, 1794.

accompanied by seven federal soldiers rode to cut them off. On the next day, the Creek had come within sight of Major Craig's station, but the Cherokee met them there. In the ensuing skirmish, one Creek was killed and scalped, and another was wounded as they fled the larger force, leaving most of their provisions and supplies behind. The Cherokee and regulars returned to Tellico Blockhouse with great joy and passed the night "dancing the scalp dance."[39]

The larger party of Creek, numbering between one hundred and two hundred warriors, reached within eighteen miles of Southwest Point on August 13. Near Crab Orchard on Cumberland Mountain, the Indians attacked a detachment of thirty-seven men from Captain Evans's company. The soldiers, under the command of Lieutenant John McClellan, were traveling along the Cumberland path when assaulted. Aided by their greater numbers, the attackers killed four of the soldiers, wounded another, and took the horses, saddles, bridles, blankets, great coats, and provisions of the entire detachment. The soldiers escaped slaughter only because of the intrepid leadership of Lieutenant McClellan. The Creek commander, "conspicuously bold," was slain. He was among "twelve to sixteen" Indians killed.[40]

As the Creek seemed to move at will along the frontiers of the territory, Governor Blount received a report from McKee stating that the upper Cherokee were determined for war with the Creek. He said they had spilled too much Creek blood for peace between them to be reestablished soon.[41]

The report was enough to cause Blount to ponder anew the possibility of involving the Cherokee, Chickasaw, and Choctaw in war against the Creek. He had mentioned it repeatedly to Robertson, and also to Hanging Maw and Double Head, pointing out to the latter that it would be better for the Cherokee to have a war with the Creek than with the United States. In such a conflict, Blount promised, "You may be sure of friends enough." Later, on November 10, he would broach the subject to Secretary Knox, but he confided to Robertson a few days later that he did not expect to see the United States allied with the other three tribes at war with the Creek until after the territory became a state with representation in Congress. Intelligence reports raising the possibility

---

39. Knoxville *Gazette*, August 25, 1794.
40. Ibid.
41. Ibid.

of a United States-Cherokee-Chickasaw-Choctaw alliance against the Creek were disconcerting to the government of Spain, which began again to see the United States as instigator of trouble in the eastern Mississippi valley.[42]

Creek marauders were busily present in the eastern districts. On August 12 fifteen miles north of Knoxville, a group of fifteen attacked the blockhouse at Bull Run, defended by eleven federal soldiers. The siege was a standoff without fatalities to either side. The besiegers fled when Captain Beard arrived with a relief party of neighboring militia.[43]

Indians leaving the settlements with a sizeable number of horses stolen from Hinds's field on August 10 were overtaken by Captain Evans and part of his command on August 12. One Indian died in the exchange of fire. All of the horses were regained.[44]

During the latter party of July, Cumberland settlers saw Indians frequently. Most were thieves looking for horses, but on one occasion, they even took milk and butter. On July 29, raiders killed Gabriel Simpson on his mother's farm about five miles from Nashville.[45]

The seeming omnipresence of hostile Indians fueled a growing resentment among the inhabitants of Mero District. They were convinced that most of their unwelcome visitors came from the lower Cherokee towns, especially those of Nickajack and Running-water. The deep frustration of the Cumberlanders was shared by many who lived in south central Kentucky, an area sometimes harassed by the same bands.

Although there had always been a certain amount of local sentiment for a strike at the lower towns, the circumstances that resulted in the frontiersmen mounting a devastating raid on Nickajack and Will's Town could hardly have been coincidence. It was not happenstance that in the summer of 1794 Joseph Brown,[46] who had spent his boyhood years in Nickajack as a captive, led a scouting party to a point on the Tennessee River opposite Nickajack to determine a feasible route for horsemen to reach it. Nor was it by chance that Governor Blount had confided to General Robertson repeatedly that he expected the national

---

42. Downs, "Indian Affairs in the Southwest Territory, 1790-1796," pp. 262-63; Holmes, "Spanish-American Rivalry Over the Chickasaw Bluffs, 1780-1795," p. 41.
43. Knoxville *Gazette*, August 25, 1794.
44. Ibid.
45. Ibid.
46. C. Somers Miller, "The Joseph Brown Story; Pioneer and Indian in Tennessee History," *Tennessee Historical Quarterly*, Vol. XXXII (Spring 1973), pp. 26-27.

government to authorize preemptive strikes at any moment against Indian towns used as bases for raids into the settlements.

In fact, Robertson was a step ahead of Secretary Knox who had written Blount on July 20, again denying authority to strike the lower towns but hinting broadly that it should be done. He wrote, "I would it were possible to strike, with the highest severity any of the parties...who should go to Cumberland to commit depredations. It would seem that an intelligent and active partisan might find some such opportunity."[47] Was Robertson the partisan Knox envisioned?

Preparation began to develop a momentum of its own. Sampson Williams, a prominent Mero public servant, surely was acting in concert with other district leaders when he persuaded Colonel William Whitley of Kentucky to bring volunteers from that state to join in the anticipated punishment of the lower towns. General Robertson could not have presumed to keep the plan secret as Colonels Ford and Montgomery busily recruited militiamen in Tennessee and Montgomery counties while Robertson was rounding up men in Davidson and Sumner.

Was it quite by accident that Governor Blount dispatched Major Ore from Hamilton District with a detachment of militia for the protection of the frontiers of Mero just in time to join the other soldiers at the appointed rendezvous? If it was not a coincidence, the gathering of the forces occurred so smoothly that cynics might doubt that it could have been planned and executed so well.

It was certainly no coincidence that many in Mero were outraged by the policies of the national government. Sometimes the outrage was directed at Secretary Daniel Smith, one of their own, who shared with Governor Blount the responsibility for implementing government policy in the territory. One volunteer for the Nickajack campaign thought of a way to show his displeasure toward Smith, if he should lose his life at Nickajack. Edmond Jennings, a bachelor neighbor of Smith's, made a will before he left. In it he provided that in the event of his death, his cattle should be driven onto Smith's plantation and there be killed and left for the wolves. He envisioned that the dead cattle would attract a host of wolves that would soon turn upon the secretary's stock and destroy them.[48]

---

47. *ASP, II, Indian Affairs,* Vol. I, p. 634.
48. Draper Manuscripts, 32S165.

By September 6 the expeditionary force had been assembled at Nashville about two miles from Buchanan's station. Although outranked by Colonels Whitley and Montgomery, Major Ore was placed in command by General Robertson. As he had been sent by Governor Blount to protect the frontiers of the district, Ore could better draw upon the public stores to supply and equip the expedition and better call upon government to pay the men involved. At the very least, his troops had been levied by public authority, and it was expected that government would honor claims for the additional soldiers.

Upon receipt of messages delivered by two expresses from the Chickasaw that a large number of Creek and Cherokee from the lower towns were "embodying" to invade Mero District, Robertson believed that he could justify a strike against them for defensive purposes. If the militia did not meet the invaders, he could see it as nothing but defensive to strike their towns to "check them in their advance." Nor was it anything but defensive to pursue parties from the lower towns that had recently committed murders and stolen horses along the Cumberland. Behind it all, however, was the principal justification: "the long repeated...almost daily sufferings of the people of the District of Mero by the hands of the Creeks and Cherokees of the Lower Towns."[49]

Blount, either genuinely opposed to Robertson's placing the militia major in command of the campaign or more likely seeking to protect his position as governor, wrote to the general on September 9 before he knew the men had left Nashville two days before. In strong official criticism of Robertson, Blount urged him to abandon the plan, reminding him that perpetrators of "lawless unauthorized acts" could not expect "pecuniary reward" from the national government.[50]

Carefully phrasing his orders to Ore, General Robertson stated that the object of the command was "to defend the District...against the Creeks and Cherokees of the Lower Towns" who, according to information lately received, were about to invade it. The secondary object was to punish those who had committed recent depredations. Robertson instructed Ore, also, to be alert to Indians returning from Mero and to pursue and punish them as an example to others.

In the main part of the order, General Robertson dealt with the expected invasion party. He told Ore that if he did not meet the party

---

49. Carter, ed., *Territorial Papers, SWT,* IV, p. 358.
50. Downs, "Indian Affairs in the Southwest Territory, 1790-1796," p. 260.

before reaching the Tennessee River, he should take his force across it and "destroy the Lower Cherokee Towns...[to] check...the expected invaders." He counseled the major to spare the women and children and to treat all prisoners with humanity.[51]

Long before the troops assembled, General Robertson had secretly submitted to the governor a conditional resignation to be brought forth at such time as circumstances might indicate. By agreement with Blount, Robertson assumed full responsibility for the expedition in his resignation.[52]

Ore left Nashville on September 7 with 550 mounted infantry. Following what he took to be the "trace of the Indians who had committed the latest murders in the district" and of those who had taken a slave woman into captivity, Ore and his men reached the Tennessee on September 12 without encountering the anticipated invaders. Following Robertson's orders, he took most of his men across the river and prepared to assault the nearest riverbank town.[53]

Nickajack and Running-water Town were close to the soldiers' place of crossing. Situated on the south side of the Tennessee River, both were surrounded on the other three sides by mountains. The towns were the "principal crossing places for the Creeks over the Tennessee for war against Cumberland and Kentucky."[54]

Nickajack was the first target. Ore's troops surprised the Indians, and "the slaughter was great." The soldiers killed fifty-four males and took nineteen women and children prisoner. Searching the village, they found two fresh scalps, lately taken in the Cumberland country, and several older ones hanging in the houses of warriors as trophies. They also found several horses and sundry articles of personal property stolen from the Mero District. They then regrouped to assault Running-water, about four miles distant.[55]

News of the attack on Nickajack reached Running-water, the largest and among the most hostile towns of the Cherokee, in time for its defenders to choose the ground on which to make a stand. Concentrating their strength at a place called the Narrows, the Indians resisted the

---

51. *ASP, II, Indian Affairs*, Vol. I. p. 530.
52. Putnam, *History of Middle Tennessee*, p. 487.
53. *ASP, II, Indian Affairs*, Vol. I, p. 632.
54. Knoxville *Gazette*, September 26, 1794.
55. Kentucky *Gazette*, October 4, 1794; *ASP, II, Indian Affairs*, Vol. I, p. 632.

militia at first, but soon gave way. Without further opposition, Ore burned the town.

Two nights before the town was sacked, Running-water had been the scene of a scalp dance "over the scalps lately taken from Cumberland," Ore learned. The celebration was made more than usually noteworthy by the presence of John Watts, Bloody Fellow, and other chiefs of the lower towns. They had come together to assure one another and their warriors that, in conjunction with the Creek, they were determined to continue the war against the frontiers. They had even discussed erecting blockhouses at each of the lower towns for defense, as suggested by the Spanish government.[56]

In the attacks on the two Cherokee towns, Ore's militia had killed fifty-five warriors, wounded several others, and taken several prisoners. There were no deaths among the men of his force, and only three were wounded. The soldiers had burned 150 houses.[57]

Learning from the prisoners that John Watts had been the only chief advocating a peaceful policy toward the settlements at the time the attacks were made, General Robertson warned him on September 20 that the Mero folk were serious about peace. The Indians must stop the killing and must not let the Creek pass through their nation to attack Mero unless they wanted the whites to return and destroy the remaining lower towns, he declared. Robertson assured Watts, "We have men enough to fight, and destroy you all, and burn your towns."[58]

On the same day, September 20, Double Head wrote to Governor Blount petitioning for peace between the lower towns and the territory. Blount received the letter at the same time he learned that General Logan of Kentucky was raising a force in contemplation of an attack on the lower towns. Without delay, the governor sent expresses to General Logan and Colonel Whitley, commander of the Kentucky troops at Nickajack, demanding that they desist. He ordered General Robertson to require them to return home if they should appear in the Mero District on their way southward. Simultaneously he told the chiefs in the lower towns of Logan's intentions. Even before Blount sent out messengers,

---

56. *ASP, II, Indian Affairs,* Vol. I, p. 632.
57. Ibid.; Kentucky *Gazette,* October 4, 1794.
58. *ASP, II, Indian Affairs,* Vol. I, pp. 531-32, 533-34, 540; Knoxville *Gazette,* November 29, 1794; Kentucky *Gazette,* October 11, 1794.

Logan had abandoned his plan because no more than thirty volunteers answered his call.[59]

As soon as he learned of the attack on Nickajack and Running-water Town, Blount officially dissociated himself from Ore's campaign. He had given no order to Robertson that would have warranted such action, he told Secretary Knox. He acted publicly as if the entire matter was a surprise to him and totally beyond his control. On October 1 Blount sent an official letter demanding a copy of Robertson's order to Major Ore and a statement of the reasons for giving it. Warning that the Ore campaign might have results quite different from those intended, Blount instructed the general to be alert to the possibility of an invasion by a large body of Creek and Cherokee to retaliate for the destruction of the two towns.[60]

Behind the scenes, Blount worked to make the expedition palatable to the national government and to protect his Mero commander from a forced resignation. In a personal letter also written October 1, the governor told Robertson that the general's private letters "heretofore written" would not be publicly disclosed. Presumably the correspondence had included plans for the attack and the general's secret resignation letter. Blount advised Robertson to defend himself by making the case for his decision as strongly and frequently as possible. He believed that the more often the explanation could be heard, the more plausible it became.[61]

When Blount forwarded Robertson's reasons for ordering Ore's attack to Secretary Knox, he offered no judgment as to whether they would justify the action taken. He left that determination to Knox who appeared to be equivocating somewhat in his letter of December 29.[62]

"The destruction of the Lower Cherokee towns stands upon its own footing; that it was not authorized, is certain," Knox wrote. He observed wearily, "The principle adopted by the president, not to authorize or direct offensive expeditions, has been so frequently brought to your view, that nothing more can be said on that subject."[63]

Unofficially, Blount was highly pleased with Ore's expedition. A visitor to Knoxville found that the destruction of the two towns was

---

59. *ASP, II, Indian Affairs*, Vol. I, pp. 531-32, 533-34, 540; Knoxville *Gazette*, November 29, 1794.
60. Carter, ed., *Territorial Papers, SWT*, IV, pp. 356-57.
61. Ibid., p. 356.
62. Ibid., p. 360.
63. *ASP, II, Indian Affairs*, Vol. I, pp. 634-35.

"spoken of by all ranks as the most brilliant thing that has happened or could have happened for this country." He said that Blount as governor disapproved of the strike because he was restricted to defensive measures only, but as a citizen of the territory, he was "highly gratified." Belief was widespread that Indian raids would be greatly diminished because of it.[64]

Apparently unwilling to serve longer as a target for official wrath and probably nudged by Blount, Robertson submitted an unconditional resignation to the governor on October 23. Although he stated that "it is not through any disgust with the public service or officers of government that I am induced to take this step," he probably meant exactly the opposite. The governor forwarded the general's resignation to Philadelphia, but no action was taken on it and Robertson continued in grade as Brigadier General, Commander, Mero District Militia.[65]

Following the Nickajack campaign, Cherokee raids on the settlements in Mero were less frequent, but the Creek filled the voids. Indians killed a certain Miss Roberts near the mouth of Red River on September 13, and on the next day they killed Thomas Reasons and his wife in their home near the same place. Other raiders killed one Chambers, wounded two others, burned John Donelson's station and a neighbor's house, and took several horses in Davidson County near Andrew Jackson's place about twelve miles from Nashville on September 16. On the same day yet another party killed a woman in Sumner County on Red River near Major Sharp's and stole several horses. About September 20, Robert Briggance met his death on a public road near Sumner Court House. On September 20, twelve-year-old Allen Nolen was killed four miles from Nashville on the plantation where his father had met the same fate six years previous.[66]

Striking again at the Bledsoe family, Indians killed and scalped Thomas Bledsoe, son of the late Colonel Anthony Bledsoe, on October 2. He was attacked near the late Colonel Isaac Bledsoe's fort. Before Thomas's death, his father, a brother, an uncle, and a cousin had fallen to Indians.[67]

Seeking to thwart raids into the Cumberland settlement from the

---

64. Keith, ed., *The John Gray Blount Papers*, Vol. II, p. 448.
65. Putnam, *History of Middle Tennessee*, p. 498; Draft of resignation, October 23, 1794, James Robertson Papers.
66. Carter, ed., *Territorial Papers, SWT,* IV, p. 358; Knoxville *Gazette*, September 26, 1794.
67. Knoxville *Gazette*, October 11, 1794.

southeast, Governor Blount ordered small detachments of mounted infantry to patrol Indian traces leading from the Tennessee River to Bledsoe's Lick and beyond. On October 1 three detachments were detailed from Captain Joseph Evans's company of militia.[68]

At first the patrols seemed effective, but after a brief lull, Indian raiders reappeared. On October 24 a party killed and scalped Evan Watkins near Colonel Winchester's mill in Sumner County. On the next day twelve warriors were seen crossing the road between Bledsoe's Lick and Shaver's cabin, and on October 26, Indians fired on a militia officer in the same neighborhood. Scouts reported seeing thirteen Indians cross the Cumberland River within five miles of Colonel Winchester's place on October 29.[69]

The inhabitants of Tennessee and Montgomery counties also felt the wrath of the southern Indians. On November 5 fifty Indians, supposed to be Creek, fell upon the families of the brothers Isaac and John Titsworth on the Red River. They killed and scalped seven whites, wounded a Negro woman, and "took a white man, three children, and a Negro fellow prisoners." Pursued by local militia, the raiders killed and scalped the children before escaping with the two adult prisoners.[70]

Six days after the Titsworth slayings, Indians attacked Colonel Sevier's station near Clarksville. They killed "Snyder, his wife, one child, Ann King and her son James, and Colonel Sevier's son Joseph and left his daughter Rebecca near death, wounded and scalped." The tragedy caused great consternation in Clarksville; women and children wept publicly and those who went to the Sevier house saw "a scene which cannot be described." There was talk on every hand of evacuating the town at once unless outside reinforcements could be provided to help defend it.[71]

Colonel John Sevier, who had earlier lost three brothers to Indian raiders, was enraged when the news from Clarksville reached him. The killings there had added eight more members of his father's family to the three who had "fallen a sacrifice to savage barbarity." Confiding to a friend the indignation of "a heart glowing with distress," Sevier

---

68. Blount to Evans, October 1, 1794, James Robertson Papers.
69. Knoxville *Gazette*, November 29, 1794; *ASP, II, Indian Affairs*, Vol. I, p. 539.
70. Knoxville *Gazette*, November 29, 1794; January 9, 1795; *ASP, II, Indian Affairs*, Vol. I, p. 539.
71. Knoxville *Gazette*, November 29, 1794; A.V. Goodpasture, "The Beginnings of Montgomery County," *American Historical Magazine*, Vol. 8 (July 1903), pp. 214-15.

lashed out sarcastically at Congress that "wisely determined . . . that we shall in this quarter, defend ourselves after the bloody hatchet is laid to our heads."[72]

On November 28, Indians killed and scalped Peter Gleaves near Sharp's station and Clinch River about twenty miles north of Knoxville. Two weeks later Indians fired a harmless salvo at Mrs. Thomas Cowan and her son as they emerged from their house on Beaver Dam Creek eleven miles from Knoxville.[73]

Most of the Indian depredations of the autumn months of 1794 came at the hands of the Creek. By October 8 General Robertson had received intelligence from the Chickasaw that Mero District, characterized by Governor Blount as "the most difficult settlement in America to protect," was yet threatened by the Creek. He was told to expect many small parties instead of a few larger forces. Within a month, however, a war party of over fifty Creek was encamped on the lower Tennessee. In the Cumberland settlements, there was talk of launching a strike into the upper Creek towns. General Robertson knew of this and warned Blount that his people could be driven to unpredictable extremes by the federal government's inaction.[74]

On November 3 Blount told Knox that there would be no real peace on the frontiers unless the upper Creek could be "induced or compelled" to follow the recent peaceful example of the Cherokee. On November 10 the governor wrote, "If the citizens of the United States do not destroy the Creeks, the Creeks will kill the citizens of the United States." He wrote to Knox again a week later, "I consider war with the Creeks unavoidable."[75]

By November 10 the Cherokee lower towns, shocked by the destruction of Nickajack and Running-water Town and claiming to have been disposed to peace before the attack, had convinced Governor Blount that they sincerely wanted peace. The inhabitants of Washington and Hamilton districts were so optimistic about improved relations with the entire Cherokee Nation that many who had taken refuge in forts and stations left them and returned to their farms. To the governor, the prospects for peace warranted the hope that for the rest of the year "no

---

72. *Dunlap and Claypoole's American Daily Advertiser*, January 2, 1795.
73. Knoxville *Gazette*, December 13, 1794.
74. Carter, ed., *Territorial Papers, SWT*, IV. p. 359; *ASP, II, Indian Affairs*, Vol. I, pp. 535, 542.
75. Carter, ed., *Territorial Papers, SWT*, IV, pp. 363, 370.

further detachments" of militia would be required to defend the frontiers of the eastern districts. "And if Cherokee faith is to be depended upon," he said, "next neither."[76]

The lower towns' newly declared interest in peace had been encouraged in part by war-ridden Spain. On July 4 the Baron de Carondelet, governor of Louisiana, had informed them that Spain wanted them to live in peace with the United States. He said they should remain at home, be prepared to defend themselves, but should not go beyond their borders to attack citizens of the United States. The government of Spain would supply guns for hunting and defense, Carondelet said, but would not support their going to war against the United States.[77]

The Cherokee knew, too, that the war in the Northwest had ended and that the United States had its full military strength free to deal with the southern Indians. They were aware, also, that Blount had erected five blockhouses in Indian country and assigned troops to each to prevent a recurrence of the events that led to Sevier's Etowah campaign and Beard's attack. The amendments to the Treaty of Holston, negotiated at Philadelphia during the summer, pleased them. But most of all, they had begun to understand that the might of the United States, unloosed upon them, could destroy their nation. Nickajack had been a convincing experience.[78]

Key chiefs from the lower towns and about five hundred warriors had come to Tellico Blockhouse to deliver messages of peaceful intent toward the settlers October 24 and 29 and November 4. Upon hearing that Hanging Maw, John Watts, John Davidson, and Tickagiskee were there and desired to see him, Governor Blount hastened to them.

On November 8 Blount and the chiefs exchanged promises of peaceful cooperation. Watts said that a short time before Major Ore's raid the lower towns had decided to stop attacks on the settlements from the upper towns. He agreed that the destruction of the two towns had been justified because of their being used repeatedly as bases to mount raids on Cumberland.[79]

The governor admitted to the chiefs of the lower towns that peace

---

76. *ASP, II, Indian Affairs*, Vol. I, p. 535; William Blount to David Henley, November 24, 1794, Blount Correspondence, McClung Collection, Knoxville Public Library.
77. Knoxville *Gazette*, November 29, 1794.
78. Downs, "Indian Affairs in the Southwest Territory, 1790-1796," pp. 261-62.
79. *ASP, II, Indian Affairs*, Vol. I. pp. 536, 537, 538; Knoxville *Gazette*, November 15, 1794.

could be threatened by irresponsible initiatives such as the reported plan of General Logan to lead an invasion of their area from Kentucky. He insisted they should not let the experience interfere with the peaceful relations now established with the inhabitants of the territory. The governor and the chiefs agreed to an exchange of prisoners, deserters, Negroes, and horses to be held on December 18 at Tellico Blockhouse. Prompt participation in the exchange by the lower towns would remove the cause that had rallied Kentuckians to attack them, Blount explained.[80]

As the governor focused his attention on the Creek threat to the territory, Judge Anderson called on the populace to obey the laws including the Indian treaties. That behavior would encourage the federal government to extend adequate protection to the frontiers. Citing the friendship of the upper Cherokee, Anderson urged his people to cultivate good relations with that nation as it was a natural buffer against the belligerent Creek. The territory folk should make certain that no one attacked the Cherokee, he insisted, because friendship—not war—with them was the answer.[81]

The Cherokee and Blount agreed that the Creek continued to be a major threat to the settlers. Asking the Cherokee to prohibit war parties from crossing their lands to attack the settlements, Blount noted that of the four Indian nations adjoining the territory, only the Creek remained combative. The Cherokee declared they would not assist the Creek, but they could not forcibly block their passage, especially in sparsely populated areas.[82]

Encouraged by the conversations at Tellico, Governor Blount ordered General Robertson on November 22 to reduce the number of militia on active duty in Mero District. He told Robertson that in the future he would not send militia from Hamilton and Washington districts to aid Mero "except in case of an invasion by a numerous party of Indians."[83]

A few weeks later, when Blount and the Cherokee were to meet again, "a great number of frontier inhabitants, sore under their many losses," showed up at Tellico to put in claims for Negroes and horses stolen by the Cherokee since the Treaty of Holston. The governor dispersed

---

80. Knoxville *Gazette*, November 15, 1794.
81. Ibid., November 1, 1794.
82. Ibid., November 15, 1794.
83. *ASP, II, Indian Affairs*, Vol. I. p. 541.

the crowd that had gathered in cold, rainy weather by explaining that the meeting was solely to exchange prisoners. Seizing upon a suggestion probably made by the governor, the frontiersmen returned to their homes planning to petition Congress for redress for their losses.[84]

The departure of the claimants relaxed the tense atmosphere. In addition to those seeking restitution for past pillaging and larceny, many whites, spurred by idle curiosity, had crowded into Tellico. Present, also, was a large number of Indians, many hoping to find the generous bounty of food and drink that was customary at public conferences.[85]

Although only a "partial exchange of prisoners" took place, the conferees set June 1, 1795, as the date for "the completion of that business." Affirming peace between the Indians and the whites seemed uppermost in the minds of the leaders of both sides. Territorial leaders and the Cherokee, with Bloody Fellow and John Watts present, discussed matters of past hostility and concluded their conversations with declarations of mutual trust and friendship. Pledging their nation to peace with the settlers, the Cherokee promised, also, to use their very best efforts to prevent the Creek from "murdering and plundering the inhabitants of Cumberland and Kentucky." The conference was concluded on January 3, 1795.[86]

Sevier's strike into their heartland in 1793, Ore's devastation of Nickajack and Running-water Town in 1794, and the constant growth of the settler population had convinced the Cherokee that peace with the whites was their only hope. For them, regrettably, that peace was only an anxious interlude that preceded their removal to Arkansas in 1838.

Notwithstanding the new relationship between the territory and the entire Cherokee Nation, peace for the Mero District was elusive indeed. Indians killed and scalped Colonel John Montgomery and seriously wounded two other men November 27 on the northwestern frontier of Tennessee County. Two days later another party killed and scalped John Lawrence, William Haines, and Michael Hampton and wounded another person on the northeastern frontier of Sumner County. On December 20, Indians killed and scalped Hugh Tenan, John Brown, and William Grimes on the Harpeth River about sixteen miles below Nashville.[87]

---

84. Knoxville *Gazette*, December 26, 1794.
85. Ibid.
86. Ibid., January 9, 1795.
87. Ibid., December 26, 1794; January 9, 1795.

CHAPTER XI

INDIAN RELATIONS AND THE GENERAL ASSEMBLY

1795

By 1795 the further development of the territorial government and its progress toward statehood depended more on good relations with the southern Indian nations than on the operation of factional politics among the settlers. How were relations to be improved? There were no new answers. The federal government demanded that settlers respect the terms of the Treaty of Holston and stay out of the Indians' country. Denying that settlers were violating treaty lines, the territorial administration argued unendingly for permission to war against the Creek.

Although there were no new answers, there were new emphases. Henry Knox, who usually had accepted Blount's assurances that settlers were not infringing on Indian territory, resigned as secretary of war and Timothy Pickering assumed his office. Pickering, a tough New England Federalist who was highly suspicious of Blount, blamed the Indian wars on the frontier people who had encroached on Cherokee lands and/or those who continually spoke and thought in terms of additional land cessions by the native Americans. The change from trust to suspicion in the office of the secretary of war would have its role in accelerating the territory toward statehood.[1]

Another significant emphasis was added by Governor Blount in the late spring of 1795 when he called the general assembly to meet in June, three months earlier than had been set when he prorogued the prior session. The governor had decided that good relations with the southern Indians and the achievement of statehood were inseparable.[2] He had even gone so far as to order the removal of United States citizens who

---

1. Symonds, "The Failure of America's Indian Policy," p. 44; Masterson, *William Blount*, p. 271.
2. Downs, "Indian Affairs in the Southwest Territory, 1790-1796," p. 268; Knoxville *Gazette*, May 8, 1795; Durham, *Daniel Smith, Frontier Statesman*, p. 179.

had settled on Cherokee lands in Powell's Valley in violation of the Treaty of Holston.³

Before reaching that decision, Blount had used every resource at his disposal to engage the Cherokee, Choctaw, and Chickasaw in war against the Creek. Confident that punitive strikes against the Cherokee had brought that nation to the conference table, he hoped that war would so diminish the strength of the Creek that they, too, would be reconciled to the frontier settlements. When the Cherokee demurred to his proposal that they stop the Creek from using their territory as a corridor to attack the settlements, Blount suggested that about sixty of their warriors be assigned to work with the militia to protect the Mero District. Under no illusion that the sixty could materially affect frontier security, Blount sought to position them so that a confrontation with Creek raiders was likely. He professed his purpose: "to induce the Cherokees to take such steps as would ultimately destroy the friendship that has...subsisted between that nation and the Creeks."⁴

Enmity between the Cherokee and the Creek had been encouraged when, near the Georgia frontier, a party of the former challenged a group of the latter "with hostile intentions" toward the United States. The Cherokee killed and scalped a Creek and brought the scalp to Tellico Blockhouse on January 1. That same night they held a scalp dance "in the presence of many of the frontier and other citizens of the United States."⁵

The Chickasaw were expecting a white attack on the Creek momentarily both as normal retaliation and as fulfillment of statements made by Blount and Robertson to Chickasaw representatives at Nashville the prior autumn. So excited were they that during the first week of January they dispatched William Colbert and seventy warriors to Nashville bearing the scalps of five Creek that had been taken when they intercepted five raiders on January 2. The force was sent to join the Mero Militia in its expected retaliation against the Creek for their depredations in

---

3. The proclamation was published in the Knoxville *Gazette* of May 8, 1795, with the notation that after it was issued, *"The persons who were the objects of it, obeyed the command."* It is doubtful that many families moved as no records of enforcement have been discovered. It was a chance for Blount to pay lip service to federal pressure.

4. Carter, ed., *Territorial Papers, SWT*, IV, p. 380; Downs, "Indian Affairs in the Southwest Territory, 1790-1796," p. 264.

5. Knoxville *Gazette*, January 23, 1795.

the Southwest Territory. The arrival of Colbert's party was considered further proof of Chickasaw loyalty to the Mero settlers.[6]

It was a mixed blessing, however. James Robertson feared the Chickasaw's readiness was premature. He confessed, "I wished the Chickasaws to kill Creeks, but lament their beginning so early." He told them that he expected an American army to march against the Creek during the summer, but stated that no orders had yet been issued. Robertson was fearful that the Chickasaw would "suffer much by the Creeks" while it was not in the power of the United States to assist them. If that happened, he predicted that the Chickasaw would lose confidence in the United States government and eventually become its enemy.[7]

Blount used the Chickasaw's eagerness to defend the westernmost settlers to persuade the Cherokee, who had declined sending warriors to Cumberland, to adopt a more vigorous stance against the Creek. Convinced that war between the Creek and the Chickasaw was certain, the governor ordered Robertson to use Colbert and his warriors in the interim to protect the Mero frontier and to dismiss an equal number of militia. He again told the secretary of war that "unless effectual measures are taken to stay the murdering hand of the Creeks...peace is not to be expected by the frontier citizens of this territory or Kentucky." Impatiently awaiting further opportunity to punish the Creek, Colbert and his warriors, entertained by the settlers at Nashville throughout a day designated in their honor, showed their readiness to fight by holding a war dance that night.[8]

Relations between the two Indian nations continued to deteriorate. On March 27 the Knoxville *Gazette* reported that the Chickasaw had lately killed and scalped ten Creek, in addition to the five killed by Colbert, and made prisoners of six others. Asserting that the violent exchanges between the nations actually constituted war, the editor urged the United States to shield the friendly Chickasaw from the Creek, who then outnumbered them sixteen to one. James Robertson, relaying a Chickasaw plea for assistance, recommended that if such were forthcoming, "the sooner it is done, the better, both for them and us." He

---

6. Kentucky *Gazette*, January 31, 1795.
7. *ASP, II, Indian Affairs*, Vol. I, pp. 556-57; Downs, "Indian Affairs in the Southwest Territory, 1790-1796," p. 265.
8. *ASP, II, Indian Affairs*, Vol. I, p. 557; Downs, "Indian Affairs in the Southwest Territory, 1790-1796," p. 265; Carter, ed., *Territorial Papers, SWT*, IV, pp. 380, 381.

had just heard from Piomingo and George Colbert who asked for the military support that they claimed Blount had offered. They requested that John Chisholm be sent at the head of the soldiers.[9]

A month later a group of Mero District volunteers of "upwards of one hundred men impressed with a high sense of the friendship of the Chickasaws and the essential services by them rendered to that infant settlement" marched from Nashville to their aid under the command of citizen Kasper Mansker, a former lieutenant colonel in the Sumner County Militia. About forty-five of the men traveled in a separate detachment with Captain David Smith. Although he did not authorize the volunteer contingent, General Robertson did not intervene, fearing that failure to aid the Chickasaw would result in losing their friendship "forever." Recognizing that the Indians would not be able to make crops due to their war with the Creek, Robertson sent them three large canoes laden with corn. He saw to it that the unauthorized volunteers took enough provisions with them to last for three months. Simultaneously, the Creek appealed to the Shawnee and other northern tribes requesting their assistance "in the total extermination of the Chickasaws."[10]

Mansker and Smith assembled the Cumberland volunteers at the Chickasaw village of Logtown on the east bank of the Mississippi River where they set up a small swivel cannon. When the Creek attacked a few days later, they were beaten off, and when the tiny cannon was fired, they went home to stay. The volunteers returned to Nashville a short time later.[11]

Although President Washington had issued a proclamation of assistance to the Chickasaw on July 21, 1794, it promised protection only against United States citizens who might invade or try to purchase their lands. Its failure to provide aid against other tribes hostile to both the Chickasaw and the United States was loudly lamented on the southwest frontier.

> Is it possible that the United States will suffer the Chickasaw nation (men, women and children) to be totally destroyed, for their friendship to them manifested, in

---

9. Knoxville *Gazette*, March 27, 1795; Robertson to David Henley, David Henley Papers, 1748-1823, TSLA; Piomingo and George Colbert to Robertson, March 5, 1795, James Robertson Papers.

10. Robertson to Blount, April 20, 1795, James Robertson Papers; Knoxville *Gazette*, May 8, July 17, 1795.

11. Walter T. Durham, "Kasper Mansker: Cumberland Frontiersman," *Tennessee Historical Quarterly*, Vol. XXX (1971), pp. 172-73.

joining the armies of St. Clair and Wayne, against the northern tribes, and in killing marauding Creeks upon Mero District?—National honor, justice, gratitude, and sound policy revolt at the idea!!![12]

But national policy could not be made in Mero District. The disapproval of the President and the secretary of war fell heavily on Robertson again. Acting on a suggestion from Blount, he again submitted his resignation as commanding general of the Mero District Militia. This time it was accepted effective August 15, 1795. James Winchester was appointed in his place,[13] but Robertson remained United States temporary agent to the Chickasaw and Choctaw nations.

Notwithstanding frontier ire, the President held firm to his course. The United States would not interfere in relationships between the various Indian nations. President Washington would defend the Chickasaw against European nations and would see that no matter who the enemy might be, they would never suffer from a lack of provisions, but he would not join them in war against the Creek. General Robertson had "done wrong" in telling the Chickasaw in 1794 that he expected the United States to send an army against the Creek the same year, he explained to visiting Chickasaw chiefs.[14]

Both the President and the Congress seemed deaf to the settlers' pleas for protection. A citizen, with tongue in cheek, observed that only the death of a federal tax collector at the hands of Indians could awaken the indifferent leaders of government to the needs of the territory.[15]

A frontiersman visiting Philadelphia in January had expressed the hope that Congress would consider the problems of the western folk as if they were their own: "It is to be hoped the members of Congress... will individually apply our sufferings to their own feelings.... The most extreme frontier family, in their poverty, are as much entitled to protection as the most wealthy member of Congress, in his ease and luxury."[16]

Throughout the first six months of 1795, sporadic raids by the Creek were reported. Settlers in each county circulated petitions to Congress

---

12. Knoxville *Gazette*, February 6, May 8, 1795.
13. Putnam, *History of Middle Tennessee*, pp. 508-9; Robertson to Winchester, August, 1795, James Robertson Papers.
14. "The Talk of the President of the United States to Major William Colbert, John Brown the Younger, and William McGillivray, Chickasaws," James Robertson Papers, 1795.
15. Augusta *Chronicle and Gazette of the State*, July 25, 1795.
16. Philadelphia *Aurora. General Advertiser*, January 12, 1795.

seeking redress, but as in past times, the effort was ineffectual. Raiders killed a mounted Mero militiaman, Elijah Walker, while he was scouting twelve miles south of Nashville on January 5. Another party killed one John Tye and wounded three of his comrades on the frontier of Hawkins County the same day. On January 28 Creek warriors killed and scalped George Man of Flat Creek about twelve miles from Knoxville. They burned his stable and stole his horses, but abandoned an attack on his house after his wife, defending their children, fired from inside, seriously wounding one of the attackers.[17]

There was no letup. One party of Creek horse thieves made off with thirty-seven animals in February. A small party of Creek fired on three settlers working in a field near Joslin's station, seven miles from Nashville, on March 5. Dangerously wounded, two of the men were shot through the body, and the third was badly beaten with a war club. On April 26, Creek marauders killed John Edwards near the house of John Williamson on Station Camp Creek in Sumner County and, three days later, seriously wounded four settlers passing down the Cumberland River with a party of Chickasaw in four canoes.[18]

Immigrating to the territory from New Madrid on the Mississippi River, Colonel Samuel T. Chew, a member of his party, and "several" of his Negro slaves were killed by Creek near the mouth of the Cumberland River on May 29. After five or six weeks of relative quiet in Sumner County, the Creek "killed, scalped, stripped, and otherwise cruelly mangled old Mr. Peyton" at Bledsoe's Lick and there inflicted multiple wounds on John, a slave owned by Nathaniel Parker.[19] Although attacks on the frontier people did not occur every day, horse thieving was an ongoing phenomenon.

On March 23 Secretary Pickering denounced Blount and Robertson's efforts to foment war between the Creek on one side and the Cherokee, Chickasaw, and Choctaw on the other. Pointing out that United States treaties with the Cherokee and Chickasaw had never included military alliances, he instructed the frontier leaders to desist from insinuating that friendly Indians could expect military support against mutual enemies. The secretary ordered, also, that Blount and Robertson should

---

17. Knoxville *Gazette*, January 9, 23, February 6, March 27, 1795; "Narrative of John Davis, Esq.," *Southwestern Monthly*, Vol. I (April 1852), p. 214.
18. Knoxville *Gazette*, March 27, April 10, May 12, 1795.
19. Ibid., June 5, 19, 1795.

refrain from encouraging warlike acts by other Indians against the Creek. Addressing himself to Governor Blount, Pickering wrote:

> Upon the whole...the complexion of some of the transactions in the Southwestern Territory appears unfavorable to the public interests.... The United States are determined...to avoid war with the Creeks. Congress alone are competent to decide upon an offensive war, and Congress have not seen fit to authorize it. The acts of individuals, and especially of public officers, apparently tending to such an event ought not to be silently overlooked.[20]

The Creek incursions were interpreted by the secretary of war as the actions of "small parties of plundering Creeks" whom he expected soon to be restrained. He was encouraged by the Creek's agreement to restore white and Negro prisoners they held and by their respect for the frontiers of Georgia "for several months past...unmolested." In fact, Pickering believed that the territory stood at the threshold of peace with all of the southern Indians if the frontier folk would follow the policies of the national government.[21]

Advising Blount that Congress had appropriated fifty thousand dollars to open trade with the southern Indians and one hundred thirty thousand dollars for the defensive protection of the frontiers, Pickering admonished, "All ideas of offensive operations are therefore to be laid aside and all possible harmony cultivated with the Indian tribes." He recommended Tellico Blockhouse as the site of a trading post to serve the Cherokee and Creek, but left the decision to the governor.[22]

In response to what the President regarded as the legitimate defensive needs of the territory, Pickering authorized Blount to establish a post on the Tennessee "at or near the Creeks' crossing place" in line with Colbert's request of January 13. Warning the governor to make certain that the specific location was satisfactory to both the Cherokee and the Chickasaw and that it was clearly on Chickasaw land, the secretary expressed hope that it could serve as a "trading house" to accommodate the lower Cherokee, the upper Choctaw, the Chickasaw and, possibly, the upper Creek.[23]

---

20. Pickering to Blount, March 23, 1795, James Robertson Papers.
21. Ibid.
22. Ibid.
23. Ibid.

The national government directed that all possible points of friction with the Cherokee be eliminated, and if the Indians objected, the garrison at Tellico Blockhouse and/or Fort Grainger should be removed. The fort at Southwest Point was not a negotiable issue, however; it was regarded as an essential anchor of the road from Holston to Bledsoe's Lick. Nor was the intrusion of settlers into Indian lands negotiable; Blount was ordered to remove those in the proscribed zone without delay and to take the necessary steps to prevent recurrences, even if it meant using military force. Pickering demanded that Blount prevent the settlers from hunting on the lands of the Cherokee, an ongoing practice clearly violating the Treaty of Holston.[24]

The Creek sent peace overtures to Governor Blount on April 3. The peace talk came after an earlier conference with the United States agent James Seagrove and originated in an assembly of the chiefs of both the upper and the lower Creek at Oakfuskeys. Having convened for the purpose of making "a firm and lasting peace with the whole of the subjects of the United States," the chiefs declared that they were determined "to bury the hatchet, guns, and all other sharp weapons, and take all the white people by the hand like brothers." There would be no more bloodshed, they promised, and frontier inhabitants could confidently expect to "work on their farms without the least fear or dread, hunt their stocks, and pass from place to place without the least apprehension of danger or molestation." They suggested that further talks between their nation and Blount should be of content similar to the peace arrangements concluded by the United States with the Cherokee. They had already begun to collect the white and Negro prisoners, horses, and other unspecified properties of the settlers to deliver to Seagrove.[25]

Blount confided to Governor Shelby of Kentucky that the talks transmitted to him seemed "to contain the best assurances of peace" that he had ever received from the Creek and Cherokee. He cautioned Shelby to understand that sporadic raids were likely to continue because the chiefs could not always control the young warriors.[26]

Some among the Cherokee believed that credit for the Creek's sudden interest in peace should be given the Chickasaw, who "had done more in a few months than the United States had done in *twenty* years—

---

24. Ibid.
25. Knoxville *Gazette*, June 19, 1795.
26. Kentucky *Gazette*, July 11, 1795.

taught the Creeks the value of peace by the dread of war." John McKee believed the Creek sought peace because the Cherokee had recommended it and because raiding into the territory had become too risky to be profitable.[27]

Probably before they knew of the Creek's overtures for peace with the United States, separate parties of chiefs from the Chickasaw and the Choctaw set out for Philadelphia to visit the President "on the affairs" of their nations. Unable to win Washington's promise of assistance in their war with the Creek, the chiefs settled for the delivery of free "goods" to their people.[28]

The prospects of improved relations with the Creek and their sometime ally Spain were dealt a serious but temporary setback May 30 when Spanish troops landed on the Chickasaw Bluffs of the Mississippi River within the limits of the Southwest Territory and began the construction of Fort San Fernando de las Barrancas. The Spanish Indian agent explained the hasty action to the Chickasaw. Falsely claiming that about three hundred United States citizens had recently settled at the Chickasaw Bluffs, he promised that the fort was to protect the Indians from further inroads by the Americans. About July 1 the Chickasaw ceded the fort site, and Spain had a foothold on United States soil.[29]

Attempting to persuade the King of Spain to abandon his reckless appropriation of Chickasaw and American land for Fort Barrancas, President Washington denounced the invasion as "an unwarranted aggression as well against the United States as the Chickasaws."[30] The Spanish governor of Natchez professed consternation at Washington's reaction; to him, the maneuver was a simple confirmation of an earlier and somewhat obscure Spanish claim to the eastern banks of the river as far north as the mouth of the Ohio.[31]

Logs, pickets, and other materials used in building the fort had been prepared on the western or, to Americans, Spanish banks of the river and moved across on boats. Reliable news of the Spanish action was

---

27. Knoxville *Gazette*, June 5, 1795; John McKee to Blount, May 27, 1795, James Robertson Papers.

28. Blount to John Chisholm, May 23, 1795; Blount to David Henley, December 8, 1785, Blount Correspondence, McClung Collection; Knoxville *Gazette*, May 22, June 5, 1795.

29. Blount to Alexander Cornell, August 12, 1795, James Robertson Papers; Holmes, "Spanish-American Rivalry Over the Chickasaw Bluffs, 1780-1795," pp. 56-57.

30. "The Talk of the President of the United States to Major William Colbert, John Brown the Younger, and William McGillivray, Chickasaws," James Robertson Papers, 1795.

31. Holmes, "The Spanish-American Rivalry Over the Chickasaw Bluffs, 1780-1795," pp. 26-28; Knoxville *Gazette*, July 3, 1795.

not printed in the Knoxville *Gazette* until July 3 when it was accompanied by editorial outrage. Reflecting the unmistakable sentiments of his readers, the editor concluded, "Certainly the United States will no longer passively behold the encroachments of the Spanish government!"

Although it is doubtful, the provocative step by Spain may have been taken to improve its bargaining position with the United States in negotiations then under way. But whatever the cause, when negotiations were concluded on October 27, the Spanish agreed to abandon the fort, recognized United States boundary claims in the area, and opened the Mississippi River to shipping. The government of Spain had been goaded to the treaty table by the wars then rumbling across Europe and the concurrent necessity of reducing the risks of overseas military involvements.[32]

In the meantime, eager to take up the question of statehood, the members of the territorial general assembly gathered at Knoxville on June 29 in response to the governor's call. Heeding Blount's recommendation that a census be taken and a yea or nay vote be registered on the question of seeking statehood, the general assembly adopted a statute to accomplish both with only one dissenting vote.[33]

Representative Thomas Hardeman of Davidson County objected to the bill because he said it would be "leading the people into a change of government" that they had not requested while "burdening them with additional taxes" with the prospect of doubtful advantages at best. He objected, also, to the possibility that travelers might be counted in each of the counties through which they passed during the census period, thus distorting the final count.[34]

When passing the statute, the general assembly had set out on a course hitherto uncharted, the first territory to propose a state under the Ordinance of 1787. The ordinance had not provided instructions detailing the route to be followed once the population appeared sufficient to

---

32. Durham, *Daniel Smith, Frontier Statesman*, p. 185.
33. *Journal of the Proceedings of the Legislative Council of the Territory of the United States of America, South of the River Ohio, Begun and Held at Knoxville, the 29th Day of June, 1795* (Knoxville: Printed by George Roulstone, Printer to the Territory, 1795), pp. 4, 5, 7 (hereinafter cited as *Legislative Council, June 29, 1795*); Knoxville *Gazette*, July 17, 31, 1795.
34. *Journal of the Proceedings of the House of Representatives of the Territory of the United States of America, South of the River Ohio, Begun and Held at Knoxville, the 29th Day of June, 1795* (Knoxville: Printed by George Roulstone, Printer to the Territory, 1795), p. 17 (hereinafter cited as *House of Representatives, June 29, 1795*).

support a state of the Union. In the absence of precedent and established courses, every move by the government of the Southwest Territory would add to the political charts by which others would later take their headings toward statehood.

The act allocated the responsibilities and set forth the methods for recording the number of persons and the votes of those eligible. The sheriff of each county, assisted by his deputies, was instructed to take the census of that county during the period of September 15 through November 15, 1795. A fine of two hundred dollars would be levied against each sheriff who failed to transmit the returns of his county to the governor by November 30, and a penalty of fifty dollars was prescribed for any deputy sheriff who failed to complete his assignment or who submitted false returns. The state would pay compensation to each sheriff at the rate of one dollar for every one hundred persons reported, an amount to be divided as the sheriff chose between his deputies and himself. All participating officers were required to take a special oath, promising to accomplish the task to the best of their abilities.[35]

The method of taking the census called for a visit by a deputy sheriff to each household where he would record the number of persons. Each person would be registered in one of six categories: "names of heads of families; free white males sixteen years and upwards, including heads of families; free white males under sixteen years; free white females including heads of families; all other free persons; [and] slaves." Indians were not to be counted, except those on the tax rolls, a negligible number.[36]

The act revised Blount's recommendation for a poll on statehood by directing the census takers to poll free males eighteen years and older to determine their wishes in the event that the population totals were less than sixty thousand, the number required to trigger statehood under the Ordinance of 1787. If affirmative responses were in the majority, the act "requested" the governor to call a special session of the general assembly for further deliberation on the question. This contingency, alluded to in Blount's opening speech to the general assembly, had arisen from discussions at the nation's capital about the possibility of Congress

---

35. Knoxville *Gazette*, July 31, 1795.
36. Ibid.

admitting the new state by legislative act irrespective of its population.[37]

Expecting the census to show that the population exceeded the minimum[38] required for statehood, the general assembly authorized the governor in that event to call for the voters of each county to elect five representatives to meet in convention at Knoxville. The representatives thus chosen would determine the permanent form of government by adopting a constitution and establishing under it a state administration.[39]

Admission to the Union as a state was not the only question before the general assembly, however. Responding weakly to the governor's request for assistance to pay for "the cutting and clearing" of a wagon road from Southwest Point to Bledsoe's Lick after the failure of a lottery for that purpose, the assembly diverted all monies—if any—in excess of two hundred pounds[40] that might be collected from the sale of the salt licks, springs, and adjoining public lands in Mero District to the use of the road commissioners.[41]

The legislators were receptive to road projects for which their limited treasury funds could make a more significant contribution. Apprised of the governor's correspondence with his counterpart in South Carolina about opening a connecting road through the eastern mountains, members of the assembly were eager to investigate the matter further. They authorized Blount to appoint three commissioners to meet with a like number from the other state to "deliberate and consult" and to report back to the next general assembly on the "practicability and probable expense of cutting and opening" the road. They set aside the sum of one hundred dollars to defray the expenses of the commissioners.[42]

As if to whet the public's appetite for road cutting, two wagons reached Knoxville from South Carolina a few weeks later. They had come through the mountains "by way of the warm springs of French Broad." The Knoxville editor trumpeted his excitement toward readers in the

---

37. Ibid., July 17, 31, 1795; *Laws*, p. 53.
38. The minimum of 60,000 persons was to be computed by "counting the whole of free persons, including those bound to service for a term of years, and excluding Indians not taxed, and adding three-fifths of all other persons." *Laws*, p. 53. The Knoxville *Gazette* estimated the number would be "upwards of 66,000 inhabitants." July 31, 1795.
39. Knoxville *Gazette*, July 31, 1795; *Laws*, p. 51.
40. Two hundred pounds had been earmarked by the previous general assembly to build a jail in Mero District. *Laws*, p. 59.
41. Ibid., pp. 59-60.
42. *House of Representatives, June 29, 1795*, p. 18.

Mero District, suggesting the road over which the wagons passed would hasten migration into all of the territory. He exaggerated wishfully when he proclaimed, "A wagon road is now open from Georgia, South Carolina, North Carolina, and the other Atlantic states by way of this place to Nashville, the capital of the rich Cumberland Country."[43]

The agenda of the general assembly was long and wide-ranging. The question of the length of term to be served by Dr. James White as the representative of the territory to Congress was resolved by adopting a resolution specifying that he was elected to serve until a permanent form of government should be established. The tax act of 1794 defining taxable property and the method of tax collection was amended to permit out-of-state landowners to pay their 1794 taxes in 1795 without penalty. An act was passed providing rules and procedures for compelling citizens to give legal testimony in out-of-state litigation.[44] Blount County was created from a portion of Knox; Sevier County was authorized to lay out a town and to build a courthouse, prison, and stocks. The town of Blountville was created in Sullivan County, and separate sets of commissioners were appointed to "regulate" the towns of Greeneville and Clarksville. Washington College was established at Salem in Washington County as an outgrowth of Martin Academy, chartered a decade prior, with the Reverend Samuel Doak as president and a board of twenty-eight trustees. Finding no revenues available to fund it, the assembly voted to suspend the operation of an act passed at the previous session for the relief of persons disabled while on duty in the militia and providing for the widows and orphans of those who had died.[45]

On no subject was there better feeling than about the prospects of peace with the Indians. Although advising caution in dealing with the "bad young men," the governor shared the pervasive optimism. Rejoicing that "the calamities arising from Indian warfare" had "in great measure ceased to exist upon their exposed frontiers," John Sevier, speaking for the legislators, praised Blount for his "unwearied and constant struggle to promote a general peace with the Indian tribes." He lamented that "the savage disposition of Indians" made it unlikely that the settlers would soon enjoy total security from them. Nonetheless,

---

43. Knoxville *Gazette*, July 31, 1795.
44. *House of Representatives, June 29, 1795*, p. 19; *Laws*, pp. 56-57.
45. *Laws*, pp. 60-65, 67; Knoxville *Gazette*, July 17, 1795.

Sevier professed "pleasing hope" that the national government would afford such defensive protection as the settlers had a right to expect from a strong and resourceful nation.[46]

On July 4 the legislators joined the citizens of Knoxville and vicinity to celebrate the nineteenth anniversary of American independence. Seventeen toasts were offered, among which there were several directed to matters currently at issue. Toasts were raised to the republic of France and the republic of Holland, to the militia, and to free navigation of the Mississippi. Fervent cheers followed tributes to "Opiomingo and our gallant *sanscullote* allies of the Chickasaw and Choctaw nations," and to "citizen Mansker and his brave associates who made bare their bosoms in defense of our faithful Chickasaw brethren." The crowd applauded friends of the territory in Congress—Dr. White, Thomas P. Carnes of Georgia, and Joseph P. G. McDowell of North Carolina—and recognized as "objects of detestation" its Federalist calumniators there—Robert G. Harper of South Carolina, William V. Murray of Maryland, and James Hillhouse of Connecticut.

The final toast reflected the purpose of the legislative session: "The Territory South of the River Ohio. May she, by a speedy admission into the Union, participate with her sister states in the advantages of representation."[47] The crowd responded enthusiastically.

---

46. *House of Representatives, June 29, 1795,* pp. 5, 11.
47. Knoxville *Gazette,* July 17, 1795.

Chapter XII

PEACE AT HAND

1795

Even as the assemblymen celebrated the political future of the territory, the federal government began a vigorous collection of the excise tax that had been extended to the Northwest and Southwest territories the year before. The effort began May 3, 1795, with the appointment of John Overton of Davidson County as supervisor of the revenue for "the district of Tennessee" embodying "the whole Territory South of the river Ohio." Chosen for the new and lucrative position over several applicants including Landon Carter of Washington District, he was simultaneously appointed inspector of the revenue for the same area. Overton would be assisted by three collectors of the revenue, Robert Houston, Baldwin Harle, and Henry Bradford.[1]

The principal taxes to be collected for the federal government were assessed against the 450 distilleries in the territory in 1795. Each was assessed according to its capacity.[2] There were also taxes on wines, teas, refined sugar, carriages, snuff, and licenses for auctioneers and realtors.[3]

The territorial citizens' resentment toward paying federal taxes was well known to the United States Commissioner of Revenue. He had heard them repeatedly cry out against "taxation without representation." He understood that he was asking the frontier folk to pay taxes to a national government that had largely ignored their cries for protection and had withheld the pay of the militia on Sevier's Etowah campaign because the secretary of war considered their action "offensive." Sensitive to public opinion on the issue, the commissioner asked for suggestions and observed that Overton's "kind" handling of the matter

---

1. Overton to Tench Coxe, April 7, 1797, Claybrooke and Overton Papers; Landon Carter to William Blount, July 27, 1794, Blount Family Papers, 1794-1829, Historic New Orleans Collection; Tench Coxe to Overton, March 3, 1795, Jacob McGavock Dickenson Papers, TSLA; Knoxville *Gazette*, June 19, 1794; July 3, 1795.
2. General account of country distilleries in the District of Tennessee [1795-96], Jacob McGavock Dickenson Papers.
3. Tench Coxe to Overton, April 9, March 3, 1795, ibid.

could reduce tensions between the taxpayers and the government.[4]

During the session of the general assembly, a delegation of five Choctaw and their interpreters joined a party of four Chickasaw and their interpreters at Knoxville to be equipped for a visit to President Washington. They were boarded at Chisholm's Tavern while awaiting delivery of their supplies. After clothing, equipment, and horses had been provided at Knoxville, the parties were escorted to their destination by Colonel Robert Hays.[5]

In an initiative unaffected by the Choctaw and Chickasaw visit to the Capitol, President Washington decided that treaty talks with the Creek Indians should be initiated. He had reached his decision after repeated requests by the state of Georgia and after he had detected what he regarded as indications of a more pacific disposition among the Creek. On June 25 he appointed three commissioners to represent the United States: Benjamin Hawkins of North Carolina, George Clymer of Pennsylvania, and Andrew Pickens of South Carolina. In that selection, the President bypassed representation from the frontier areas most immediately affected, Georgia and the Southwest Territory.[6] By so doing, he could expect the commissioners to hold to a broader national view than was held by those who shared especially volatile boundaries with the Creek.

Washington emphatically placed the Mero District on the agenda. He charged the commissioners to inquire into "the dissatisfaction of the Creeks...manifest since the treaty of New York, by their numerous and distressing depredations" on the southwestern frontiers. He believed that the frequent, destructive raids in the Mero District were inspired by "some claim to the lands" along the Cumberland River. Washington ordered the commissioners to explore the causes of the hostilities "and to enter into such reasonable negotiations as will remove them and give permanent peace to those parts of the United States."[7]

Before the commissioners could initiate contacts with the Indians, the Creek asked Blount to intercede with the Chickasaw in their behalf.

---

4. Tench Coxe to John Overton, July 25, 1795, ibid; "A Statement of the Grievances of the Grand Jury of Hamilton District, Superior Court of Law, April Term, 1795," *American Historical Magazine*, Vol. II (October 1897), p. 336.
5. William Blount to David Henley, May 15, 23, 29, July 23 (2), 25, 29, Blount Correspondence, McClung Collection.
6. Knoxville *Gazette*, July 31, 1795.
7. Ibid.

If the Chickasaw would return their prisoners, the Creek said, they would bury the hatchet. Simultaneously the Creek sent word to the Chickasaw that they wanted to end the war between their nations and to exchange prisoners. The Creek implored, "Do exert yourselves in restoring peace between us that whenever we meet we may hunt, smoke, eat and drink together in peace." Their petition for Blount's help came with a reaffirmation of their commitment to peace with the frontier people and a request for a meeting with the governor at Tellico Blockhouse. Blount responded by suggesting they meet in the early part of October. He immediately wrote Pickering of the Creek request and asked for instructions.[8]

Territorial leaders and the public as well had been heartened by testimony given by Colonel Isaac Titsworth of Tennessee County when he returned in August from the Creek Nation where he recovered from captivity his daughter and a slave black. He said that when he demanded their release, the Creek readily delivered them and asked no ransom. Based on extensive talks there, Titsworth concluded that practically all the Creek were eager to end the war with the Chickasaw and that the chiefs and all, except some of the young warriors or "bad young men," were equally eager for peace with the United States. He attributed their turn toward peace to the receipt of messages urging that course from such diverse but important sources as the Spanish governor, the Choctaw and Chickasaw nations, James Seagrove, and Governor Blount. Although optimistic about the Creek's change in attitude toward the United States, the deputy Indian agent Alexander Cornell warned Blount that the settlers "should not be lulled to sleep or be off their guard as there are rash men on both sides."[9]

Delegations of Creek and Cherokee chieftains and smaller deputations of Choctaw and Chickasaw met with the governor on October 10 at Tellico Blockhouse under a white silken flag ordered by Blount "as an emblem of peace." Among the early arrivals were the Cherokee chiefs John Watts, Bloody Fellow, The Glass, Richard Justice, Double Head, Talotiska, and Otter Lifter. At the governor's side were Dr. James White, delegate to Congress from the territory; Colonel James White, commander of the Knox County Militia; Captain Rickard, commander

---

8. Alexander Cornell to the leaders of the Chickasaw Nation, July 27, 1795; Blount to Pickering, August 9, 1795, James Robertson Papers; Carter, ed., *Territorial Papers, SWT*, IV, p. 400.

9. Isaac Titsworth Report, August 9, 1795; Cornell to Blount, July 27, 1795, James Robertson Papers.

of the detachment of federal troops; and the agents to the Cherokee John McKee and Silas Dinsmoor. [10]

The result of their negotiations was to concentrate mutual efforts for peace between the Creek and the Chickasaw and peace between the Creek and the United States. There was agreement to exchange prisoners and a date was set—April, 1796—for surveying the Cherokee boundary indicated in the Treaty of Holston. The conference would prove "highly beneficial" to the United States, Blount predicted at its conclusion, because it has "heighten[ed] the chain of friendship" between the states and the three Indian nations.[11]

Even before the conference had begun, Blount sent word from Tellico to a large number of families gathering at Knoxville to cross through the wilderness to Nashville that they could expect a safe crossing, unchallenged by Indians. He said they would need no military escort nor should they have "the least apprehension of injuries at the hands of the Cherokees or Creeks." His optimistic prediction was based upon the "repeated assurances of peace" by the Indians during the prior six months, upon informal consultation with the chiefs at Tellico prior to the conference,[12] and upon his own selfish desire to see land values in Mero enhanced by the increase in settlement.

During the conversations Blount realized that he needed to set his people on a positive course to peaceful relations with all the tribes, and he turned to Judge Campbell for assistance. Asking the judge to use his influence for peace and goodwill toward the Indians, Blount specifically wanted him to help keep the settlers calm. He would also help them understand that peace was at hand and that they must treat the Cherokee as good neighbors.[13]

In the wake of the Tellico conference, Blount was besieged at home by Indians who attended it, as well as others coming into Knoxville, for supplies and gifts. He ordered blankets, coats of coarse wool, flaps, leggings, linen for shirts, silk handkerchiefs, thread, binding, hats, ribbon, and buckles for the forty Creek who came to Tellico Blockhouse. To certain Creek chieftains, he gave rifles, and to those of their party

---

10. Broadside, William Blount to Joseph Dorris, October 11, 1795, ibid.
11. Philadelphia *Aurora. General Advertiser,* December 14, 1795; January 4, 1796; Masterson, *William Blount,* p. 276; Blount to Colonel David Henley, October 6, 24, 1795, Blount Correspondence, McClung Collection.
12. Broadside, William Blount to Joseph Dorris, October 11, 1795, James Robertson Papers.
13. *Dunlap and Cl̄ ͞ poole's American Daily Advertiser,* November 18, 1795.

who needed it, he supplied iron to shoe their horses. A few Creek chiefs even accepted the hospitality of the governor's home where he entertained them "without expense to the United States."[14]

Bringing selected young warriors to Knoxville to show them that not only the government but the people at large were friendly toward them, the seven Cherokee chiefs gathered their party at Chisholm's Tavern where they were entertained at government expense. Blount gave a rifle to Hanging Maw, replaced a pair of brass pistols stolen from Double Head, and sent thirty gallons of whiskey and two beaver traps with chains and grapples to Little Turkey. He provided supplies of salt to all seven chiefs.[15]

To implement the agreements reached at Tellico dealing with prisoner exchange and peace between the Creek and the Chickasaw, Blount dispatched his trusted aide Captain John Chisholm to the Creek Nation on November 9. Chisholm was to return a Creek prisoner held at Knoxville, to obtain from the Creek "all the prisoners of this territory both black and white," and to bring back all horses "stolen from this country . . . [that] yet remain in the nation." He was charged, also, with the general task of restoring peace between the Creek and the Chickasaw but the method of achieving it was left to his judgment. Blount advised him that the task would require the "perfect understanding" of both parties and, echoing Secretary Pickering, warned that he should be careful to avoid "every species of deception whatever may be the object obtained thereby."[16]

After the Tellico conference, the citizens of Washington and Hamilton districts could relax their vigilance against Indians for the first time since creation of the territory. Willie Blount, the governor's half brother, exuded confidence:

> The Indians and the frontier people are together in the settlements, the nation, and the wilderness without the least apprehension of danger from each other. All is peace and friendship. . . . This country . . . is . . . in as great, if not greater state of peace and order, than any other part of the United States.[17]

---

14. Blount to David Henley, October 20 (3), 24, 26, 28, December 17, 1795, Blount Correspondence, McClung Collection.
15. Blount to David Henley, November 17, October 26 (2), November 9, December 17, 1795, ibid.
16. Blount to John Chisholm, November 6, 1795, ibid.
17. Philadelphia *Aurora. General Advertiser*, January 4, 1796.

His optimistic assessment was shared by many in the coastal states. It was evident in the increase in migration from those areas to the territory. The Knoxville *Gazette* estimated that twelve thousand new settlers had arrived in the Mero District during the year and that larger numbers had settled in each of the districts of Washington and Hamilton. The editor's enthusiasm enveloped Kentucky and other western lands.

> The immigration to Kentucky, this year, has been uncommonly great. The day is not far distant, when the country west of the Appalachian Mountain[s] will be the most populous part of America. It affords every encouragement to settlers—a very rich soil, the best water, a temperate climate and health, uninterrupted by *yellow* or other *contagious fevers*.[18]

The governor's half brother, probably reflecting the attitudes of the principal land speculators, was as excited about the population growth in the territory as he was about the coming of peace. Immigration to the three districts had exceeded their "most sanguine expectations." Funds for the long-desired wagon road across the wilderness had been found, and it had been cut and cleared enough to provide much improved passage to the Cumberland settlements. He elaborated, "Sixty-six wagons have already passed this for Nashville and...there are upwards of forty...between this place [Knoxville] and the iron works upon Mossy Creek; pack horses have passed without number."[19]

Not all of the new settlers were the kind sought by Blount and his fellow land speculators. Many of them had North Carolina grants to lands lying within areas guaranteed by treaty to the Indians. Insisting that ownership carried with it the right of immediate possession, the new landowners by their presence threatened the peace so recently concluded. The governor envisioned four possible answers to the problem: extinguish the claims of either the grantees or the Indians to the lands in question, take measures to prevent the grantees from taking possession, or "again be involved in an Indian war by their so doing."[20]

Receiving reports that white settlers were crossing into Cherokee territory in violation of the Treaty of Holston, Blount ordered both the

---

18. Knoxville *Gazette* quoted in Philadephia *Aurora. General Advertiser*, December 30, 1795.

19. Philadelphia *Aurora. General Advertiser*, January 4, 1796; Knoxville *Gazette*, July 31, 1795; William R. Garrett, ed., "Correspondence of General James Robertson," *American Historical Magazine*, Vol. IV (1899), p. 267; John Summerville to James Robertson, August 2, 1795, James Robertson Papers.

20. *ASP, II, Indian Affairs*, Vol. I. p. 584.

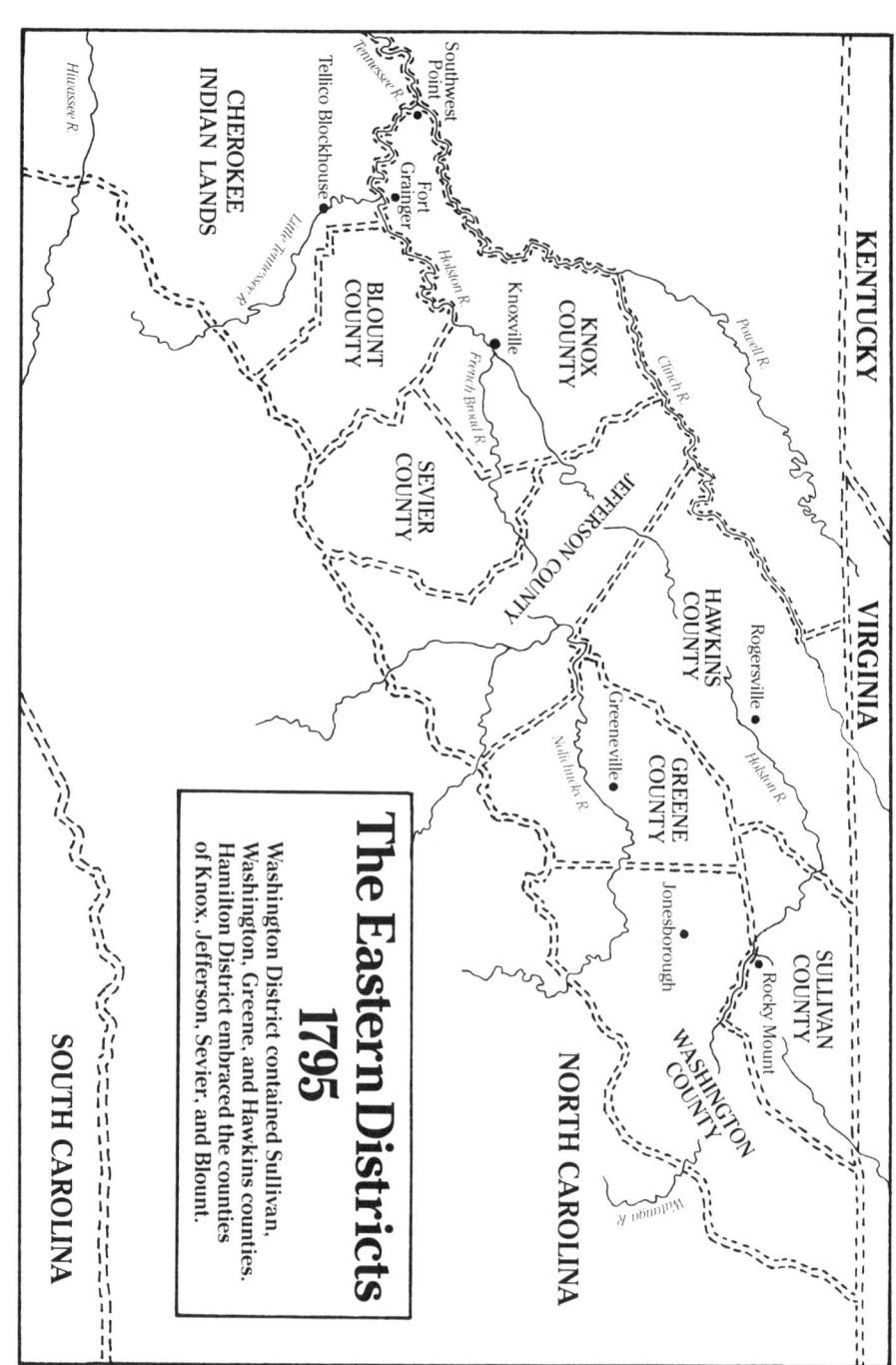

sheriff and the colonel commandant of Blount County on December 1 to investigate the situation below the experimental boundary line run in 1792. If they found settlements in the area, they were to order the settlers "to withdraw to the northward of the line" within forty-eight hours or be removed by military force. He hoped the officers, Alexander Kelly and Littlepage Sims, could use their "address and influence with the objects of it to obey without compelling the necessity of military force." The settlements that they found must not have been numerous as Kelly and Sims worked only eight days "removing the frontier citizens off the Indian lands."[21]

Blount used the boundary problem as part of the justification for a recommendation made December 14 that the United States purchase the approximately two hundred thousand acres north of the Tennessee River between the Clinch River and Chilhowee Mountain. He was prompted to suggest the purchase because the President had just appointed commissioners to make a land purchase from the Creek. By the purchase from the Cherokee, the boundary line would become the Tennessee River, a natural barrier that would stop easy or casual passage into or out of the Cherokee Nation. Blount denied personal interest in the land and sent his recommendation through Dr. White at Philadelphia.[22]

On November 28, 1795, based on the census reports from all eleven counties, Governor Blount certified to Secretary of State Timothy Pickering that there were 77,262 inhabitants in the Southwest Territory, a total that comfortably exceeded the minimum requirement of 60,000 for statehood. A generous count had been virtually assured by tying the sheriffs' pay for conducting the census directly to the totals reported. The larger the numbers reported, the more the sheriffs were paid.[23]

Doubts about the census taking were plentiful in Mero. Blount's popularity had sunk to new lows with many there. Sampson Williams was probably speaking for most in the district when he asked David Henley to make a fair representation to members of Congress of "the manner in which the census had been taken in this territory, as well as other impositions."[24]

---

21. Carter, ed., *Territorial Papers, SWT*, IV, pp. 408-10; "Bill for Services Rendered to U.S.A.," Kelly and Sims, December 10, 1795, Blount Correspondence, McClung Collection.
22. Carter, ed., *Territorial Papers, SWT*, IV, pp. 411-14.
23. "Census Schedule," ibid., pp. 404-5, 406.
24. Williams to Henley, November 17, 1795, David Henley Papers, 1748-1823.

Persistence of the doubts suggested there were concerns in Mero relating to more than the methodology of the census takers. There was uncertainty about the statehood proposed. A few in Mero hoped that by delaying action a while longer, there would be an opportunity later for that district to achieve separate statehood. Probably the majority were apprehensive of becoming an isolated western minority in a new state controlled in the eastern Washington and Hamilton districts.[25]

Although the Southwest Territory could have been divided into a maximum of two states under the cession act, the frontier leaders had not given that option serious consideration. The area of the territory was comparable to that of North Carolina and Kentucky, for example, but more persuasive than that coincidence was the settlers' perceived need to join the Union for protection against the Indians. If two states were laid off, each would find itself waiting indefinitely for the population growth necessary to qualify as a state, and the majority of settlers were unwilling to wait any longer.

The poll for independent statehood, important only if the census total should have been less than the minimum required, showed 6,504 in favor and 2,562 opposed. In the poll, statehood was preferred in every county except the three in Mero District. There the most populous county, Sumner, did not report the "yeas" and "nays." Davidson County reported only 96 yeas to 517 nays, and Tennessee County had 58 yeas to 231 nays.[26]

After certifying the census, Governor Blount called for each county to elect five persons to represent them in convention at Knoxville to determine the form of state government. The elections would be held by the sheriffs of the respective counties on December 18 and 19 in the same manner that they had held elections for members of the general assembly. All free white males, twenty-one years of age "and upwards," were eligible to vote, and the sheriffs would certify the five candidates receiving the largest number of votes in each county as being duly elected members of the convention. Blount announced January 11, 1796, as the date for convening the delegates.[27]

The leaders of the territory had been uncertain about the specific course to take once the population requirement for statehood had been met.

---

25. Corlew, *Tennessee, A Short History*, pp. 106-7.
26. "Census Schedule," Carter, ed., *Territorial Papers, SWT*, IV, pp. 404-5, 406.
27. Carter, ed., *Territorial Papers, SWT*, IV, pp. 407-8.

Should the Congress invite the territory to join the Union? Should the President apprise Congress that the territory was now eligible for statehood? Should the territory simply apply for admission? Should the territory proceed to convert itself into a new state, organize state government, and present itself to Congress ready for admission, with constitution and elected officials in place?

Dr. James White believed that Congress would take no action regarding the sixteenth state until "we come forward with a petition for that purpose." White suggested that it would be proper to call a convention for the formation of the proposed government to take effect immediately after the congressional act of admission. Informal discussions between members of Congress and their friends in the territory had resulted in suggestions in 1794 that an act should be proposed to create the new state and bring it into the Union, but nothing was done.[28]

Blount and his political allies decided to establish the new state, adopt its constitution, elect its officials, and petition Congress to accept it on an equal basis with the other states. Under this plan, Congress would admit a state organized prior to the act of admission. It was an interesting prospect, and one that would not go unchallenged.

---

28. Knoxville *Gazette*, February 6, April 24, 1795; White to William Blount, March 19, 1795, James Robertson Papers.

Chapter XIII

THE PEOPLE AND THE LAND

1793-96

Although peace with the neighboring Indians was achieved only a few months before 1796, the year of statehood, the population of the territory increased twofold between 1791 and 1795. When faced on arrival with raids, killings, and thefts, many of the immigrants must have questioned their decision to cross into the disputed lands.

Yet the settlers—old and new—never wavered in their passion for becoming landowners. They surveyed, cleared, and improved the land, often with armed guards standing by. Many of them clustered in the towns of Nashville, Clarksville, Knoxville, Jonesborough, Rogersville, Blountville, and Greeneville. Some settled on larger tracts away from close neighbors and survived by stockading their places or, at times of distress, going to the nearest station to join others in defending themselves.

The vast majority of houses were built of logs using easily mastered techniques and the help of family and friends. House "raisings" were commonplace. General Sevier attended two separate raisings in Hamilton District on successive days in the summer of 1795.[1]

Although details are not available, several houses were built in Knoxville during the period 1793-96. A nearby sawmill and abundant clay taken from near the riverbanks provided lumber and hard bricks. By the latter part of the period, houses of frame construction and brick chimneys began to appear. They were built with the methods used earlier in constructing Governor Blount's residence[2] but on a more modest scale.

A "neat little box of a courthouse" was erected in Knoxville in 1793, and a prison and stocks were put up at the same time. Typical of others in the West, the courthouse was a square log pen with sides sixteen feet long. The floor was laid with two layers of squared logs, the top layer at right angles to the under layer. A loft was floored with thick

---

1. DeWitt, ed., "Journal of Governor John Sevier, 1790-1815," p. 178.
2. Patrick, *Architecture in Tennessee, 1768-1897*, p. 60.

oak planks, and the roof was made of wide boards spiked to the rafters.[3]

Even smaller log buildings were erected as jails in Knox and the other counties, but they drew protests from sheriffs. They were too small, and escape from them was too easy. In 1795 Sheriff George Gillespie of Washington County complained to the superior court that the county jail was "insufficient." During the same year, Sheriff George Conway of Greene County filed a similar complaint about the jail in Greeneville. And in 1796 Thomas Hardeman, sheriff of Davidson County, registered his second protest with the county court over the inadequacy of the jail at Nashville.[4]

For reasons not discovered, the Sumner County courthouse, crudely built of logs a few years before on West Station Camp Creek, was abandoned at the end of 1792. The quarterly court then began a practice that would continue nearly ten years; each session of court was held in the house of one of the magistrate members.[5]

At Greeneville, Thomas Alexander built a modest log house in 1795, later called "Antrim." A more commodious log house of two stories, set on a stone foundation, was erected by Valentine Sevier there in 1795. As was often the case with other larger log houses, the exterior walls of the building were later covered with wood clapboard.[6]

A few fine homes were erected despite the delays attending their construction. The building of Rock Castle, the plantation home of Secretary Daniel Smith on Drake's Creek in Sumner County, languished through the late 1780s and early 1790s before it was finished in 1795 or 1796. Beset with injuries to the chief mason when he was thrown from his horse, the failure of sawmill operators to produce lumber when needed, the poor quality of the shingles supplied, and the unsettling effects of frequent Indian raids into the area, construction of the large stone house proceeded by fits and starts. The pace of construction was slowed further by the frequent extended absence of the owner while he fulfilled his duties as secretary of the territory in Knoxville.[7]

---

3. Ibid., p. 6; Knoxville *Gazette*, April 6, 1793; Goodspeed, *History of Knox County*, p. 809.
4. WCR, Superior Court Minutes Book, 1791-1805, Roll 167, p. 68; Greene County, Tennessee Records, Quarterly Court Minutes, 1783-1796, Microfilm, Roll 10, TSLA, p. 402 (Greene County Records on microfilm at TSLA are hereinafter cited as GCR); DCR, Quarterly Court Minutes, Book B, 1791-1797, Roll 1597, Microfilm, TSLA, p. 314.
5. Durham, *The Great Leap Westward*, p. 67.
6. Doughty, *Greeneville, One Hundred Year Portrait, 1775-1875*, p. 271.
7. Durham, *Daniel Smith, Frontier Statesman*, pp. 191-93.

When completed, however, Rock Castle was probably the finest house in the new state. Although its architectural details were neither as elaborate nor as handsome as those embodied in some houses built soon after 1795, Rock Castle represented frontier architecture in transition. It bridged the gap between the houses hurriedly raised during the preceding decades and the buildings of a more permanent type that featured design and ornamentation reminiscent of the fine houses of Virginia and Maryland.[8]

Two other noteworthy houses were built about the same time. In 1794 Thomas Craighead erected Glen Echo, a two-story brick house, across the road from Spring Hill Meetinghouse in Davidson County. In 1795 Charles Elliott built a two-story stone house called Walnut Grove on a high bluff overlooking East Station Camp Creek in Sumner County.[9]

Notwithstanding the slow progress of construction measured in terms of commercial and residential structures of better quality, the land acquisition mania continued unabated. The larger speculators like William Blount, John Sevier, and Stockley Donelson understood that they could make good profits only with increased population in the territory. They understood, also, that peace with the Indians, by negotiation or by suppression, was necessary to attract settlers.

One of the first efforts to tell the story of the Southwest outside its area was embodied in *A Short Description of the Tennessee Government, or the Territory of the United States South of the River Ohio, To Accompany and Explain a Map of that Country*, a booklet published at Philadelphia by Mathew Carey in 1793. Authorship of the text is usually attributed to Daniel Smith.[10]

Using the surveys made by Smith, Carey published the first map of the territory in 1794 and called it "A Map of the Tennessee Government formerly Part of North Carolina." The booklet was distributed before the map was printed, but when the map became available, reprints of both appeared in gazetteers, geographies, and atlases and as separate

---

8. Ibid., p. 195.

9. Brandau, ed., *History of Homes and Gardens of Tennessee*, p. 151; Durham, *The Great Leap Westward*, p. 148.

10. Although unlikely, it may have been written by Hugh Williamson who put Smith's surveys together and turned them over to Carey to print. Williamson told Governor Blount in 1793 that he had written a description of the territory to be published by Carey. Keith, ed., *The John Gray Blount Papers*, Vol. II, pp. 300-301, 313.

pieces for several years thereafter in this country and abroad.[11]

Probably for the first time in public print, the Carey imprint spoke of making the homelands of the Chickasaw in the western extremity of the territory available for settlement. It suggested that the United States should purchase the entire area and pay the Chickasaw a price that would enable them to live in a reserved territory "in a degree of ease and affluence, which otherwise they can never expect."[12]

The Philadelphia *Gazette* contributed to the promotion in 1795 by featuring a long description of the Southwest Territory in its October 17 edition. Making lavish claims for the area, the *Gazette*'s correspondent said it was much more desirable as a place of residence than Kentucky or the Northwest Territory. There was no spot of ground in the well-watered country, he said, that was more than twenty miles from "boatable navigation" connecting southward to Natchez and New Orleans. The soil was fertile, and there was plenty of timber, salt, sugar, iron, lead, saltpeter, and copperas. It was, in short, a transmontane paradise.[13]

Letters and articles by citizens of the territory extolling its virtues to prospective settlers often appeared in the Knoxville *Gazette*. The only writer identified as a woman, Eliza Campbell, wrote of her family's "country seat" southwest of Knoxville near the confluence of the Tennessee and Holston rivers, Campbella. Rehearsing the advantages of "fertile meadows" and "streams of crystaline water," Eliza asserted that the climate was "extremely healthy." With peace at hand, she invited readers in faraway places to "come...and possess this beautiful region."[14]

Anxious to see faster growth in the population of the territory, William Blount and his brothers tried unsuccessfully to sell western land to European buyers. James C. Mountflorence, a native of France and an early settler at Nashville, had been the Blounts' agent in Paris since returning

---

11. Durham, *Daniel Smith, Frontier Statesman*, pp. 179-81. Governor Blount had encouraged Colonel William Tatham to compile a map of the territory and, at one time, understood that he had done so, but the project was never completed. To acquire materials for the map, Tatham had made a public call through the columns of the Knoxville *Gazette* on June 15, 1793. Keith, ed., *The John Gray Blount Papers*, Vol. II, p. 313; G. Malvin Herndon, *William Tatham, 1752-1819* (Johnson City, Tennessee: Research Advisory Council, East Tennessee State University, 1973), pp. 100-101.
12. [Smith], *A Short Description of the Tennessee Government*, p. 17.
13. Reprinted in Imlay, *A Topographical Description of the Western Territory*, pp. 525-26.
14. Knoxville *Gazette*, July 31, 1795.

there in 1791. His own ineptness combined with the turmoil of the French Revolution nullified his every effort, however. He claimed to have been on the verge of concluding several substantial sales when the revolutionary convention decreed that anyone who traveled outside the country would be banished.[15]

During the winter of 1795-96, he visited England to arouse interest there, but he failed to dispose of a single acre. It became a familiar story: Mountflorence was often at the threshold of success but something beyond his control always prevented his stepping across. John Gray Blount formally dismissed Mountflorence from their service by letter on March 18, 1796, and directed him to deliver the land grants in his possession to James Monroe, the United States Minister at Paris.[16]

The possibilities of interesting foreign investors in the western lands were in the dreams of many. In the spring of 1795, a prospective partner for the Blount brothers proposed to "lay out a large city two miles square, five lots to the acre" adjoining Knoxville. "Laid out upon some new and elegant plan...[and] handsomely delineated," the new city was to be called Palmyra. The proposal was advanced by Dr. Nicholas Romayne who expected to attract enough buyers from Europe to realize a net profit of about eighty thousand dollars. The project was not undertaken, however.[17]

Failure to make sales abroad seemed only to whet the Blounts' already insatiable appetite for trade in western lands. During the summer of 1794, William Blount platted out a tract of 95,370 acres in Hawkins County on Clinch River "between Powell's and Clark mountains." At once he dispatched the plat and "a good description...signed by respectable characters" to David Allison, his agent in Philadelphia, to offer it for sale. The fact that Blount had not yet obtained a grant did not concern him. "It is known as mine and will be so considered and not meddled with by anybody," he advised brother John Gray.[18]

Former clerk of the Superior Court of Mero District and later deputy paymaster for United States troops and the militia in the territory, Allison

---

15. Keith, ed., *The John Gray Blount Papers*, Vol. II, pp. 173-74, 174n; Keith, "Letters From Major James Cole Mountflorence," p. 267.

16. Keith, "Letters From Major James Cole Mountflorence," pp. 254, 270-75; Alice Barnwell Keith, ed., *The John Gray Blount Papers*, Vol. III (Raleigh, North Carolina: State Department of Archives and History, 1965), pp. 36-37, 36n, 80-81.

17. Keith, ed., *The John Gray Blount Papers*, Vol. II, pp. 534-35.

18. Ibid., pp. 416-17.

had begun to represent the Blounts' business interests at Philadelphia about 1793. In addition, during his first two years there, Allison joined William Blount in partnership land speculations in South Carolina, Arkansas, and the Southwest Territory. In 1795 he would become a partner in the Philadelphia mercantile firm of John B. Evans and Company, a supplier to merchants in the territory and elsewhere.[19]

Admitting Stockley Donelson to a partnership interest in another venture, the governor planned to add to the Blount holdings in the autumn by making "a sweeping survey between the Clinch and Holston so as to include the mouths of both of these rivers say at least 150,000 acres." Operations on such a scale set the Blounts and their associates apart from lesser speculators. In addition to large tract transactions, however, the brothers bought and sold numerous grants ranging in size from a few hundred to a few thousand acres.[20]

When the end of the Indian wars approached in 1795, the governor gave renewed attention to land in the Mero District. On April 20 he told John Gray to suspend sales of any of their properties in Mero and four days later counseled him "to purchase all the Cumberland lands you can." William Blount, heeding his own advice, increased his investment in Mero lands during the late summer and early autumn months.[21]

Probably no one was a partner in more real estate ventures than Stockley Donelson. As district surveyor, he was privy to all surveys made for grants, and in many instances, he made the surveys in the field. His fees were usually paid by conveying to him a portion of the tract surveyed or by making him a partner in the ownership of the land. In his capacity as surveyor of warrants granted to the Continental Line of North Carolina and surveyor of the Western District, he was perhaps the person most knowledgeable about land opportunities and probably the largest landowner in the entire territory.[22]

When Stockley Donelson sought a partner, he looked in high places. On June 12, 1794, he and Martin Armstrong invited James Glasgow,

---

19. That relationship quickly led to Allison's financial ruin; bankruptcy would overtake him in 1797. Sent to a Philadelphia debtors' prison, he died there September 30, 1798. Smith and Owsley, eds., *The Papers of Andrew Jackson, 1770-1803,* Vol. I, p. 58n.
20. Keith, ed., *The John Gray Blount Papers,* Vol II, pp. 396, 415, 417.
21. Ibid., pp. 535-36, 595.
22. Knoxville *Gazette,* April 24, 1795; Kincaid, ed., "History of the Southwest Territory, 1790-1796, by Samuel Cole Williams," pp. 127-28.

secretary of state of North Carolina, to become a partner with them in buying, assembling, and selling a large tract of land. Seeking to buy "military and state land warrants" such as would cover a tract of sixty thousand acres, Donelson and Armstrong assured Glasgow that their undertaking was sound. They promised to discuss the matter face-to-face with him soon, but in the meantime "we keep these matters... secret, nor does the right hand know what the left is doing."[23]

Throughout the years of the territory, John Sevier, Sr., invested heavily in land in the valley of the Cumberland. One such investment was made in October, 1795, when Stockley Donelson surveyed and combined the land represented by 36 warrants into a single tract of 32,000 acres for Sevier on the Cumberland River in Sumner County. Donelson located the parcel so that it adjoined another tract of 25,000 acres that had been surveyed previously for Sevier. He assured Sevier that the location did not include any lands for which grants had been issued.[24]

On another occasion, Sevier sent George Gordon to the North Carolina secretary of state to deliver 150 land warrants each for 640 acres and to receive in exchange a patent representing the total of 96,000 acres. The land was "to be laid on each side of the Cumberland [River] near the mouth of Obed River." Were these lands part of the warrants covering 128,000 acres that he and Landon Carter had owned as partners since 1792? The answer is uncertain because when the partners obtained titles, none was taken in Carter's name, some were in Sevier's, and many in the names of persons they thought "fit...to receive them" in behalf of the partners. Sevier engaged, also, in numerous smaller transactions.[25]

Although the risk was high, the prospect of amassing quick fortunes through land speculation was an ever-present temptation on the frontier. In the Mero District two young attorneys, John Overton and Andrew Jackson, entered into a formal partnership on May 12, 1794, "for the purpose of purchasing lands as well those lands without as within the military bounds." Theirs was a frank avowal; they, like many of their contemporaries, would deal in lands within Indian territory. Most of

---

23. Armstrong and Donelson to Glasgow, June 12, 1794, Coffee Papers, Dyas Collection, TSLA.
24. These 57,000 acres were located in the area that became Jackson County in 1801. Survey by Stockley Donelson for John Sevier, Sr., October 25, 1795, John Sevier Papers, McClung Collection.
25. DeWitt, "Journal of Governor John Sevier, 1790-1815," p. 178; Driver, *John Sevier, Pioneer of the Old Southwest*, pp. 68-69.

the transactions involved grants made under the "land grab" act of 1783 that briefly opened to claim by North Carolinians all of the Indian lands in that state's transmontane west. While the act was in force, citizens had staked claims to two or three million acres of Chickasaw and Cherokee land.[26]

As an individual proprietor, John Overton already owned several tracts in the Chickasaw Nation at the Chickasaw Bluffs and along the Hatchee River. He actively sought to sell them with the help of an agent at Philadelphia in 1794 and 1795. Other lands may have been in his inventory as well, as is indicated by his sending grants totaling 50,000 acres to the agent on February 17, 1795. Since George Roulstone at Knoxville was to forward the documents to Philadelphia, Overton reminded him of "that important rule in business, *secrecy* and *dispatch.*"[27]

Overton later sold partnership interests in a tract he had acquired during this period to Andrew Jackson and James Winchester. Containing 5,000 acres and known as the John Rice grant, it became the site of the city of Memphis, laid out and promoted by Overton and Winchester in 1819.[28]

Jackson was, in addition, a partner of Henry Bradford, a deputy surveyor with whom he sent plats of discoveries for 150,000 acres to Stockley Donelson on June 9, 1795. Donelson was to sell the land for them, retaining the customary one-fourth for his services.[29]

The excitement about land was evident on every side. The Knoxville *Gazette* of March 27, 1794, displayed a list of Mero District grants recently issued by the secretary of state of North Carolina and awaiting the grantees at Captain Stone's in the territorial capital. The documents had just arrived from North Carolina, brought by William Terrell. There were 55 grants in Davidson County, 47 in Sumner County, and 35 in Tennessee County. Conspicuously absent from the roll of grantees were the names of Blount, Donelson, Sevier, Robertson, Overton, and Jackson.

The land market in the territory was undergirded by agriculture. Most settlers wanted their own land from which they could support their

---

26. Smith and Owsley, eds., *The Papers of Andrew Jackson, 1770-1803*, Vol. I, pp. 47-48, 48n.
27. Overton to J. Grant, October 18, 20, November 8, 1794; Overton to Roulstone, February 17, 1795, Claybrooke and Overton Papers.
28. Durham, *James Winchester, Tennessee Pioneer*, pp. 220-24.
29. Smith and Owsley, eds., *The Papers of Andrew Jackson, 1770-1803*, Vol. I, p. 59.

families, and they planned to live on it. There was not much interest manifest in farm villages where the owners of farmland would live among close neighbors for the pleasure and security of it. Land tracts suitable for farming were the parcels for which there was the readiest market.

Farmers produced corn, wheat, oats, barley, peas, beans, both Irish and sweet potatoes, flax, hemp, indigo, tobacco, cotton, rice, and green vegetables. A portion of almost every farm was devoted to poultry, including geese and ducks, milk cows, hogs, livestock, and sheep. Apple, pear, and peach orchards were often planted, and many farmers kept beehives.[30]

The breeding and raising of horses was a significant activity. The services at stud of stallions with names such as Chatham, Laburnum, Brilliant, Rainbow, and Raven were advertised periodically in the *Gazette*. Perhaps typical of the owners was Charles Gilliam, the owner of Rainbow, who stood the stallion at his plantation near the confluence of the Holston and French Broad rivers, offering stud services for twenty shillings for the season. He offered "ferriage gratis to any person bringing mares" to his horse.[31]

Vitally important to the development and operation of farms was the availability of cheap labor. To fill that need, farmers employed black slaves in ever-increasing number, bringing them in as needed from Virginia and the Carolinas. A typical acquisition of slaves was made by Joseph Greer who bought a young single man and a man with a wife and five children at Petersburg, Virginia, and brought them to the territory in 1795.[32]

Sometimes slave owners did not have enough work to employ all of their slaves and, in that case, leased their services to others. In his journal for 1795, John Sevier noted the locations of slaves that he had leased to others.[33]

In Davidson County William T. Lewis leased Hercules, a slave cabinetmaker, to David Hay for twelve months for twenty-five pounds Virginia currency payable in corn at two shillings per bushel and "in making a complete and workman like desk and bookcase with sashes,

---

30. [Smith], *A Short Description of the Tennassee Government*, p. 8; DeWitt, ed., "Journal of Governor John Sevier, 1790-1815," p. 180.
31. Knoxville *Gazette*, January 16, February 13, 27, March 27, May 8, 1794.
32. Bill of sale, November 27, 1795, Joseph Greer Papers, TSLA.
33. DeWitt, ed., "The Journal of Governor John Sevier, 1790-1815," p. 182.

and three cherry bedsteads." Hay agreed to keep Hercules "constant at the carpenter's trade" except for a fortnight in the corn field so that Lewis would not suffer the loss of Hercules' valuable skills.[34]

As slaves were valuable chattels, owners were invariably alarmed when one ran away. A newspaper advertisement appealing for the apprehension of the runaway usually appeared soon after the escape. Three ran away from James Richardson at Southwest Point on April 10, 1795.

> Ranaway...two negro men and a negro woman. One of the men called Dave is about 36 years old, 6 feet high, very black, a very likely active fellow.... Bob, about 38 years of age, yellow complexion, inclined to be corpulent.... The woman is named Pegg, pock marked...and about forty years of age. Whoever takes up said negroes, or either of them, and delivers...or secures them, shall be generously rewarded for their trouble.[35]

Often escapees were apprehended by white citizens who printed notices that they had "taken up" a runaway, giving a description of the person and such information as they could obtain from him. Alexander Carmichael of Knoxville advertised:

> Taken up, as a run-away, at Connor's Creek block house, on the 14th instant, a negro fellow who calls himself Jemmy. He had with him a horse, and was making for Cumberland to his master Joseph Davis, who he says, left him with one John Hayes on Holston. Said negro is about five feet seven inches high, about 35 years old; has a scar in his forehead.... His owner is desired to come prove his property, pay charges and take him away.[36]

Most sales and purchases of slaves were privately negotiated between white buyers and sellers. Often, however, prospective sellers would advertise for buyers. When slaves with special skills or capabilities were offered, the owner could expect a prompt response in the market place. George Roulstone inserted this notice in his newspaper in 1794.

---

34. Davidson County, Tennessee, Records, Minutes of the Superior Court of North Carolina Including Mero District, 1788-1803, Part I, 1788-1798, Historical Records Project, Works Progress Administration, May 16, 1938, TSLA, p. 183.
35. Knoxville *Gazette*, April 24, 1795.
36. Ibid., March 27, 1795.

> For Sale
> A LIKELY NEGRO FELLOW
> about twenty-four years of age, healthy and sound, who understands all kinds of farming business.—For terms apply to
> G. Roulstone and Co.[37]

When interest lagged in the Greeneville Lottery in 1794, the managers added prizes to attract attention. Prominent on the list were "two prime likely Negroes," Joe and Luce, the property of Joseph Dunham valued at ninety-five pounds sterling each.[38]

On another occasion, three slave girls between the ages of twelve and twenty-five were pledged as security for a bond posted by their owner. If their owner did not pay in due time a debt of three hundred pounds "good money," he would be forced to deliver the girls to his creditor.[39]

Notwithstanding their value as chattels, slaves were sometimes set free. A highly regarded black woman at Nashville, Nelly, purchased her freedom from her owner William Taitt for one hundred dollars. The agreement specified that she could not become a slave again but must remain forever free.[40]

Slaves did not often appear as defendants in criminal court cases. An exception to this rule was Dick who was charged with burning James Bosley's barn near Nashville on July 22, 1793. Convicted on strong circumstantial evidence provided by nine white and three black witnesses, Dick was sentenced to the same punishment usually given to horse thieves. He received fifty lashes on his bare back and lost both ears to the sheriff's knife.[41]

Skilled labor was supplied in some instances by young white men who had learned their trades by serving stipulated periods of apprenticeship. In 1794 the Knoxville newspaper office sought a well-recommended fourteen- or fifteen-year-old "lad" as an apprentice to the printing business. Quarterly court records refer to binding out orphan children both male and female as apprentices, usually until they reached

---

37. Ibid., June 19, 1794.
38. Ibid.
39. Davidson County Records, Minutes of the Superior Court of North Carolina Including Mero District, 1788-1803, Part I, 1788-1798, p. 117.
40. DCR, Wills and Inventories, Vol. II, 1794-1805, Roll 427, p. 32.
41. DCR, Quarterly Court Minutes, Book B, 1791-1797, Roll 1597, pp. 119-21.

their twenty-first birthday.[42] That not all apprentices performed their tasks satisfactorily was demonstrated in a scathing denunciation of a runaway published in a reward notice in 1793. It offered a reward of one penny to anyone who would bring the "rogue" home. Characterizing the sixteen-year-old boy as "*young* in age but *old* in iniquity; *small* in stature, but a *great* scoundrel," the notice alleged that he was guilty of "every . . . practice annexed to infamy." It concluded that he, John Hutchinson, was a "*candidate for the gallows.*"[43]

---

42. Knoxville *Gazette*, March 27, 1794; DCR, Quarterly Court Minutes, Book B, 1791-1797, Roll 1597, pp. 93, 238; KCR, Quarterly Court Minutes, Book O, pp. 127, 137, 148.

43. Knoxville *Gazette*, September 14, 1793.

CHAPTER XIV

COMMERCE, TRADE, AND TRAVEL
1793-96

The growing population of the territory resulted in increased trade and commerce. That was nowhere more evident than in the proliferation and growth of mercantile establishments, nearly all of which were operated by single proprietors or partnerships. Although there was an obvious need for household and farm supplies that could not be furnished by local producers, merchants had problems sustaining profit enough to survive. With much of their business done by exchanging goods imported from Philadelphia or Baltimore for farm produce, hides, skins, pelts, and other local products, the merchants often experienced difficulty when trading frontier produce for their next shipment of merchandise. To make sales in the first place, merchants often had to extend credit for long periods of time and, inevitably, losses followed.

The prospects of success seemed always good enough to attract new venturers when others failed or withdrew from the market or when increases in population suggested additional merchants could be supported. A partnership, John Summerville and Company, established in 1792 on German Creek, enlarged its operation the next year by opening a store in Knoxville, across the street from the governor's office, and setting up another at Henry's station on Nine Mile. In a newspaper advertisement appearing January 26, 1793, Summerville promised "a large and general assortment of winter goods" would be offered beginning in February. He would sell merchandise in exchange for "bear and deer skins, furs of all kinds, bees wax, etc." At the same time, he offered to purchase linsey, seven hundred linen, and "public securities of every denomination, that are or may be issued for the protection of the frontiers of the Territory."[1]

The Summerville partnership was dissolved in October, 1793, but John Summerville, proprietor, reopened at the same stand in Knoxville a few weeks later. Trying to avoid the hazards of extending credit,

---

1. Knoxville *Gazette*, January 12, 26, March 9, 1793.

Summerville closed his store one day in the spring of 1794 and reopened the next as "John Summerville's Cheap Ready Money Store, where no credit whatever will be given." He would sell for cash or the usual pelts and farm produce, but he would not accept deferred payment.[2]

The results of the merchant's change to the "Cheap Ready Money" concept are not certainly known. At best, they must not have been overwhelmingly favorable. In November, 1794, he closed the store and quit the mercantile business in Knoxville.[3]

After closing the store, Summerville was employed by the partners William Blount and Stockley Donelson to operate a mercantile and land speculation business for them at Raleigh, North Carolina, under the firm name of John Summerville and Company. The Raleigh location was chosen as the best place "to purchase military and other lands," the principal "objects" of the company. The names of the partners did not appear in the company name because they did not want to be identified publicly with it.[4]

David Deaderick maintained stores at Jonesborough and Greeneville. About December 1, 1793, he returned from Baltimore with a sizeable assortment of merchandise for both stores that he would barter for skins, furs, beeswax, and flax. He offered to pay cash for skins of the otter, black fox, wild cat, mink, and muskrat. By midsummer of the next year, Deaderick had imported goods from Philadelphia.[5]

The opening of a shipment of goods from Baltimore by Robert Wyly in Greeneville illustrates many of the mercantile operations of the period. Although he had sold merchandise previously in Greeneville, he liquidated each shipment and had no remaining stock until the new order arrived. The intervals between his sales were long enough that he apparently had no storehouse, but rented space when receipt of goods was imminent. Giving notice of the arrival of his merchandise, Wyly said that it was being opened at his store, "the house formerly occupied by Mr. John Hacker." He solicited the return of his former customers, declaring that he would sell for cash or bear and deer skins, furs of all kinds, flax, and beeswax.[6]

---

2. Ibid., December 7, 1793; March 13, 1794.
3. Ibid., December 26, 1794.
4. Keith, ed., *The John Gray Blount Papers*, Vol. II, pp. 596, 597-98.
5. Knoxville *Gazette*, December 7, 1793; June 19, 1794.
6. Ibid., December 7, 1795.

James Ore announced on March 27, 1794, that he was opening a new store in Knoxville at No. 23 and the corner of State Street. He would continue his store business located on German Creek as he expanded operations to Knoxville. In addition to the usual produce accepted in trade, Ore would take "hogs lard in white walnut kegs, butter, pork...new feathers, [and] a few good horses."[7]

Ore's store on German Creek incorporated a blacksmith's shop in its operation as it was a gathering place for travelers about to go through the wilderness to Kentucky. During the autumn of 1794, departures to Kentucky from Ore's store were scheduled about twice each month.[8]

Ore often accepted militia discharges in lieu of cash for his merchandise, holding the certificates until the paymaster for the War Department received funds to pay the men for their respective terms of service. When, in 1795, the agent for the War Department at Knoxville still had not received money for tours of duty originating as early as 1792, Ore called on the militiamen who owed him "to come forward and settle their respective sums." He offered to take good merchantable beef cattle as payment.[9]

Another business, the Bent Creek Store operated by Patrick Nenney, closed its books on Bent Creek and relocated and reopened on a plantation a few miles distant. Periodically James and Samuel Miller received and sold Philadelphia merchandise at Knoxville.[10]

The mercantile firm of Stephen Duncan and Company, located adjoining Captain John Wood's at Knoxville, featured dry goods and groceries. On January 1, 1794, Charles McClung, a protégé of Governor Blount, displayed a new shipment of goods at his store on State Street, and in the summer of that year Edward McFarling opened shipments of dry goods and groceries at the "fording of Big Pigeon."[11]

Nathaniel and Samuel Cowan's stores at Jonesborough and Knoxville seemed to prosper during the 1790s. Like other merchants, the Cowans experienced difficulties getting possession of military discharges assigned to them until the soldiers were paid. In 1793 they gave notice

---

7. Ibid., March 27, 1794.
8. Ibid., August 25, 1794.
9. Ibid., July 17, 1795.
10. Ibid., May 18, 1793; March 27, 1794.
11. Ibid., December 19, 1793; January 2, April 10, May 8, 1794.

that they would hold militia captains responsible for delivery of the discharges with a lawful power of attorney, citing the captains' practice of standing as security for soldiers' purchases until their pay came down from the War Department.[12]

The partners King and Crozier imported soft goods, hardware, and miscellaneous articles including cutlery, bar iron, iron castings, groceries, saddles and bridles, books and stationery, window glass, nails, pottery, glassware, Irish linens, gunpowder, chocolate, teas, and spices. They sold their goods at Captain John Stone's in Knoxville for cash or various skins, furs, and farm produce.[13]

Tavern keeper James Armstrong of Abingdon, Virginia, doubled for a while as a merchant in the lower Holston country. His last shipment of goods was opened in June, 1795, at Evans's Ferry about fifteen miles from Knoxville, after which time he quit the mercantile business.[14]

The merchant Titus Ogden, who was virtually a ward of William Blount, sold general merchandise ranging from law books to iron castings. In February, 1793, he advertised "a few copies" of the 1791 revised edition of *Laws of the State of North Carolina Published According to Act of Assembly by James Iredell Now One of the Associate Justices of the Supreme Court of the United States* and Francois Xavier Martin's book that would be published the following year, *A Treatise on the Jurisdiction of Justices of the Peace in Civil Suits According to the Laws of the State of North Carolina*. Three months later he had kettles, pots, Dutch ovens, skillets, "sod irons and fire dogs." After Ogden's death in the summer of 1793, Blount characterized him as "only a nominal merchant though he appeared to be a man of much business."[15]

Another of Blount's men, John Chisholm, often busy with matters of government, understood that there was no credit risk in doing business with the War Department. He was a bidder to supply rations to troops on duty in the Southwest Territory in 1794.[16]

Records are less clear about the mercantile business in Mero District. In 1793, James Winchester brought two separate shipments to his

---

12. Ibid., March 9, April 6, May 4, 1793; February 13, March 27, 1794.
13. Ibid., March 27, May 22, July 3, 1795.
14. Ibid., June 19, 1795.
15. Ibid., February 23, May 18, 1793; Keith, ed., *The John Gray Blount Papers*, Vol. II, pp. 121, 325.
16. John Chisholm to David Henley, October 31, 1794, David Henley Papers, 1748-1823.

Cragfont plantation from Philadelphia. They were among the first sizeable stocks of assorted goods shipped into the district.[17]

At Nashville, George M. and John Deaderick; Seth Lewis, Howell Tatum, and Robert Searcy; William Taitt; Sampson Williams; William Black; and John Edgar and Company engaged separately in the mercantile trade. Williams, Lewis and his associates, and the Deadericks competed as suppliers of materials purchased by the government for the Chickasaw and Choctaw. Williams and the Deadericks curried favor with Indian agent James Robertson by selling him his needs at "a reduction over going market prices," but neither won the contract; the business was divided among all the merchants of Nashville. Black obtained merchandise wherever it was available. On at least one occasion, he bought a variety of items offered at an estate sale including beds, tables, dishes, saddles, pots and pans, horses, cows, and hogs.[18]

In August, 1795, Andrew Jackson and David Allison of Philadelphia bought an assortment of merchandise and shipped it to Nashville. Although the exact contents are not known, an account of the freight expenses shows that the lot was made of a shipment from Philadelphia and another from Baltimore. Both were transported overland to Pittsburgh and then sent by riverboat to Limestone, a port on the Ohio. At that point Jackson's young brother-in-law and law partner Samuel Donelson met the boat and brought the goods "around to Nashville."[19]

The merchandise was offered for sale in Jackson's first store, operated with Samuel Donelson, at Nashville. Entries in the store's account book, made between August 6 and September 3, 1795, show sales of shoes, hats, writing paper, coffee, linen, silk, thread, calico, muslin, ribbon, knives, loaf sugar, wine, chocolate, spices, tea, raisins, bridles, teakettles, books, cigars, needles, buttons, cotton hose, spoons, pans, and saddles.[20]

From 1792 to 1794, a series of financial reverses reduced the operations of Lardner Clark, Nashville merchant and tavern keeper since 1784, to a shambles. Forced to sell his house, Clark left the city in 1794 to

---

17. Durham, *James Winchester, Tennessee Pioneer*, pp. 38, 39.
18. Deposition of Sampson Williams, July 7, 1795, Seth Lewis to David Henley, May 5, 1795, David Henley Papers, 1748-1823; "War Department Collection of Post Revolutionary War Manuscripts, Territory Southwest of Ohio River," National Archives, Record Group 94, M-904, Roll 4, p. 335; DCR, Quarterly Court Minutes, Roll 1603, pp. 109, 189; DCR, Wills and Inventories, Vol. II, 1794-1805, pp. 15, 32.
19. Smith and Owsley, eds., *The Papers of Andrew Jackson, 1770-1803*, Vol. I, p. 58.
20. Ibid., pp. 455-76.

seek a new beginning in the Northwest Territory. He died there in 1801.[21]

The growing population needed processors as well as purveyors of goods. The demand for leather for shoes, saddles, and harnesses invited several into tanning. Peter McNamee opened a tanyard at Knoxville on Second Creek in June, 1793, employing "an excellent good workman from the northward." Adam Peck opened a tannery at his plantation on Mossy Creek near Perkins's ironworks. Both tanned on shares. Nathaniel Cowan, a partner in the mercantile firm of Nathaniel and Samuel Cowan, announced in the spring of 1794 that he would open a tanning business in the ensuing autumn. He advertised to buy chestnut and oak bark by the cord delivered to the northeast side of the creek, opposite the town spring of Knoxville. He would pay twelve shillings per cord for chestnut and ten shillings for oak bark in cash or store goods.[22]

Succeeding the partnership of Lard and McCoy formed the year before, Stephen Duncan and David Lard opened a tanyard in Knoxville on Second Creek in 1794 where they offered "tanning and currying" services. They were paid by taking one-half of the hides brought for treatment. They also purchased hides for their own use and produced leather from them that they sold to make shoes, saddles, and bridles. By January, 1795, Duncan and Lard were making shoes. Soon thereafter, they were probably the promoters of the saddler's shop opened by John and Robert Hunter in Stephen Duncan's storehouse. Advertising "a quantity of good Liverpool salt" for sale at their shop to attract customers, the Hunters said they would accept beef cattle and public securities in payment for their products and other goods.[23]

Only a few silversmiths and cabinetmakers appeared during the territorial years, and records of their work are rarely discovered. George Bean, son of the legendary first settler of North Carolina's western lands, offered his services as a silversmith in 1792. His shop was on German Creek in Hawkins County. William A. Atkinson worked as a silversmith at Jonesborough about 1793, and John Sapp opened a shop in Knoxville in 1795 to "carry on all kinds of work in gold and silver," including

---

21. W.A. Provine, "Lardner Clark, Nashville's First Merchant and Foremost Citizen," *Tennessee Historical Magazine,* Vol. III, Nos. 1 and 2 (March and June 1917), pp. 44, 50, 121, 123-25.
22. Knoxville *Gazette,* April 20, June 15, 1793; March 27, 1794.
23. Ibid., July 13, 1793; April 10, 1794; January 23, June 15, 1795.

plating on iron, steel, brass, and copper. George Hopkins, a chair maker of Greene County, and Thomas Murray, a cabinetmaker of Sumner, were only two of an otherwise unknown but sizeable number who made furniture between 1790 and 1796.[24]

Iron castings made at the foundries and furnaces of the upper Holston River region quickly found their way into Knoxville and Nashville. Along with other merchants at Knoxville, Alexander Carmichael had bar iron and castings "of every kind, well assorted" for sale in 1793 for cash, country linen, or linsey. By the summer of 1795, riverboats were moving shipments of castings to both Nashville and New Orleans. "Commanded" by Alexander Moore, four boats of about fifteen tons each left Knoxville bound for Nashville on June 14, 1795, "loaded with bar and cast iron, and a variety of articles belonging to the inhabitants of Mero District, which from their bulk or weight could not be transported through the wilderness." On the same day, Rawleigh Hogan pushed off a boat of twenty tons "burthen," loaded with "bar and cast iron, whiskey, bacon, lime, and many other...products of this country."[25]

The iron industry in the eastern district had grown slowly from 1792 to 1795. New works appeared at Mossy Creek and Beaver Creek, and the John Seviers, father and son, joined Walter King to open at Pactolus in Sullivan County. The fever even spread to the Cumberland where James Robertson had already begun to develop an iron furnace and forge when Governor Blount attempted to discourage him from the undertaking. Acting as if the project were beyond Robertson's ability to develop, Blount noted that at least ten thousand dollars would be required to make it operational. He pointedly remarked to Robertson that he planned to "raise a company" to erect an ironworks in the Cumberland country as soon as circumstances would admit of success. But the governor's advice was for naught. Robertson put his works in operation without Blount's assistance.[26]

In 1795 Governor Blount, who had previously explored the possibility of joining Colonel Thomas King in ownership of a bloomery near

---

24. Ibid., October 6, 1792; January 9, 1795; Benjamin Hubbard Caldwell, Jr., *Tennessee Silversmiths* (Winston-Salem, North Carolina: The Museum of Early Southern Decorative Arts, 1988), p. 28; Derita Coleman Williams and Nathan Harsh, *The Art and Mystery of Tennessee Furniture and Its Makers Through 1850*, ed. C. Tracey Parks (Nashville: Tennessee Historical Society and Tennessee State Museum Foundation, 1988), pp. 294, 306.

25. Knoxville *Gazette*, April 3, 1793; June 19, 1795.

26. Holt, "The Economic and Social Beginnings of Tennessee," p. 204; Williams, "Early Iron Works in the Tennessee Country," pp. 44-45.

Blountville, became interested in a slitting mill and a nail factory, both of which would draw their raw material from that and other bloomeries in the area. He had been inspired by Thomas Hart's report of financial success with a nail factory at Lexington, Kentucky.[27]

Among the basic needs of frontier settlers was access to a grain mill that could grind corn and wheat as well as foodstuffs for their poultry and farm animals. Most mills were driven by water power, but smaller grinding facilities sometimes drew their power from beasts of burden, mules, horses, or oxen. The water-powered mills often included sawmills for producing lumber and squared timbers. Every stream with a year-round flow had at least one good mill seat and often more. In 1795 alone, the quarterly court of Blount County approved the locations for eight new mills and Washington County authorized four. Between 1793 and 1796, Greene County approved seven; Jefferson County, five; Davidson, eight; and Sumner, four.[28]

Mill dams, necessary to hold water in reserve to supply mill race flows to the wheel, often impaired water supplies downstream, especially at dry times of the year. Was this issue, riparian rights, behind action taken by the Knox County Quarterly Court on November 6, 1793?

> On petition of sundry, the inhabitants of Knoxville, it is ordered that the upper mill dam of James White be broken *down,* against the first day of July next, and that the petition of James McCullough for liberty to build a mill on Second Creek be not granted.[29]

Vital supplies such as lead and powder could be had through the merchants periodically, but both were available at the lead mines on the French Broad River in Jefferson County. Customers could make purchases with "cash or country produce."[30]

The growth of the territorial capital meant men required clothing made

---

27. Keith, ed., *The John Gray Blount Papers,* Vol. II, pp. 521-22, 535.
28. Blount County, Tennessee, Records, Quarterly Court Minutes, 1795-1818, Microfilm, Roll 101, TSLA, pp. 3, 4, 5, 9, 10, 12, 14, 16; WCR, Quarterly Court Minutes, pp. 523, 537, 539, 557; Jefferson County, Tennessee, Records, Quarterly Court Minutes, 1792-1798, Microfilm, Roll 25, TSLA, pp. 6, 10, 17, 49, 79, (Jefferson County Records on microfilm at TSLA are hereinafter cited as JCR); GCR, Quarterly Court Minutes, pp. 285, 293, 347, 354, 410, 428; DCR, Quarterly Court Minutes, Book B, Roll 1597, pp. 71, 104, 133, 141, 277, 317, 319; Sumner County, Tennessee, Records, Quarterly Court Minutes, 1787-1796, Microfilm, Roll 327, TSLA, pp. 59, 60, 66, 74 (Sumner County Records on microfilm at TSLA are hereinafter cited as SCR). Records for the other counties unavailable.
29. KCR, Quarterly Court Minutes, Book O, p. 89.
30. Knoxville *Gazette,* June 15, 1793.

outside the home. A Knoxville tailor, Joseph West, advertised to hire two journeymen tailors in 1794.[31]

Throughout the territory the needs of travelers were furnished by the rise of hostelries and eating houses known variously as taverns, houses of entertainment, public houses, and ordinaries. The first three categories usually provided food, drink, and lodging for the traveler and grain, fodder, and pasturage for his horse. The latter usually offered only food and drink.

The ordinaries were as various as their keepers. Most were kept for the convenience of passersby, and advertising was by word of mouth. Others were opened to serve specific needs. When the county court of Sumner County began to hold sessions at the residence of Ezekiel Douglass, one of its members, he sought and was granted a license to keep an ordinary. His food service was patronized by some of the lawyers, jurors, and many citizens who had lawsuits or other business to be conducted during the court sessions.[32]

Some of the larger establishments advertised occasionally in the *Gazette*. Readers learned in the spring of 1794 that John Chisholm had opened a house of entertainment at No. 17 State Street in Knoxville with "boarding...by the quarter, half year or year, on the usual terms," and that Alexander Carmichael's house of entertainment, closed by the proprietor, had been reopened by William McNutt and John Hiltebrand. They offered the traveler "boarding by the week" and all kinds of liquor; for his horse there were corn, fodder, hay, and oats. The *Gazette*'s subscribers read, also, that Alexander Purdom had opened a tavern in Greeneville.[33]

Travelers' needs were provided at Nashville, too. There the Big House Tavern, owned by Howell Tatum, offered food, drink, and lodging in 1794.[34]

Probably the largest hostelry in the territory, the Nashville Inn, was opened in the latter part of 1795 or the first part of 1796 by William T. Lewis. Located on the public square of Nashville, the inn became a favorite stopping place for visiting politicians and businessmen for the next half century. In 1793 the county court had canceled Lewis's

---

31. Ibid., August 27, 1793; July 3, 1794.
32. SCR, Quarterly Court Minutes, 1787-1796, p. 62.
33. Knoxville *Gazette*, January 30, April 10, 1794; March 27, 1795.
34. DCR, Quarterly Court Minutes, Book B, Roll 1597, p. 143.

license to keep an ordinary after strong representations by attorneys John Overton and Andrew Jackson who stated that they appeared "only for the good of society." The subsequent issuance of a license to Joel Lewis suggests that a way had been found to circumvent the attorneys' objections. On January 16, 1795, the court granted a license to keep an ordinary to William T. Lewis and renewed it the year following.[35]

While the magistrates were slapping Lewis on the wrist, they willingly granted a permit to "a certain Negro called Bob" to sell liquor and victuals "on his good behavior." After Bob built a house on public ground next to the courthouse, the court voted to permit him to continue his business there.[36]

Although records of tavern operations are virtually nonexistent for the period, the minutes of the Washington County Quarterly Court for 1795 mention five taverns licensed for Jonesborough and another for a location elsewhere in the county. The licenses for Jonesborough were issued to Joseph Sevier, John Adams, Thomas Miller, Gabriel Blackburn, and John Waddell. The other went to James Carmichael.[37]

County courts regulated charges made at houses of entertainment, public houses, taverns, and ordinaries. On January 26, 1793, these rates were set for Knox County:

Diet	16 cents	Rum 1/2 Pint	16 cents
Corn per gallon	10 cents	Wine 1/2 pint	16 cents
Oats per gallon	10 cents	Beer qt.	8 cents
Fodder per bundle	3 cents	Cider qt.	8 cents
whiskey 1/2 pint	8 cents	Lodging per night	6 cents
brandy 1/2 pint	12 cents	Pasturage per day	8 cents[38]

The demand for merchandise and services on the frontier was not always supported by buying power. Merchants were especially vulnerable, and the demise of some was an ongoing phenomenon. When a merchant's customers were unable to pay him, he was unable to pay his suppliers in Baltimore or Philadelphia.

Faced with the failure of his Philadelphia partnership with John B.

---

35. John Egerton, *Nashville: The Faces of Two Centuries, 1780-1980* (Nashville: Plus Media, Incorporated, 1979), p. 47; DCR, Quarterly Court Minutes, Book B, Roll 1597, pp. 133, 243, 315.
36. DCR, Quarterly Court Minutes, Book B, Roll 1597, pp. 150, 203.
37. WCR, Quarterly Court Minutes, pp. 524, 545, 547, 558, 566, 578.
38. KCR, Quarterly Court Minutes, Book O, p. 37.

Evans, David Allison bitterly blamed the merchants of the Southwest Territory for much of his financial distress. When William Blount canvassed and reported the bleak prospects of payment from his accounts in the territory, Allison was outraged. Offered "a pittance" at best, he asked, "Is it possible they are so ignorant of address in business or have they an intention to ruin me that they may rise on my downfall?"

Allison said the merchants had dug their own financial graves by trying to "undersell each other and weekly advertise, at an expense, that they are still lowering their price." Frustrated because they did not promise future payment or explain why payment had been delayed, Allison was deeply disturbed. He could not accept their indifference to his plight. In a letter to Blount he exploded, "I have often and do now say, *God damn them all.*"[39]

News of Allison's collapse was received with apprehension. John Overton of Nashville learned the news on December 10 and relayed it by letter to Colonel Henley at Knoxville, correctly predicting that Allison's fall would cause financial reverses for many in the territory. Although some of the merchant debtors might be relieved of their obligations to Allison, many individuals in the area were owed large sums by the Philadelphia firm, primarily for land. Overton was convinced that Governor Blount had played a significant role in the Allison and Evans debacle. "All I can wish (and God forgive me for it) to complete the scene is that Blount, the *primum mobile,* may break, too," he wrote. "That he is broke in *credit* with all the world, except a few, is certain."[40]

There was no more important element in the commerce and politics of the day than travel; people and goods required movement through space for myriad reasons. Some of the most frequently encountered obstacles were streams of such depth, width, and/or current that they could not be forded. It followed that a vital link in overland travel was ferriage. With most transportation centered on beasts of burden, crossing the larger streams during all but the driest months was virtually impossible without a ferry. Andrew Evans operated a ferry at his plantation not far from Knoxville on the French Broad River for several months, and William McBee maintained a ferry across the Holston River

---

39. Allison to William Blount, January 4, 1795, Blount Family Papers, 1794-1829, Historic New Orleans Collection.
40. Overton to Henley, December 10, 1795, David Henley Papers, 1748-1823.

on the main road leading southward to Knoxville. At McBee's, ferriages were "gratis" to travelers who purchased from the proprietor's offerings of liquors, corn, oats, and fodder. Alex Cunningham was proprietor of a ferry; Benjamin Rogers was his "ferryman."[41] Samuel L. Doak's ferry continued to ply the Holston, about six miles upriver from Knoxville. James Haralson's and Robinson's ferries were also located near Knoxville on the Holston. Abraham McCleary operated a ferry in Knox County on the French Broad River.[42]

During the decade ending in 1795, several ferries were operated to accommodate traffic across the Cumberland at Nashville. Among them were Lockett's, Thomas's, Nichols's, Cripps's, the Academy's, Baker's, and White's ferries.[43] From 1793 to 1796, the Sumner County Quarterly Court licensed three ferries to operate on the Cumberland above Nashville. The licensees were William Dillard, James Carson, and William Gillespie, the latter for a ferry at Fort Blount.

The Fort Blount tavern and ferry rates, higher than charges for comparable service and fare elsewhere in the district, were published by the quarterly court during its term held in January, 1796.

Dinner	25 cts.	Ferriage:	
Breakfast or supper	16¼ cts.	Man and horse	12½ cts.
Brandy 1/2 pt.	25 cts.	Wagon and four horses	1.00
Whiskey 1/2 pt.	12½ cts.	Cart with horses	50 cts.
		Single person or horse	4 cts.
		Pack horse and load	12½ cts.
		Corn per qt.	4 cts.
		Oats per qt.	3 cts.[44]

In Greene County, Isaac Baker kept a ferry on the Nolichucky River, and James Guthrie had one on Lick Creek. In Jefferson County, ferries on the French Broad River were operated by Peter Fine, Matthew Roulston, William Small, Benjamin Rogers, James Neely, Andrew Russell, Thomas Stockton, James Hubbert, John Seehorn, William Webb and Seth Rogers, and John Neely. A ferry on the Nolichucky River was kept by James Hill, and Thomas Flippin had one on the Holston.[45]

---

41. Knoxville *Gazette*, August 13, 1793; May 22, December 26, 1794.
42. Ibid., January 26, 1793; KCR, Quarterly Court Minutes, Book O. p. 137.
43. DCR, Quarterly Court Minutes, Book B, 1791-1797, Roll 1597, pp. 62, 71, 95, 126, 179, 305.
44. SCR, Quarterly Court Minutes, 1787-1796, pp. 56, 82, 95, 99.
45. GCR, Quarterly Court Minutes, 1783-1796, pp. 403, 428; JCR, Quarterly Court Minutes, 1792-1798, pp. 13, 14, 24, 43, 45, 49, 52, 59, 60, 68.

River transportation was used primarily to float heavy cargo downstream, but even that utility was denied most of the time below Knoxville by the Indians. With the achievement of peace with the Creek and Cherokee in 1795, passage of the lower river was relatively secure. Natural barriers in the Tennessee such as the "Suck" and Muscle Shoals made travel in those areas hazardous in the extreme. At times of high water, however, passage could be made with little difficulty. By June 19, at least three riverboats had put off with cargo for New Orleans and four to Nashville.[46]

When goods from the War Department finally arrived at Knoxville for transshipment to the Chickasaw and Choctaw, Governor Blount directed that a boat be built to carry the cargo to its destination. Negotiating for the governor, John Chisholm engaged David Moore to build "a large flat-bottomed boat" nine feet wide and forty feet long and take it downstream to the Ohio River, thence up to the Cumberland and up that stream to Nashville to deliver the Indian goods. Construction details specified that the boat was to be built of "plank at least two inches thick, to be well caulked and pitched and covered with a good roof." A "good floor" was to be laid inside the hull, a sufficient pump supplied, and enough oars and poles furnished "for the working" of the boat. Moore agreed to have it completed in six weeks and to pilot it to its destination.[47]

The travel activity within the territory that involved the largest number of people was the journey through the wilderness to the Mero District. Typically, families traveling westward to Bledsoe's Lick and Nashville would gather at Knoxville or Southwest Point to make the passage, accompanied by guards from Mero Militia companies. The most widely noticed of those was the annual autumn crossing that set out from Southwest Point for Bledsoe's Lick. A typical call for the westward bound to gather in October, 1794, was made through the columns of the *Gazette* on June 19, July 3, and August 4.

> On the 26th of October next a large company of armed persons will leave Southwest Point for the District of Mero. This notice is thus early published, that families and others, coming from a distance, may embrace the opportunity of passing the

---

46. Knoxville *Gazette*, January 23, June 19, 1795.
47. Articles of Agreement, September 21, 1795, between John Chisholm and David Moore; Blount to Chisholm, September 18, 1795, Blount Correspondence, McClung Collection.

wilderness with safety. A military post will be established, by order of the government, prior to that time, at the passage of the Cumberland River, which will render the journey through the wilderness more agreeable than heretofore.

Similar announcements were made in 1793 and 1795. In the latter notice, it was claimed that the wagon road would be opened ahead of the concourse enabling travel by wagon for the first time.[48]

From time to time there were crossings of groups assembled on short notice, sometimes with guard escorts and sometimes without. In 1793 one unidentified group announced its impending midsummer departure from Knoxville for the Cumberland barely a week ahead of time. Sometimes the fellow travelers were undisciplined ruffians, and on those occasions, men with their families usually withdrew into a separate company. Even Bishop Asbury changed travel plans when he found his party made up of "rowdies and unprincipled men." He recruited fourteen or fifteen reliable men and crossed from Kentucky to Holston without incident.[49]

Travelers bound for Kentucky from Virginia, North Carolina, and the Southwest Territory had found Robert Wyly's place at Greeneville a good rendezvous and departing point for crossing through Cumberland Gap on the Wilderness Road. Once in a while Wyly announced the impending departure in the direction of Kentucky of a large armed party.[50]

Among the thousands who came down the Holston Valley through Jonesborough and Greeneville to Knoxville before crossing to Nashville in 1795 was the celebrated French botanist André Michaux. Intent on observing plant life in the American West, Michaux joined a party of fifteen armed men with about thirty women and children to make the journey from Knoxville to the Mero District. They traveled without serious mishap and reached Bledsoe's Lick on June 12. After a night at the late Isaac Bledsoe's fort, he rode the short distance to James Winchester's place where he slept two nights to rest himself and his horse.[51]

Of necessity county government focused thoughtful attention on roads connecting settlements, mills, and courthouses. County quarterly courts

---

48. Knoxville *Gazette*, January 9, 23, 1795.
49. Ibid., July 27, 1793; Asbury, *The Journal of the Rev. Francis Asbury*, p. 165.
50. Knoxville *Gazette*, June 15, 1793.
51. Reuben Gold Thwaites, ed., *Travels West of the Alleghanies Made in 1793-96 by André Michaux; in 1802 by F.A. Michaux; and in 1803 by Thaddeus Mason Harris, M.A.* (Cleveland, Ohio: The Arthur A. Clark Company, 1904), pp. 58-61.

initiated and/or approved the routes to be followed as new roads were cleared. Typically, the court would appoint a committee to select the best route to connect two or more points. The court would next select a crew of men who lived along its right-of-way to cut and maintain the road under the oversight of one of their number. In 1793 the Davidson County Court appointed an overseer for the repair and maintenance of the city streets of Nashville.[52]

The development of a network of roads, although primitive indeed, contributed not only to a sense of place for those living along their routes, but to a sense of connection to the rest of the United States. In 1795 John Sevier noted in his journal that the distance "by road" from his farm to Charleston, South Carolina, was 255 miles. He must have recognized that his place was about equidistant from Charleston and Clarksville, the farthest western extremity of the settled part of the Southwest Territory.[53]

Monopolized by the Knoxville *Gazette*, the territorial press was successful in favorably representing the territory's position vis-a-vis the southern Indians to the rest of the country. The *Gazette*'s accounts of whites' suffering at the hands of Indians and its reassurances that the settlers were complying faithfully with the terms of the Treaty of Holston were copied in other newspapers throughout the country.[54] The message was clear. It was the Indians who were responsible for the hostilities that existed between them and the whites.

At the same time the *Gazette* depicted Blount to territory folk as hamstrung and hog-tied by the national government. The newspaper adroitly whetted its territorial readership's appetite for preemptive strikes against the Cherokee and Creek and contributed in no small way to the ready responses that came from volunteers when strikes were made both with and without authority.

Publishing the newspaper, not unlike many other activities conducted on the frontier, was no easy task. Even the paper on which it was printed was not always readily available. A wagoner absconded with a load

---

52. DCR, Quarterly Court Minutes, Book B, 1791-1797, Roll 1597, pp. 61, 62, 98, 104, 115, 126, 149, 152, 169, 170, 269, 305.

53. DeWitt, ed., "Journal of Governor John Sevier, 1790-1815," p. 182.

54. Some of the newspapers reprinting extensively from the *Gazette* were the Kentucky *Gazette*, the Boston *Gazette and Republican Weekly Journal*, *Columbian Museum and Savannah Advertiser*, *Dunlap and Claypoole's American Daily Advertiser* (Philadelphia), New York *Daily Advertiser*, and the Augusta *Chronicle and Gazette of the State*.

of paper destined for the *Gazette* in 1793, but publication was "retarded" for only a few weeks. Keeping apprentices on the job to learn "the art and mystery" of printing was almost impossible, and the editor frequently advertised for young, trainable men. At least one slave was employed in the operation.[55]

The partnership of Roulstone and Ferguson, publishers of the *Gazette* and general printers, was dissolved April 20, 1793. George Roulstone and Company succeeded the partnership, and the *Gazette* did not miss an issue. He had enlisted the services of leading citizens to receive subscriptions and accept payments on accounts in arrears. In Jefferson County, the *Gazette* was represented by Alexander Outlaw, James Roddye, George Doherty, and John Tatham; in Greene County, James Richardson and Robert Wyly; in Washington County, James Charter; in Sullivan County, James Brigham; in Hawkins County, Joseph Rogers; in Mero District, Lardner Clark and Andrew Jackson. Roulstone continued as printer for the territorial government and printed for the public as well.[56]

His office was, in addition, a place for the delivery and pick up of North Carolina land grants, and Roulstone occasionally acted as the agent for others as when he represented H. Dunlap to stop timber thieves from cutting logs on Dunlap's lands near Knoxville. His printing shop was often listed as a place to return stray horses when the owner advertised to recover them.[57]

Dealing in farm produce, Roulstone's company advertised in the spring of 1793 that it would give a generous price for "bacon, country manufactured sugar, and flax." A few months later, Roulstone wanted to buy "clean, well-made country sugar" and a milk cow.[58]

On February 27, 1795, George Roulstone became the sole proprietor of the *Gazette*. By that time he had become a recognized leader in public affairs, serving as clerk of the legislative council, a commissioner for the city of Knoxville, postmaster at Knoxville, and trustee of Blount College.[59] He was also propagandist without peer for Governor Blount, the territorial government, and for the westward movement.

---

55. Knoxville *Gazette*, August 27, September 14, December 7, 1793; October 11, 1794; KCR, Quarterly Court Minutes, Book O, p. 64.
56. Knoxville *Gazette*, January 12, April 20, 1793.
57. Ibid., June 15, 1793; November 1, 1794; January 23, March 27, 1795.
58. Ibid., May 4, 1793; January 2, 1794.
59. John Dobson, *The Lost Roulstone Imprints* (Knoxville: The University of Tennessee Library, 1975), pp. 5, 9.

CHAPTER XV

IN COMMUNITY

1793-96

Schooling, religious training, legal services, medical care, and the militia function were not overlooked during the period 1792-96. The development of educational opportunities for young people on the frontier was left to parents and community leaders who had the interest and resources to do something about it. Students were tutored by itinerant schoolmasters, by ministers of the few churches, by teachers at established schools such as Washington College or Davidson Academy, and by their parents and older brothers and sisters. Some were instructed by a private teacher like Nicholas Honore Sidone Fournier at Knoxville, but few were privileged to attend school outside the territory, as did the sons of William Blount and Daniel Smith who were students at Abingdon, Virginia.[1]

An academy was kept by an unknown schoolmaster on Drake's Creek in Sumner County near Daniel Smith's home. On at least one occasion, David Allison brought books for the academy from Philadelphia to Knoxville at Smith's order.[2]

A school sponsored by the Lebanon in the Fork Presbyterian congregation was taught by one Thompson. It was located on the Dandridge Road where the deacons of the church paid regular visits to be certain that instruction in the Bible and the catechism was not neglected.[3]

Throughout the years of the territorial government, Martin Academy, which became Washington College in 1795, and Davidson Academy seemed to thrive. John Sevier was in the audience at Washington College September 27, 1795, when the school held an exhibition of the work of its scholars. Sevier was impressed by the ability of the young speakers who addressed the assembly. To make the transition from academy to college, Samuel Doak, president, had convened the trustees on July 23, 1795, at Salem, Washington County.[4]

---

1. "Papers of General Daniel Smith," p. 226; Keith, ed., *The John Gray Blount Papers*, Vol. II, p. 450.
2. "Pioneer Documents," *American Historical Magazine*, Vol. V (October 1900), p. 297.
3. Goodspeed, *History of Knox County*, p. 892.
4. DeWitt, ed., "Journal of Governor John Sevier, 1790-1815," p. 180; Knoxville *Gazette*, July 17, 1795.

Scholars were instructed without major interruption at Davidson Academy under the supervision of a board of trustees that in 1793 included Thomas B. Craighead, president; Daniel Smith, secretary; and James Robertson, James Winchester, Hugh Williamson, Robert Hays, Ephraim McLean, Lardner Clark, and Andrew Jackson. The trustees generated income for the school by operating a Cumberland River ferry at Nashville and by selling farm produce from a two-hundred-acre tract of academy land that adjoined the town of Nashville on its southern boundary. During this period, President Craighead continued holding classes for the academy in his meetinghouse, a practice that would continue until the trustees erected a schoolhouse on the academy tract in 1803.[5]

Chartered in 1794, Greeneville College seems to have begun to establish itself at once, but records of the period are scanty. One of the first meetings of its trustees was held at Mount Bethel Church in Greeneville on February 10, 1795. President Hezekiah Balch presided.[6]

A month later the trustees of Greeneville College petitioned the United States government for such "benefaction or endowment" as they might think proper. Addressing identical memorials to President Washington, the Senate, and the House of Representatives, the trustees declared that they had no funds to open the college and thereby relied on "divine providence and such donations as may be given by those who are friends to religion and education." They approached the central government because Congress had the "power to encourage the promotion of learning and useful knowledge by endowing colleges for that purpose." The trustees' appeal, although eloquently made, produced none of the results sought.[7]

After personally delivering the memorials, Hezekiah Balch visited in New England where he raised $1,350 in cash, $350 in subscriptions, and a large number of books for the library. By the late summer of 1796, the trustees had authorized construction of an eight-room two-story frame structure to house the school. The site selected was close

---

5. Putnam, *History of Middle Tennessee*, pp. 639, 641-42; Durham, *Daniel Smith, Frontier Statesman*, pp. 95, 212-13; Durham, *James Winchester, Tennessee Pioneer*, p. 83; Smith and Owsley, eds., *The Papers of Andrew Jackson, 1770-1803*, Vol. I, p. 29.

6. Knoxville *Gazette*, February 6, 1795.

7. Carter, ed., *Territorial Papers, SWT*, IV, pp. 393-94.

by Balch's country home near Greeneville on land he donated.[8]

The trustees of Blount College at Knoxville, also chartered in 1794, first met October 18 of the same year. At a meeting in December they directed President Samuel Carrick to begin enrolling students in the latter part of January, 1795. Carrick had previously conducted a small private school at his residence and was well known as a teacher of Latin and Greek.[9]

Although most settlers were of Protestant Christian religious persuasion, the organization of congregations and the establishment of churches were not high priorities with them. The Presbyterian Church seems to have made the most significant advances. The leadership of Doak, Balch, Carrick, and Gideon Blackburn was formidable. Blackburn, who had begun his ministry as pastor of the New Providence and Eusabia congregations in 1792, preached to a number of groups in the eastern districts that later became Presbyterian congregations. His sense of mission took him into several villages of the neighboring Cherokee. Samuel Carrick had continued his relationship with the congregation at Lebanon in the Fork, and in 1793 they built a log meetinghouse forty by sixty feet on a nine-acre tract provided by a member. He was pastor of the first Presbyterian congregation in Knoxville and functioned in the capacity even after he became president of Blount College. Balch, who had come to the territory from Mecklenburg County, North Carolina, built his ministry around the Mount Bethel Presbyterian Church at Greeneville where he also served as president of the college. By 1794, he had published at least one of his sermons.[10] In terms of numbers of congregations established, Samuel Doak was unsurpassed anywhere in the territory. Like Carrick and Balch, he was a scholar and schoolmaster as well as missionary and preacher.

The ministry of Thomas B. Craighead dominated Presbyterian activities in Mero District from his home near Nashville. Like Doak, he was a graduate of the College of New Jersey that later became Princeton. One of the early churches that fed on his ministry was Shiloh, established in 1793 about seven miles west of Bledsoe's Lick. William McGee was

---

8. Doughty, *Greeneville, One Hundred Year Portrait, 1775-1875*, pp. 155-56.
9. Knoxville *Gazette*, October 11, December 26, 1794; Keith, ed., *The John Gray Blount Papers*, Vol. II, p. 450.
10. Goodspeed, *History of Knox County*, pp. 890-91; Knoxville *Gazette*, January 30, 1794; Herman A. Norton, *Religion in Tennessee, 1777-1945* (Knoxville: University of Tennessee Press, 1981), p. 6.

the pastor at Shiloh from 1793 to 1800.[11]

Craighead's church and all Presbyterian congregations in the Mero District were included in the Transylvania Presbytery that covered Kentucky and some areas north of the Ohio River. Uncomfortable with the practice of slavery, Transylvania ordered Presbyterian slaveholders in 1794 to teach their blacks "not above the age of fifteen years to read the word of God and give them such good education as may prepare them for the enjoyment of freedom." Two years later, the presbytery urged its members to emancipate such of their slaves as were ready for freedom and to prepare those who were not.[12]

The Methodist Church, measured in terms of the numbers of its members, stabilized, then declined slowly during the latter years of the territory. Its survival was bolstered by the western visits of Bishop Asbury and the increase in the ranks of the itinerant preachers.[13]

Three circuits had been established to serve Methodist congregations in the districts of Washington and Hamilton. They were Holston, Greene, and New River, the latter including part of southwestern Virginia. In 1795 that part of New River circuit within the Southwest Territory was merged into the Holston circuit. From 1793 through 1796, Jacob Kobler was presiding elder for those circuits. Pastors appointed to Holston circuit were John Simmons and Stith Meade, 1793; Francis Acuff and John Lindsey, 1794; Tobias Gibson and Aquila Jones, 1795; and Obadiah Strange, 1796. Appointments to Greene circuit were Samuel Rudder and John Ray, 1793; Williams Kavanaugh, Barnabas McHenry, and Lewis Garrett, 1794; Benjamin Lakin and Nathaniel Munsey, 1795; and John Page and Munsey, 1796. New River had Jacob Peck, 1793, and Samuel Rudder and John Ray in 1794.[14]

Three notable congregations of the period were the Ebeneezer Church, Vanpelt's Chapel, and Acuff's Chapel. The Ebeneezer Church, located on the south side of Nolichucky River a few miles east of Greeneville,

---

11. Durham, *The Great Leap Westward*, p. 159; Shiloh Presbyterian Church, 1793-1847, Historical Records Project, TSLA, p. 1.

12. Walter Brownlow Posey, *The Presbyterian Church in the Old Southwest, 1778-1838* (Richmond, Virginia: John Knox Press, 1952), pp. 20, 74.

13. Richard Nye Price, *Holston Methodism. From Its Origin to the Present Time*, Vol. I (Nashville and Dallas: Publishing House of the Methodist Episcopal Church South, 1903), pp. 197, 199, 235; McFerrin, *History of Methodism in Tennessee*, Vol. I, pp. 134, 188, 217; Cullen T. Carter, *Methodism in the Wilderness, 1786-1836* (Nashville: Parthenon Press, 1959), p. 35.

14. McFerrin, *History of Methodism in Tennessee*, Vol. I, pp. 135, 157, 197, 216; Knoxville *Gazette*, May 8, 1794.

was the site of the annual meeting of the Western Conference in 1795. That congregation had been organized around the large families of the brothers Henry and Felix Earnest. In 1793 the Western Conference had been convened in Nelson's Chapel on the land of James Nelson in Washington County near Jonesborough.[15]

Vanpelt's Chapel, located on the north side of Lick Creek, was named for Benjamin Vanpelt who had emigrated from Alexandria, Virginia, in 1790. Vanpelt was a local preacher whose new home was usually a place of rest for Bishop Asbury when he was in the area.[16]

The congregation recognized as the cradle of Methodism in the eastern districts was Acuff's Chapel in Sullivan County near the twentieth-century site of Blountville. Construction of the meetinghouse antedated the territory and is generally thought to have been the first Methodist house of worship erected in North Carolina's western lands. Francis Acuff, son of the founder of the congregation, became a Methodist preacher in 1793 at the age of twenty-three. He died in 1795 while serving the Danville, Kentucky, circuit.[17]

By 1793 there were Methodist congregations or "societies" at the County Line Meetinghouse on the line between Hawkins and Jefferson counties, at Beth-car, sometimes referred to as Moore's Chapel, on the Nolichucky about nine miles from what is now Morristown, and at Pine Chapel on the south bank of the French Broad in Jefferson County.[18]

Methodism in the Mero District was organized under the aegis of the Cumberland circuit embracing an area that included the counties of Davidson, Sumner, and Tennessee in the territory and part of Logan County, Kentucky. John Dickens and Henry Birchett were assigned to the circuit in 1793, and after the latter's death in 1794, Jacob Lurtin and Moses Speer shared the appointment. William Burke, who had served the church in the Holston area previously, and Peter Guthrie were assigned to the Cumberland circuit for the first time in 1795. Francis Poythress was elder of the district from 1793 through 1796. In 1796 John Buxton and William Duzan shared the Cumberland circuit.[19]

The most significant meetinghouse of the period in Mero was built

---

15. Price, *Holston Methodism*, Vol. I, pp. 184-85, 188.
16. Ibid., p. 196.
17. Ibid., pp. 135, 223, 224.
18. Ibid., pp. 136-38.
19. McFerrin, *History of Methodism in Tennessee*, Vol. I, pp. 135, 157, 197, 216, 445; Carter, *Methodism in the Wilderness, 1786-1836*, pp. 32-33.

on the public square in Nashville, a stone structure that stood for a few years without windows and doors. Methodists erected it in 1795 or 1796, and they shared it with other Christian denominations. Another rallying place for Methodists was established in 1793 when Norris's Meetinghouse, a log building, was raised in Sumner County on Station Camp Creek.[20]

To hold their audiences and drive home their messages, the frontier preachers had to be a resourceful lot. In his *Early Times in Middle Tennessee,* John Carr recalled a memorable summer day with Henry Birchett at Norris's Meetinghouse. Preaching from a stand in the woods to a large congregation, Birchett watched a "dark and angry" cloud spread across the heavens just above the heads of the people. When it began to issue "terrific thunder and lightning," the crowd became alarmed and began to scatter.

> But just then the preacher succeeded in getting their attention, and told them to stay and unite with him in prayer to God. He bowed, and I have never heard such a prayer! He prayed for the clouds to be dispersed, that they might have a quiet and peaceable waiting upon God.... When we arose from our knees, the cloud had changed its course, and passed away, and we were not interrupted by rain. This direct answer to prayer, so evident to all, had a most gracious effect upon the congregation, even the wicked believing that God had heard the prayer of the preacher.[21]

The relatively minor role that organized religion played in the settlement of the territory was explained in part by Bishop Asbury. He wrote, "When I reflect that not one in a hundred came here to get religion, but rather to get plenty of good land, I think it will be well if some or many do not eventually lose their souls."[22] The low estate of the church was shown clearly in the lives of the territorial leaders, virtually none of whom gave it time or energy.[23]

The Baptist Church, represented in the Holston Valley below the Virginia state line by Jonathan Mulkey, Tidence Lane, William Murphy,

---

20. W. Woodford Clayton, *History of Davidson County, Tennessee, with Illustrations and Biographical Sketches of Its Prominent Men and Pioneers* (Philadelphia: J.W. Lewis, 1880; Nashville: Charles Elder, 1971), p. 197; John Carr, *Early Times in Middle Tennessee* (Nashville: Parthenon Press, 1958), p. 61.
21. Carr, *Early Times in Middle Tennessee,* p. 50.
22. Asbury, *The Journal of the Rev. Francis Asbury,* Vol. II, p. 342.
23. William Blount, Daniel Smith, John Sevier, James Robertson, James Winchester, Landon Carter, Dr. James White, Andrew Jackson, Griffith Rutherford, Stockley Donelson, William Cocke, and John Overton all had one characteristic in common; they gave little time to the organized church.

and other ministers since the 1770s, seems to have experienced modest growth from 1793 to 1796. Few surviving records document that progress in terms of numbers of members, however.[24]

In the East, the Holston Association of Baptist churches, formed in 1786, was convened periodically to afford exchanges of information and inspiration among the member churches. By 1796, five congregations in the Cumberland country had organized the Mero Association for the same purpose. The member churches, all in or near the valley of the Red River, were Mouth of Sulphur Fork later called Red River, Head of Sulphur Fork, and Middle Ford of Tennessee County; White's Creek later called New Bethel of Davidson; and West Fork of Station Camp Creek in Sumner.[25]

At least eighteen Baptist congregations are known to have existed during this period in Washington and Hamilton districts and nine in Mero. Of the former the largest membership was in the church at Buffalo Ridge—about two hundred and fifty persons. Other congregations were known as Cherokee Creek, Bent Creek, Lower French Broad, French Broad at Koonts's Meetinghouse, Forks of Little Pigeon, Limestone, Kendricks Creek, Sinking Creek, and Muddy Creek. There were also Fall Branch, Beech Creek, Clear Fork, Robertson's Creek, Beaver Creek, Greasy Cove, North Fork of Holston, and Mouth of Richland Creek. The four in Mero, in addition to those in the Mero Association, were Concord, Mill Creek, Rock Spring, and Providence.[26]

The leadership of the Baptist Church in the eastern section was provided primarily by the elders Mulkey and Lane and certain of their contemporaries, including Isaac Barton, Uriah Hunt, William Murphy, Caleb Witt, James Fears, Duke Kimbrough, and Thomas and Richard Murrel. In the Mero Association, John Dillahunty, Garner McConnico, Jesse Fears, James Whitsett, and Patrick Mooney were principal advocates of the faith.[27]

---

24. J.J. Burnett, *Sketches of Tennessee's Pioneer Baptist Preachers*, Vol. I (Nashville: N.p., 1919), pp. 318, 388; Samuel W. Tindall, *The Baptists of Tennessee* (Kingsport: Southern Publishers, Inc., 1930), p. 20; *Minutes of the Tenn. Baptist Association, Holston, 1786-1850*, Pub. no. 836 (Nashville: Historical Commission, Southern Baptist Convention, n.d.), Microfilm, Southern Baptist Convention Archives and Library, Nashville.

25. Walter Brownlow Posey, *The Baptist Church in the Lower Mississippi Valley, 1776-1845* (Lexington, Kentucky: University of Kentucky Press, 1957), p. 116; R.D. Brooks, *One Hundred and Sixty-Two Years of Middle Tennessee Baptists* (Nashville: N.p., 1958), p. 1.

26. Burnett, *Sketches of Tennessee's Pioneer Baptist Preachers*, Vol. I, pp. 37, 38, 41, 157, 227, 256, 287, 319, 390, 393, 528, 563.

27. Ibid., pp. 37-38, 157, 256, 285, 360, 361, 391, 393, 528; Durham, *The Great Leap Westward*, p. 160.

Baptist congregations attempted to police the behavior of their members. The few extant records of the French Broad River Church provide examples of that effort. In 1794 Samuel Johnson gave "satisfaction" after being charged with drinking whiskey to excess, and Abraham Carlock was cited to attend "the next church meeting" in order to "give satisfaction for making a shooting match." Later, Carlock was "excommunicated" for the sin of "gameing." Women did not escape the watchful eyes of their brothers and sisters. In 1795 Elizabeth Johnston was excommunicated "for the sin of speaking disrespectfully of sister Nancy Johnston and contradicting her own words and neglecting to hear the church."[28]

From the professions, the territory seemed to have adequate numbers of attorneys, but very few medical doctors. In 1796 at least thirty-two lawyers were licensed to practice in the courts of the territory. Among those who had been practicing at some time since 1793 were Andrew Jackson, John Overton, Howell Tatum, Josiah Love, Bennett Searcy, James Cole Mountflorence, James Doherty, James Mulherrin, Samuel Donelson, Seth Lewis, Isham Allen Parker, Isaac McNutt, Randal McGavock, Robert Knox, and Thomas Stuart from Mero District.[29]

Washington and Hamilton districts were served by attorneys John Sevier, Jr., Samuel Mitchell, John Shields,[30] Luke Bowyer, John Cocke, Thomas Gray,[31] Hopkins Lacy, David Greer,[32] Willie Blount, William Cocke, W. C. C. Claiborne, John Lowry, William Tatham, Joseph Hamilton, James Reese, and Archibald Roan.[33]

From 1793 to 1796 the *Gazette* took notice of only two doctors, although there were probably others. Both set up practices at Knoxville in 1794. Dr. Thomas McCombs announced that he was "entering the practice of physic." He promised to have constantly on hand a large assortment of "genuine medicine," which he would dispense on short notice "on the most moderate terms." He claimed to have had "long studies and experience under the most eminent physicians in the Atlantic states."[34]

---

28. French Broad River Baptist Church, Minutes, 1786-1842, Historical Records Project, TSLA, pp. 3-5.
29. Eastin Morris, *The Tennessee Gazetteer* (Nashville: W. Hasell Hunt & Co., 1834), p. 36; DCR, Quarterly Court Minutes, Book B, 1791-1797, Roll 1597, pp. 69, 70, 99, 231, 264, 301, 317.
30. GCR, Quarterly Court Minutes, 1783-1796, pp. 286, 288, 301.
31. JCR, Quarterly Court Minutes, 1792-1798, pp. 54, 56, 100.
32. WCR, Superior Court Minutes Book, 1794, Roll 167, p. 19.
33. KCR, Quarterly Court Minutes, Book O, pp. 38, 163, 164, 165; Knoxville *Gazette*, April 6, 1793.
34. Knoxville *Gazette*, May 8, 1794.

Dr. Robert Johnston was represented as a "surgeon and physician" practicing at Knoxville. He, too, kept a stock of "the most genuine medicines" from which he would supply "private families...on the shortest notice." Four months later he had a wallet full of bills that he could not collect.[35]

Dr. Mark B. Sappington practiced medicine at Nashville. The creator of "Sappington's Pills," the frontier doctor had covered them "with *mystery* and a coat of sugar," according to a nineteenth-century historian.[36] In 1795 Dr. Morgan Brown came from South Carolina to Montgomery County to practice medicine,[37] and in 1796 Dr. William Holt was attending clients in Washington and Greene counties.[38] Doctors William Ward and William P. Chester practiced in Washington County. Dr. James White of Nashville practiced more politics than medicine during this period as he represented the territory as its delegate to Congress.

Life on the frontier demanded the best of settlers, but sometimes elicited the worst. Law enforcement officers had their work cut out for them. Thievery was not uncommon, but horse stealing was the most heinous larceny of all. There was a consensus that horse thieves should be dealt with summarily and severely. When Peter Stacey was convicted of horse stealing by the Washington District Superior Court meeting at Jonesborough on September 23, 1793, the sentence was typical for the crime.

> The sentence...is that he, Peter Stacey, stand in the pillory one hour, and shall be publicly whipped on his bare back with thirty-nine lashes well laid on, and at the same time both of his ears nailed to the pillory and cut off. And shall be branded on the right cheek with the letter "H" of the length of three-quarters of an inch and the breadth of half an inch, and on the left check with the letter "T."

The execution of the sentence was carried out by the sheriff at five o'clock in the afternoon of the same day on which it was passed.[39]

---

35. Ibid., July 31, November 29, 1794.
36. Putnam, *History of Middle Tennessee*, p. 242; DCR, Wills and Inventories, Vol. II, 1794-1805, p. 9.
37. Edythe Rucker Whitley, *Red River Settlers* (Baltimore: Genealogical Publishing Company, Inc., 1980), pp. 17, 79.
38. GCR, Quarterly Court Minutes, p. 435; Gump, "Possessions and Patterns of Living in Washington County: The 20 Years Before Tennessee Statehood, 1777-1796," pp. 80-82.
39. WCR, Superior Court Minutes Book, 1793, Roll 167, p. 13.

Convictions for petit larceny, whether stealing a small gold coin or a handkerchief, called for public punishment. The Mero District Superior Court gave each of two such criminals "thirty-nine lashes well laid on" their bare backs at the public whipping post in Nashville.[40]

County courts frequently called to account the bearers and begetters of illegitimate children. Both parents were fined in many cases, and the father was often required to post bond to provide for the child's care and upkeep. On May 19, 1793, in Jefferson County, the mother of an out-of-wedlock child was fined fifty shillings for having a "base begotten child and refusing to declare the father."[41]

In Sumner County both parents of an illegitimate child were required to post bond for its care and upkeep. Another variation of the courts' resolve to protect the county from the expense of caring for the progeny was demonstrated in Sumner when the courts, unable to determine the paternity of the infant, required two of the mother's male friends to post bond jointly.[42]

The county courts were charged with the care and oversight of orphans. Responding to cases made known to them, the magistrates customarily put the individual children in the care of a family that would provide food, lodging, and a modest education for them in exchange for their labor as soon as they were old enough to work. When orphans were abused by those responsible for their care, the courts intervened and often placed the children with another family.[43]

An important event that occurred periodically during the territorial years was the arrival and disbursement of payroll funds to the militia. Sent by a courier from the War Department in Philadelphia, the funds were received at Knoxville by the agent of the department for the territory or by his coworker, the paymaster. Then notices were placed in the newspaper designating times and places for captains to pick up the payroll monies due their respective companies for specified dates of service.

---

40. Davidson County Records, Minutes of the Superior Court of North Carolina Including Mero District, 1788-1803, Part I, 1788-1798, pp. 115, 123.

41. GCR, Quarterly Court Minutes, 1783-1796, p. 297; SCR, Quarterly Court Minutes, 1787-1796, p. 61; JCR, Quarterly Court Minutes, 1792-1798, p. 19.

42. SCR, Quarterly Court Minutes, 1787-1796, pp. 57, 66.

43. KCR, Quarterly Court Minutes, Book O, pp. 42, 146; DCR, Quarterly Court Minutes, Book B, Roll 1597, pp. 62, 93, 238; JCR, Quarterly Court Minutes, p 33; GCR, Quarterly Court Minutes, p. 435.

Although tours of duty typically lasted only a few days, the total cash funds disbursed were significant to a frontier economy that had comparatively little money in circulation. In 1794, militia pay amounted to $29,555.56 for the Mero District. For the same period the militia in Washington and Hamilton districts received $25,838.66.[44]

The payroll payouts occasionally were subject to petty abuse. When one of his men pointed out to the captain in command at Fort Blount that instead of the authorized number of thirty men he had far less on duty, a padded payroll resulted. For each vacancy on the roster, the soldiers solicited powers of attorney from men who had not been present. Their plan was to divide the pay "for those that did no duty... between the captain and those that did."[45]

The settlers were seriously disturbed by the stubborn refusal of the War Department to pay the militia who were part of General John Sevier's Etowah expedition in 1793 and other militia who participated in the Nickajack campaign of 1794 on orders given by General James Robertson. When Colonel James King arrived at Knoxville in April, 1795, with bank notes sent by the secretary of war to pay militia claims to the end of 1794, he did not have the pay due for the expeditions against Etowah and Nickajack that the Congress considered offensive in nature.[46]

Even payment for approved duty was often slow in reaching the militia. Although soldiers of the Mero District Militia, due to their remoteness, were generally the last to be paid, Sullivan County leaders, tormented by their slow-paid soldiers, demanded the agent for the War Department to pay. They wrote to Henley: "We call upon you... in the name of the *people of Sullivan, our constituents,* to inform us why these certificates have not been paid. And when you suppose that they may draw their hard-earned pittance."[47]

The national government, through the War Department, pumped additional funds into the territory as it purchased rations and supplies for the small number of federal troops and the larger number of militia.[48] Other monies of significant totals were added as the department purchased supplies for the Indians. In the spring of 1794, proposals were

---

44. National Archives, Record Group 94, M-904, Roll 4, pp. 150-55.
45. Ibid., pp. 172-73.
46. Knoxville *Gazette*, April 24, 1795.
47. John Rhea, George Rutledge, and W.C.C. Caliborne to Colonel David Henley, January 31, 1796, David Henley Papers, 1748-1823.
48. Ration Claims List, Sumner County Archives, Gallatin, Tennessee.

solicited for delivery of several items to Southwest Point or the mouth of Nine Mile Creek. Prices were sought for corn and salt by the bushel, bacon, pork, flour, Indian meal, and tobacco by the pound, and whiskey by the gallon.[49]

Collection of the taxes on land, polls, and distilleries reminded many who had opposed enlargement of the territorial government that they had forecast correctly; bigger government meant higher taxes. Each county set the rates for its land and poll taxes, and the federal government laid and collected the tax on distilleries. Tax collector for the county, the sheriff gathered in the revenues at the appointed times. Knox County Sheriff Robert Houston scheduled appointments to receive tax payments at thirteen different places in the county from December 1 through December 15, 1794.[50] Similar practices were carried out in other counties.

---

49. Knoxville *Gazette*, April 24, 1794.
50. Ibid., November 15, 1794.

CHAPTER XVI

THE STATE OF TENNESSEE

1796

With the advent of the year 1796, statehood for the inhabitants of the territory was in reach at last. Five representatives from each of the eleven counties, chosen at the mid-December elections of the prior year, stood ready to gather in convention at Knoxville "for the purposes of forming a constitution, or form of government for the permanent government of the people."[1]

On January 11, 1796, the convention assembled in David Henley's office, a large one-room log house. The amenities were modest. James White had provided accommodations for the delegates at minimal expense. The total cost for seats was $10.00, and tables for the presiding officer and secretary were covered with three and one-half yards of oilcloth for $2.62. Firewood, candles, and candle stands were supplied for an additional expenditure of $22.50.[2]

The delegates to the convention were David Craig, James Greenaway, Joseph Black, John Houston, and Samuel Glass from Blount County; John McNairy, Andrew Jackson, James Robertson, Thomas Hardeman, and Joel Lewis from Davidson; Samuel Frazier, Stephen Brooks, William Rankin, John Galbreath, and Elisha Baker from Greene; James Berry, Thomas Henderson, Joseph McMinn, William Cocke, and Richard Mitchell from Hawkins; Alexander Outlaw, Joseph Anderson, George Doherty, James Roddye, and Archibald Roane from Jefferson; William Blount, James White, Charles McClung, John Adair, and John Crawford from Knox; George Rutledge, William C. C. Claiborne, John Shelby, Jr., John Rhea, and Richard Gammon from Sullivan; Peter Bryan, Samuel Wear, Spencer Clack, John Clack, and Thomas Buckenham from Sevier; Thomas Johnston, James Ford, William Fort, Robert Prince, and William Prince from Tennessee; Landon Carter, John Tipton, Leroy Taylor, James Stuart, and Samuel Handley from

---

1. Carter, ed., *Territorial Papers, SWT,* IV, pp. 407-8.
2. *Journal of the Proceedings of a Convention, Begun and Held at Knoxville, January 11, 1796* (Knoxville: printed by George Roulstone, 1796), p. 31 (hereinafter cited as *Journal, January 11, 1796*).

Washington; and Daniel Smith, David Shelby, Isaac Walton, William Douglass, and Edward Douglass from Sumner. They chose William Blount to be president; William Maclin, secretary; John Sevier, Jr., reading and engrossing clerk; and John Rhea, doorkeeper. They appointed a committee to develop rules to be observed "in doing business during the session of the convention."[3]

The delegates formed a distinguished group. Among them were a future president of the United States, Andrew Jackson; six future United States senators, Blount, Cocke, Anderson, Jackson, Claiborne, and Smith; four future congressmen, Jackson, Claiborne, Rhea, and Sevier; two former congressmen, Sevier and Blount; three future governors of the state, Sevier, McMinn, and Roane; a future governor of Louisiana, Claiborne; two of the territorial judges, McNairy and Anderson; the governor and speaker of the legislature of the ill-fated state of Franklin, Sevier and Carter; and the Mero District stalwart, James Robertson.[4] Observers were reminded of the newness of the settlements when sixteen of the delegates gave Virginia as their birthplace; eight listed Pennsylvania; seven, North Carolina; four, South Carolina; and three, Maryland.[5]

The delegates had been followed into Knoxville by citizens from all over the territory. Most came only as spectators, but others, like John Sevier, Sr., were present to lobby for matters of special interest to them. Working openly for positions supported by Blount, Sevier was certainly fulfilling his part of their unwritten agreement that would ultimately see Sevier as the first governor of the new state and Blount as one of its United States senators.[6] Another effective worker for Governor Blount at the convention, though not a delegate, was his half brother Willie who would become governor of Tennessee in 1809.

After hearing a sermon by Samuel Carrick to open the session on the second day, the body approved the recommendations of its rules committee that, with a few modifications, followed the rules adopted by the house of representatives of the territorial assembly on August 6,

---

3. Ibid., pp. 3-4.
4. *Biographical Directory of the American Congress, 1774-1971*, pp. 64, 71, 73, 83, 92, 95, 99, 103, 106, 515, 605, 739, 760, 1176, 1601, 1678, 1711; Robert H. White, ed., *Messages of the Governors of Tennessee, 1796-1821*, Vol. I (Nashville: Tennessee Historical Commission, 1952), pp. 1, 105, 445; Putnam, *History of Middle Tennessee*, p. 553.
5. Corlew, *Tennessee, A Short History*, p. 97.
6. Ramsey, *The Annals of Tennessee*, p. 650.

1794. The convention then reviewed the pay rate of $2.50 per person per day for its members, set by the last general assembly and, noting that "economy is an amiable trait in any government," reduced it to $1.50 per day. Travel reimbursement was set at $1.00 for every thirty miles traveled to and from Knoxville.[7]

Having attended to those and other matters essentially of a housekeeping nature, the convention turned to its primary task: drafting a state constitution and bill of rights. To begin the process, each county delegation selected two of its number to sit on a committee charged with bringing drafts of both documents before the entire body. The committee members thus elected were Craig and Black of Blount County; McNairy and Jackson of Davidson; Frazier and Rankin of Greene; William Cocke and Henderson of Hawkins; Roddye and Anderson of Jefferson; Blount and McClung of Knox; Claiborne and Rhea of Sullivan; Shelby and Smith of Sumner; Wear and John Clack of Sevier; Johnston and Fort of Tennessee; and Tipton and Stuart of Washington.[8]

After two days of deliberations, Daniel Smith, who had been elected chairman of the committee, presented a draft of a "bill of rights" to the convention. On January 27 he returned with a draft of the constitution. The contents of both documents were examined, and on February 3 the convention voted to approve the bill of rights, containing thirty-two separate provisions. It was agreed to change its title to Declaration of Rights and to incorporate it into the body of the constitution as the last section, Article XI.[9]

Not unlike the practices of older states, the Declaration of Rights closely paralleled the Bill of Rights of the Constitution of the United States. In its final form, however, the Declaration reflected two distinctly western concerns. Trumpeting the West's need to have access by river to the sea, Section 29 proclaimed:

> That an equal participation of the free navigation of the Mississippi, is one of the inherent rights of the citizens of this state: it cannot therefore, be conceded to any prince, potentate, power, person or persons whatever.[10]

---

7. *Journal, January 11, 1796*, pp. 3-5.
8. Ibid., pp. 5-6.
9. Ibid., pp. 24-25.
10. *Constitution of the State of Tennessee, Unanimously Established in Convention at Knoxville, the Sixth Day of February, One Thousand Seven Hundred and Ninety-Six* (Philadelphia: Printed for Thomas Condie, No. 20 Carter's Alley, 1796), p. 27.

Section 31 mirrored the West's passion for land as it declared:

> That the people residing south of French Broad and Holston, between the rivers Tennessee and the Big Pigeon, are entitled to the right of pre-emption and occupancy in that tract.[11]

The constitution provided for the organization of a government "republican in form and relatively democratic in character." Containing the executive, legislative, and judicial departments, it was similar to other state constitutions, but drew heavily upon the work of the constitution makers of North Carolina and, to a lesser extent, Pennsylvania.[12]

A vigorous debate developed around provisions for a general assembly. At length a proposal to have a unicameral legislature was defeated, and the original provision for a house of representatives and a senate, "both dependent upon the people," was sustained. Elections to both bodies would be held at intervals of two years. The number of members of the house would exceed that of the senate by a ratio of no more than three to one, and representation in both houses would be apportioned according to the taxable inhabitants. The legislature was required to make an apportionment of its seats every seven years after the taking of a census for that purpose. Members of the house of representatives would be elected from each county, but senators would be elected from districts drawn by the legislature. Membership of the house was initially fixed at a minimum of twenty-two and a maximum of twenty-six, but provision was made to increase the number when the population should increase sufficiently. Each county was entitled to one senator until the first apportionment.[13]

The constitution established qualifications for holding office in the general assembly that limited candidates to resident adult male property owners. To be elected to either house, one had to be a male at least twenty-one years of age and must have resided three years in the state and one in the county from which he sought election. The candidate also had to own at least two hundred acres of land in that county.[14]

---

11. Ibid., p. 27.
12. Philip M. Hamer, ed., *Tennessee, A History, 1673-1932*, Vol. I (New York: The American Historical Society, Inc., 1933), p. 173; Joshua W. Caldwell, *Studies in the Constitutional History of Tennessee* (Cincinnati: The Robert Clarke Co., 1895), p. 81.
13. *Constitution of the State of Tennessee*, pp. 5-6; *Journal, January 11, 1796*, pp. 10, 12, 25, 26.
14. *Constitution of the State of Tennessee*, p 7.

The convention specified that the general assembly, the dominant branch of government under this constitution, would meet regularly in the odd-numbered years but could be called into special session by the governor. The governor had no power of veto, however. The general assembly was the lawmaking body, but also had the power to appoint all officers of government—including judges—except certain county and all militia officers. It had the power to remove state officials for any misdemeanor in office through impeachment by the house and trial before the senate. Virtually the only constraints imposed on the members of the house and senate were provisions that they could not raise their salaries until the year 1804, and when creating new counties, they could not reduce the existing counties below a stated minimum size.[15]

The reconciliation of the free practice of religion and the majority's determination to maintain a judicious separation of church and state was not easy. In Article VIII, the delegates provided that ministers of the gospel and priests, "by their professions dedicated to God and the care of souls," were ineligible to hold a seat in either house of the legislature. On the other hand, the same article stipulated that "no person who denies the being of God, or a future state of rewards and punishment, shall hold any office in the civil department of this state." But there was no provision requiring belief in the Protestant religion as was maintained in the North Carolina Constitution until 1835.[16]

The convention vested the supreme executive power of the state in the office of governor. Limited to serving three terms of two years each, the governor was required to be at least twenty-five years of age, a resident of the state for four years, and the owner of at least five hundred acres of land. The office had little power. The governor could make appointments only to fill vacancies that occurred when the legislature was not in session. He could recommend legislation to the general assembly, but could do little or nothing if it ignored or disapproved his recommendations. Directed to "take care that the laws be faithfully executed," the governor was commander in chief of the army, navy, and militia of the state, except when they were in the service of the United States. He was empowered to grant pardons and reprieves and to call the legislature into special session. Perhaps his most important responsibility was to report to the legislature on the status of government

---

15. Ibid., pp. 7, 15, 17-18.
16. Ibid., p. 19; Caldwell, *Studies in the Constitutional History of Tennessee*, p. 97.

and to recommend such action as he deemed appropriate.[17]

The constitution makers broke with the traditions of some of the older states by providing for universal manhood suffrage. The right to vote was extended to all white and to all free black men twenty-one years and older. Nonetheless, the voters would not be burdened by frequent visits to the polls as the constitution reserved most elections for state and local office to the legislature and to the county quarterly courts whose members were appointed by the legislature.[18]

Debated at length, the proposed provision governing taxes was rewritten and adopted in the following form for Article I, Section 26:

> All lands liable to taxation, in this state held by deed, grant or entry, shall be taxed equal and uniform, in such manner, that no one hundred acres shall be taxed higher than another, except town lots, which shall not be taxed higher than 200 acres of land each; no free man, shall be taxed higher than 100 acres, and no slave higher than two hundred acres on each poll.[19]

On Friday, February 5, 1796, the delegates made their last changes in the draft of the constitution and committed the engrossed copy to Daniel Smith, John McNairy, and John Rhea who functioned as a committee to verify that it correctly reflected the actions of the convention. After reviewing it overnight, they delivered it to be read to the convention on Saturday morning, February 6.[20]

While the engrossing clerk read the preamble, cheers of pride and fulfillment rocked the meetinghouse:

> We, the People of the Territory of the United States south of the river Ohio, having the right of admission into the general government as a member state thereof, consistent with the Constitution of the United States, and the act of cession of the state of North Carolina, recognizing the ordinance for the government of the Territory of the United States north west of the river Ohio, do ordain and establish the following constitution, or form of government: and do mutually agree with each other to form ourselves into a free and independent state, by the name of THE STATE OF TENNESSEE.[21]

---

17. *Constitution of the State of Tennessee*, pp. 11-13.
18. Ibid., pp. 5, 6, 11, 14.
19. Ibid., p. 10.
20. *Journal, January 11, 1796*, pp. 31-32.
21. *Constitution of the State of Tennessee*, on back of title page, unnumbered.

After the entire instrument was read, the convention approved it by unanimous vote.[22]

Before adjourning, the delegates instructed the president of the convention to send a copy of the constitution by express to the secretary of state at Philadelphia. The prompt adoption of the constitution had met an urgent though publicly unstated goal of the convention leadership; the constitution and their application for statehood would be brought before Congress prior to its adjournment.[23]

To expedite the organization of the government under the new constitution, the delegates authorized and directed Governor Blount "to issue writs of election to the sheriffs of the several counties, for holding the first election of members of the general assembly and governor, under the authority of the constitution of the state of Tennessee." Blount issued the orders at once calling for the elections to be held on the second Thursday and Friday of March.[24]

The convention adjourned *sine die* the same day. After celebrating their achievement for a day or two, the delegates turned homeward, and Joseph McMinn, a member of the convention acting as Blount's express to Philadelphia, set out to deliver the constitution and a message to Dr. White to apply at once for statehood.[25]

The adjournment of the convention found the constitution firmly in place. Compiled and approved by duly elected representatives of the people, the constitution faced no referendum. It had to be reviewed by no other body except the Congress of the United States and that only for the purpose of determining that it and the government to be formed under its provisions were truly republican.[26]

Throughout the drafting and debates, Blount and his supporters had generally prevailed. The strength of their control was demonstrated not only in the final product of the convention but also in Blount's election as president with Daniel Smith presiding in his absence, in James Robertson's presiding over sessions when they were conducted as a committee

---

22. *Journal, January 11, 1796*, p. 32.
23. Ibid.; Corlew, *Tennessee, A Short History*, p. 98.
24. *Journal, January 11, 1796*, pp. 31-32; Corlew, *Tennessee, A Short History*, p. 99; *Constitution of the State of Tennessee*, p. 6.
25. Carter, ed., *Territorial Papers, SWT*, IV, p. 419.
26. Masterson, *William Blount*, p. 291.

of the whole, and in Smith's chairing the committee to draft the constitution and its Declaration of Rights.[27]

The governor had worked hard to get his friends elected to the convention. And he had lost no time in warning them of the courses of action that his enemies might take to thwart the organization of government. He had been apprehensive of what might be done by political adversaries like David Henley, Sampson Williams, Judge Anderson, and the Cocke-Tipton crowd.[28]

Public acceptance of the convention's work was generally favorable. The governor's ineffectual enemies had hurt themselves with the Mero District people, Andrew Jackson was pleased to write Blount on February 29. Returning delegates had told anxious listeners of the efforts led by Judge Anderson and Alexander Outlaw to weaken the constitution, and it had "detracted from their popularity" while Blount's popularity had "greatly increased." Jackson concluded, "Calumny, that fiend to virtue, had fled, a calm has arrived, imprecations cease, and Caesar is rendered his due... if I may hazard an opinion, your election [to the Senate] will be unanimous."[29]

Probably the most positive reaction to the constitution came from Thomas Jefferson, former secretary of state and future president, who described it as "the least imperfect and most republican constitution yet adopted by any state." Surely the lengthy Declaration of Rights appearing in the constitution had struck a responsive chord with him.[30]

Arthur Campbell, the articulate Southwest Virginian who had given gratuitous advice often to the territory people, was predictably negative about the constitution of Tennessee. Disparaging it as "the instrument called a constitution," he wrote to President Washington to counsel delay of two years or more before accepting Tennessee into the Union. He raised the question of which government—national or state—would dispose of the unoccupied lands and hinted darkly that there might be other serious objections to the constitution. Admitting that the exercise of drafting a constitution would be useful to the citizens, he added, with

---

27. *Journal, January 11, 1796,* pp. 11, 12, 32; Corlew, *Tennessee, A Short History,* p. 97; Masterson, *William Blount,* p. 287.
28. Masterson, *William Blount,* p. 285.
29. Smith and Owsley, *The Papers of Andrew Jackson, 1770-1803,* Vol. I, p. 82.
30. Ramsey, *The Annals of Tennessee,* p. 657.

biting sarcasm, that it would add to their stock of knowledge, "a treasure they need almost as much as that of gold."[31]

By the middle of February, sheriffs throughout the territory had received writs issued by the governor calling for elections to be held in each county. Voters would elect a governor and representatives and senators for the general assembly of the new state. Local politicians scrambled to line up candidates while negotiations among the territorial leadership seemed to develop a consensus that would bring Sevier to the office of governor, Blount and Cocke to the United States Senate and, later, Andrew Jackson to the House of Representatives. The position of speaker of the state senate, who was also by virtue of the office interim successor to the governor, was probably designated in the informal caucus to go to James Winchester. The need to bring it into the arrangement was dictated by the eastern districts having the three highest offices—and the voters to elect them—when the West had only the fourth. The addition of Winchester made the situation more palatable in the Mero District, however.[32]

The first session of the first general assembly of the state of Tennessee was convened at Knoxville on Monday, March 28, 1796. After eleven senators and twenty-two representatives subscribed the oath of office, both houses chose officers and prepared for further deliberations the next day. James Winchester was elected speaker of the senate and James Stuart speaker of the house of representatives. The senate elected Francis A. Ramsey clerk with George Roulstone and Nathaniel Buckingham assistants to him. The house chose Thomas H. Williams clerk with John Sevier, Jr., his assistant. Thomas Bounds and John Rhea were made doorkeepers of the senate and house respectively.[33]

On the second day of the session, a joint meeting of both houses ordered the election returns from the counties to be opened, and after the results had been tallied, Speaker Winchester announced that John Sevier had been "duly and constitutionally elected governor" of the

---

31. Carter, ed., *Territorial Papers, SWT*, IV, p. 420.
32. Smith and Owsley, *The Papers of Andrew Jackson, 1770-1803*, Vol. I, p. 82: McMillan, "A Biographical Sketch of Joseph Anderson (1757-1837)," pp. 86-87.
33. *Journal of the Senate of the State of Tennessee, Begun and Held at Knoxville, on Monday, the Twenty-Eighth of March, One Thousand Seven Hundred and Ninety-Six* (Knoxville: Printed by George Roulstone, Printer to the State, 1796), pp. 3, 4, 48, 49 (hereinafter cited as *Journal of the Senate, March 28, 1796*); *Journal of the House of Representatives of the State of Tennessee, Begun and Held at Knoxville, on Monday, the Twenty-Eighth of March, One Thousand Seven Hundred and Ninety-Six* (Knoxville: Printed by George Roulstone, Printer to the State, 1796), pp. 3, 4, 53, 54 (hereinafter cited as *Journal of the House, March 28, 1796*).

state of Tennessee. Acting at once on the confirmation of Sevier's election, William Blount, as governor of the territory, announced to Secretary of State Pickering that the government of the state of Tennessee was organized and established and that the government of the Territory of the United States South of the River Ohio "has terminated." Sevier was inaugurated the next day to the roar of sixteen rounds of cannon fire discharged in his honor.[34]

Preparing for a joint session on Thursday, March 31, to elect United States senators and a secretary of state, the house nominated William Blount, William Cocke, and Joseph Anderson for the Senate and William Maclin for secretary. The senators accepted the nominees and added only one, Dr. James White for the Senate. Before the balloting began, the house withdrew the name of Anderson, and the senate withdrew the name of Dr. White. In joint session, there was no contest. Blount and Cocke were elected to the Senate and Maclin became secretary of state. Eager for Blount and Cocke to take their places in the United States Senate, the general assembly instructed its clerks to make a transcript from the journals relative to the election of senators, have it signed by the speakers of both houses, attested by their clerks, and forwarded to Governor Sevier for his "certificate and seal of office." The documents thus developed would become the credentials of office necessary for "their obtaining seats in the senate of the United States."[35]

Undaunted by the fact that the political entity they were setting out to govern was by the declaration of its territorial governor no longer a federal territory and, by the hesitance of the federal government, not yet a member state of the Union, the legislators addressed legislation to situations that required it and acted generally as if they were confident in their roles. Many of them had been members of the territorial general assembly, some had been delegates to the constitutional convention, and a few had been legislators in other states, notably North Carolina.

The general assembly debated and passed a total of thirty-five acts. The most extensive legislation dealt with implementing the new government itself. The first act passed set the number of judges for the superior

---

34. Carter, ed., *Territorial Papers, SWT*, IV, p. 422; *Journal of the Senate, March 28, 1796*, pp. 6-8; DeWitt, ed., "Journal of Governor John Sevier, 1790-1815," p. 185.

35. *Journal of the Senate, March 28, 1796*, pp. 7, 9, 11.

court of law and equity, established the qualifications for office, prescribed the required oath, set the salaries, and provided that they would be elected by the legislature. Other acts specified a method for qualifying the secretary of state into office, gave directions for safekeeping the acts and records of the state, and called for the creation of a treasury department.[36]

The legislators provided for the election of an attorney general for each of the three districts of the state, the appointment of electors to cast the state's vote for president and vice president of the United States, and the repeal of an act of the territorial general assembly of 1794 that defined "property deemed taxable." They passed rules and procedures for electing the governor and members of the general assembly, representatives to Congress and militia officers. They acknowledged the governor's compensation set by the constitution and required him to have his residence at the seat of state government. By another act they authorized constitutional rates of compensation for the legislators, clerks, and doorkeepers, and provided for the payment of expenses incident to holding sessions of the general assembly.[37]

A uniform method of presenting memorials to the general assembly that sought the division of counties and/or the placement of courthouses was adopted. Two acts dealt with the collection and appropriation of state revenues, and another repealed all prior fee schedules for county and state offices and set new ones.[38]

Before launching into a sea of legislation primarily of local interest, the general assembly attended to several matters of more general interest. It passed a law to amend an existing statute regulating the descent of real estate through inheritance by declaring daughters' rights of inheritance to be the same and coequal with those of sons. It repealed an act of the territorial general assembly that provided for the relief of such persons as had been disabled by wounds, accidents, or illness suffered while on duty in the militia. Looking with ever more attention to roads and ferries, the legislators provided that a jury of five instead of the former requirement of twelve was adequate to lay out roads in the counties. They ordered ferries to transport electors free of charge

---

36. *Acts Passed at the First General Assembly of the State of Tennessee, Begun and Held at Knoxville, on Monday, the Twenty-Eighth of March, One Thousand Seven Hundred and Ninety-Six* (Knoxville: Printed by George Roulston, Printer to the State, 1796), pp. 2-9. 12-14 (hereinafter cited as *Acts, First General Assembly*).
37. Ibid., pp. 10-12, 22, 23-25, 27-33, 39, 40-41.
38. Ibid., pp. 14-24, 36-37, 39-42.

on election days and gave ferry operators the responsibility for maintaining the riverbanks at their landings. They also agreed on a law for correcting mistakes made in surveying or platting tracts of land.[39]

Nine acts primarily affecting the Mero District were passed. One of them expanded the board of trustees of Davidson Academy and directed it to construct certain buildings for the school "on the hill above Nashville near the road leading to Buchanan's mill" and employ tutors "as soon as the funds will permit." Another provided relief for those who had suffered by the loss of the records of the court of equity in Mero, recently destroyed by fire. An act with maritime overtones prevented the obstruction of the navigation of that part of the Red River from its entrance into the state from Kentucky until it empties into the Cumberland River. The general assembly, responding to confusion over boundary lines and land titles in Nashville, amended the act establishing the town by directing that designated trustees resurvey the town, marking its bounds and laying off such additional lots as they considered appropriate. Authorized to sell the new lots, the trustees were to use the monies received to build a jail and stocks for the district. They were authorized, also, to convey the stone building used by the Methodists as a meetinghouse and the public land on which it stood to that denomination with the provision that, when vacant, it could be used by other sects, and that if the Methodists ceased to use it, title would revert to the city.[40]

As the name Tennessee had been given the state by the constitutional convention, it was decided to divide Tennessee County by creating two counties with new names. The general assembly created Montgomery and Robertson counties, in the latter instance adding to the area by appropriating a small area of western Sumner County. A subsequent statute provided for the location and establishment of the town of Springfield to be the county seat of Robertson. Clarksville was designated the seat of Montgomery, and commissioners appointed to oversee the construction of a jail and stocks there, and another act authorized the establishment of the town of Palmyra, although it was already in existence as Blountsborough, with 246 lots on the south bank of Cumberland River and on both sides of Deason Creek near Clarksville.[41]

In the first of a series of statutory efforts to select a site and name

---

39. Ibid., pp. 38, 44, 45-46, 51-52.
40. Ibid., pp. 9-10, 47-51, 52-53, 64-67.
41. Ibid., pp. 54, 59-60, 67-70, 74-75.

for the county seat of Sumner, the legislature appointed commissioners to determine the location and trustees to buy two hundred acres of land, lay out the town, and sell lots. The act named the town Ca Ira and authorized the construction of a courthouse, prison, and stocks.[42]

Local political maneuvering forestalled the fulfillment of the law, and it was repealed and replaced by successive acts in 1797, 1799, and 1801. The Act of 1801, designating Gallatin as the name for the county seat town to be laid out, withstood opposition, and the town was established the following year.[43]

Fewer acts dealt with the eastern districts. The existence of the town of Maryville, previously authorized as the seat of Blount County, was confirmed, and the county was given the privilege of holding two fairs each year at Maryville "for the purpose of selling all kinds of goods, wares, and merchandise" with free admission to every citizen of the state. The legislature created the new counties of Grainger in Hamilton District and Carter in Washington District. The land for Grainger was taken from Hawkins and Knox; Carter County was formed from the northern extremity of Washington. The usual courthouse, prison, and stocks were authorized for both counties at places to be chosen by commissioners designated for the purpose. Other acts provided for "regulation" of the town of Jonesborough and the repair or new construction there of a courthouse, prison, and stocks; a survey to mark the line between Knox, Jefferson, and Sevier counties; and a survey to delineate the line between Blount and Sevier counties.[44]

Prompted by Governor Sevier, the general assembly took up the question of land rights south of the French Broad River that had been addressed in the Declaration of Rights, Article XI. The governor recommended that the Indians' claim should be extinguished or the "adventurers" compensated for the lands granted to them by North Carolina. By resolution, the state's representatives and senators in the Congress were instructed to advise that body that it was essential to the preservation of peace between the southern Indians and the United States to resolve the land question promptly. The resolution asserted that measures must be taken to "relieve and quiet the grantees of lands under the state of North Carolina, the possession of which is guaranteed

---

42. Ibid., pp. 55-57.
43. Durham, *The Great Leap Westward*, pp. 76-77.
44. *Acts, First General Assembly*, pp. 58-59, 60-63, 71-74, 75-76, 82-83.

to the Indians by treaty, which claim we wish extinguished, and the claimants put in peaceable possession of their lands."[45]

As the session neared its end, Governor Sevier sent a short message to the general assembly in which he reported favorably on relations with the Indians and insisted that "a few years peace would be the most legal and eligible mode to reduce our neighboring tribe to reason and good order." Fearing that further Indian wars would discourage immigration and retard the development of the state, Sevier reminded the legislators they must be aware of the plight of the settlers already in the area:

> Many thousands have moved to our government, not many are wealthy, their resources small, and their wants great; and were they reduced to the melancholy dilemma of entering into forts and blockhouses, I am assured their condition would be distressing and painful in the extreme.[46]

The House responded to Sevier's message on the last day of the session. Agreeing that "peace was a most desirable object," the representatives promised they would "take care that the citizens of this state commit no encroachments upon the Indians; that the conditions of the Treaty of Holston be preserved inviolate."[47]

The general assembly adjourned its first session on April 23. According to William Blount's calculation, the new state was twenty-six days old.[48]

The question of statehood, resolved in the territory, had been in the hands of the Congress since April 8. On that day President Washington had submitted the Tennessee constitution, the enumeration of the inhabitants, and other pertinent documents to both houses. In a letter of transmission, the President commented that the act establishing the Southwest Territory appeared to have extended to its people

> the right of forming a permanent constitution and state government, and of admission, as a state, by its delegates, in the Congress of the United States, on an equal footing with the original states, in all respects whatever, when it should have therein sixty thousand free inhabitants: provided the constitution and government so to be

---

45. *Journal of the Senate, March 28, 1796*, pp. 24, 26.
46. *Journal of the House, March 28, 1796*, pp. 70, 71.
47. Ibid., pp. 74-75.
48. Carter, ed., *Territorial Papers, SWT*, IV, p. 422.

formed should be republican, and in conformity to the principles contained in the articles of said ordinance.[49]

Washington made no recommendation as to the action Congress should take. Perhaps his failure to point a direction was occasioned by the fact that the admission of a state created from a territory was a new experience for the federal government. His cautious attitude was more likely caused by concern for the Federalist party, which had not yet picked a candidate to succeed him. The Federalists feared that a western state would vote for Thomas Jefferson, the likely Republican candidate, in the upcoming presidential election.[50]

In the House of Representatives, the President's message was referred to a committee that, four days later, reported a resolution admitting Tennessee into the Union.

> *Resolved,* That, by the authenticated documents accompanying the message from the President of the United States to this house on the eighth day of the present month, and by the ordinance of Congress bearing date the 13th of July, 1787, and by the law of the United States, passed on the 26th of May, 1790, it appears that the citizens of that part of the United States which has been called the Territory of the United States, South of the River Ohio, and which is now formed into a state under a republican form of government by the name of Tennessee, are entitled to all the rights and privileges to which the citizens of the other states in the Union are entitled, under the Constitution of the United States; and that the state of Tennessee is hereby declared to be one of the sixteen states of the United States of America.[51]

The resolution came before the House for debate on May 5, and it encountered opposition aplenty. Opponents advanced five principal objections. First, they argued that Congress, not the inhabitants of a territory, should initiate by act the formation of a new state. Next, they contended that a census to qualify the region for statehood should have been taken under the direct authority of Congress. Third, the census as taken by Governor Blount was inaccurate because it included "people within" and not "people resident in" the territory, a procedure that may have enumerated travelers and transients who were not inhabitants of the area. Next, opponents claimed that the new state constitution had

---

49. *Annals of the Congress of the United States, Fourth Congress-First Session,* Vol. V (Washington, D.C.: Gales and Seaton, 1849), pp. 891-92.
50. Corlew, *Tennessee, A Short History,* p. 101.
51. *Annals of the Congress of the United States, Fourth Congress-First Session,* Vol. V, p. 1300.

been drawn too hastily and was, in some respects, at odds with the United States Constitution and the act that established the territory. Finally, they asserted that admitting Tennessee under the circumstances would set a dangerous precedent.[52]

Most of the representatives in opposition were willing for Tennessee ultimately to become a state, but the Federalists wanted to delay admission until after the presidential election. In the first speech by members of the opposition, Congressman William L. Smith of South Carolina presented the five points of objection, but concluded that he was willing for the new state to be admitted "provided it was done in a constitutional manner." To him, that meant having Congress declare the territory a state, direct the enumeration of inhabitants, and recognize statehood when the population exceeded the minimum required.[53]

Congressional advocates for admitting Tennessee were led by Thomas Blount of North Carolina, brother of the territorial governor; Albert Gallatin, a Pennsylvania representative who became secretary of the treasury of the United States under President Jefferson; and the future president James Madison. Speaking first, Blount told his colleagues that the House had been dilatory in acting on statehood as "the government of Tennessee had a month ago gone into operation." Reminding them that the President had been advised of "every step taken toward the proposed change of government," Blount explained that the people of the new state believed they were exercising rights guaranteed under compact with the United States.[54]

In a tightly reasoned argument, Albert Gallatin held that "the people of the Southwest Territory became *ipso facto* a state the moment they amounted to sixty thousand free inhabitants, and that it became the duty of Congress, as part of the original compact, to recognize them as such, and to admit them into the Union whenever they had satisfactory proof of the fact." The leadership of the territory had followed the terms of the Ordinance of 1787, and the Congress must do the same or declare that it will not be bound by that law of the land, he said. Nothing in the ordinance prohibited any of the steps taken by the territory, and although Congress might have taken some facilitating or clarifying action

---

52. Ibid., pp. 1300-1304; Hamer, ed., *Tennessee, A History, 1673-1932*, Vol. I, p. 179; *Claypoole's American Daily Advertiser*, May 28, 1796.
53. *Annals of the Congress of the United States, Fourth Congress-First Session*, Vol. V, pp. 1300-1304.
54. Ibid., pp. 1315-16.

along the way, its failure to do so could not fairly be deemed reason to oppose the resolution.

Taking up the question of the accuracy of the census, Gallatin admitted that the law passed by the territorial assembly "differed from that under which the census of the states had been taken," but reminded his listeners that it was acquiesced in by the federal government. To the question of the fairness of its taking, he responded that "on this they [the opposition] had not a shadow of proof."[55]

James Madison said that the only question was the enumeration of inhabitants. If there were sixty thousand more or less, he said, that was all that mattered. If the number exceeded sixty thousand as the governor of the territory had reported, the citizens were being held in a degraded situation, he said, deprived of the right of representation in Congress. He explained that the census had been taken by the governor, appointed by the President with the advice and consent of the Senate, and that until the debate began no question had been raised by either the executive or the legislative branch about the propriety of the taking.[56]

On May 6 after a final bit of ineffectual parliamentary maneuvering by opponents, the resolution admitting Tennessee to the Union was passed in the House by a vote of 43 to 30. Voting followed party lines. Only three Federalists voted in favor, and only two Republicans against admission. There was a sectional dimension to the voting, also. Only one representative from below the Potomac voted against admission, and only three of twenty congressmen from New England voted in favor. Congressmen from the mid-Atlantic states did not align with either section but split their votes.[57]

The debate in the upper house would be quite different, however. The Federalists were in control there.

The Senate committee, to whom the Tennessee statehood application had been referred, reported May 5 that it was of the opinion that the inhabitants of the Southwest Territory were not at that time entitled to be received into the Union as a new state. The committee recommended that leave be given to bring in a bill laying out the territory into one

---

55. Ibid., pp. 1320-22.
56. Ibid., pp. 1308-9.
57. Charlotte Williams, "Congressional Action on the Admission of Tennessee into the Union," *Tennessee Old and New*, Vol. I (Nashville: Tennessee Historical Commission and Tennessee Historical Society, 1946), p. 42.

state and providing for the enumeration of the inhabitants thereof according to the census act of March 1, 1790. The recommendation would delay the admission until after the presidential election, but would bring the state into the Union within the next year or two.[58]

Developing the point that Congress was obligated to lay off the boundaries of a state-to-be before the enumeration was taken, the Senate committee suggested that a territory was not entitled to admission as a state when its population reached sixty thousand, but that a part of the territory, designated by Congress, could attain statehood with the required population. In its report the committee declared:

> The number of inhabitants which establishes a claim of admission must be the number of inhabitants of a state previously laid out, and defined in its boundaries by Congress, and not the number of inhabitants of a Territory which, for the purpose of temporary government, composes a district which may be divided by Congress into several states.[59]

Dr. White, the territorial representative to Congress, believed there was little hope for favorable action by the Senate. He predicted that the "whole business" would be pronounced "a nullity." He had been stunned by the Senate's refusal to permit the reading of Senator-elect William Cocke's credentials upon his arrival. Reaching Philadelphia ahead of Blount, Cocke had drawn the sneers of several Federalist senators who concluded that he had been permitted that honor in order unwittingly to shield the former governor from the first of their hostile darts.[60]

The committee report was taken up by the Senate on May 14, and after debating it for most of the day, the group offered an amendment to admit the new state. It failed by a vote of 14 to 9. On May 18 the Senate passed on first reading a bill incorporating the essence of the committee's original report. A week later it beat back amendments that would have made it agree with the House bill, and on the next day, May 26, the Senate bill entitled "An Act Laying Out into One State the territory ceded by the State of North Carolina to the United States,

---

58. *Annals of the Congress of the United States, Fourth Congress-First Session,* Vol. V, p. 94.
59. Ibid., p. 93. In the case of the Southwest Territory, it could be divided into no more than two states, according to the North Carolina cession act.
60. Dr. White to John Overton, May 13, May 27, 1796, Overton Papers, Murdock Collection.

and providing for an enumeration of the inhabitants thereof" passed third and final reading.[61]

On May 23 the Senate had grudgingly received Cocke and Blount "as spectators" and had provided chairs for them "for that purpose until the final decision of the Senate shall be given on the bill proposing to admit the Southwestern Territory into the Union." The resolution to permit them to observe the proceedings had carried by a single vote, 12 to 11.[62]

With the session nearing adjournment, the Senate bill was considered by the House select committee, which proposed to amend it by declaring Tennessee a state of the Union and, based on the 1790 census, giving it one representative instead of the two expected from the census of 1795. Thus amended, the Senate bill was passed by the House on May 30 and sent to the Senate. When that body refused to concur in the amendment granting statehood, the House was insistent, and a conference committee undertook to reconcile the opposing views. On May 31 the Senate receded from its position, and on June 1, the last day of the session, the act admitting Tennessee into the Union was passed and signed by the President. Senate opponents took satisfaction in refusing the same day to seat Blount and Cocke in their chamber because they had been elected before the state had been accepted into the Union.[63]

Among onlookers during the final day of the session was Andrew Jackson who had arrived from Nashville on the evening of May 31. He had reached Philadelphia too late to lobby for statehood, but he was present when Tennessee became the sixteenth state of the Union. When Congress next assembled, in January, 1797, Jackson would be present as Tennessee's first member of the House of Representatives.[64]

The bill as passed into law reduced Tennessee's representation in the House of Representatives to one instead of the two previously expected and the number of presidential electors from four to three. Senate language in the final version did not recognize that the state existed prior to the passage of the act, a turn that would necessitate a special session

---

61. *Annals of the Congress of the United States, Fourth Congress-First Session*, Vol. V, pp. 89-91, 97, 109.
62. Ibid., p. 103.
63. Ibid., pp. 116, 117, 119, 120-21.
64. Dr. James White to John Overton, June 1, 1796, Overton Papers, Murdock Collection; Corlew, *Tennessee, A Short History*, p. 104.

of the Tennessee legislature to provide for the legal election of Cocke and Blount to the Senate.[65]

About two weeks later Governor Sevier received the news.[66] Elated that Tennessee had been accepted as the sixteenth state of the Union, he called a special session of the general assembly to be convened at Knoxville on July 30, 1796. He explained that he had called both houses to take the action necessary to put the state in full compliance with the statute on Tennessee statehood adopted by the Congress June 1. They must elect two United States senators, provide for the election of a single member of the house of representatives instead of two as previously contemplated, and reduce the number of presidential and vice-presidential electors from four to three.[67]

Probably the first news to reach Nashville from Philadelphia came by letter from Dr. James White. Writing to John Overton on June 1 moments after the admission was passed and prior to the vote on the question of seating the senators, he pointed out that victory had been won in the waning hours of the last day of the session after certain opponents of the measure had left the chamber.[68]

The governor's call for the special session had prompted James Winchester, speaker of the senate, to apprise him of the views of those in Mero District who were questioning the legality of the new state. Noting that Congress had not considered the state to be in existence until it was admitted into the Union, Winchester advanced the opinion that the state constitution and all acts of the legislature were void because a state that did not exist could not act. To remove all doubt, he suggested that a convention should be called to form another or confirm the present constitution, and organize the government anew. He did not pursue the matter further, however, and was present, although a day late, to preside over the senate at the special session.[69]

On August 2, the general assembly in joint session elected Blount and Cocke to the United States Senate and during the following few

---

65. Hamer, ed., *Tennessee, A History, 1673-1932*, Vol. I, p. 182.
66. Cocke and Blount to Sevier, June 2, 1796, Stanley F. Horn Collection, Jean and Alexander Heard Library, Vanderbilt University, Nashville.
67. *Journal of the Senate of the State of Tennessee, Begun and Held at Knoxville, on Saturday, the Thirtieth Day of July, One Thousand Seven Hundred and Ninety-Six* (Knoxville: Printed by George Roulstone, Printer to the State, 1796), pp. 3-5 (hereinafter cited as *Journal of the Senate, July 30, 1796*).
68. Overton Papers, Murdock Collection.
69. Winchester to Sevier, July 19, 1796, Governors Papers, TSLA; Durham, *James Winchester, Tennessee Pioneer*, p. 50.

days provided for the election of a single congressman and three presidential and vice-presidential electors. The requirements of the congressional act had been met. The state of Tennessee would be a full and equal member state of the federal Union until the Civil War when it would find that leaving and reentering the Union was fraught with even more trauma than the entry experience of 1790 to 1796.[70]

The Southwest Territory had vindicated those who drafted the Ordinance of 1787 and had validated their work as a proven blueprint to statehood. With sufficient population growth, a raw, remote frontier had followed the step-by-step progression from a territorial administration to a state of the Union, equal to the older states in all rights and responsibilities. For more than one hundred years after Tennessee became the sixteenth state, other territories spawned governments that followed essentially the same path specified by the ordinance and tested successfully by the Southwest Territory. The process did not end until forty-eight free, equal, and contiguous states blanketed the land from sea to sea.

---

70. *Journal of the Senate, July 30, 1796*, pp. 6-7, 7-16.

BIBLIOGRAPHY

PUBLISHED MATERIAL

BOOKS AND
BOUND OFFICIAL PUBLICATIONS

Acts and Ordinances of the Governor and Judges of the Territory of the United States South of the River Ohio, 1792 and 1793, and Acts of the Territorial General Assembly, 1794 and 1795, included in *Laws of the State of Tennessee*. Knoxville: Printed and Published by George Roulstone, 1803.

Acts Passed at the First General Assembly of the State of Tennessee, Begun and Held at Knoxville, on Monday, the Twenty-Eighth of March, One Thousand Seven Hundred and Ninety-Six. Knoxville: Printed by George Roulstone, Printer to the State, 1796.

Annals of the Congress of the United States, Fourth Congress-First Session. Vol. V. Washington, D.C.: Gales and Seaton, 1849.

Annals of the Congress of the United States, Third Congress-First Session. Vol. IV. Washington, D.C.: Gales and Seaton, 1849.

Arnow, Harriet Simpson. *Flowering of the Cumberland*. New York: The Macmillan Company, 1963.

Asbury, Francis. *The Journal of the Rev. Francis Asbury, Bishop of the Methodist Episcopal Church, From August 7, 1771, to December 7, 1815*. Vol. II. New York: Published by the Methodist Episcopal Church, 1821.

Biographical Directory of the American Congress, 1774-1971. Washington, D.C.: Government Printing Office, 1971.

The Blount Journal, 1790-1796. Nashville: Tennessee Historical Commission, 1955.

Brandau, Roberta Seawell, ed. *History of Homes and Gardens of Tennessee*. Nashville: Parthenon Press, 1936.

Brooks, R. D. *One Hundred and Sixty-Two Years of Middle Tennessee Baptists*. Nashville: N.p., 1958.

Burnett, J. J. *Sketches of Tennessee's Pioneer Baptist Preachers*. Vol. I. Nashville: N.p., 1919.

Caldwell, Benjamin Hubbard, Jr. *Tennessee Silversmiths*. Winston-Salem, North Carolina: The Museum of Early Southern Decorative Arts, 1988.

Caldwell, Joshua W. *Studies in the Constitutional History of Tennessee*. Cincinnati: The Robert Clarke Co., 1895.

Carr, John. *Early Times in Middle Tennessee*. Nashville: Parthenon Press, 1958.

Carter, Clarence Edwin, comp. and ed. *Territorial Papers of the United States, Northwest Territory, 1787-1803*. Vol. II. Washington, D.C.: Government Printing Office, 1934.

_____, comp. and ed. *The Territorial Papers of the United States, Territory of the United States South of the River Ohio, 1790-1796*. Vol. IV. Washington, D.C.: Government Printing Office, 1936.

Carter, Cullen T. *Methodism in the Wilderness, 1786-1836*. Nashville: Parthenon Press, 1959.

Clark, Walter, ed. *The State Records of North Carolina*. 26 vols. Goldsboro, North Carolina: Nash Brothers, 1886-1907.

Clayton, W. Woodford. *History of Davidson County, Tennessee, with Illustrations and Biographical Sketches of Its Prominent Men and Pioneers*. Philadelphia: J. W. Lewis, 1880. Nashville: Charles Elder, 1971.

Constitution of the State of Tennessee, Unanimously Established in Convention at Knoxville, the Sixth Day of February, One Thousand Seven Hundred and Ninety-Six. Philadelphia: Printed for Thomas Condie, No. 20 Carter's Alley, 1796.

Corlew, Robert E. *Tennessee, A Short History.* 2d ed. Knoxville: University of Tennessee Press, 1981.

De Pauw, Linda Grant, ed. *Documentary History of the First Federal Congress of the United States of America, March 4, 1789-March 3, 1791.* Vol. II, *Senate Executive Journal and Related Documents;* and VI, *Legislative Histories.* Baltimore: Johns Hopkins University Press, 1972, 1986.

Deaderick, Lucile, ed. *Heart of the Valley, A History of Knoxville, Tennessee.* Knoxville: East Tennessee Historical Society, 1976.

Dobson, John. *The Lost Roulstone Imprints.* Knoxville: The University of Tennessee Library, 1975.

Doughty, Richard H. *Greeneville, One Hundred Year Portrait, 1775-1875.* Greeneville, Tennessee: Published for the author, 1975.

Driver, Carl. *John Sevier, Pioneer of the Old Southwest.* 2d ed. Nashville: Charles and Randy Elder, Booksellers, 1973.

Durham, Walter T. *Daniel Smith, Frontier Statesman.* Gallatin, Tennessee: Sumner County Library Board, 1976.

_____. *The Great Leap Westward.* Gallatin, Tennessee: Sumner County Library Board, 1969.

_____. *James Winchester, Tennessee Pioneer.* Gallatin, Tennessee: Sumner County Library Board, 1979.

Eblen, Jack Ericson. *The First and Second United States Empires, Governors, and Territorial Government, 1784-1912.* Pittsburgh: University of Pittsburgh Press, 1968.

Egerton, John. *Nashville: The Faces of Two Centuries, 1780-1980.* Nashville: Plus Media, Incorporated, 1979.

The Gentleman's Magazine for April, 1791. Vol. LXI, No. 1, Part I. London: Printed by John Nichols for David Henry, 1791.

Gilmore, James Roberts. *The Advanced Guard of Western Civilization.* New York: D. Appleton and Company, 1888.

Hamer, Philip M., ed. *Tennessee, A History, 1673-1932.* Vol. I. New York: The American Historical Society, Inc., 1933.

Haywood, John. *The Civil and Political History of the State of Tennessee.* Reprint. Knoxville: The Tenase Company, 1969.

Henderson, Archibald. *The Conquest of the Old Southwest.* New York: The Century Co., 1920.

Hening, William Waller, ed. *The Statutes at Large; Being a Collection of all the Laws of Virginia, from the First Session of the Legislature in the Year 1619.* 13 vols. Richmond: Printed by and for Samuel Pleasants, Jr., Printer to the Commonwealth, 1809-1823.

Herndon, G. Malvin. *William Tatham, 1752-1819.* Johnson City, Tennessee: Research Advisory Council, East Tennessee State University, 1973.

History of Tennessee, From the Earliest Times to the Present: Together with an Historical and a Biographical Sketch of the County of Knox and the City of Knoxville, Besides a Valuable Fund of Notes, Original Observations, Reminiscences, etc., etc. Easley, South Carolina: Southern Historical Press, 1982. Reprint of portions of a volume originally published at Nashville: Goodspeed Publishing Co., 1887.

Imlay, Gilbert. *A Topographical Description of the Western Territory.* 3d ed. London: Printed for J. Debritt, 1797.

Journal of the House of Representatives of the State of Tennessee, Begun and Held at Knoxville, on Monday, the Twenty-Eighth of March, One Thousand Seven Hundred and Ninety-Six. Knoxville: Printed by George Roulstone, Printer to the State, 1796.

BIBLIOGRAPHY

Journal of the House of Representatives of the United States, Being the Second Session of the First Congress, Begun and Held at the City of New York, January 4, 1790. Washington, D.C.: Gales and Seaton, 1826.

Journal of the House of Representatives of the United States, Being the Third Session of the First Congress, Begun and Held at the City of Philadelphia, December 6, 1790. Washington, D.C.: Gales and Seaton, 1834.

Journal of the Proceedings of a Convention, Begun and Held at Knoxville, January 11, 1796. Knoxville: Printed by George Roulstone, 1796.

Journal of the Proceedings of the House of Representatives of the Territory of the United States of America, South of the River Ohio, Begun and Held at Knoxville, the 25th day of August, 1794. Knoxville: Printed by George Roulstone, Printer to the Territory, 1794.

Journal of the Proceedings of the House of Representatives of the Territory of the United States of America, South of the River Ohio, Begun and Held at Knoxville, the 29th Day of June, 1795. Knoxville: Printed by George Roulstone, Printer to the Territory, 1795.

Journal of the Proceedings of the Legislative Council of the Territory of the United States of America, South of the River Ohio, Begun and Held at Knoxville, the 25th Day of August, 1794. Knoxville: Printed by George Roulstone, Printer to the Territory, 1794.

Journal of the Proceedings of the Legislative Council of the Territory of the United States of America, South of the River Ohio, Begun and Held at Knoxville, the 29th Day of June, 1795. Knoxville: Printed by George Roulstone, Printer to the Territory, 1795.

Journal of the Senate of the State of Tennessee, Begun and Held at Knoxville, on Monday, the Twenty-Eighth of March, One Thousand Seven Hundred and Ninety-Six. Knoxville: Printed by George Roulstone, Printer to the State, 1796.

Journal of the Senate of the State of Tennessee, Begun and Held at Knoxville, on Saturday, the Thirtieth Day of July, One Thousand Seven Hundred and Ninety-Six. Knoxville: Printed by George Roulstone, Printer to the State, 1796.

Journal of the Senate of the United States of America, Being the Second Session of the Second Congress, Begun and Held at the City of Philadelphia, November 5, 1792. Philadelphia: Printed by John Fenno, in Fifth Street, 1792.

Keith, Alice Barnwell, ed. *The John Gray Blount Papers.* 4 vols. Raleigh, North Carolina: State Department of Archives and History, 1952-82.

Laws of the State of Tennessee including Acts and Ordinances of the Governor and Judges of the Territory of the United States South of the River Ohio, 1792 and 1793, and Acts of the Territorial General Assembly, 1794 and 1795. Knoxville: Printed and Published by George Roulstone, 1803.

Lefler, Hugh T., and Albert R. Newsom. *North Carolina, The History of a Southern State.* Chapel Hill: University of North Carolina Press, 1954.

Letter From the Secretary at War Accompanying His Report Relative to the Running of a Line of Experiment From Clinch River to Chilhowee Mountain, By Order of the Governor of the Territory of the United States South of the Ohio, In Pursuance of a Resolution of the House of Representatives of the 28th Ultimo. Philadelphia: Printed by Order of the House of Representatives, 1798.

Lindley, Harlow, Norris F. Schneider, and Milo M. Quaife. *History of the Ordinance of 1787 and the Old Northwest Territory.* Marietta, Ohio: Northwest Territory Celebration Commission, 1937.

Lowrie, Walter, and Matthew St. Clair Clarke, eds. *American State Papers, Class II, Indian Affairs.* 2 vols. Washington, D.C.: Gales and Seaton, 1832.

Masterson, William Henry. *William Blount.* New York: Greenwood Press, 1969.

McFerrin, John B. *History of Methodism in Tennessee.* 3 vols. Nashville: A. H. Redford, Agent, Methodist Episcopal Church South, 1875.

McLoughlin, William G. *Cherokee Renascence in the New Republic.* Princeton, New Jersey: Princeton University Press, 1986.

McRee, Griffith J. *Life and Correspondence of James Iredell, One of the Associate Justices of the Supreme Court of the United States.* Vol. II. 1857. Reprint. New York: Peter Smith, 1949.

Morris, Eastin. *The Tennessee Gazetteer.* Nashville: W. Hasell Hunt & Co., 1834.

Nevins, Allen. *The American States During and After the Revolution, 1775-1789.* New York: The Macmillan Company, 1927.

The New Encyclopaedia Britannica. Vol. 4. Chicago: Encyclopaedia Britannica, Inc., 1988.

Norton, Herman A. *Religion in Tennessee, 1777-1945.* Knoxville: University of Tennessee Press, 1981.

Patrick, James. *Architecture in Tennessee, 1768-1897.* Knoxville: University of Tennessee Press, 1981.

Picken, Mary Brooks. *The Fashion Dictionary; Fabric, Sewing and Dress as Expressed in the Language of Fashion.* New York: Funk and Wagnalls Company, 1957.

Posey, Walter Brownlow. *The Baptist Church in the Lower Mississippi Valley, 1776-1845.* Lexington, Kentucky: University of Kentucky Press, 1957.

_____. *The Presbyterian Church in the Old Southwest, 1778-1838.* Richmond, Virginia: John Knox Press, 1952.

Price, Richard Nye. *Holston Methodism. From Its Origin to the Present Time.* 5 vols. Nashville and Dallas: Publishing House of the Methodist Episcopal Church South, 1903-19.

Putnam, Albigence W. *History of Middle Tennessee or Life and Times of General James Robertson.* Nashville: N.p., 1859.

Ramsey, J. G. M. *The Annals of Tennessee to the End of the Eighteenth Century.* 1853. Reprint. Kingsport: East Tennessee Historical Society, 1967.

Return of the Whole Number of Persons Within the Several Districts of the United States, According to "An Act providing for the enumeration of the inhabitants of the United States," passed March the first, seventeen hundred and ninety-one. Washington City: Printed by William Duane, 1802.

[Smith, Daniel]. *A Short Description of the Tennassee Government, or the Territory of the United States South of the River Ohio to Accompany and Explain a Map of that Country.* Philadelphia: Mathew Carey, Bookseller, 1793.

Smith, Sam B., and Harriet Chappell Owsley, eds. *The Papers of Andrew Jackson, 1770-1803.* Vol. I. Knoxville: University of Tennessee Press, 1980.

Sparks, Jared. *The Works of Benjamin Franklin.* Vol. X. Boston: Tappan and Whittemore, 1840.

_____. *The Writings of George Washington.* Vol. X. Boston: American Stationers' Company, 1836.

Thwaites, Reuben Gold, ed. *Travels West of the Alleghanies Made in 1793-96 by André Michaux; in 1802 by F. A. Michaux; and in 1803 by Thaddeus Mason Harris, M.A.* Cleveland, Ohio: The Arthur A. Clark Company, 1904.

Tindall, Samuel W. *The Baptists of Tennessee.* Kingsport: Southern Publishers, Inc., 1930.

Wagstaff, H. M., ed. *The Papers of John Steele.* 2 vols. Raleigh, North Carolina: Publications of the North Carolina Historical Commission, 1924.

Weeks, Stephen B. *Southern Quakers and Slavery, A Study in Institutional History.* Baltimore: The Johns Hopkins Press, 1896.

Whitaker, Arthur P. *The Spanish-American Frontier, 1783-1795.* Boston and New York: Houghton Mifflin Company, 1927.

White, Robert H., ed. *Messages of the Governors of Tennessee, 1796-1821.* Vol. I. Nashville: Tennessee Historical Commission, 1952.

Whitley, Edythe Rucker. *Red River Settlers.* Baltimore: Genealogical Publishing Company, Inc., 1980.

Williams, Derita Coleman, and Nathan Harsh. *The Art and Mystery of Tennessee Furniture and Its Makers Through 1850.* Edited by C. Tracey Parks. Nashville: Tennessee Historical Society and Tennessee State Museum Foundation, 1988.

Williams, Samuel C. *The Lost State of Franklin.* Rev. ed. New York: The Press of the Pioneers, 1933.

_____. *Phases of Southwest Territory History.* Johnson City, Tennessee: The Watauga Press, 1940.

ARTICLES

Allen, Ben, and Dennis T. Lawson. "The Wataugans and the 'Dangerous Example.'" *Tennessee Historical Quarterly,* Vol. XXVI (Summer 1967).

Allison, John. "The 'Mero' District." *Tennessee Old and New.* Vol. I. Nashville: Tennessee Historical Commission and Tennessee Historical Society, 1946.

Arnow, Harriet Simpson. "Education and Professions in the Cumberland Region." *Tennessee Historical Quarterly,* Vol. XX (June 1961).

_____. "The Pioneer Farmer and his Crops in the Cumberland Region." *Tennessee Historical Quarterly,* Vol. XIX (December 1960).

Bentley, George F. "Printers and Printing in the Southwest Territory, 1790-1796." *Tennessee Historical Quarterly,* Vol. VIII (December 1949).

Berkhofer, Robert F., Jr. "The Northwest Ordinance and the Principle of Territorial Evolution." *The American Territorial System.* Edited by John Porter Bloom, National Archives Conferences. Vol. V. Athens: Ohio University Press, 1973.

Boniol, John Dawson, Jr. "The Walton Road." *Tennessee Historical Quarterly,* Vol. XXX (Winter 1971).

Cobb, P. L. "William Cobb—Host to Governor William Blount." *Tennessee Historical Magazine,* Vol. IX (January 1926).

Corbitt, D. C. "Exploring the Southwest Territory in the Spanish Archives." East Tennessee Historical Society *Publications,* No. 38 (1966).

Corbitt, D. C., and Roberta Corbitt, eds. "Papers from the Spanish Archives Relating to Tennessee and the Old Southwest." East Tennessee Historical Society *Publications,* Nos. 14-22 (1942-50).

Cox, Isaac Joslin, and Reginald McGrane, eds. "Documents Relating to Zachariah Cox." *Quarterly Publication of the Historical and Philosophical Society of Ohio,* Vol. VIII, Nos. 2 and 3 (combined issue; April-June, July-September 1913).

De Friece, Pauline Massengill, and Frank B. Williams, Jr. "Rocky Mount: The Cobb-Massengill Home, First Capitol of the Territory South of the River Ohio." *Tennessee Historical Quarterly,* Vol. XXV (Summer 1966).

Deschamps, Margaret Burr. "Early Days in the Cumberland Country." *Tennessee Historical Quarterly,* Vol. VI (September, 1947).

DeWitt, John H., ed. "Journal of Governor John Sevier, 1790-1815." *Tennessee Historical Magazine,* Vol. V (October 1919).

Dickinson, W. Calvin. "Frontier Splendor: The Carter Mansion at Sycamore Shoals." *Tennessee Historical Quarterly,* Vol. XLI (Winter 1982).

Downs, Randolph C. "Indian Affairs in the Southwest Territory, 1790-1796." *Tennessee Historical Magazine,* Series II, Vol. III (January 1937).

Durham, Walter T. "Kasper Mansker: Cumberland Frontiersman." *Tennessee Historical Quarterly,* Vol. XXX (1971).

_____. "Thomas Sharp Spencer, Man or Legend." *Tennessee Historical Quarterly*, Vol. XXXI (1972).
Fink, Paul M. "The Bumpass Cove Mines and Embreeville," East Tennessee Historical Society *Publications*, No. 16 (1944).
Folmsbee, Stanley J., and Susan Hill Dillon. "The Blount Mansion." *Tennessee Historical Quarterly*, Vol. XXII (June 1963).
Garrett, William R., ed. "Correspondence of General James Robertson." *American Historical Magazine*, Vols. I-V (January 1896-April 1900).
Goodpasture, A. V. "The Beginnings of Montgomery County." *American Historical Magazine*, Vol. 8 (July 1903).
_____. "Dr. James White, Pioneer, Politician, Lawyer." *Tennessee Historical Magazine*, Vol. 1 (December 1915).
_____. "William Blount and the Old Southwest Territory." *American Historical Magazine*, Vol. 8 (January 1903).
Goodstein, Anita. "Black History on the Nashville Frontier, 1780-1810." *Tennessee Historical Quarterly*, Vol. XXXVII (Winter 1979).
Hamer, Philip M. "The British in Canada and the Southern Indians." East Tennessee Historical Society *Publications*, No. 2 (1930).
_____, ed. "Letters of Governor William Blount." East Tennessee Historical Society *Publications*, No. 4 (1932).
_____, ed. "A Muster Roll of Captain Jacob Tipton's Company in St. Clair's Campaign." East Tennessee Historical Society *Publications*, No. 3 (January 1931).
Henderson, Archibald. "Richard Henderson: The Authorship of the Cumberland Compact and the Founding of Nashville." *Tennessee Historical Magazine*, Vol. 2 (September 1916).
Holmes, Jack D. L. "Spanish-American Rivalry Over the Chickasaw Bluffs, 1780-1795." East Tennessee Historical Society *Publications*, No. 34 (1962).
Holt, Albert C. "The Economic and Social Beginnings of Tennessee." *Tennessee Historical Magazine*, Vol. VII (October 1921).
Keith, Alice Barnwell. "Letters From Major James Cole Mountflorence to Members of the Blount Family (William, John Gray, and Thomas) From on Shipboard, Spain, France, Switzerland, England, and America, January 22, 1792—July 21, 1796." *North Carolina Historical Review*, Vol. XIV (July 1937).
Kincaid, Robert L. "The Wilderness Road in Tennessee." East Tennessee Historical Society *Publications*, No. 20 (1948).
Livingood, James W. "The Tennessee Country at the Birth of a Nation." *Chattanews*, Vol. XVIII (December 1987).
Masterson, William H. "The Land Speculator and the West—The Role of William Blount." East Tennessee Historical Society *Publications*, No. 27 (1955).
_____. "William Blount and the Establishment of the Southwest Territory." East Tennessee Historical Society *Publications*, No. 23 (1951).
McMillan, Fay E. "A Biographical Sketch of Joseph Anderson (1757-1837)." East Tennessee Historical Society *Publications*, No. 2 (1930).
McMurry, Donald L. "The Indian Policy of the Federal Government and the Economic Development of the Southwest, 1789-1801." *Tennessee Historical Magazine*, Vol. I (March 1915).
Miller, C. Somers. "The Joseph Brown Story; Pioneer and Indian in Tennessee History." *Tennessee Historical Quarterly*, Vol. XXXII (Spring 1973).
"Narrative of John Davis, Esq." *Southwestern Monthly*, Vol. I (April 1852).
"Papers of General Daniel Smith." *American Historical Magazine*, Vol. VI (July 1901).
"Pioneer Documents." *American Historical Magazine*, Vol. V (October 1900).
"Pioneer Letters." *American Historical Magazine*, Vol. II (January 1897).

Provine, W. A. "Lardner Clark, Nashville's First Merchant and Foremost Citizen." *Tennessee Historical Magazine,* Vol. III, Nos. 1 and 2 (March and June 1917).

Sioussat, St. George L. "The North Carolina Cession of 1784 in its Federal Aspects." *Proceedings of the Mississippi Valley Historical Association, 1908-1909.* Vol. II. Cedar Rapids, Iowa: The Torch Press, 1910.

"A Statement of the Grievances of the Grand Jury of Hamilton District, Superior Court of Law, April Term, 1795." *American Historical Magazine,* Vol. II (October 1897).

Storm, Colton, ed. "Up the Tennessee in 1790: The Report of Major John Doughty to the Secretary of War." East Tennessee Historical Society *Publications,* No. 17 (1945).

Symonds, Craig. "The Failure of America's Indian Policy on the Southwestern Frontier, 1785-1793." *Tennessee Historical Quarterly,* Vol. XXXV (Spring 1976).

Turner, Frederick Jackson. "The Policy of France Toward the Mississippi Valley in the Period of Washington and Adams." *American Historical Review,* Vol. X (1905).

Whitaker, Arthur P. "The Muscle Shoals Speculation." *Mississippi Valley Historical Review,* Vol. 13 (1926).

White, Kate. "John Chisholm, A Soldier of Fortune." East Tennessee Historical Society *Publications,* No. 1 (1929).

Williams, Charlotte. "Congressional Action on the Admission of Tennessee into the Union." *Tennessee Old and New.* Vol. I. Nashville: Tennessee Historical Commission and Tennessee Historical Society, 1946.

Williams, Samuel Cole. "Colonel David Henley." East Tennessee Historical Society *Publications,* No. 8 (1946).

_____. "Early Iron Works in the Tennessee Country." *Tennessee Historical Quarterly,* Vol. VI (March 1947).

_____. "The South's First Cotton Factory." *Tennessee Historical Quarterly,* Vol. V (September 1946).

_____. "The Southwest Territory to the Aid of the Northwest Territory, 1791." *Indiana Magazine of History,* Vol. XXXVII (June 1941).

NEWSPAPERS

Augusta *Chronicle and Gazette of the State.*
Claypoole's American Daily Advertiser.
Connecticut *Courant* (Hartford).
Dunlap and Claypoole's American Daily Advertiser.
Dunlap's American Daily Advertiser.
Dunlap's Daily Advertiser.
Kentucky *Gazette.*
Knoxville *Gazette.*
New York *Daily Advertiser.*
Philadelphia *Aurora. General Advertiser.*
Philadelphia *Gazette of the United States.*

MAPS

"A Map of the Tennassee Government formerly Part of North Carolina taken chiefly from surveys by Gen'l D. Smith and Others, J. T. Scott, sculp." *Guthrie's Geography.* Philadelphia: Mathew Carey, 1794. Plate 31.

UNPUBLISHED MATERIALS

Blount Correspondence. McClung Collection, Knoxville Public Library.

Blount County, Tennessee, Records:
Quarterly Court Minutes, Microfilm, TSLA.

Blount Family Papers, 1794-1829. Historic New Orleans Collection.

Blount, William. Letters. Special Collections, Hoskins Library, University of Tennessee, Knoxville.

Claybrooke and Overton Papers. Tennessee Historical Society, TSLA.

Coffee Papers. Dyas Collection, TSLA.

The Cumberland Compact, Tennessee Historical Society, TSLA.

Davidson County, Tennessee, Records:
Deed Books B and C, Microfilm, TSLA.
Minutes of the Superior Court of North Carolina Including Mero District, 1788-1803, Microfilm, TSLA.
Quarterly Court Minutes, Microfilm, TSLA.
Wills and Inventories, Microfilm, TSLA.

Dickenson, Jacob McGavock. Papers. TSLA.

Donelson, John. Journal. Tennessee Historical Society, TSLA.

Draper Manuscripts. The Collection of Lyman C. Draper held by the State Historical Society of Wisconsin, Madison.

First Presbyterian Church, Knoxville, Tennessee, Church Records, 1792-1967. Church Records—Presbyterian, TSLA.

French Broad River Baptist Church, Minutes, 1786-1842. Historical Records Project, TSLA.

Governors Papers. TSLA.

Greene County, Tennessee, Records:
Quarterly Court Minutes, Microfilm, TSLA.
Minutes of Court of Pleas and Quarter Sessions, 1783-1796, Microfilm, TSLA.

Greer, Joseph. Papers. TSLA.

Gump, Lucy K. "Possessions and Patterns of Living in Washington County: The 20 Years Before Tennessee Statehood, 1777-1796." Thesis, East Tennessee State University, 1989.

Hagy, James W. "Frankland: The Dream of Southern Appalachian Statehood, 1769-1786." Typescript. Piney Flats, Tennessee: Friends of Rocky Mount, 1989.

BIBLIOGRAPHY

Henley, David. Letters. Special Collections, MS 736, Hoskins Library, University of Tennessee, Knoxville.

Henley, David. Papers, 1748-1823. TSLA.

Henley Papers. William R. Perkins Library, Duke University, Durham, North Carolina.

Horn, Stanley F. Collection. Jean and Alexander Heard Library, Vanderbilt University, Nashville.

Jefferson County, Tennessee, Records:
Quarterly Court Minutes, Microfilm, TSLA.

Johnson, Liz M. "Construction Analysis of Rocky Mount." Typescript. Rocky Mount Historical Association, January, 1981, Tennessee Historical Commission.

Kincaid, Robert L., ed. "History of the Southwest Territory, 1790-1796, by Samuel Cole Williams." Typescript. Nashville: Tennessee Historical Commission, 1960.

Knox County, Tennessee, Records:
Minutes of the Quarterly Court of Knox County, Book O, 1792-1795, Transcribed and prepared by the Tennessee Historical Records Survey, Work Projects Administration, March, 1941, TSLA.

Minutes of the Tenn. Baptist Association, Holston, 1786-1850, Pub. no. 836. Nashville: Historical Commission, Southern Baptist Convention, n.d., Microfilm, Southern Baptist Convention Archives and Library, Nashville.

Miscellaneous Manuscript File, Tennessee Historical Society, TSLA.

National Archives:
Record Group 46, Records of the United States Senate, "Territorial Papers of the United States Senate, 1789-1873, Territory of the United States South of the River Ohio, 1789-1808," M-200, Roll 2.
Record Group 94, Department of the Army, Records of the Adjutant General's Office, 1780s Through 1917, "Compiled Service Records of Volunteer Soldiers Who Served from 1784 to 1811, Territory South of the River Ohio," M-905, Rolls 26-32.
Record Group 94, "War Department Collection of Post Revolutionary War Manuscripts, Territory Southwest of Ohio River," M-904, Roll 4.

North Carolina Legislative and Gubernatorial Papers Relating to Tennessee. TSLA.

Overton, John. Papers. Murdock Collection, Tennessee Historical Society, TSLA.

Ration Claims List. Sumner County Archives, Gallatin, Tennessee.

Robertson, James. Papers. TSLA.

Sevier, John. Papers. McClung Collection, Knoxville Public Library.

Shelby County, Tennessee, Records:
Grant Book 1, 1819-20, Microfilm, TSLA.

Shiloh Presbyterian Church, 1793-1847. Historical Records Project, TSLA.

Sumner County, Tennessee, Records:
    Quarterly Court Minutes, Microfilm, TSLA.

Washington County, Tennessee, Records:
    Quarterly Court Minutes, Microfilm, TSLA.
    Superior Court Minutes Book, 1793-1795, Microfilm, TSLA.

Index

A

Abingdon, Va., 16, 100, 139, 140, 227, 240
Abongpohigo, 173-74
Abraham, a slave, 102
Absalom, Morris, 107
Academy's ferry, the, 235
Acuff, Francis, 243-44
Acuff's Chapel, 243-44
Adair, Edward, 133
Adair, John, 99, 103, 252
Adams, John, 151, 233
Alexander, Thomas, 213
Alexandria, Va., 37-38, 244
Algerines (Algerians), 152
Allison, David, 44, 140, 148-49, 216-17, 217n, 228, 234
American Revolution, 3, 7, 19, 32, 57
Amis, Thomas, 98, 105
Anderson, James, 128
Anderson, John, 10
Anderson, Joseph, 33, 33n, 45, 55, 94, 173-74, 186, 252-54, 259, 261
Antrim, 213
Appalachian Mountains, 3, 18-19, 25-26, 27, 41, 95, 207
Armstrong, James, 227
Armstrong, James ("Trooper"), 59
Armstrong, John, 20, 28, 52
Armstrong, Martin, 56, 217-18
Arthur, T., 106
Asbury, Bishop Francis, 105-06, 237, 243-45
Ashe, John B., 32
Atkinson, William A., 229
Augusta *Chronicle and Gazette of the State*, 238n

Avery line of 1777, 6, 12
Avery's Trace, 7

B

Baker, Elisha, 252
Baker, Isaac, 235
Baker's ferry, 235
Balch, Hezekiah, 241-42
Bald Mountain, 27
Ball, Nicholas, 122, 166
Baltimore, Md., 93, 99, 224-25, 228
Baptists, 104-05, 245-47
Barton, Isaac, 246
Bastille, 30
Bean, George, 99, 229
Bean, William, 4
Bean's station, 100
Bear Creek, 49, 75, 78-79, 99, 164
Beard, Hugh, 57, 85, 116
Beard, John, 131-36, 140, 150, 159, 165, 176, 185
Bearden, John, 98
Beaver Creek (Baptist Church), 246
Beaver Dam Creek, 167, 169, 184, 230
Beech Creek (Baptist Church), 246
Benge, Bob (The Bench), 121, 171
Bent Creek (Baptist Church), 246
Bent Creek Store, 226
Berry, James, 252
Beth-car, *see* Moore's chapel
Betty (daughter of Nancy Ward), 132
Betty (wife of Hanging Maw), 132
Big Pigeon River, 29, 137, 226, 255
Big Tellico, 137, 169
Big Hatchie River, *see* Hatchee River
Big Valley town, 137
Big House Tavern, 232

283

Birchett, Henry, 244-45
Bird, Francis, 99
Bird's station, 122
Black, Joseph, 252, 254
Black, William, 228
Black's blockhouse, 84
Blackburn, Gabriel, 233
Blackburn, Gideon, 242
Blackmore, George D., 118
Bledsoe, Anthony, 14, 18n, 19, 21-22, 102, 112, 168, 182
Bledsoe, Anthony (son of Anthony), 168
Bledsoe, Anthony (son of Isaac), 168
Bledsoe, Catherine Montgomery, 116
Bledsoe, Isaac, 18n, 22, 115, 168
Bledsoe, Thomas, 182
Bledsoe's fort, 115, 182, 237
Bledsoe's Lick, 7, 18, 20, 22, 81-82, 115, 118, 162, 183, 193, 195, 199, 236-37, 242
Bloodworth, Timothy, 32
Bloody Fellow, 58-61, 69, 74-76, 83, 170, 180, 187, 204
Blount College, 161, 239, 242
Blount County, 200, 209, 231, 252, 254, 264
Blount, John Gray, 20, 32, 43, 101, 139, 148, 164, 169, 216-17
Blount, Mary Sumner, 95
Blount, Thomas, 32, 95, 101, 152, 216-17, 267
Blount, William, 20, 26-27, 29, 32-34, 36-39, 41-47, 49, 51, 53-57, 57n, 58-63, 66-67, 69, 71-83, 85-87, 89-91, 93-97, 100, 109-10, 112, 115-17, 119, 123-31, 133, 139-40, 142, 144-53, 155-56, 159, 163-65, 167, 169, 173, 175, 177-79, 181-86, 188-89, 189n, 191-95, 198-200, 203-04, 206-07, 209-12, 214, 214n, 215, 215n, 216-17, 219, 225-27, 230, 234, 238-40, 245n, 252-54, 258-61, 265-66, 269-71
Blount, Mrs. William, 95
Blount, Willie, 206, 247
Blountsborough, 263

Blountville, 97, 200, 212, 231, 244
Bob, a free black, 233
Bob, the slave, 221
Boggs, John, 173
Bold Hunter, 133
Bosley, James, 102, 222
Boston *Gazette and Republican Weekly Journal*, 238n
Bounds, Thomas, 260
Bowen, William, 98
Bowles, William Augustus, 52, 70, 73, 74n
Bowyer, Luke, 247
Bradford, Henry, 109, 202, 219
Breath of Nickajack, the, 74-75
Briggance, Robert, 182
Brigham, James, 239
Bristol, 39
Brooks, Stephen, 252
Broom, the, 74
Brown, Jacob, 85
Brown, John, 187
Brown, Joseph, 176
Brown, Dr. Morgan, 248
Brown's station, 22, 80
Brushy Creek (of Red River), 85, 98
Bryan, Peter, 252
Buchanan's mill, 263
Buchanan's station, 84, 86, 178
Buckenham, Thomas, 252
Buckingham, Nathaniel, 260
Buffalo Ridge (Baptist Church), 246
Buffalo Town, 171
Bull's Gap, 98
Bull's Run, 131, 165, 176
Bumpass Cove, 99
Burke, William, 244
Buxton, John, 244

C

Ca Ira, 264
Cabin, the, 74
Cage, William, 10-11
Campbell, Arthur, 16, 50, 259
Campbell, David, 10, 33, 33n, 41, 43, 64, 66-67, 81, 94, 119, 162, 205

Campbell, Eliza, 215
Campbella, 215
Campbell's station, 98, 135
Caney Fork River, 4, 116, 118
Carey, James, 58, 69-70
Carey, Mathew, 214, 214n, 215
Carlock, Abraham, 247
Carmichael, Alexander, 98, 221, 230, 232
Carmichael, David, 132
Carmichael, James, 233
Carmichael's tavern, 158n
Carnes, Thomas P., 201
Carondelet, Luis Francisco Hector-Baron de, 67, 68, 73, 126, 185
Carr, John, 245
Carrick, Samuel C., 103-04, 151, 242, 253
Carson, James, 235
Carter County, 264
Carter, John, 98
Carter, Landon, 10, 11, 42, 45, 67, 99, 202, 218, 245n, 252-53
Casteel, William, 168
Castleman, Abraham, 138
Caswell, Richard, 13-14, 39
Catholics, 106
Cavet, Alexander, 121, 141-42
Charleston, S.C., 69, 156, 238
Charley (of Running Water), 74
Charter, James, 239
Chattanooga, 20, 72
Cherokee Creek (Baptist Church), 246
Cherokee Indians, 5-7, 12-13, 17, 20, 23, 40, 45, 47n, 48-52, 54-55, 57-59, 61-62, 67, 69-79, 82-89, 91, 93, 102, 110-12, 116-18, 121-29, 131-38, 140-42, 151, 155, 157-58, 162-63, 165, 167, 169-71, 173-76, 178-82, 184-89, 193-96, 204-07, 209, 219, 236, 242
Chester, Dr. William P., 248
Chew, Samuel T., 193
Chickamauga Creek, 174
Chickamauga Indians, 20-21, 23, 60, 72, 80, 172

Chickasaw Bluffs, 6, 114, 196, 219
Chickasaw Indians, 5-6, 17, 23, 38, 47, 47n, 52, 56, 69, 70, 74, 76-79, 93, 101, 112, 114, 116, 126, 128-29, 134, 138-39, 157-58, 164, 175-76, 178, 184, 189-96, 201, 203-06, 215, 219, 228, 236
Chilhowee Mountain (village), 88, 91, 170, 209
Chisholm, John, 58, 75-76, 94, 96, 98, 100, 139, 157, 163, 191, 203, 206, 227, 232, 236
Choctaw Indians, 5, 38, 47n, 69-70, 74, 76-79, 93, 116, 175-76, 189, 192-94, 196, 201, 203-04, 228, 236
Chota, 93, 123
Christian, Gilbert, 42, 141
Christian, Robert, 103
Cincinnati, Ohio, 65
Clack, John, 252, 254
Clack, Spencer, 252
Claiborne, W. C. C., 247, 252-54
Clark, George Rogers, 154
Clark, Lardner, 228, 239, 241
Clark Mountain, 216
Clarksville, 7, 97, 111, 183, 200, 212, 238, 263
Clayton, Seward, 84
Clear Fork (Baptist Church), 246
Clinch Mountain, 21
Clinch River, 4, 17, 40, 56, 60, 87-88, 91, 119, 124, 141, 165, 184, 209, 216-17
Cloyd's plantation, 120
Clymer, George, 203
Cobb, Ethelred, 66n
Cobb, William, 39, 39n, 40, 43, 56, 66n, 95
Cocke, John, 247
Cocke, William, 11, 55, 85-87, 150, 159, 162, 245n, 247, 252-54, 260-61, 269-71
Colbert, George, 78, 157, 190-91, 194
Colbert, William, 78, 157, 189, 190, 194
Coldwater, 21-22

INDEX

Columbian Museum and Savannah Advertiser, 238n
Colyer, William, 99
Concord (Baptist Church), 246
Connor's Creek blockhouse, 221
Conway, George, 213
Coody, Arthur, 123
Coosa River, 141
Cornell, Alexander, 204
Cotton, John, 84
County Line Meetinghouse, 244
Cowan, Nathaniel, 99, 226, 229
Cowan, Samuel, 99, 226, 229
Cowan, Mrs. Thomas, 184
Cox, Zachariah, 50, 52, 56, 66-67, 93
Coyatee, 12, 73-74
Crab Orchard, 168, 175
Cragfont, 228
Craig, David, 167, 170, 252, 254
Craig, John, 120, 122, 167
Craighead, Thomas B., 103-04, 214, 241-43
Crawford, John, 84, 252
Creek Indians, 5-6, 21-24, 29, 38, 47n, 48-52, 59, 62, 69-70, 72, 74-75, 82-83, 86, 88-90, 93, 102, 111-12, 114-18, 121-24, 126, 128, 132, 134, 138-39, 141-42, 151, 154-55, 158, 162-63, 165-67, 170-71, 173-76, 178, 180-84, 186, 188-90, 192-96, 203-06, 209, 236
Cripps's ferry, 235
Crooked Creek, 84, 118
Crow, David, 111, 122
Crow Town, 72
Cumberland circuit, 244
Cumberland Compact, 18-19
Cumberland country, 4, 6-7, 16, 18-20, 22-26, 29, 36, 39, 41, 43-44, 48-49, 59-60, 62, 72, 83, 90, 101-02, 105, 107, 112, 116-18, 123, 126-27, 138, 143, 167, 176-77, 179-80, 182, 184-85, 187, 190-91, 200, 207, 218, 221, 230, 246
Cumberland Gap, 16, 17n, 65, 237
Cumberland Mountains, 7, 39, 45, 85, 123, 175

Cumberland River, 4, 6-7, 17, 17n, 18-19, 21, 23, 52, 62, 73, 111-12, 115-16, 155, 162, 183, 193, 203, 218, 235-37, 241, 263
Cunningham, Alex, 235
Cunningham, James, 173
Cunningham, Jonathan, 120

D

Dandridge, 121
Danville, Ky., 100, 144
Dave, a slave, 221
Davidson Academy, 103-04, 235, 240-41, 263
Davidson County, 10, 18, 20, 33n, 44, 54, 57, 102, 107, 147, 150-52, 155, 158-59, 177, 182, 197, 202, 210, 213-14, 219-20, 231, 238, 244, 246, 252, 254
Davidson, John, 185
Davis, Joseph, 221
Deaderick, David, 99, 225
Deaderick, George M., 228
Deaderick, John, 228
Deason Creek, 263
DeKalb County, 23
Detroit, Mich., 167
Dick, a slave, 222
Dickens, John, 244
Dier, John, 166
Dillahunty, John, 246
Dillard, William, 235
Dinsmoor, Silas, 205
Disturber, the, 69
Doak, Samuel, 103-04, 200, 240, 242
Doak, Samuel L. (ferry operator), 100, 235
Dodson, R. (Dodson's ford), 100
Doherty, George, 137, 150, 239, 252
Doherty (Dougherty), James, 247
Donelson, John, 17, 102, 182
Donelson, Samuel, 228, 247
Donelson, Stockley, 42, 56, 151, 156, 162-63, 214, 217-19, 225, 245n
Doublehead, 61-62, 121, 124, 133, 156, 167, 175, 180, 204, 206
Douglass, Edward, 253

INDEX

Douglass, Ezekiel, 232
Douglass, James, 82
Douglass, William, 253
Drake, John, 165
Drake's Creek, 168, 213, 240
Dripping Spring, 111, 172
Duck River, 4, 138
Duncan, Stephen, 229
Duncan, Stephen, and Company, 99, 226
Dungan, Jeremiah, 98
Dunham, Joseph, 222
Dunham's station, 80
Dunlap and Claypoole's American Daily Advertiser, 238n
Dunlap, H., 239
Dunmore, Lord (John Murray), 8
Duzan, William, 244

E

Early Times in Middle Tennessee, 245
Earnest, Felix, 244
Earnest, Henry, 244
East Station Camp Creek, 214
Ebeneezer Church, 243
Edgar, John, and Company, 228
Edmiston, John, 82
Edwards, John, 193
Elizabethton, 98
Elk River, 4
Elliott, Charles, 214
Embree, Thomas, 98
Emory River, 40-41
Eskaqua, *see* Bloody Fellow
Estanaula, 69, 75-76, 123
Etowah, 141-42
Etowah Campaign, 141, 185, 202, 250
Europe, 9
Eusabia, 242
Evans, Andrew, 234
Evans, John B., 234
Evans, John B., and Company, 217
Evans, Joseph, 175, 183
Evans, Nathaniel, 166
Evans, Thomas, 21, 176
Evans's Ferry, 227, 234

F

Fall Branch (Baptist Church), 246
Fame, the brig, 156
Farragut, George, 37
Fayetteville *Gazette*, 37
Fayetteville, N.C., 26
Fears, James, 246
Fears, Jesse, 246
Ferguson, James, 167
Ferguson, Robert, 37, 41, 97, 239
Fine, Peter, 235
Flat Creek, 99, 131, 193
Flippin, Thomas, 235
Fool Charley, 132
Ford, James, 44, 150-51, 177, 252
Forked Deer River, 5
Forks of Little Pigeon (Baptist Church), 246
Fort Blackmore, 17
Fort Blount, 73, 155, 235, 250
Fort Grainger, 195
Fort Patrick Henry, 17
Fort San Fernando de las Barrancas, 196
Fort Washington, 65, 70, 114
Fort, William, 151, 252, 254
Fournier, Nicholas Honore Sidone, 240
France (French), 3, 7, 92, 143, 154, 201, 215
Frankland, 16
Franklin, state of, 10-16, 33, 33n, 40, 49, 109
Frazier, Samuel, 252, 254
Freeland's station, 102
French Broad (Baptist Church) at Koonts's Meetinghouse, 246-47
French Broad River, 4, 7-8, 12-13, 16, 23, 29, 45, 48, 50, 54, 56, 66, 90, 93, 104, 121, 163, 168, 199, 220, 231, 234-35, 244, 255, 264
French and Indian War, 7
French Lick, *see* Nashville
French Revolution, 30, 92, 140, 167, 216
French War of 1755, 6

287

INDEX

G

Galbreath, John, 252
Gallatin, 264
Gallatin, Albert, 267-68
Gamble, James, 166
Gamble's station, 122, 127, 137
Gammon, Richard, 151, 252
Gardoqui, Don Diego, 24
Garrett, Lewis, 243
Gaskins, Malachia, 111
Gee, Jonathan, 84
Genet, Edmund C., 154
German Creek, 99-100, 103, 119, 224, 226, 229
Gibson, Tobias, 243
Gilbert, Thomas, 50
Gillespie, George, 98, 102, 213
Gillespie, William, 235
Gilliam, Charles, 220
Gist, Joshua, 10
Glasgow, James, 217-18
Glass, the, 83, 204
Glass, Samuel, 252
Gleaves, Peter, 184
Glen Echo, 214
Gordon, George, 218
Gordon, John, 138, 172
Grainger County, 264
Grassy Valley, 99
Gray, Deliverance, 166
Gray, Thomas, 247
Greasy Cove, 122
Greasy Cove (Baptist Church), 246
Great Britain (British), 3-4, 7, 38, 96, 114, 123, 167, 172, 216
Great Iron Mountain, the, 27
Green, Adam, 119
Green, William, 168
Greenaway, James, 252
Greene circuit, 243
Greene County, 8, 10, 25, 42-43, 48, 54, 65, 98, 110, 141, 147, 150-51, 161, 213, 230-31, 235, 239, 248, 252, 254
Greene Court House, 100, 120, 121, 141

Greeneville, 12, 33, 97, 99, 141, 200, 212-13, 225, 232, 237, 241-43
Greeneville College, 161, 241
Greeneville lottery, 222
Greenfield station, 20, 115
Greer, David, 247
Greer, Joseph, 129, 220
Gregg, Thomas, 58
Grimes, William, 187
Guilford County, N.C., 37
Guthery (Guthrie), James, 99, 235
Guthrie, Peter, 244

H

Hacker, John, 225
Hadley, Joshua, 7n
Hague, John, 98
Haines, William, 187
Half Pone (Creek), 111
Halifax, N.C., 8
Hall, James, 20
Hall, William, 115
Hall, Major William, 20
Hall, Thankful Doak, 20
Hamblen, David, 98
Hamilton District, 119, 146, 160, 162-63, 166, 168, 174, 177, 184, 186, 206-07, 210, 212, 243, 246-47, 250, 264
Hamilton, Joseph, 247
Hampton, Michael, 187
Handley, Samuel, 252
Hanging Maw, the, 58, 71, 74-75, 85, 87-89, 123-25, 132-35, 166, 169-71, 173-75, 185, 206
Haralson, James, 235
Hardeman, Thomas, 197, 213, 252
Hardin, Joseph, 10, 26, 150
Harle, Baldwin, 202
Harper, Robert G., 201
Harpeth River, 4, 187
Harris, James, 111
Harrodsburg, Va., 16
Hart, Thomas, 230
Hatchee River, 5, 101, 219
Hawkins, Benjamin, 31-32, 203

INDEX

Hawkins County, 42, 48, 54, 56-57, 93, 100, 110, 147, 150-51, 161, 166, 193, 216, 229, 244, 252, 254, 264
Hawkins Court House, 80, 119, 239
Hayes, John, 221
Hays, David, 33, 220-21
Hays, Robert, 44, 162, 203, 241
Hazel Patch, 119
Head Man of Hiwassee, the, 74
Head of Sulphur Fork, 246
Heaton, Thomas, 112
Henderson, Richard, 17-18, 18n, 90-91
Henderson, Thomas, 252, 254
Henderson, William, 136
Henderson's line, 91-92
Hendricks's station, 20
Henley, David, 140, 148-49, 209, 234, 252, 259
Henley, Samuel, 88, 123
Henry, Patrick, 32
Henry's station, 120, 124, 166, 178, 224
Hercules, a slave, 220-21
Hetler, Sebastian, 120-21
Hightower River, 141
Hill, James, 235
Hillhouse, James, 201
Hillsborough, N.C., 37
Hiltebrand, John, 232
Hinde's valley, 81
Hiwassee (old town), 174
Hiwassee River, 4, 12, 136-37
Hodge, Welcome, 107
Hogan, Rawleigh, 230
Holland, 201
Holmes, Francis, 125
Holston Association, 105, 246
Holston circuit, 243
Holston River, 4, 7, 17, 49-50, 56, 60-61, 71, 88, 91, 93-94, 97-99, 106, 119, 125, 158, 164, 215, 217, 220-21, 235, 255
Holston River Valley (settlements), 9, 11, 14, 17, 17n, 20, 24-25, 34, 36, 40, 43, 71, 100, 104-07, 122, 156, 195, 227, 234, 237, 244-45

Holt, Dr. William, 248
Hopkins, George, 230
Houston, John, 252
Houston, Robert, 202, 251
Hubbert, James, 235
Hunt, Uriah, 246
Hunter, John, 7n, 229
Hunter, Robert, 229
Hutchinson, John, 223

I

Iredell, James, 38
Iron Mountain, 27
Ish, John, 173-74
Ish's mill, 141

J

Jackson, Andrew, 55, 143, 170, 182, 218-19, 228, 233, 239, 241, 245n, 247, 252-54, 259-60, 270
Jackson County, 218n
Jackson Purchase, the, 6
Jackson, Samuel, 120
Jacobins, 167
Jefferson County, 89, 110, 118-19, 121-22, 137-38, 147, 150, 151, 153, 161, 169, 231, 235, 239, 244, 249, 252, 254, 264
Jefferson County Court, 110
Jefferson Court House, 100
Jefferson, Thomas, 8, 14, 16, 53, 67, 90, 114, 135, 148, 150, 259, 266-67
Jemmy, a slave, 221
Jennings, Edmond, 177
Joe, a slave, 222
Johnson, Samuel, 247
Johnston, Elizabeth, 247
Johnston, Nancy, 247
Johnston, Dr. Robert, 248
Johnston, Samuel, 22, 23n, 26, 31
Johnston, Thomas, 252, 254
Jones, Aquila, 243
Jones, Stephen, 171
Jonesborough, 9, 10, 33n, 40, 42, 65, 97, 99-100, 107, 120, 122, 127, 146, 161, 212, 225-26, 229, 233, 237, 244, 248

289

Joslin's station, 138, 193
Justice, Richard, 74, 204

K

Kavanaugh, Williams, 243
Kelly, Alexander, 126, 150, 159, 167-68, 209
Kelly's station, 120
Kendricks Creek (Baptist Church), 246
Kennedy, Daniel, 42, 141
Kentucky *Gazette*, 116, 238n
Kerr, Joseph, 125, 128
Kimbrough, Duke, 246
King, Ann, 183
King and Crozier, 227
King Fisher, 69
King George III, 4
King, James, 99, 132, 174, 183, 250
King, Robert, 58, 173
King of Spain, 24
King, Thomas, 42, 99, 230
King, Walter, 230
Kirk, John, Jr., 13
Kirk, John, Sr., 12
Kittagiska, 74
Knox County, 96, 98, 110, 119, 137, 150-51, 159, 161, 168, 174, 200, 213, 233, 252, 254, 264
Knox County Militia, 131-32, 167, 204
Knox County Quarterly Court, 96, 110, 231
Knox, Henry, 41, 64, 70-71, 74-75, 77, 93, 117, 125, 128-29, 135, 142, 148, 155-56, 172, 175, 177, 181, 184, 188
Knox, Robert, 247
Knoxville, 39, 41, 71, 73-74, 79-81, 86, 88-89, 93-95, 97-100, 103, 107, 109-10, 116, 118-23, 125-26, 128-29, 132, 138-40, 145-47, 149-50, 153, 157-58, 161, 163-65, 167-69, 173, 176, 181, 184, 193, 197, 199, 201, 203, 205-07, 212-13, 215-16, 221-22, 224-27, 229-32, 234-37, 239-40, 242, 248-50, 254, 260, 271

Knoxville *Gazette,* 41, 71-72, 82, 85-88, 92, 96-97, 99, 109-10, 115, 117, 121, 124-25, 134, 143, 153, 157-58, 161, 163, 165, 167, 190, 197, 207, 215, 215n, 219, 220, 232, 236, 238, 238n, 239, 247
Kobler, Jacob, 243

L

Lacy, Hopkins, 150, 247
Lakin, Benjamin, 243
Lambert, Jeremiah, 105
"land grab" act of 1783, 6, 20, 52
Lane, Tidence, 105, 245-46
Lard, David, 229
Lard and McCoy, 229
Lawrence, John, 187
Lea, Luke, 121
Lebanon in the Fork, 104, 240, 242
Leslie, Robert, 75n
Lewis, Joel, 233, 252
Lewis, Seth, 228, 247
Lewis, Mrs. William, 122
Lewis, William T., 220-21, 232-33
Lexington, Va., 16, 116, 231
Lick Creek (Greene County), 235, 244
Limestone, 98, 228
Limestone (Baptist Church), 246
Lindsey, John, 243
Linsey, Benjamin, 166
Little Pigeon River, 89, 106, 118-19, 120, 171
Little River, 7, 12, 61, 88, 91, 122, 137
Little Tennessee River, 4, 12-13
Little Turkey, 72, 75, 117, 132-33, 169, 206
Lockett's ferry, 235
Logan, Benjamin, 180-81, 186
Logtown, 191
London, England, 8, 52
Long Hair, 23
Long Island of Holston, 98
Long Island Villages, 72, 173
Lookout Mountain Town, 72
Louis XVI, 140

INDEX

Love, Josiah, 247
Love, Robert, 98
Lower French Broad (Baptist Church), 246
Lowry, John, 247
Luce, a slave, 222
Luis Francisco Hector-Baron de Carondelet, *see* Carondelet
Lurtin, Jacob, 244
Lusk, Joseph, 82, 85
Lyle, John, 66n

M

Maclin, William, 253, 261
Mad Dog, chief, 102
Madison, James, 267-68
Man, George, 193
Mansker, Kasper, 18n, 103, 191, 201
"A Map of the Tennassee Government formerly Part of North Carolina," 214
Marie Antoinette, 167
Martin Academy, 103, 200, 240
Martin, Alexander, 10, 37, 56
Martin, Joseph, 32
Martin, Samuel, 166-67
Martin, William, 7n
Maryville, 264
Massey, William, 119
Matthews, Jeremiah, 110
Mayfield, Isaac, 172
Mayfield's station, 22
McAdam, Joseph, 172
McBee, William, 234-35
McClain, Thomas, 98
McCleary, Abraham, 235
McClellan, John, 175
McClung, Charles, 99, 226, 252, 254
McCombs, Dr. Thomas, 247
McConnico, Garner, 246
McCoy, John, 170
McCullough, James, 231
McDowell, Joseph P. G., 201
McFarling, Edward, 226
McGavock, Randall, 247
McGee, William, 242
McGillivray, Alexander, 24, 48-52, 74n, 83, 111
McHenry, Barnabas, 243
McKee, John, 125, 169-71, 196, 205
McLean, Ephraim, 241
McLugen, John, 111
McMinn, Joseph, 150, 252-3, 258
McNabb, John, 137
McNairy, John, 33, 33n, 38, 44, 252-54, 257
McNamee, Peter, 98, 229
McNutt, Isaac, 247
McNutt, William, 232
McRory, Robert, 172
Meade, Stith, 243
Mebane, Alexander, 156
Meek, Adam, 151
Memphis, 219
Mero Association, 246
Mero District, 20-21, 23-24, 26, 32-33, 37, 39-44, 53, 55-56, 58, 60, 62, 65, 73-74, 80-85, 88, 96, 98, 101-02, 105, 109, 111-12, 114-17, 122-23, 128, 143, 146, 149, 155-56, 158-59, 161-63, 165-66, 170, 172, 174, 176-80, 182, 184, 186-87, 189-93, 199, 199n, 200, 203, 205, 207, 209-10, 216-19, 227, 230, 236-37, 239, 242-44, 247, 249-50, 253, 259, 263, 271
Methodists, 104-05, 243-45
Michaux, André, 237
Middle Ford, 246
Middle Striker, 123, 173
Middleton's station, 167
Military Reservation, 19-20, 28, 52
Mill Creek, 22
Mill Creek (Baptist Church), 246
Miller, George, 69, 71-72
Miller, James, 99, 226
Miller, Samuel, 138, 226
Miller, Thomas, 233
Miro, Don Estevan, 15, 20, 24, 26, 29, 51, 67
Mississippi River, 1, 3-6, 14-15, 23-25, 36, 52, 56, 80, 91, 94, 143, 154, 176, 191, 193, 196-97, 201, 254
Mitchell, Richard, 252

INDEX

Mitchell, Samuel, 119, 247
Monroe, James, 216
Montgomery County, 177, 183, 248, 263
Montgomery, John, 177-78, 187
Mooney, Patrick, 246
Moore, Alexander, 76, 230
Moore, David, 164, 236
Moore's chapel, 244
Morgan, John, 82
Morgan's station, 166
Morganton, N.C., 15
Morris, John, 128-29
Morrison, Peter, 99
Morristown, 244
Mossy Creek, 207, 229-30
Mount Bethel Church, 241-42
Mount Vernon, 38
Mountflorence, James Cole, 41, 215-16, 247
Mouth of Richland Creek (Baptist Church), 246
Mouth of Sulphur Fork, 246
M'Tear's station, 120
Muddy Creek, 120
Muddy Creek (Baptist Church), 246
Mulherrin, James, 247
Mulkey, Jonathan, 205, 245-46
Munford, Robinson, 101
Munsey, Nathaniel, 243
Murphy, William, 245-46
Murray, John, Earl of (Lord) Dunmore, 8
Murray, Thomas, 166, 230
Murray, William V., 201
Murrell, Richard, 246
Murrell, Thomas, 246
Muscle Shoals, 14, 21, 45, 49, 51, 56, 59, 66, 70, 75, 87, 173, 236

N

Nashville, 6, 17-18, 21, 23, 27, 41, 44, 76-81, 83, 88, 91, 93, 97, 101-03, 107, 114, 116, 138, 155, 158, 161, 166, 168, 172, 176, 178-79, 182, 187, 189-91, 193, 200, 205, 207, 212-13, 215, 222, 228, 230, 234-38, 241-42, 245, 248-49, 263, 270-71
Nashville Inn, 232
Natchez, 172, 215
Natt, a slave, 102
Neely, James, 235
Neely, John, 235
Neely, William, 115
Nelly, a slave, 222
Nelson, A., 99, 103
Nelson, James, 118, 244
Nelson, Thomas, 118
Nelson's chapel, 244
Nenney, Patrick, 99, 226
New Boston, 125
New Hope, 106
New Madrid, 193
New Orleans, 15, 20, 94, 99, 143, 154, 215, 230, 236
New Providence, 242
New River circuit, 243
New York City, 12, 31, 38, 48, 157
New York *Daily Advertiser*, 26, 238n
New York Treaty of 1790, 48
Nichols's ferry, 235
Nickajack, 72, 176-77, 179-82, 184-85, 187, 250
Nine Mile Creek, 170, 224, 251
Nolen, Allen, 182
Nolichucky River, 7, 33, 106, 120-21, 137, 235, 243-44
Nontuaka, 74
Noon-Day, 128
Norris's Meetinghouse, 245
North Carolina General Assembly, 10, 12, 14, 16, 21, 27, 33
North Fork of Holston (Baptist Church), 246
Northward, the, 69
Northwest ordinance, *see* Ordinance of 1787
Northwest Territory, *see* Territory of the United States Northwest of the River Ohio

O

Oakfuskeys, 195

Oates, Roger, 122, 166
Obed River, 4, 218
Obion River, 5
Observer, 87
Occochappo, *see* Bear Creek
Ogden, Benjamin, 105
Ogden, Titus, 227
Ohio River, 1, 4-5, 17, 94, 236, 243
Opiomingo, *see* Piomingo
Ordinance of 1787, 1, 28, 32, 34, 36-37, 44, 54, 140, 145-47, 150-51, 197-98, 267, 272
Ore, James, 103, 177-81, 185, 187, 226
Osalotiska, 84
Otter Lifter, 204
Outlaw, Alexander, 239, 252, 259
Outlaw, Patience, 33n
Overall, William, 111
Overton, John, 158, 202, 218-19, 233, 234, 245n, 247, 271

P

Pactolus, 230
Page, John, 243
Paine, Thomas, 92
Painted Rock, 27
Palmyra (Knox County), 216
Palmyra (Montgomery County), 263
Panton, Leslie, and Company, 52, 73, 75n
Panton, William, 75, 75n, 89
Paris, 215-16
Parker, Isham Allen, 247
Parker, Nathaniel, 193
Pates, John, 118
Pearcifield, Peter, 169
Peck, Adam, 229
Peck, Jacob, 243
Pegg, the slave, 221
Pensacola, Fla., 75, 93
Perkins, Nicholas Tate, 98
Perkins's ironworks, 200, 229
Perry, William, 45, 55
Petersburg, Va., 220
Pevahouse's station, 165
Philadelphia *Gazette*, 215

Philadelphia, Pa., 34, 57, 65, 69-72, 74, 81, 89, 93, 96, 99, 124-25, 127, 129, 131-33, 135, 139-40, 142, 145, 148, 152, 157, 164, 182, 185, 192, 196, 209, 214, 216-17, 217n, 219, 224-26, 228, 233-34, 240, 249, 258, 269, 270-71
Phillips, Joseph, 102
Pickens, Andrew, 50, 76, 79, 139, 203
Pickering, Timothy, 188, 193-95, 204, 206, 209, 261
Pine Chapel, 244
Piomingo, 23, 78-79, 134, 138, 157, 164, 191, 201
Pistol Creek, 120
Pitchlyn, John, 78
Pittsburgh, Pa., 228
Pittsylvania County, Va., 17
Powell's Valley, 43, 98, 189
Powell's Mountain, 119, 216
Poythress, Francis, 244
Presbyterians, 103-04, 240-43
Prince, the, 69
Prince, Robert, 252
Prince, William, 252
Proclamation Line, the, 8n
Providence (Baptist Church), 246
Pruet, St. Clair, 111
Pugh, Jonathan, 15
Purdom, Alexander, 232

Q

Quakers, 106

R

Raccoon Valley, 122
Radcliff, Mrs. Harper, 80
Rains, John, 138
Rains's station, 22
Raleigh, N.C., 19, 225
Ramsey, Francis A., 42, 119, 260
Ramsey, Josiah, 85
Rankin, William, 252, 254
Ray, John, 243
Reasons, Thomas, 182
Reasons, Mrs. Thomas, 182
"Red Bird," 87-88

Red River, 4, 155, 166, 182-83, 246
Reedy Creek, 98
Reelfoot River, 5
Reese, James, 247
Rhea, John, 252-54, 257, 260
Rhea, Matthew, 65-66
Rice, John, 219
Richardson, James, 86, 221, 239
Richmond, Va., 65, 93, 95, 100, 131
Rickard, William, 125, 139, 165, 204
Rights of Man, the, 30, 92, 109
Roane, Archibald, 247, 252-53
Robert, a slave, 102
Roberts, Obadiah, 85
Robertson, Charles, 22
Robertson County, 263
Robertson, Elijah, 23n
Robertson, James, 4, 17, 18n, 19, 21-27, 29, 32, 39, 42-44, 50, 58, 77, 79, 81-82, 101-02, 107, 114-18, 126, 134, 138, 151, 155, 157, 166-67, 175-82, 184, 186, 189-93, 219, 228, 230, 241, 245n, 250, 252-53, 258
Robertson's Creek (Baptist Church), 246
Robinson's ferry, 235
Rock Castle, 98, 213-14
Rock Island ford, 118
Rocky Mount, 39-41, 45, 54, 109
Roddye, James, 239, 252, 254
Rogers, Benjamin, 235
Rogers, Joseph, 239
Rogers, Seth, 235
Rogersville, 40-41, 97-99, 105-06, 161, 212
Romayne, Dr. Nicholas, 216
Ross, Davis, 98
Roulston, George, and Company, 239
Roulston, Matthew, 235
Roulstone, George, 37, 41, 94, 97, 146, 159, 161, 219, 221-22, 239, 260
Rudder, Samuel, 243
Running Water (town), 72, 87, 124, 173, 176, 179-81, 184, 187
Russell, Andrew, 42, 235

Russell, David, 151
Russell, William, 167
Rutherford, Griffith, 151, 156, 158, 245n
Rutledge, George, 150, 252

S

Salem, 200, 241
Salisbury, N.C., 125
Sam, a slave, 102
Sapp, John, 229
Sappington, Dr. Mark B., 248
Scantee, 132
Seagrove, James, 77, 114, 165, 167, 195, 204
Searcy, Bennett, 247
Searcy, Robert, 228
Second Creek, 229, 231
Seehorn, John, 235
Sequatchie River, 4
Sevier County, 160-61, 200, 252, 254, 264
Sevier, John, Jr., 247, 253, 260
Sevier, John, Sr., 9-12, 14-16, 20, 27, 29, 33, 42, 45-46, 57n, 65, 86-88, 95, 109, 132, 136, 140-42, 144-46, 151, 156, 162, 164, 183, 185, 187, 200-02, 212, 214, 218-19, 230, 233, 238, 240, 245n, 250, 253, 261, 264-65, 271
Sevier, Joseph, 183
Sevier, Rebecca, 183
Sevier, Valentine, Jr., 183
Sevier, Valentine, III, 213
Sharp's station, 184
Sharpe, Anthony, 81, 117, 182
Shaw, Leonard S., 70, 72, 124, 169
Shawanese Warrior, the, 84
Shawnee Indians, 5, 17, 72-73, 83-84, 112, 114
Shelby, David, 253-54
Shelby, Evan, Jr., 111
Shelby, Evan, Sr., 14
Shelby, Governor Isaac, 111, 117, 195
Shelby, John, Jr., 99, 252
Shelby, Moses, 111
Shelton, William, 103

Shields, John, 247
Shiloh (Presbyterian Church), 242-43
A Short Description of the Tennassee Government, or the Territory of the United States South of the River Ohio, 214
Simmons, John, 243
Simpson, Gabriel, 176
Sims, Littlepage, 209
Sinking Creek (Baptist Church), 246
Sitgreaves, Joseph, 44
Slate Creek, 167
Slavery (slaves), 28, 102, 167-68, 172, 220-22, 243
Small, William, 235
Smart, William, 84
Smith, Daniel, 23-26, 32-33, 37, 39, 41-42, 44, 54, 56, 58, 62, 67, 69, 78, 90-91, 94, 98, 107, 109, 116, 125-26, 131-36, 136n, 140-41, 144, 146-49, 152-53, 168, 177, 213, 240-41, 245n, 253-54, 257-59
Smith, David, 191
Smith, William L., 267
Snoddy, William, 118
South Carolina Yazoo Company, 51
Southwest Point, 88-89, 116, 125, 162, 168, 171, 175, 195, 199, 221, 236, 251
Southwest Territory, *see* Territory of the United States South of the River Ohio
Spain, 3, 6-7, 14-15, 23-26, 38, 48, 51, 68, 73, 79-80, 83-84, 88-90, 96, 112, 114, 118, 126, 135, 143, 154, 169, 176, 180, 185, 196-97, 204
Speer, Moses, 244
Spencer, Thomas Sharp, 168
Spring Hill Meetinghouse, 104, 214
Springfield, 263
St. Clair, Arthur, 65-66, 73, 112, 128, 192
St. Lawrence River, 36
Stacey, Peter, 248
Station Camp Creek, 20, 80, 84, 172, 193, 245
Staunton, Va., 71

Steele, John, 86
Stockton, Thomas, 235
Stokes County, N.C., 56
Stone, John, 93, 96, 129, 158, 219, 227
Stone's Mountain, 27
Stone's River, 4, 80
Stony Point, 98
Strange, Obadiah, 243
Strother, John, 50
Stuart, James, 252, 254, 260
Stuart, Thomas, 247
Sullivan County, 8, 10, 14, 42, 52, 54, 57, 65, 99, 141, 147, 150, 161, 200, 230, 239, 244, 250, 252, 254
Sullivan Court House, 99-100
Sulphur Fork of Red River, 23
Summerville, John, 99, 225
Summerville, John, and Company, 224-25
Sumner County, 13, 20-22, 33n, 44, 54, 57, 80-81, 98, 115, 118, 122, 142, 144, 147, 149-51, 155, 158-59, 168, 172, 174, 177, 182-83, 187, 191, 193, 210, 213-14, 218-19, 230-32, 235, 240, 244-46, 249, 253-54, 263-64
Surgoinsville, 98
Sycamore Creek, 85

T

Taitt, William, 222, 228
Talbot, Matthew, 105
Talohteske (Talotiska), 85, 171, 204
Tarborough, N.C., 95, 102
Tatham, John, 239
Tatham, William, 215n, 247
Tatum, Howell, 228, 232, 247
Taylor, John, 71
Taylor, Leroy, 150, 252
Taylor, Parmenas, 151, 156
Taylor's Trace, 84
Tedford, George, 120
Telford, John, 120
Tellassee (Tallassee), 88, 136, 167-70
Tellico, 171, 186-87, 205-06

INDEX

Tellico Blockhouse, 173-75, 185-86, 189, 194-95, 204-05
Tellico Plains, 166
Tennessee Company, the, 50-51, 70
Tennessee County, 20, 23, 44, 54, 57, 80, 85, 147, 150-51, 158, 160, 177, 183, 187, 210, 219, 244, 246, 252, 254, 263
Tennessee district, 202
Tennessee River, 4, 14, 17, 21, 23, 29, 40, 45, 49-52, 60, 71-73, 75, 78, 83, 87, 90-91, 93, 115, 117, 121, 126, 131, 136-38, 142, 146, 148, 164, 166, 168, 170, 172, 174, 176, 179, 183-84, 194, 209, 215, 236, 255
Tennessee, state of, 3, 33, 266-68, 270, 272
Terrell, William, 219
Territory of the United States Northwest of the River Ohio, 1, 32, 47, 57, 147-48, 202, 215, 229
Territory of the United States South of the River Ohio:
  origins: cession of 1784, 8-10; state of Franklin, 9-16; cession of 1789, 25-30; slavery protected, 28; Congress creates territory, 31-33
  governance: officers appointed, 33; Ordinance of 1787 to govern, 32-36; powers of governor, 37-38; seat of government, 39-42; elected assembly 109-10, 142-48, 150-53, 158-64; council, 151, 155-56, 158-64; Federal taxes, 202-03
  statehood: advocated, 197-201, 209-11; constitution adopted, 252-58; governor and general assembly elected, 260; assembly convened, 260-65; Congress accepts Tennessee, 265-70; U.S. senators, congressmen, presidential electors chosen, 270-71
Third Estate, 30
Thomas's ferry, 235
Thompson, James, 80
Thompson, John, 58, 123, 133-34

Tickekisky (Tickagiskee), 134, 185
Tinnan, Hugh, 111, 187
Tipton, Jacob, 66
Tipton, John, 13, 15, 42, 109, 127, 150, 252, 254
Tipton-Sevier feud, 40, 109
Titsworth, Isaac, 183, 204
Titsworth, John, 183
Town Creek, 168
Transylvania Presbytery, 243
Transylvania Purchase, 18, 60
Treaty of 1783, 3
Treaty of Dumplin Creek, 12
Treaty of Fort Stanwix, 1766, 6n
Treaty of Holston, 51, 55, 61-62, 64, 67, 69-71, 73, 75, 82, 87, 90, 110, 123-24, 126, 132-33, 156, 167, 173, 185-86, 188-89, 195, 205, 207, 238, 265
Treaty of Hopewell, 1785, 6, 7, 12, 33, 45, 48-50, 78
Treaty of Hopewell, 1786, 38
Treaty of New York, 48-49, 52, 59, 82, 87, 98, 174, 203
"Trenk," 109-10
Tuckasegee River, 137
Tusculum College, 161
Tuskeega, 169, 171
Tuskigatahee (Tuskegatahe), 74
Tye, John, 193
Tynoila, 137

U

Unaka Mountain, 27
University of Tennessee, 161

V

Vance, Dr. Patrick, 107
Vanpelt, Benjamin, 244
Vanpelt's Chapel, 243-44
Versailles, 30
Virginia Yazoo Company, the, 51

W

Wabash River, 66
Waddell, John, 233
Walker, Elijah, 193

INDEX

Walker, Francis, 152
Walker's line, 91-92
Wallace, Joel, 120
Walnut Grove, 214
Walnut Hills, 56
Walton, Isaac, 253
Ward, Nancy, 132
Ward, Dr. William, 248
Washington College, 200, 240
Washington County, 8, 10, 13, 15, 33n, 39-44, 52, 54-55, 65-66, 88, 98-99, 102-03, 120, 122, 127, 147, 150-51, 161, 200, 213, 231, 233, 239, 241, 244, 248, 253-54, 264
Washington District, 8-10, 16, 40, 42, 48, 53, 58, 60, 65-66, 76, 80, 83, 85, 88-89, 132, 160-61, 163, 166, 172, 186, 202, 206-07, 210, 243, 246-47, 250, 264
Washington District Superior Court, 33n, 51, 55, 66, 107, 146, 184, 248
Washington, George, 1, 31-34, 36-38, 43-45, 47-50, 55, 61-64, 67, 69-70, 73-74, 77-79, 81, 86, 90-91, 117, 123-26, 128-30, 132-33, 135, 137-40, 142, 146, 150
Washington, N.C., 37
Watauga River, 4, 7, 39
Watauga settlement, 8, 17, 103-04, 107
Watkins, Evan, 183
Watts, John, 50, 58, 71, 74-76, 83-84, 89, 112, 117, 121, 123-26, 133, 169-71, 180, 185, 187, 204
Wayne, Anthony, 114, 157, 192
Wear, Samuel, 136, 150, 252, 254
Wear's Cove, 122, 136-37, 169
Wear's mill, 122
Webb, Hugh, 172
Webb, William, 235
Wells, Abraham, 120
Wells, Robert, 111
Wells's station, 120, 122
West, Joseph, 232
West Station Camp Creek, 213
White, James (of White's fort), 24, 39, 93, 95, 127, 129, 131, 158n, 159, 162, 204, 231, 252
White, Dr. James, 150, 152, 154-55, 159-60, 200-01, 204, 209, 211, 245n, 248, 258, 261, 269, 271
White's Creek, 85, 246
White's ferry, 235
White's fort, 56, 93
Whitley, William, 177-78, 180
Whitsett, James, 246
Wilderness Road, 17, 17n
Will (of Running Water), 74
Will's Town, 138, 169, 173, 176
Williams, Edmond, 45
Williams, Sampson, 177, 209, 228, 259
Williams, Thomas H., 260
Williamson, Hugh, 32, 117, 140, 214n, 241
Williamson, John, 193
Willioe, 174
Wilmington, N.C., 29, 33
Wilson, Benjamin, 80
Wilson, David, 122, 144, 149-50, 155, 158, 174
Wilson, Samuel, 82
Wilson, William, 115
Winchester, George, 174
Winchester, James, 23, 44, 58, 118, 127, 151, 156, 159, 162, 174, 183, 192, 219, 227, 237, 241, 245n, 260, 271
Witt, Caleb, 246
Wolf River, 5
Wolf's Friend, 78
Wood, John, 98, 167, 226
Woolsey, Zephaniah, 121
Woolsey, Mrs. Zephaniah, 121
Wyly, Robert, 225, 237, 239

Y

Yancey, Ambrose, 98-99
Yancey, William, 39

Z

Zeigler's station, 81, 86

TEN

S.Wn T

F. Massac
Fort Johnson
Iron Bank
Ohio R.
KEN
Obian R.
Mississippi River
Forked R.
Wolf R.
Chickasaw Bluff
Tennessee R.
Cumberland R.
Buffalo C.
Yellow C.
Red R.
Clarksville
Nashville
Stones C.
Cumb
Barren
Duck R.
Crow R.
Muscle Shoals
Elk R.
Rocky R.
Nick
Crow T.
Creek's cross
Watts
Tombigbee R.
E
O
R
Yazoo R.
Coosee R.
Turkey's